Pitchpole

THE UPENDING OF A BOAT in gigantic seas where the stern passes over its bow and the vessel is dropped upside down. The most violent action a vessel can experience, it is usually fatal to the boat and its crew.

Le Dauphin Amical *anchored off the beach in Mexico*

CAPE HORN

One Man's Dream
One Woman's Nightmare

RÉANNE HEMINGWAY-DOUGLASS

FineEdge.com

Editing: Alice H. Klein; Kathryn Wilkens
Book design: Melanie Haage Design
Cover design: Diego Carlos Linares
Cover photo: Rick Doyle/CORBIS
Photos: Réanne Hemingway-Douglass and Don Douglass

~~~

Library of Congress Cataloging-in-Publication Data
Hemingway-Douglass, Réanne.
    Cape horn : one man's dream, one woman's nightmare / by Réanne
Hemingway-Douglass.—Rev. 2nd ed.
      p. cm.
    Includes bibliographical references (p.).
    ISBN 0-938665-83-9
      1. Hemingway-Douglass, Réanne.—Journeys. 2. Douglass, Don.
—Journeys. 3. Dauphin Amical (Sailboat). 4. Survival after airplane
accidents, shipwrecks, etc. 5. Cape Horn (Chile). I. Title.
G478.H46 2003
910.4'5—dc21   2002192843

Published by FineEdge.com
13589 Clayton Lane
Anacortes, Washington
Printed in the United States of America.

To the memory of my parents whose love paved the way

To Don—co-pilot for life—who taught me to soar

To Lois SeCheverell Buell, my guiding Polaris

Contents

List of Maps and Charts vii
Le Dauphin Amical: Sail and Deck Layout. viii
Le Dauphin Amical: Cockpit and Interior Layout ix
Preface to First Edition x
Preface to Second Edition xii
Author's Notes xiii
Prologue. xiv

1   *The Shattering* 1
2   *Attitude Adjustment* 18
3   *Isla de Pascua—the Long Wait.* 47
4   *South Pacific High* 73
5   *One Week to Cape Horn* 91
6   *Pitchpoled* 99
7   *The Morning After.* 109
8   *Oil on the Water & Towing Warps* 122
9   *Decision* 134
10   *Patagonia—the Lee Shore.* 149
11   *Dársena Aid* 168
12   *Rescue Be Damned!* 189
13   *Good Friday Encounter* 204
14   *Strait of Magellan Ahead* 220
15   *Pacific Winds, Atlantic Tides* 233
16   *End of a Nightmare* 245

Epilogue to First Edition. 267
Epilogue to Second Edition 272
Afterword: *Stateside Headlines: Missing at Sea*
by Katherine Wells. 280

Appendices
A Original Itinerary. 285
B Specifications of Le Dauphin Amical. 286
C State Department Telegram 289
D Newspaper Articles. 290
E Lloyd's Surveyor's Report 291
F Beaufort Scale 293
G Captain's Notes: The Ultimate Wave 294

Glossary 295
Bibliography. 298
Acknowledgments 300
About the Author 301

List of Maps & Charts

Easter Island (Rapa Nui). 47
Golfo Trinidad 150
Puerto Henry and Dársena Aid. 168
Canal Trinidad to Canal Inocentes 190
Canal Inocentes to Canal Sarmiento 198
Canal Sarmiento 205
Sarmiento to Collingwood 221
Canal Smyth to Isla Tamar. 226
Paso Roda (Isla Tamar, Puerto Tamar) 236
Caleta Notch 246
Cabo Crosstide 249
Bahía Snug. 254
Puerto del Hambre (Port Famine) 258
Punta Arenas 264
Tierra del Fuego 268

Chart reproductions used in this book are from the U.S. Hydrographic Office, the Defense Mapping Agency, the British Admiralty, or the Chilean Navy. They are for illustrative purposes only and are not to be used for navigation.

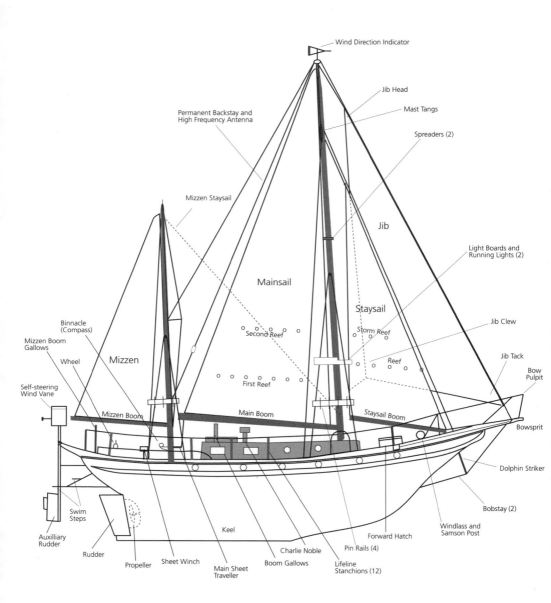

Le Dauphin Amical – Sail and Deck Layout

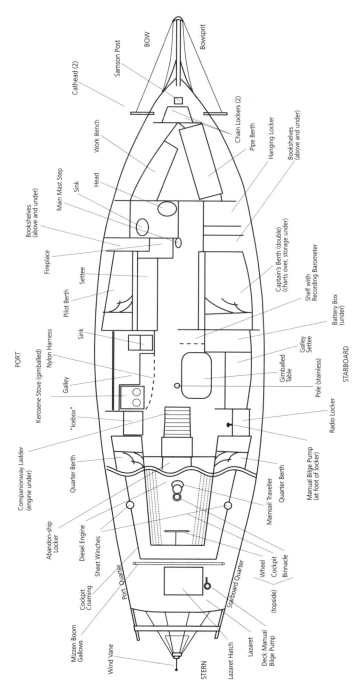

BOW

Bowsprit

Samson Post

Cathead (2)

Chain Lockers (2)

Pipe Berth

Hanging Locker

Bookshelves
(above and under)

Work Bench

Main Mast Step

Sink

Head

Bookshelves
(above and under)

Captain's Berth (double)
(charts over, storage under)

Fireplace

Settee

Shelf with
Recording Barometer

Pilot Berth

Battery Box
(under)

PORT

Sink

Nylon Harness

Kerosene Stove (gimballed)

Galley

Galley
Settee

Gimballed
Table

STARBOARD

Pole (stainless)

"Icebox"

Radio Locker

Companionway Ladder
(engine under)

Quarter Berth

Manual Bilge Pump
(at foot of locker)

Quarter Berth

Abandon-ship
Locker

Diesel Engine

Sheet Winches

Mainsail Traveller

Mizzen Boom
Gallows

Cockpit
Coaming

Port Quarter

Starboard Quarter

Wheel

Cockpit

Binnacle

(topside)

Wind Vane

Lazaret Hatch

Deck Manual
Bilge Pump

Lazaret

STERN

Le Dauphin Amical – Cockpit and Interior Layout

Preface to the First Edition

On October 12, 1974, my husband, Don Douglass, and I headed out of Los Angeles Harbor aboard our 42-foot sailboat, le Dauphin Amical, to begin what was meant to be a two-year circumnavigation of the Southern Hemisphere. With us were four teen-age boys: Don's sons Jeff (eighteen), and Michael (sixteen), my son Sean (fourteen), and his best friend Carl (fourteen).

We had spent the previous eighteen months renovating and modifying a Porpoise ketch designed by William Garden (a well-known, highly respected naval architect of British Columbia). Constructed of strip-planked Port Orford cedar over oak frames, she was a 20-ton boat, 42 feet in deck length with a 13-foot beam. Although just four years old when we left, she was in every respect an old-fashioned, traditional wooden vessel, which had been strengthened and outfitted, according to Don's plans, for high latitude sailing. Sailors and boaters of the 1990s may think it incredible that we carried no auxiliary generator, no radar, no Loran, no GPS (it didn't even exist yet). But since we were headed for the high latitudes of the Southern Ocean—where spare equipment is nonexistent and repairs impossible—Don didn't want to rely on electronic "gadgets" that frequently corrode in salt air.

What follows is the true account of an edge-of-life adventure. But Cape Horn is not just a story about a sailing voyage. It is the story about how I, as first mate, experienced the voyage—how I felt about the Captain, the sea, the boat, the crew.

During the years we planned and prepared for the voyage I searched the literature for stories by women who, like me, followed their mates for love or adventure. What I found were books by sailing couples who had made the sea their life; stories by famed singlehandlers—men, or the exceptional woman; or highly romanticized accounts by men who "took" their wives aboard.

Wonderful books, all, but nothing to help me understand what I, as a "nonsailor," might face emotionally on a two-year voyage. I found little that described the problems I might face cooped up in a 42-foot boat with four teenagers and a husband who was my opposite in temperament.

Why could I find so little? Because the sea has traditionally been a male-dominated world. Because it takes machismo to sail around the world—self-confidence that verges on arrogance; a love of risk, of pitting oneself against nature; an ability to endure pain and privation. Did the sailors who wrote their adventure also chronicle their emotional ups and downs—even if they took a female partner? No! They wrote about hourly sail and course adjustments, about storms that carried away rigging, about seas that sent their boat on beam ends. Stuff that sells to the nautical market!

Where were the stories by women? How did the women partners handle the experience? I couldn't find a clue. I began to suspect that ordinary partners, like me, gave a resounding No at the first mention of a sailing voyage. Or they bailed out along the way. (I met many dreamy skippers along California docks who told me with a faraway stare, "My wife would never agree to a trip like this." I met others who dumped their wives to follow their dream.) I also began to suspect that if women wrote about their experiences in anything less than happy-sailor tones, their chances of finding a publisher were slim.

Spurred by female friends to "tell it like it is," I began to keep a detailed journal before we set out, resolved to publish an account of my own, in my own words, from beginning to end.

Why then, readers may ask, have I waited nearly two decades to publish this account when I was so eager to tell my story?

To begin with, I had used my journal to pour out such heavy psychological details that nobody would have been interested in the raw stuff, and by the time I was able to stand back and sort out my own feelings from a more objective view, several years had already passed.

Sample chapters of my first draft came back from a reputable agent who urged me to fictionalize my story. "I can place it immediately," he told me, "if you'll rewrite it as a novel." I wasn't willing.

Sample chapters came back from two mainstream sailors who told me, "Forget all that emotional stuff. We want to hear Don's story."

In fact, Don, did want to tell his own story. He wanted to publish what I considered a highly dramatized account of our trip, emphasizing its "heroic aspects" and covering the nautical minutiae found in most cruising books. Although I respected Don's expertise and knew that many sailors might value a book from his point of view, the end product would have gone straight to the nautical shelves.

I considered handing it over to a ghost writer, but it wouldn't have been my story. I considered trying to find a publisher, but in the end I would have had to adapt my story to meet the publisher's editorial constraints. Friends suggested a back-to-back story—his and hers—but our two stories were as dissimilar as my diary was from the logbook. How could any bookseller market it?

Our respective egos dug in. I refused to water down my story, but Don wasn't ready to support my endeavor. We couldn't agree on any approach. Tension between us came to the boiling point. I was not ready at the time to press to the wall. I backed off.

A decade passed. The diaries and notes filed away in drawers simmered all the while in my brain.

Fortunately, as I hit the high side of my fifties, I began to sense my mortality. In 1989, a few months after Don had suffered a near-fatal heart attack, he asked me his favorite question, "What do you want to accomplish in the next five years?"—the question he had asked on our first date.

Without flinching, I answered: "Publish our story in my words." And so, I dug out my files and began again.

Preface to the Second Edition

When I began writing *Cape Horn: One Man's Dream, One Woman's Nightmare* a decade ago, I had originally anticipated publishing a limited number of copies for our family, friends and business associates. Instead, at Don's urging, we printed copies of the book in the five-figure range.

I was convinced, at the time, that women would be the primary market; that men would shrink at the first mention of any emotional descriptions or dialogue. However, to my delight, of the hundreds of letters and emails I've received in response to the First Edition, men (Alpha males included!) as well as women, balance the scale. And not only has the book been a commercial success, it is now considered a classic in Cape Horn literature; it has also been published in France and in Italy.

With the exception of a couple of fishermen who would have keel-hauled me,[1] and an anonymous reader who thought I should title the book, *Whine Around the Horn,* all have thanked me for my forthrightness and willingness to tell my point of view, as a novice sailor, and one whose marriage to an obsessed adventurer was tenuous at the beginning.

In this Second Edition, I have tried to address the many comments or questions I've received from readers by adding a second Epilogue that carries on, in capsule form, where I ended our story. And, to the many readers who don't know the "Rest of the Story", yes, Don and I are still together. Our thirty-five year-marriage, with its ups and downs, including over 160,000 cruising miles under sail and power, has just gotten better and better!

---

[1] Keel haul: an archaic punishment that involves roping a sailor by hand and foot and dragging him from side to side under the keel of a vessel.

Author's Notes

Source documents for this book are the ship's logbooks, my three journals, Don's two diaries, letters to our family and friends, newspaper clippings, and a deeply etched set of memories. Where I have recreated dialogue, I tried to be as true as possible to what I recorded in my journals. With a few exceptions, names mentioned in the narrative are real.

Although I tried to avoid using too much unfamiliar vocabulary, nautical terminology is such a rich and precise language that it's impossible at times to avoid its use without compromising accuracy. For this reason, a glossary of nautical terms has been included, as well as diagrams and sketches of le Dauphin Amical.

In most cases, I have used the Spanish place names throughout the text, following their usage in the British South America Pilot. (See Glossary.)

In addition, I followed several conventions in technical details. Although we kept the ship's clock and chronometer on Greenwich Mean Time (GMT)—now called Universal Coordinated Time—I adjusted time in the narrative to reflect local time, using the 24-hour clock in four digits (for example: 1330 hours = 1:30 p.m.). Most of the compass headings or bearings given in the text are recorded as true (not magnetic) in three digits. (For example, at latitude 50° south, there is a deviation of 25° west; therefore, when the heading is recorded in the text as 090° due east, the compass was actually reading 065° and is noted as such in our logbook.)

Distances are given in nautical miles (a nautical mile being equivalent to one minute of latitude or 1/60 of a degree). Speed over the ocean is given in nautical miles per hour, known as knots. (One nautical mile is equivalent to 1.15 statute miles; therefore, wind speed of 50 knots is equivalent to 57.5 statute miles per hour.) Wind speeds were recorded in our logbook using the Beaufort Scale. (See Appendix.)

Prologue

"Come on, you can do it," the voice from below shouted. "You can do it, Réanne!"

I wanted to screech, "Hell no, I'm not going over that lip!" I was terrified of sheer drop-offs, and forty vertical feet separated me from the top of a boulder and the ground below.

"Come on! Lean back." The voice was becoming impatient.

With my left hand I clutched a climbing rope that was fixed to a permanent eyebolt hammered into coarse granite. The rope was "threaded" through my crotch, around my right buttock, up and across my chest, over my left shoulder, and diagonally across my back to my right hand. With my right arm held straight down along the side of my hip, I was supposed to feed the loose end out slowly while I leaned back and "sat" on the rope, keeping my legs perpendicular to the rock face as I rappelled over the lip and down the vertical wall to earth. It was a technique called *dulfersitz*.

A chilling autumn wind whipped across the rock, blasting my cheeks with sand. I clutched tighter and wondered what the hell I was doing all wrapped up like a package being sent to China.

The voice from below belonged to a man I'd met two weeks earlier through a mutual friend. (We were both single parents and the friend had been eager to get us together.) It was a Saturday in late November 1966, and the Sierra Club "picnic" to which he'd invited me and my two sons turned out to be a class in basic rappelling.

On our first encounter, two weeks before, we had sipped wine across a table from each other, and Don had described his Dream. A dream that had simmered since he was a kid—to sail around Cape Horn following the old clipper ship route and circumnavigate the Southern Hemisphere.

"I want to make that dream come true," he said. "And I think I have what it takes. It's a gift I'd like to give my kids before they grow up and leave home."

Abruptly changing the subject, he asked what was important to me, what I wanted to do with my life.

His directness jarred me, and although he spoke softly he was intense. He wasn't making small talk; he wanted an answer. "What's important to you?" he repeated.

The Sierra Club "picnic" was only our second date. I felt I was being tested, judged. Like a new car. See if it has guts; see how far you can push it; see how it holds up under adverse conditions; see if you really want to commit to it. I was furious.

"Come on. You can do it!" I heard again. "You can do more than you think you can."

I wondered what had attracted me to this guy that first night. *This is it,* I thought. *I send him packing the minute we get home!* But I had to go over the lip—or unwrap myself and let everyone know I was a coward.

Ego goaded me on. I'd show him what I could do. Besides, five little faces from his brood and mine were glued on me from below. I couldn't let them think I was chicken.

I rappelled down the cliff, shaking from terror.

I hesitated a few minutes before answering his question that first night. I had been so caught up in the struggle to support my children that I hadn't had time to give much thought to what *was* important to me. As I thought about it now, I studied him.

He was prematurely bald, and his high rounded forehead was etched with a permanent crease. He had small, nearly lashless blue eyes, and his eyebrows were so blond they were barely visible. When he laughed, crow's feet appeared at the corner of his eyes and his face softened. But when he was intent on getting his point across, his eyes riveted on me like laser beams, making him seem as fierce as if he'd just come out of battle on the plains of Outer Mongolia. He wasn't handsome in a conventional sense, but his energy and intensity excited me.

What was important to me? Love was important—for my two young boys, my family, my friends. My career as a French teacher and language consultant—that was important to me, too. And a passion for France, stemming from college days. I wanted to complete my master's degree, raise my two boys, travel, learn new languages, lead trips to France, write, study piano. These were my dreams—pretty tame in comparison to Don's. I stressed that although I wanted adventure in my life, love was most important to me.

Our mutual friend had told me that Don was an entrepreneur and an adventurer who climbed mountains, hiked, and sailed and was raising his daughter and two sons by himself.

He took a moment before he spoke again. "Love is important to me, too. But I think I'd rank adventure ahead of love." He paused, his eyes probing my face. "My ex-wife thought my dream was crazy," he said. "You don't, do you?"

I felt instant sympathy and murmured, "Of course not." His honesty and the way he was trusting me by sharing his dream sent chills through me. He was a man with goals and drive, in charge of his own life. It had been years since I'd met a man like that, and I let him know it.

Driving home from the Sierra Club outing, Don chatted incessantly while I sat silent and confused. How could this man have been so warm and intense, so interested in me on our first date, so pushy on the second? I liked him that first evening. Now I didn't.

When he pulled into my driveway to drop us off he seemed suddenly aware of my anger, and—as if making a peace offering—he handed me a book and asked, "Would you be willing to read this and tell me what you think about it?" He was soft and human again. But I wondered if this were another test.

Instead of telling him I didn't want to see him again, I read the book, *Once Is Enough*. He'd already given me a brief idea about the story when we talked about his "Dream." I knew it was about Miles and Beryl Smeeton, a renowned British sailing couple who, in 1957, had pitchpoled in their sailboat, *Tzu Hang*, near Cape Horn.[1]

The term *pitchpole* was new to me. Don had explained that huge seas can cause a boat to surf down a wave, trip its bow on the following wave, and be upended stern over bow—in some cases, a gigantic wave simply lifts a boat and drops it upside down. It was the most violent action a boat could experience, and it had happened to the Smeetons *twice!*

The first chapters of their book began as typical sailing narrative—preparations in Melbourne, Australia; leaving port and heading south through the Tasman Sea toward the Great Southern Ocean; problems with rigging and equipment; dreary weather (days without sun, incessant rain squalls)—nothing that excited me. But my disinterest turned to fascination as I got into the heart of the story.

Seven weeks out of Melbourne, and still 900 miles from Cape Horn at the 50th parallel, the Smeetons and their crew, John Guzzwell, encountered the infamous seas that roll unimpeded around the Antarctic continent, sometimes building to exceptional heights. Then the "ultimate wave" hit, and their sailboat was pitchpoled, tossed over, and torn apart.

They managed to jury rig *Tzu Hang* and limp to the coast of Chile, where they spent nine months repairing the boat before setting out again to round Cape Horn (this time without Guzzwell). Approaching 50° south latitude, they were pitchpoled a *second* time.

The Smeetons were strong and unusual people, but I was convinced that much of their story was fiction—an ordeal like that didn't happen to real people. At least not the people in my life. And when Don asked what I thought about their story, I answered, "Incredible. Almost too much to be true—especially Beryl swimming back to the boat with a broken collarbone and a smile on her face."[2]

He agreed it did sound unbelievable, but fiction or not, the Smeetons were his heroes. Then he added offhandedly, as if wanting to reassure me, that there was about one chance in a million of being pitchpoled twice. He asked, "Do you suppose you could do something like that?"

I laughed and answered, "I assume you mean sail around the world, not pitchpole!"

Guts. Did I have what it would take to round the world in a sailboat? Although I had read *Once Is Enough*, I really had no concept of what sailing around the world involved. But the thought of adventure like that appealed to me.

As a child, I wasn't afraid of things little girls were supposed to fear. Fun for me meant seeing how high I could climb in huge trees, jumping off thirty-foot sand cliffs along the dunes of Lake Michigan, playing Robinson Crusoe and building my own hut in the woods. It meant ice skating on the local pond during a blizzard and belly-flopping onto my sled and bombing downhill in pitch dark. Guts meant beating up boys who picked on my friends. It meant jumping in after my best friend when she got caught in an undertow, and having to knock her unconscious so she couldn't pull me under. Guts meant wrapping a four-foot-long garter snake around a boy's neck in retaliation for his having put it down my dress.

As an adult, though, I had never pushed the limits of adventure the way Don did. Pleasure, not risk, motivated me. Sure, I was a good swimmer, a good canoeist, and a passable cyclist, but I'd never climbed a mountain higher than 6,000 feet, never done more than daysail on Lake Michigan or San Francisco Bay, never been out of sight of land on anything smaller than an ocean liner. The gutsiest thing I did in college was hitchhike in France and Italy and fight off rich old men who wanted to bed me in exchange for a ride. But could I sail around Cape Horn? Don's question sparked my sense of adventure, stirred up my dormant sense of daring. Could I? Yes, I thought I could!

Other considerations loomed, however, as we got to know one another. Don and I were totally different—in personality and background. He was a man of passion—loud; quick to laugh, interrupt, or talk about himself; quick to get angry, chastise with sarcasm, then just as quick to forget.

I'd been taught to keep my emotions in check. Not to laugh too loudly; not to show anger. Talking or bragging brought on a look from my mother that was devastating, and I still had a hard time expressing my feelings or talking about my accomplishments.

Steeped in liberal arts, not math and physics as Don was, I didn't understand the "physical laws of the universe"—forces, momentum, magnetism, electricity. Don loved to talk about those things, as well as about money, finance, and economics. He made budgets for one year, two years, or five, and discussed them with his family. He loved to make deals, and he was good at negotiating. To him business was exciting— "the creative stuff of life." To me it was a mystery.

I'd been taught not to bargain, rather to accept a price and pay it. *Business,* especially *big business,* was almost a dirty word in my family, and high risk was always to be avoided. And until my father was put on "extended leave" during the McCarthy witch-hunts of the 1950s, money was simply not a topic to be discussed.

Good books and classical music were our home entertainment—we didn't even own a television. Piano lessons, private college, junior year in France—our parents were indulgent with education, not consumer goods. They were loving but extremely strict with my brother and me.

Don's childhood during World War II was disrupted by constant moving—he attended eight different schools in ten years—and he had missed the socialization process a normal teenager goes through. Although he had nice manners, he had never learned how to read "body language" or acquired a sense of timing. He blurted out whatever came to his mind the minute it occurred to him, catching people off guard, annoying them, and making them defensive.

My mother and father had stressed honesty, courtesy, manners, and correct grammar. I was concerned with social form and very sensitive to body language.

Don had attended "the school of hard knocks," and he liked telling me that he had completed a two-year stint in the army during the Korean conflict, then put himself through engineering school while he held down a full-time job to support a wife and three kids. He was a self-made man, and my private liberal arts college seemed like a country club to him.

Maybe I hadn't "had it hard" growing up, but for five years as a single parent, I had learned what it meant to fight for survival. Nothing in my past had prepared me for raising two sons without child support. After I finally got my teaching credential, I'd had to juggle two teaching jobs and tutoring on weekends to scrape together enough money for food and rent. I'd had to renegotiate loans; had to convince people to accept partial payments; had to be firm (or even nasty) when simple courtesy didn't work. I'd had to loosen my tongue, screw up my courage, and go against everything my temperament and upbringing had dictated. For me, this was just as challenging as going over the lip of a forty-foot cliff.

And nothing could have prepared me, either, for the risks and pitfalls of partnership with a man whose desire for adventure outranked even his desire for love. I liked and admired Don's enthusiasm and passion for life. And sometimes he was a teddy bear—warm, thoughtful, and loving. But at other times I hated his all-consuming drive and his apparent relish for undergoing duress. Our differences would prove to be a lethal mix, but I didn't give it much thought. The man and his way of life fascinated me too much to reject.

His Dream? . . . Well, with both of us deeply in debt and struggling to combine our families, the chances that we'd ever own a boat and sail around the world seemed pretty slim. I figured I wouldn't have to face that for a while, so when Don asked me to marry him, I answered with a spirited, "Yes!" and signed on for whatever life brought.

NOTES

1. The Smeetons' story, which is a classic account of pitchpoling, appears in almost all nautical literature about survival or exceptional waves. (See Bibliography.)

2. After I had read their biography, *High Endeavours*, I understood that the Smeetons were, indeed, an exceptional couple.

H omme libre, toujours tu chériras la mer!
La mer est ton miroir; tu contemples ton âme
Dans le déroulement infini de sa lame,
Et ton esprit n'est pas un gouffre moins amer.

—BAUDELAIRE, *Les Fleurs du Mal,*
XIV L'Homme et la Mer

Free man, you will always cherish the sea!
The sea is your mirror; you contemplate your soul
In the infinite rolling of the waves,
And your spirit is not an abyss less bitter.

—*Author's translation*

CHAPTER 1

The Shattering

ACAPULCO, DECEMBER 4

Don's Dream exploded just eight weeks after we sailed out of Los Angeles Harbor. The last shards of his grand mosaic—a two-year circumnavigation of the Southern Hemisphere—had shattered, an unwanted gift shoved back in his face.

We were just preparing to head uptown to clear port for Easter Island when Jeff asked, "Uh . . . you going to the Port Captain's?"

"Yes, why? Do you want to go with us?"

"Uh . . . no . . . I think I might wanna be going home."

"Might wanna be going home . . . "

Nausea spread through my gut like I'd been KO'd. I leaned over to control the urge to vomit.

"You can't be serious," I said without thinking. Jeff never uttered a word unless he meant it and I knew it. I glanced at Don, who had started up the companionway ladder. Favorite son was defecting, as the three younger ones had, and he was stunned speechless, tears in his eyes.

A long discussion we'd had a week earlier flashed through my mind. We had just received word from Tex—our amateur radio contact in California—that the Ecuadorian government had denied our request for a permit to visit the Galapagos Islands. Don had planned our original itinerary to take maximum advantage of currents and winds, and the Galapagos were a perfect takeoff point for sailing to Easter Island.

We were disappointed. Not only would we miss the famed tortoises, seals, iguanas, and bird life, but by having to change course we faced a miserable four weeks' beat into the wind to get to Easter Island.

Equipment malfunctions, crew defections, and a two-week trip home to accompany Michael and Carl had already delayed our progress and caused us to change our itinerary. Our families and friends were upset; they'd sent mail to ports we would never visit, and with the latest word about the Galapagos, we had begun to talk about further changes.

The *Sailing Directions for South America* that covered Isla de Pascua (Easter Island) had discouraged me: "The weather is never good for more than a few days at a time at Isla de Pascua. Ships anchoring off the island must be kept ready for sea. Often, almost without warning, the wind will change and set a vessel on the shore within a few minutes. . . . Chilean authorities strongly advise all shipping and small craft to avoid coming to Isla de Pascua, except in an emergency."

I asked Don why we should go at all if we couldn't get off the boat because of weather.

"Come on, it's never as bad as you read in the *Sailing Directions*," he said. "They put all that stuff in to cover their ass. Except for beating into the wind on the way, we won't have any problems."

My discouragement ignited Jeff. "Dad, I don't want to go around Cape Horn."

I was stunned and reminded him about a ripping family discussion we'd had a year before leaving California. Don and Jeff had been trying to get the rest of us to catch the excitement of rounding Cape Horn: "Because, like Mt. Everest, it's there"—a cliché both of them loved to use.

Mike, Sean, and Carl hadn't liked the idea. I hadn't either. A recurring nightmare about pitchpoling off Cape Horn had stifled any initial curiosity I'd had about rounding the Horn.

I'd had the nightmare three times, and each time I would awaken panicked and drenched with perspiration. Each dream was identical: we were heading toward Cape Horn; the boat, caught by a tremendous wave, was catapulted through space at zero Gs, rolled over, and shattered; Sean

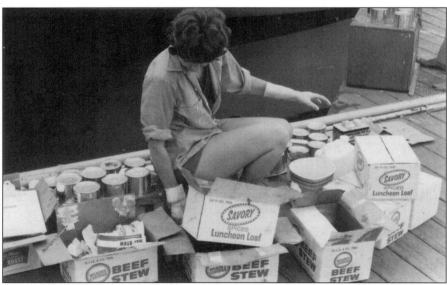

Shellacking 600 cans to prevent corrosion

was thrown out of the cockpit and lost forever. Although I had recorded the details in my diary, I never told anyone about the nightmare, as if voicing it would make it come true.

I'd read all the "horror" stories and I didn't want to be the first female to go down off Cape Horn. I'd cast my vote with Mike, Sean, and Carl. But, like Don, Jeff had persisted. "Sure we might die, Mom. But what a way to go!"

Strengthening and remodeling le Dauphin Amical *(ex-*Liddle Mae*)—October 1973*

When Jeff said he didn't want to go around the Horn, I reminded him of his flip remark a year earlier. "Yeah, but that was when I thought all six of us would be going. I don't think three of us can handle it. Can't we come up with a different plan?"

That same day, we had discussed alternatives to Cape Horn: transiting the Panama Canal, the Caribbean, then down the coast of Brazil and across the South Atlantic. But Don reminded us the diesel engine wasn't powerful enough to buck the currents in the Caribbean.

I proposed crossing the North Atlantic and heading to France. *My* dream was a leisurely trip around the canals of Burgundy, Bordeaux, or Provence; tying up to a barge in a small village and sharing bread and sausage with the captain and his family; watching old men in berets play *boules* in the town square; buying cheese in an outdoor market; cycling along poplar-lined roads; living the seasons of the Impressionists and the Fauves. My dream was interesting, but it lacked adventure, risk. It was the type of cruise septuagenarians took, and I didn't expect Don to give it much thought. Besides, at that time, he didn't share my love of France. A short, unpleasant visit to Paris when he was a young GI had soured him on the French.

"Nope," he said, forcing me to think pragmatically. "Too many shipping lanes to cross and we're too shorthanded to maintain night watches. Besides, winter in the North Atlantic is *bad*."

"Worse than Cape Horn?" I gasped.

"We're headed for Cape Horn in the summer. Sure, there are storms down there, but there's only a 10 percent chance of a bad one in January."

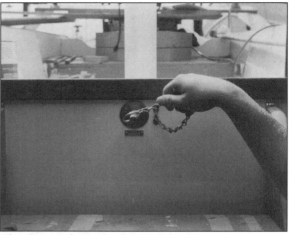

The release pin for our abandon-ship locker

Jeff suggested heading for the Marquesas, then down to New Zealand and Australia. "We talked about that route at home a year ago, Dad, remember?"

"Yeah, but that was only a possibility if we'd left in May. Now it's the wrong time of year to head in that direction—it's hurricane season down there."

All of our suggestions had hit the wall and bounced off. We didn't have a chance. Don wanted to head to Cape Horn and we would head to Cape Horn.

That night, particularly annoyed, I wrote:

> *The cards are stacked. I feel like Carmen drawing her Queen of Spades: "Cap Horn. Cap Horn. Toujours Cap Horn." Don says the winds are right for Cape Horn, there are no shipping lanes to cross, and that if it gets too rough we can go through the Strait of Magellan. Like Moitessier, he thinks it's the "Logical Route."[1] He was a little too cheery explaining all this—I'm suspicious of his "logic." Can't he just be honest and clean and say "I want to round Cape Horn; it's my dream." Nope. He plays a role— the logical man. We must take la Route Logique. Acapulco to Easter Island; Easter Island to Cape Horn. La suite comme prévue. Subject closed.*

Now Jeff looked at Don standing motionless and white-faced on the ladder, and he read his thoughts. "Dad, I'm not leaving for the same reasons the other guys did. I don't think it's that bad on the boat, but I miss my friends. You've got Mom . . . I've got nobody . . . no friends to talk to. You and Mom like different things, classical music and small anchorages without people. I don't mind places like that, but when there's no

Before the defections

other eighteen-year-old to share them with, it's no fun. If I can find someone to come back with me maybe I could meet you later, like at Easter Island or Punta Arenas."

In the seven years I'd been his stepmother, I had never heard Jeff utter that many words at once and with such obvious care for Don's feelings. His determination to rejoin us seemed genuine, but I could envision the future: he'd go home and have so much fun he'd forget that he ever mentioned it.

What now? I thought. *What now?* I looked at Don again. His face was beginning to regain color, his fighting mode returning. "You've really thought about this? . . . Are you sure? . . . What are your plans? . . . " He was testing, verifying.

My mind did tail spins while he and Jeff talked. *What now?* We were supposed to leave the next day for our 3,500-mile passage to Easter Island.

The memory of the high-pitched voice of a cruising acquaintance twanged at my eardrums. "Why are you taking teenage boys? Little kids are okay, but teenagers . . . Can't you leave them home?" She and her husband had just returned from a two-year trip to the South Pacific. "We

A world chart, showing the itinerary, had hung on our wall at home for over a year

fought more than we ever have in twenty years of marriage, just the two of us. You're crazy to take four teenagers!"

I should have known it would come to this. I should have been prepared.

Maybe I was. There had been an undercurrent I couldn't put my finger on—whisperings that stopped the minute Don or I appeared. Then there were sarcastic remarks flying between the captain and crew. After ten days of listening to them, I had flown into a screaming rage at everyone—the boys as well as Don—that had ended in a shaky truce for a few days.

Then, on October 27, before we'd even left Baja California, the torpedo hit. Michael asked if we could make a "slight" detour to La Paz to drop him and Carl off—he wanted to go home, "couldn't handle the captain."

The detour involved two hundred extra miles, and he had acted as if he were just asking to be let off at the movies. I could have pummeled him. I had sensed that he didn't want to come on the trip; he'd been so ugly for six weeks before we left California—gritting his teeth about having to help get ready, complaining, swearing, shouting obscenities at Don and the boatóthat Iíd written in my diary:

I wish Michael would just say he doesn't want to go and get it over with. But I have a hunch he wants to make Don so angry he'll tell Mike to stay the hell home. That way, he won't have to make a decision himself.

Michael's announcement had angered me, but Carl's floored me. As our "adopted" son and Sean's best friend, he had always been a cheerful addition to our family. As a crew member, he had taken his watches without complaining, and he seemed to enjoy the sea life and the art of sailing. He took his studies seriously and kept his sense of humor, and he never used sarcasm like Don and the other three. When Carl said he wanted out, I felt I was losing my support team and wondered whether our frank and bombastic exchanges had shocked him, whether the sarcasm had gotten to him. But at fourteen, he'd never been away from home before, and he said he missed his father.

"Besides," he told me, "I'm not used to the way you and Mr. Douglass live." That was it! He wasn't used to our emotional outbursts, the captain's digs at character, and the pressure. The hours he'd spent at our house weren't enough to get used to "the way we lived." He had never heard Don and me arguing because Don was usually gone, and the kids and I had good times together without tension.

Michael and Carl left, and three weeks later, in Puerto Vallarta, Sean got off too.

Now, after Jeff's announcement, I thought about *my* father, the groans he would utter when he heard the latest news; his frustration and his fear for us, which he never showed outwardly. When I had last talked to him, on November 23, I told him we were omitting Guatemala from our itinerary. We couldn't afford to go there considering the time we'd lost delivering the boys.

"You keep changing your plans," he complained. "I just mailed a letter to Guatemala about your finances. Now you won't receive it. There's no money left in your checking account. What shall I do?"

I wished I had insisted that Don's partner manage our personal finances—it was too much for Daddy. "No money" meant we were into our $5,000 bank credit line, which we'd expected to use until Don's lump-sum sabbatical payment was deposited in January. But credit financing was anathema to my father. He always paid his bills before they were due, set aside reserves for emergencies and taxes and followed an elaborate system even my mother couldn't figure out. When I suggested turning the bookkeeping over to PJ, Don's partner, he balked. We had to "keep it in the family." He would have been horrified to let anyone else know the balances on our bank card, our boat loan, our graduate student loans, or the fact that all he could do was make monthly payments—*small* monthly payments—slowly, slowly.

The inability to cope was a side of my father I'd never seen before. He had always been in charge, quick to react to emergencies, able to handle financial difficulties. He was in his early seventies, but he seemed to be going downhill rapidly. I wondered if fear for us could be dragging him down, or whether something was wrong with him.

But Daddy's frustrations were the least of my worries. Discouraged and suddenly afraid, I stared at the interior of the cabin. A boat chosen for six people—rebuilt, strengthened, and outfitted for Cape Horn—and provisioned for six people for six months. Years of planning, saving, doing without; the time and effort we, and especially Don, had put into this project. I didn't know whether to feel sorrier for him or for me. Would he be open to another plan? What else was possible, given the weather and the season? It seemed we'd exhausted all the ideas in our discussion the week before.

Memory of my recurrent nightmare pushed at my temples, and I tried to brush it away. I couldn't allow myself to think about the negatives. I had to keep my mind focused on the present; we would have to hustle to get everything done for Jeff. Don and I would have to think about ourselves later.

I came to and heard, "Okay. If that's really what you want, do you have enough money to pay your way home?"

Jeff nodded. Don had insisted that the kids save enough to pay for a flight home in case they bailed out and that they also make prior living arrangements. Maybe he had sensed more than I gave him credit for.

"We'd better make radio contact with Tex and let your mom and stepfather know you'll be coming home."

I glanced at my watch. It was almost noon; everything closed between 1200 and 1400 hours. I took a deep breath and said, "Let's have lunch, then Jeff and I can head uptown."

We were anchored off a gringo hotel. Jeff and I rowed ashore and headed to the lobby where we found a travel agent who efficiently booked a flight for the next morning.

We headed uptown to run errands: buy extra fan belts for the alternator, tubing for the water filter, hose clamps. This was Jeff's first in-depth glimpse of local color and he was animated.

Acapulco crowds were thick with every level of society. Small children were selling cheap knickknacks and shoe shines; Indian women balanced baskets on their heads or sat cross-legged on the ground in their long skirts, surrounded by garishly decorated clay pots.

We found the open-air market—a cave of covered stalls that stretched fifty feet into the shadows. Fresh carcasses had just been delivered to the meat shop. Two bare-chested butchers in blood-spattered aprons were skillfully carving beef heads, whole livers, intestines, and legs and suspending them on gigantic iron meat-hooks at the side of their booth.

Long stalks of bananas hung from every green-grocer's stall. Zucchini, chayote, carrots, tomatoes, onions, leeks, cilantro, parsley, Swiss chard, potatoes, Mexican broccoli, and fresh herbs filled plastic buckets or huge cardboard bins. Open sacks of beans, rice, dried peas, flour, and maize displayed the harvest of a rich farmland.

A pair of slim, thick-lipped maids bargained for vegetables while their long-nailed, elegantly dressed and coiffed mistresses waited, double-parked in air-conditioned Mercedes. Stout widows, dressed in black, piled wicker hand baskets high with fruits and vegetables. Slick-haired, hot-eyed young men in tight-fitting pants made me clutch my shoulder bag across my bosom.

Jeff and I filled our *bolsas* with small bananas, squash, beets, potatoes, with dried beans, rice, and fresh bread. I stayed clear of the meat. Flies feasting on the purple blood were too vivid for my antiseptic American mind.

Jeff was excited, solicitous, and talkative, full of "what ifs." He'd never flown before, never used public transportation. A mountain man who'd hiked over a thousand miles in the backcountry, he was nervous about taking the plane.

"What if I get lost in the Mexico City airport? What if I miss the transfer in Mexico City?"

I explained what to do.

"What if I miss the plane in Phoenix?"

I reminded him that they speak English in Arizona and that he could manage a pay phone.

"Oh, yeah," he grinned.

We were friends, equals, that afternoon; he was fun to be with and I felt good, in a melancholy way, sorry that it couldn't always be like this.

I bought *La Prensa* at a newsstand and turned to the day's horoscope for Aquarius: "Don't move from where you are if you want to preserve tranquillity. Abandon your wishes to make changes and visit other places. There is a love that will offer you peace and security, although without the emotion you crave. . . ."

I never read horoscopes—I thought the whole idea was ridiculous. But I couldn't put it down. I kept rereading it. How could it be so accurate? What had prompted me to buy the newspaper and read the silly thing? It was uncanny. I tore it out to tape it in my diary. What was happening to me? I'd never considered myself superstitious and had always made fun of people who were. But fear was taking charge of me—my subconscious was turning inside out.

That evening after sundown, Don and I sat in the cockpit sipping Dubonnet while Jeff packed. Both of us were physically and mentally exhausted, and the wine loosened our tongues immediately.

"How do you feel now that Jeff's leaving?"

"Like a failure. That's the worst part of it. I realize how little emotional sharing I've done with him and the other boys." His eyes filled and he was silent.

I wondered if that was what it took for him to realize how much he'd withheld from me, from the whole family, for the last year. He was holding the reins of a burgeoning manufacturing and retail business; making plans for this voyage and overseeing the rebuilding of the boat. And he had refused to give up all his other activities: he climbed a dozen peaks in six days in the Northwest, went to Mexico to bag a peak at Christmas, to the desert to rock climb at Easter. He led four-week trips to the Sierra in the summer, taught snow-survival classes in the San Bernardino Mountains in winter. This was stuff that would have felled an ordinary man, and it had nearly wiped out the rest of us.

Don was the planner, the thrill seeker, the risk taker who swept us along with rationalizations about educational experience, the test of will, the need to set one's sights higher and higher. But he never took time for introspection: "emotional sharing." It was as if he set goals to avoid facing himself.

I had nearly signed off the trip myself eighteen months earlier. Don had wanted me to commit, to share actively in his dream. But I had had trouble committing to him when he wasn't committed to me *emotionally*—he was too busy running all the time. It had been a rough decision for everyone, but we had finally come to an understanding, and Don had kept assuring me the trip would bring us closer together as a family—like a couple who think they'll improve their marriage by having a child. I could foresee the problems we'd have in such tight quarters, but I confined my remarks to diary entries only; Don would have accused me of negativism.

Just two weeks out of Los Angeles, as we sailed along the coast of Baja, I'd written:

> *Am beginning to think this trip will make us detest one another instead of bringing us together. It's hard enough for a husband and wife to live like this, but increase the number by four, as we've done, and the probability for disagreements shoots up like a thermometer in molten lead.*

Don had often criticized parents who relive their own dreams through their children, and I wondered if he was thinking about the same thing now. He knew he had pushed the boys hard trying to "shape them up" for Cape Horn. But he had used sarcasm and insults, thus achieving the reverse of what he wanted: they balked and bailed out.

Happy sailing along the coast of Mexico

Now Don felt "like a failure." This was the first time I had ever heard him say that. I put my arms around him. I liked him better when he could admit weakness than when he played the indomitable captain.

"I feel bad for you. If you could just practice getting your anger and frustration out in a more positive manner, we'd both be a lot better off."

He nodded. "I know. I don't understand why I'm so nasty at times, I guess I just expect too much from people."

He went to bed, too drained to talk about our own plans. Before I turned in I wrote:

> I wonder if it's better to set your sights lower, like I do, and perhaps not fail at all, or set your sights so high, as Don does, that failure comes hard.
>
> Jeff keeps insisting he's only going home to enlist a friend who'll fly to Easter Island or Punta Arenas, Chile, to help crew, but I don't think we'll see him again. I'm scared. Yesterday I thought of a name for our book— And Then There Were None—but I was afraid to say it out loud. Today Don came up with the same idea.

DECEMBER 5

0600 hours. The airport limousine stopped at the hotel, and Jeff hopped in as casually as if he were taking a ride around town.

We rowed back to the boat and Don said, "For godsake, let's clear port before anything else happens.

I agreed. I wanted to get the formalities of clearing port over no matter what direction we might head. Neither of us had wanted to come to Acupulco, but we'd agreed so the boys could have one last spree before we hit the high seas.

The day we arrived (and before Jeff dropped his bomb), I had written:

We are here in a port for the benefit of a crew that has jumped ship. But the boys would have been disappointed—this is a city of middle-aged and elderly American tourists on $499 three-day packages—no teenage fun here. We're down to our last teenager and he hasn't seen one young English-speaking female lolling on the beach or sunning at the edge of a pool.

I cannot imagine what draws people here. Sure, the beach that curves around the bay is beautiful, the water warm. But it's so damn hot I drip just breathing. What draws people? I do know the answer. It's the package—deluxe, air-conditioned, guaranteed. Limousines that whisk you to a hotel with casino and swimming pool. "English spoken here." No need to mix with the natives. No need to go outdoors.

But we have no air-cooled package, no deluxe accommodations. We are "camped" in the middle of a quarter-million people. The water here in the boat harbor is too dirty for swimming, too dirty to pump saltwater for dishes. Thievery abounds. We are warned not to leave our boat unattended, warned that even though we lock it, thieves will strip the deck clear in broad daylight. I'm torn between wanting to get out of here as fast as possible and the desire to keep an attachment to land, as unpleasant as it is. No more sight of land when we leave here, just thirty days at sea—no sand dunes, hills, trees, or mountains—nothing but water, endless water.

We removed everything from deck that would tempt a thief, locked the boat, and headed uptown to clear with immigration, customs, and the port authorities. I was happy we wouldn't have to do this again for a while—it had become a drag.

It was 1000 hours when we arrived at *Migración*. We had been waiting more than thirty minutes for the chief to sign our release papers when his assistant returned and informed us we had to pay a fine because we were checking out of Mexico early, instead of heading to Puerto Angel as our papers indicated.

"Here, sign this receipt," he told Don. It was our first encounter with *la mordida*—"the bite." Firmly and politely, Don said, "No."

I had learned by then to keep my mouth shut and not reveal that I spoke Spanish. If we played "dumb Americans," the officials would finally become exasperated and give us our way. If I argued in Spanish, they became angry.

The assistant excused himself to report Don's response. Fifteen minutes later, he returned. The *mordida* was lowered.

Don pulled both of his pockets inside out. They were empty. The assistant laughed, headed back to his chief again, and returned promptly to say, *"Jefe dice oke."* (The Chief says it's okay.)

The customs office was on the first floor of the same building; we had another wait. I checked my watch. It was after 1100. I knew that everything in the government offices would come to a screeching halt in sixty minutes. If we didn't get out of there by noon we'd have a two-hour wait. Drenched and uncomfortable, I complained that the women didn't seem to perspire.

"Study them, and you'll understand why," Don said.

I studied. One middle-aged man among two dozen young women was working diligently, his shirt sleeves rolled up, his hand fumbling periodically in his pocket for a handkerchief to wipe his brow. The others looked cool and unrumpled. I saw what Don meant—they weren't working; they were just sitting.

After fifteen minutes, frustrated with the waste of time, I pulled a pad of paper out of my *bolsa* and began recording what I saw. Don did the same. I stared at the workers, as if I were making notes about their behavior. It made them nervous. An older woman approached the counter and asked what we wanted.

Don shoved our papers across the counter. Within three minutes they were returned, stamped, and we headed to the port captain's office where we cleared with uncommon speed just before noon.

Jeff's name still appeared on the crew list, and we hadn't mentioned a word to the authorities. A month earlier in Puerto Vallarta, we had learned a lesson the day Sean was supposed to fly home. His duffels, scuba gear, and cartons of textbooks were stacked in the cockpit ready to offload, as soon as Don returned from town where he'd gone to clear Sean's departure.

We were anchored a quarter-mile off the town wharf, and I could see Don untie the dinghy and row back toward the boat. His strokes suggested we were in for an ugly scene, and by the time the dinghy bumped against the side of the boat, his face was red, his eyes bulging.

"Kid, you're not leaving today. You may never leave this fucking place the way things are going—we have to write a letter to the immigration officer explaining all these exits of crew members."

Two days later, Sean was "cleared" to fly home. If the authorities in our next port thought we'd dumped Jeff overboard, we'd deal with our crime at that point.

1730 hours on a winter's evening. The sun had set, but the air still steamed and I still dripped. It was 90°F, 95 percent humidity—the *cool* season in Acapulco—and the misplaced Midwesterner in me longed for cold weather, the smell of dead leaves burning, leafless silver branches stretching against a pale yellow sky, lacy patterns of ice along creek banks, the air-sting that presages snow's arrival. I'd always thought winter should be a time for stripping the bark, a scrubbing down with harsh soap. A time for nature to pause, rest, and take stock before the *renouvellement*. But the only resemblance to winter's spirit in Acapulco was the quiet, wistful time Don and I were sharing that night.

"I want to talk about us now," I said. Don flushed. "I suppose you've been wondering whether I'm going to stay with you."

"Yes, I've been wondering if you were planning to bail out, too. We could abort the whole trip, you know . . . How do you feel about continuing?"

His question triggered a memory—a conversation I'd had with Carl's father after I took Michael and Carl back to California in early November. I had just received the message that Sean wanted to bail out too and fly home to live with Carl and his dad. Fred Kowalski had taken me to breakfast to "talk" and asked pointedly how I felt about continuing with just Jeff as crew. I had had trouble fighting off self-pity, and with my chin quivering, my nose dripping, my eyes overflowing with brine, replied that I didn't know what would happen but that I'd made a commitment to Don and I intended to fulfill it. The big difference between then and now was that there were just two of us left.

I've been wondering if you were planning to bail out, too. How do you feel about continuing? How did I feel about continuing? . . . Things had changed so drastically since we left California on Columbus Day. When we first started planning the voyage, I had "hired on" as teacher, cook, chief sail repair person, helmsman, and assistant navigator. (I'd taken a celestial navigation class along with Don, but I hadn't mastered the calculations yet or learned how to use the sextant.) The boys were supposed to do the heavy work—raise and douse the sails, handle the anchor, swab the decks. It was the traditional nautical separation of duties. Now I would have to learn skills I never dreamt I would—skills I didn't want to learn, that I didn't have the muscles for. If the four boys had been there at that moment I would have screamed at them: "You let me down. I can't handle this 20-ton boat and you know it!" But I knew that if I continued, I was going to have to learn.

I knew, also, that before I could answer Don, I had to know how much Cape Horn ultimately meant to him. I'd heard so many of his rationalizations—*the Great Circle Route, the Logical Route, the educational experience, the excitement, the first family to round Cape Horn*—but, since we first met, I hadn't heard him say plainly, with honesty, "I want to do this for me." Was it still a passion, or had he lost his drive? If he couldn't be honest with me at this point and admit it was still *his* life's dream, it meant he hadn't learned anything about himself in the last eight weeks, and probably never would.

"How important is it to you to round Cape Horn?" I spoke softly, stressing each word carefully.

He was silent for a long time.

Impatient for a reply, I raised my voice, exaggerating each word. "How . . . important . . . is . . . it?"

His face reddened. He looked at me and hesitated, as if he were afraid to let down his guard. Then slowly and quietly he answered, "I guess . . . it's . . . pretty important." His eyes filled. "I'm beginning to realize this really is my trip. Mike and Sean were so ugly about leaving that it was easy for me to blame them, not to see my part in the whole thing."

He took a breath, and I could see he was struggling with his feelings. "Losing Jeff really hits hard—he seemed to take to sailing like I do. But all the boys had different expectations than I did, and I couldn't see it. Now I do."

He paused again. "Yeah. I guess rounding Cape Horn is pretty important to me." He wiped the tears off his face with the back of his hand. "It really is *my* dream, isn't it? . . . Will you continue to share it with me?"

I didn't answer immediately. *The Horn . . .* I thought. *I am afraid. But something in me wants to be able to shout—"I did it! I went around the Horn!"—when it's over.*

It was the same theme that had recurred again and again during my life, and in our marriage—I wanted to, but I didn't. It was the same fascination with risk I had when I first met Don. I could follow the advice of *La Prensa's* horoscope, look for peace and security, and my parents would be happier. But—as the horoscope warned—that wasn't the kind of life I wanted. I craved emotion, not just stability. The kind of passion for life that Don had—an enthusiasm that so many people lacked. On the other hand, as exciting as life could be with him, it could also be hell. Could I deal with the tempestuous nature of the Great Southern Ocean, as well as that of the captain?

"I want to, but I'm worried about two things," I said. "Cape Horn is one. The second is us." He flushed.

"I'm not in love with sailing like you are, and Cape Horn isn't my choice. What I wanted out of this trip in the first place was to see new countries and meet new people—not spend all my time at sea in extreme conditions."

He was listening, pensive and quiet. I continued. "Now that the boys are gone, I'm worried about becoming your scapegoat. I'll try to be a good first mate, but if I don't measure up to your expectations, I don't want to become your whipping boy."

He nodded. "I hope I've learned something from the experience with the boys," he said, his eyes filling again. "I know it's been hard on you. You were caught between the boys and me, and I appreciate the support you've given me. I need you . . . and I want you to go with me."

"Let's go below and study the chart," I said. "Last month, when you and Jeff and I discussed the route around Cape Horn you pretty much ignored our concerns. I need more details."

We climbed below, and Don took down the pilot chart for the South Pacific, unrolled it, and laid it on the galley table.

To me, a pilot chart looks like a Kandinsky print. "Satellites" with feathered tails, called *wind roses,* indicate the direction and force of the wind for each 10-degree square of a particular ocean. Sweeping lines in red, blue, and green indicate paths of storms, barometric pressure, and annual variation. Underneath these sea-like creatures lie the edges of continents, clusters of islands, and printed phrases such as *Extreme Limit of Icebergs, Great Circle Route.* I found Easter Island, an obscure dot among the wind roses, between 20° and 30° south latitude, 110° and 120° west longitude. I peered at the wind roses near Cape Horn—they had twice as many feathers.

"What's the percentage of gales off Cape Horn for the summer months?"

Don reached up to the bookcase, pulled out our *Marine Climatic Atlas,* and spread it open on the pilot berth. He thumbed to Chart 20, February. Swirling blue and red lines that looked as if someone's pen had gone awry covered the chart. Percentage of gales of more than 34 knots were indicated by red lines that hung along the high latitudes of both hemispheres.

Don pointed. "See this line here? Ten percent. That's maybe three days out of a month." He turned to the chart for March. The percentage doubled. "If we can get past Cape Horn before the end of February we should be fine. But if the weather gets bad, we'll head for the Strait of Magellan. I promise."

"I want to continue," I said. "I've always thought this could be the greatest adventure of my life. We haven't had much fun together the past year—getting ready was too intense—but maybe that can change now. If you can yield a little to my expectations, then I'm with you till my sabbatical leave is over next year."

He studied my face, not sure I was serious, waiting for me to repeat what I'd just said. I sensed his insecurity and took his hand. "I'm not going to abandon you. I'll continue to share your dream with you . . ."

NOTES

1. *La Route Logique* is the term used by Bernard Moitessier in *Cap Horn à la Voile*. In 1965, he and his wife, Françoise, left France aboard the *Joshua* for a honeymoon voyage to the Galapagos, Tuamotus, and Tahiti. Instead of returning home through the Panama Canal, they took *la Route Logique*—the logical, fast route around Cape Horn—in order to be back in France with Françoise's children by Easter of the following year. At that time, Françoise was the first woman to round Cape Horn in a sailing vessel under 50 feet. in December 1967, Miles and Beryl Smeeton made their third and (this time) successful attempt in *Tzu Hang* to round the cape from east to west, making Beryl the second woman to round Cape Horn in a small yacht.

CHAPTER 2

Attitude Adjustment

DECEMBER 9

"Attitude. It's your attitude that makes you seasick," Don said.

We were 130 miles south of Acapulco, and I didn't have my sea legs yet. I was miserably sick.

"You're sick because the kids left, aren't you? You've got to get over them."

His comment made me angry. He'd never been seasick in his life, and he had always attributed seasickness to "mental illness."

Rolling seas had always made me seasick, but I usually grew accustomed to the motion of the boat after a day or two. The trip down the coast of Mexico to Acapulco had been fairly easy. The wind had been steady, and once we set the sails, the boat heeled consistently on one tack, allowing me to adjust to a single motion. Now, with less wind, we had to motor. The odor of diesel didn't blow away, and the boat rolled erratically. Early in our practice runs, I had tried all the antiemitics on the market. They either made me dopey or irritated my stomach. I had known when we began the trip that I would just have to "tough it out," but I hadn't anticipated such a violent reaction.

We had been at sea three days, and I couldn't keep a thing in my stomach. My head pounded; each hour the vise at my temples tightened. Everything bothered me: the odor of diesel and kerosene, the stickiness of the air, the motion of the boat, the lack of breeze, the sun. Topside or below, I felt the same. Awful.

Don had been patient and thoughtful these three days, teaching me to read messages from the clouds and from the water—explaining how the temperature of the water would drop as we headed south and entered the Humboldt Current. He pointed out the navigational stars—Aldebaran, Betelgeuse, Bellatrix, and Pollux—and talked about how primitive peoples used certain stars to guide them. He showed me how to judge the altitude of a star above the horizon.

I liked what I was learning, but I was too ill to feel any enthusiasm. I wrote:

Don has had the concern of a father sitting at the edge of a child's sickbed. "I'll tell you stories to cheer you up." But this child doesn't care. She's apathetic. She thinks only of her nausea. She wants it to go away and tries not

to think about it. "Be an adult," she tells herself. "Adults don't get sea-
sick," she's heard "real" sailors say. But nothing helps. The child is nause-
ated day and night. She's afraid to eat but knows she needs something on
her stomach. Dehydrated from vomiting and dry heaves, she's afraid to
drink but knows she should. She knows that fresh air is best for her, but she
can't sit up in the cockpit without vomiting, can't lie down because the sun
cooks her. And yet she doesn't want to go below because the odor of the
diesel fuel makes her gag.

After seventy-two hours at sea, the father lost patience. He felt the
child was malingering, that she should have gotten her sea legs by this
time, should have followed a conventional recovery pattern.

"Enough of this. Get up and work and forget about yourself. Forget
about the smells. Get engrossed in something," he told her.

The day before we left Acapulco I had mailed a letter to a colleague, saying, "We sail tomorrow for Easter Island and will be on the seas for four
weeks. This will be the real test of how well Don and I can do as a team
since the 'defection' of our crew. I have been learning to do things I
never wanted to learn and never thought I'd have the strength to do.
Perhaps I'll become a sailor in spite of myself."

So far, I hadn't done that. Aside from cooking, pumping the bilge,
and writing in the log, I was useless. Navigating, adjusting sails, and
checking equipment and conditions on the boat was a full-time job, and
Don was pulling that weight, while I was coping with continual nausea.

We began to have equipment failures: the galley freshwater pump was
sucking up air, not water; the fluorescent light over the galley counter quit;
the tape-deck speakers worked only intermittently; the switch on the cockpit spotlight broke. Also, two months earlier, off Cedros Island 330 miles
south of Los Angeles, the boat had suddenly lurched and crashed down on
an uncharted rock. Jeff and Don had epoxied the damage, and although it
had set well, we had been shipping water in the salon bilge ever since.

December 10

Don dove overboard to check the hull but couldn't find any obvious
leaks. Our only solution was to pump and pump, every few hours. The
motion of the boat hadn't changed, and I was still feeling miserable. And
because it didn't require me to think, pumping became my chore. As
long as I caught the water before it washed over the floorboards, my
efforts took a maximum of five minutes.

Cooking was a different story. I had to think, and it was no five-
minute job. I tried following Don's advice to keep a positive attitude as I

prepared lunch. *Relax. Think positively,* I told myself. *Practice your breathing. Inhale deeply. Exhale fully. Be positive.*

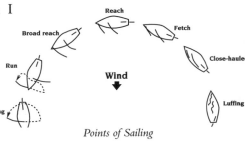

Points of Sailing

I tried lighting the stove, but the pressure in the kerosene fuel tank had dropped and I couldn't get a flame. To increase the pressure we used a bicycle tire pump that was mounted along the port side of the engine, aft of the galley. While I crawled back to retrieve it, seas slammed against the boat, knocking me against the galley lockers. I inhaled a lungful of diesel fumes; exhaled, held my breath, gagged; crawled back to the stove, opened the locker door below the stove, and attached the pump to the pressure valve. *Ten, twelve, fifteen, sixteen. Sixteen—pressure's good; enough to light the stove.* I detached the pump, crawled aft to restow it, and returned to the stove. I stood up and secured the safety belt around my rump. *Relax. Take a deep breath. Exhale.*

I poured alcohol into the burner cup, lit the alcohol, and let it burn off. The odor, antiseptic and sickeningly sweet, made me gag. I hung over the sink to heave—dry heaves, nothing came up.

I turned back to the stove. The alcohol had burned off. I turned on the valve, lit a match, and held it over the element. Black smoke hissed out. The burner wasn't hot enough yet to vaporize the kerosene.

Don came below to get his sextant. It was time for his noon shots.[1] About to ask for my help, he saw me struggling with the stove, hesitated, turned, and climbed back up the ladder. I poured more alcohol into the burner cup, repeated the process, and gagged. "Relax, think positively," I said aloud. I covered my nose with my hand. It smelled of alcohol and kerosene. An acute sense of smell was my curse on this boat. I grabbed a towel to cover my nose.

The alcohol burned off. I relit the burner. It grabbed this time, sending forth a clean blue flame. I poured a spoonful of olive oil into the frying pan; added fresh zucchini, tomatoes, onions, garlic, olives; crumbled a sausage bar over the mixture; put slices of Velveeta cheese on top. A poor man's *ratatouille*. It smelled good. *Maybe I can even eat a little of it myself,* I thought.

I served Don's plate and set it on the gimballed table so it wouldn't fly onto the floor while I was dishing up my own portion. I unbuckled myself, hung onto the pole, grabbed Don's bowl, crawled up the ladder, passed his bowl out to him, crawled down the ladder, grabbed my bowl, crawled back up, wedged my feet against the cockpit combing (sides), and took a bite. My esophagus revolted; the zucchini reversed itself. I hung over the lee rail.

Don said, "This is great. Can I finish yours?"

Before heading back to the berth I pumped the bilge for the fifth time since 0800. Forget sea legs—the biceps in my right arm were the only muscles I was building.

DECEMBER 11

By the fifth day we had settled into a routine, or rather, Don had. Breakfast before 0800. Juice, cocoa, fresh fruit, granola with canned milk. Today Don prepared his own breakfast, opened a can of V-8 juice for me, and made me a cup of hot chocolate. I drank the V-8 and took a sip of cocoa. The flavor of the creamer—the only chemical ingredient in my homemade mix—made me burp and gag. I slipped out of the berth and ran for the toilet, where the whole mess came up. The motion in the forward part of the boat made me all the more nauseated.

"Bring me a bucket," I yelled.

He brought it, and I inched my way up to the cockpit with the bucket under my chin. I prostrated myself on the sun-seared deck. *Better to burn on deck than die in the head*, I thought.

Afterward, Don took sun sights with his sextant. I timed for him listlessly, making errors. It took me five minutes to do correctly what should have taken one minute. He snarled, startling me to attention.

"Dammit, when I say 'mark,' push the stopwatch button and record the time. How are we going to find Easter Island if we don't start taking navigation seriously?"

Afternoon. The wind stopped, and le *Dauphin* flopped about. The mainsail and jib slapped noisily from side to side. Don lowered the sails, secured the booms, lashed the helm, came below, and snuggled up with me in the berth. Our sticky bodies reacted like contact glue.

Oh God, please don't let him get turned on, I thought.

Too late—God didn't do what I asked.

I groaned aloud, "How can you be turned on by a sick partner?" I knew he'd been suppressing his primal urge too long.

"I get turned on seeing you in your bikini. My desire doesn't turn off just because you're nauseated," he said gently, stroking my thighs.

His tender side always surfaced when we made love, and as much as I could have used some tenderness at the moment, lovemaking was the farthest thing from my mind. I hoped he would reconsider and fall asleep. He didn't. And I yielded, figuring one more refusal would turn him into a raving maniac. As the boat rolled—great jolting rolls without rhythm, without warning—I struggled to brace myself against the side of the berth.

I lay beside him, afterward, wondering how other women handled sex when the boat was heeling at a forty-five-degree angle. Even when I wasn't seasick, my libido seemed to do a nose-dive when we were sailing. I promised to do my own *Hite Report of Sailing Mates*. I had always suspected sailors were as horny[2] as the average *Penthouse* reader, but sex—like seasickness or feelings—is such a taboo in nautical literature that I could never find out how sexual urges were handled at sea, with or without a woman. Never.

Don awoke, unglued himself, and went topside to check the helm. The breeze was freshening. Black clouds gathered in the west, and noisy raindrops clattered on deck.

I fell asleep and dreamt that E. and I were attending a ball together. *A high-ceilinged room is edged in relief with gilded vines. Forests of faded green tapestries—knights in full mail, damsels in headdress, solitary unicorns—hang on paneled walls. An orchestra plays Viennese waltzes as E. and I weave a dance across the parqueted floor made uneven by centuries of ballroom feet. Our bodies are exquisitely tuned to each other's, and my white chiffon dress floats high and filmy above my knees as I twirl in three-quarter time. The ball ends, and the morning newspaper plasters the story of our love affair on its front page. The whole world knows about us now. Should we deny it?*

The sound of sloshing water awakened me before E. and I came to a decision. The dream disturbed me. The dancing—romantic and sensuous—uplifted me, delivered me from the daily sameness of nausea and

Don had to practice his navigational skills without my help

inactivity. But the newspaper story pulled me down—my damn subconscious wouldn't allow me even an hour of pleasure, real or imagined.

The sound of the water penetrated my consciousness. I listened; it wasn't the usual soothing sound of water rushing past the hull.

"Oh Christ!" I jumped down from the berth. I had slept over four hours and the cabin sole (floor) was awash; two inches of water covered my feet. The transverse frames of the hull in the forward part of the salon were acting as a dam, preventing the water from draining aft toward the lowest part of the bilge where I could pump it out. Heeling on this tack had increased the inflow from the leak in the bow.

I screamed to Don. He came below and removed the floorboards. "Get the bucket and a cup. We'll have to scoop the water out." He went back to the helm, and I spent the next thirty minutes scooping, dumping, and retching. It was 1745 when I finished, and time to start supper.

I wrote:

Oh dear God, if you ever listen to agnostics, help me get over this nausea. I want to get on with living.

Our destination—Easter Island—lies 3,500 miles south of Acapulco, and slightly west at 26°28' south, 105°23' west. After a week at sea we had covered nearly five hundred miles and were ten degrees from the Equator. Not a bad record, we thought, when the freshest winds rarely blew more than 10 knots (12 mph) or not at all. Our ship's log for each twenty-four-hour period read like a tennis volley: "Drop genoa and drift. Wind rising. Raise genoa. Light winds, start engine. Drop genoa. Raise genoa. Slight easterly, stop engine, set mizzen staysail."

The weather was sunny, hot, and muggy. Everything on deck and below—including the crew—perspired. The bulkhead began sprouting green fuzz; the nautical almanac began to wilt, its pages sticking together; the bath towels, toilet paper, and our clothes smelled like mildew.[3] It was the "typical cruising" described in the books I'd read. I'd expected it; but the reality was always worse than the literature, and I hadn't counted on being seasick.

December 13

Discouraged about not getting my sea legs, I had a weeping spell in the morning. As usual, Don came up with his own interpretation: "You're crying because you hate this trip, aren't you?"

"I am not. I'm crying because I feel wretched and useless. I'm not being good crew. I've tried to relax, tried to keep a good attitude, but nothing does any good, I keep having the dry heaves. Have you noticed how much weight I've lost? You can see my ribs now."

"Don't any of the books you've read say what to do for seasickness?"

"Hell, no," I said. "We've been through all this before. Nobody writes about the negative stuff—endless days of seasickness; grubby, humid, sticky, breathless days. No one complains about their boat being in shambles. No one tells you that everything gets wet, mildewy, and stinky. No one talks about body odor or dirty hair. No one talks about screwing on board. How was I supposed to know?"

I kept on—nausea hadn't slowed my tongue. "Remember how Al teased you when he was working on the boat about your unrealistic expections? You didn't believe those stories he told about his trip to Tahiti, did you? They were too real—realism doesn't sell. People want adventure, fantasy, heroism; man against nature, conquering, competing, setting records. People like me just don't come on trips like this—they *shouldn't* if they get seasick. But I never dreamt it would be this bad." I wept, engulfed in self-pity. Don shook his head and climbed back up the companionway ladder. Again I knew what he was thinking—"mental illness"—and my child-mind thought, *If I die of dehydration or starvation, he'll be sorry.*

The voices of friends who had filed by the dock in Los Angeles before we left streamed through my mind now. As they watched me shellacking two thousand tins of meats and vegetables, they chatted, eagerly supplying their own helpful and not-so-helpful comments about combating seasickness: You get seasick, and you're taking a world cruise? . . . Hey, I've got just the remedy—a tablespoon of white corn syrup before each meal. . . . Mix apple cider vinegar and honey and take a swig after each meal. . . . Drink tomato juice every hour—it works great! . . . Try hypnosis. . . . Stay plastered and you'll never know what happened . . . I continued to dip cans and nod, thanking people for their tips. Secretly, with the exception of hypnosis and getting drunk, I tried them all. Nothing worked.

Despite my nausea, my mind was beginning to appreciate the sea:

I like this wind that drives us forward, sometimes rhythmically, sometimes impulsively, across a great undulating plain of gentle hills and valleys. The patterns on the water look like wheat waving blue in the wind. Puffs of inky grey clouds balance at the horizon's edge, framing infinity. We are on a downhill run, galloping down, down, down to the Equator. My mind likes this sailing. My stomach likes nothing.

DECEMBER 15

Although I still felt rotten, I was now managing to cook two meals a day, reef the sails, set them, douse them, and stand watch during the night. I could identify the navigational stars without having to ask which constellation they were in, and I had been able to time for Don as he took his shots. But it was only a small percentage of what he needed. He was wearing out.

Not only had he been single-handling the 20-ton boat, he'd had to practice his navigational skills without my help. Since this leg of the cruise was the first time we'd been out of sight of land, he wanted to be sure his sun and star shots were on the mark. Taking the shots and doing the calculations demanded uninterrupted time, and because of me, he didn't have that time.

The self-steering vane didn't give him any help either. It gyrated so much as we beat into the wind that he was afraid it would break if we used it for any length of time. When conditions were stable, he could lash the helm, let the boat sail itself, and accomplish some chores, but that was rare; most of the time one of us had to stand watch.

Don had been filling my slot, but as the dark lines under his eyes deepened, so did his irritability—and my discouragement.

That night during our radio schedule, Tex made a phone patch (telephone call) to my friend Katherine Wells. Kathy, who was sharing details from our letters with the local newspapers, told us one of them had printed a story about why the boys bailed out.

"Either the boys didn't want to incriminate you, or the reporter didn't ask the right questions when she interviewed them," she said. "The article was pretty bland—the usual stuff about sailing. It entirely missed the point that their fantasies about the trip didn't match reality."

At the end of my night watch—0300 hours—we saw a mysterious green glow in the water. About thirty feet wide and fifteen feet deep, the spot passed slowly to starboard, then seemed to follow behind our stern. At first, Don thought it might be the reflection of our running lights and asked me to turn them off. I did. He looked over the stern. No luminescence. "If that was our running lights, the spot should return when we turn the lights on." I turned them back on; the spot had disappeared.

Could the spot have been Noctiluca, a luminescent micro-flagellate—the sea's version of a microscopic firefly—that gathers in vast groups and gives off an eerie green glow? When we pumped saltwater into the head we frequently witnessed a tiny fireworks display, as these tiny light-emitting creatures shot around the bowl. Or—a jarring thought—could the spot have been a whale covered with bio-luminescence?

We were approaching the same area where the Robertsons—an English family of six—had lost their 43-foot schooner. The boat had been hit and sunk by a pod of killer whales two hundred miles west of the Galapagos. The story of their thirty-eight days in a life raft, *Survive the Savage Sea*—published a year before we left—had given us pause. They were positive the thirty-foot whales had attacked their boat!

"That spot was about the same length as our hull," Don said. "It could have been a whale checking us out."

The luminescent spot disappeared, but Don and I were too uneasy to leave the cockpit. I thought about our own six-man life raft, stowed in our "bombproof" abandon-ship locker aft of the companionway. Don and Al Ryan—a friend who had rebuilt *le Dauphin Amical*—had spent hours designing the locker, a space of 18 cubic feet that held our Avon life raft, survival food, water and watermaker, spare sextant, nautical almanac, fish hooks and line, first aid supplies, life jackets, and warm clothing. Were there enough supplies in that locker? Could we offload everything in that locker within minutes? Would we be able to survive as the Robertsons had?

DECEMBER 16

We were 6 degrees north of the Equator, beneath a cloud belt that hangs over the Equatorial Trough.[4] We had hit the doldrums, an area infamous for flat seas and torrid temperatures, where sailing ships flounder in windless days, where men—like the Ancient Mariner—died with lips parched. Not so for us. The seas rolled along, like Iowa hills heaving slowly and gently. Squalls and thunderstorms, characteristic of the Trough, moved across the sky in endless procession, and for a change we had favorable winds. In these stable conditions, the steering vane took over the helm, relieving us from constant watches.

A squall hit mid-afternoon. Don was in heaven, hollering and screaming—"Isn't this great!"—racing down the ladder to get the bottle of liquid Joy, back up to lather himself and wait for the pelting downpour. Back down the ladder to ask for a towel, while I struggled with the stove at a thirty-five-degree angle.

"I'm clean now," he said, hoping his cleanliness would awaken my sex drive.

I ignored the implication and asked him if he could take down some canvas to make the boat ride a little easier—she had been leaping and galloping all afternoon and acted as if she would trip any moment.

"Nope. We'll never get to Easter Island unless we drive as hard as we can when the wind blows."

"You promised great sailing once we got to the Trade Winds," I whined.

"That was if we'd gone to the Galapagos."

"So it'll be like this all the way, even when we hit the Trades?"

"Probably," he answered.

Shortly afterward, I made the mistake of thinking out loud: "If I haven't kicked this nausea by the time we get to Easter Island, how would you feel about my flying to the coast of Chile and meeting you?"

The prospect of being forever nauseated was almost as appalling to me at this point as rounding Cape Horn, and I hoped Don would give me some sympathy, some sign that he understood what I was going through. But my timing was

Rooted to the helm during a squall

all off. His face quick-froze into what I called his Mongolian scowl, and he nearly exploded.

Of course he couldn't offer me sympathy after I'd just given him a replay of Mike, Carl, Sean, and Jeff. All he could see ahead were thousands of miles of water, the most difficult leg of the trip, the worst seas, and in a boat that wasn't designed to be sailed singlehandedly. *Abandoned.* He was going to be abandoned!

One side of my brain thought: *Maybe I'll get over this nausea soon.* The other side had already spoken.

I added timidly: "Maybe we could find someone at Easter Island who'll crew with us . . . or with you."

"Yeah. Maybe," he said icily.

If I could have retracted my words, I would have; but there was nothing I could do to make amends. And to make matters worse, conditions the next ten hours were the most trying we had experienced—repeated squalls, constant sail changes, an inaccurate chronometer, inability to get time ticks on the radio (we were out of range), batteries that wouldn't charge properly, corroding electrical fixtures, and—for Don—a seasick first mate who might defect. He had had it. Every gram of patience in his body had been depleted.

The next morning, vacillating between disdainful sarcasm and saccha-

rine sweetness, he launched into a completely illogical soliloquy: "If I
ever do this sort of trip again, I'll have an all-girl crew." (Understood that
I wouldn't be part of it.) "Girls are less competitive, easier to train, more
subservient." (Meaning *I* wasn't.) "Men are too competitive. They argue
all the
time about the captain's decisions." (Meaning that I was like a man at that
point. He was forgetting that *real* men never get seasick.) "Girls just
accept what the captain says." (Meaning *I* didn't.)

As little sense as this soliloquy made, it was designed to provoke me,
and it did. I wanted to scream at him: "You hypocrite—you consider
yourself a supporter of equal opportunity for women and you have the
gall to talk like this." Instead, I let the blood vessels in my temples expand,
gritted my teeth, and kept my mouth shut. We didn't need another fight.

DECEMBER 17

*Lava-blue clouds churn and roil. Steel sheets advance across the horizon like
an army on the march, leaving a trail of smoke in their path. Rain driven
by wind shoots across deck like volleys of machine-gun fire.*

*I love this weather! It's clean, honest weather. No pretenses, no indeci-
siveness, no vacillation—the sky knows what it wants to do and does it.*

The weather was a cathartic, and as long as I stayed in the cockpit I
felt better. Rooted to the helm under a poncho, I was wearing only my
foul weather jacket and a pair of underpants—but they were the first
clothes besides a bikini that I'd worn since Acapulco!

I had been at the helm for over four hours. Don was hungry and
wanted me to fix something to eat, but the minute I went below and
smelled diesel, alcohol, and kerosene, my gagging responses took over. I
didn't want to leave the helm, and I told him I'd make a deal: swap cooking for all-day helm duty.

He looked surprised. "I don't know how to cook, you know that."

"You can do it if I give you step-by-step directions. You know how
to open a can, don't you?"

"If it would help you get over your seasickness, I'm willing to give
anything a try."

That night, he filled an entire page in his journal with his disastrous
first attempt:

The cruising life is enough to make a grown man cry. While I'm putting the
sextant back in its case the boat takes a particularly sharp roll and the Ovaltine
jar flies off the galley counter where I left it open after fixing a cup for
Réanne. Ovaltine and glass all over the floor. Ovaltine must be hydroscopic
because it immediately picks up the moisture on the floor, congealing into
something like brownie crumbs. So I crawl around on all fours trying to push

this glue into little piles with the dust pan. Wham! The door under the sink swings open and clobbers me in the head. (I didn't close it properly when I took out the dustpan.) I take the dustpan topside to shake the stuff into the water; it blows all over the deck instead. Back down to get paper towels. There aren't any on the holder. And as if once wasn't enough, I do the same thing with a jar of homemade plum jam.

DECEMBER 18

After ten hours at the helm, I was sleeping a relaxed five hours—my first good sleep in days—when Don's shout awakened me. Panicked, I jumped down from the berth and bounded up the ladder.

"What's the matter?" I yelled.

"What do you mean?"

"You hollered for me, didn't you?"

"No. You must have been dreaming."

I was sure I'd heard him call. Perhaps I *had* been dreaming. Or was I losing my mind? "What ifs" had been creeping into my subconscious— *What if I fell overboard on watch while Don was asleep? What if a gust of wind hit the boat with all sails set, knocked it horizontal, and threw Don overboard? What if a freak wave swamped the cockpit while I was at the helm?* What if? What if? With the wind howling, the water swishing against the hull, the sails flapping and knocking, the one below would never hear a thing. The boat would sail blindly on, taking Don or me to a solitary fate. Perhaps my subconscious was telling me to be more vigilant. We hadn't been wearing our safety harnesses. It was time to use them.

Wide awake after that episode, I didn't want to go below again and took a four-hour watch in the rain. I was inching my way up from the bottom.

DECEMBER 21

Fifteen days from Acapulco, we crossed the Equator. It was winter solstice in the Northern Hemisphere, the shortest day of the year; summer solstice, the longest day, in the Southern Hemisphere. Until we reached a higher latitude, however, we wouldn't notice much difference in daylight. Near the Equator the length of daylight remains the same all year; just the time of the sunset and sunrise varies.

The temperature of the water and air were nearly equal at the Equator, and they had both dropped over 13 degrees since Acapulco. The air felt good. For the first time since we'd left California, I needed socks and shoes.

We have finally hit the southeast Trade Winds. It's wonderful, consistent, predictable sailing. The helm is lashed, the sails are set as they have been for three days, and le Dauphin takes us lopingly down the Southern Hemisphere. We are still beating into the wind, as we will all the way to Easter Island, but the beat is regular this time.

It was a day of celebration: we had crossed the Equator, I was beginning to pull out of my seasickness, and I was hungry!

"Would you make me some creamed tuna if I told you how to fix it?" I asked Don.

"Baby, I'll make *anything* you want if you'll just eat."

A can of albacore mixed with a can of shrimp soup, a dash of salt, pepper, onion powder, and basil tasted wonderful and stayed down.

Four hours later, still at the helm, I asked Don to bring me a raw potato and the peeler. I was hungry again.

"Good Lord, you'll get sick for sure if you eat a raw potato."

"Why would I crave a raw potato if my body didn't want it?"

One bite, I thought, would cure my craving, but it didn't. I ate the whole potato and asked for another. Two potatoes, raw and alkaline. My body was ignoring conventional wisdom. The trick at that point seemed to be to keep my stomach filled and to eat what I craved.

We had avoided talk about the future, but questions plied my brain constantly. Should I leave Don at Easter Island and fly to Chile? Should we look for someone else to help him? Although I was getting over my seasickness, I was concerned about what would happen once I set foot on land at Easter Island. Would I lose my sea legs and have to repeat the whole process when we went back to sea? And the thought of just the two of us rounding the Horn had begun to gnaw on me again. If I did continue, would we be able to find crew to help us? Unlike the sky I vacillated daily.

Don flip-flopped, too. Aloud. He was giving me the sweet-sour treatment again, and I hated it. We had begun to fight unmercifully, and one night, we had the ultimate showdown.

While I was on watch,

Trade wind sailing at last!

he came up to the cockpit to take some star shots and asked me to time for him. I loved this time of night and was in a good humor. The sky was a mass of stars, and I had fun playing a game with myself, trying not to look at the compass, and steering instead by the navigational stars whose positions I had finally memorized.

Earlier in the day, Don had rigged up a little 12-volt trouble-light that I could use at night to see the stopwatch when I timed his star shots. The idea was to hang it over my shoulders so my hands would be free for the stopwatch.

The seas had been extremely choppy all night, and as I tried to time I was having trouble managing both the helm and the stopwatch. At the very second Don called, "Mark!" the little bulb popped out of its socket and dropped onto my bare leg, burning it. I jumped up without thinking and quickly tried to replace the bulb in its socket without letting go of the helm. I was about to explain what happened when Don hollered, "Did you get it?"

Wedged against the main boom gallows, eight feet away, he was oblivious to my problems.

I started to explain, "No, the bulb—"

His wires crossed. Pent-up anger at a prospective defector poured out, and he screamed through clenched teeth, "What! You didn't get it? I ask you to do a simple thing and you can't even do that right, you stupid bitch. All you do is lie around and play sick. You don't do a goddam thing right."

This time he had jabbed too far. Something snapped in me, and I screamed back with all the might I could muster. "You sonovabitch, you don't even know what happened. I was trying to help, but your home-made job fell apart. You don't give a damn about me—all you care about is this damn boat—and you're doing the same thing to me that you did to the boys. You think I like being nauseated? I hate it! No matter what you may think, I didn't *plan* to be sick!"

"I'm sick of you," he said.

"I'm sick of you, too! And as soon as I can get off this goddam boat I'll go home, get a divorce, and you can find some other broad who loves sailing and can screw standing on her head."

Totally out of control and oblivious to fairness on my own part, I kept screaming.

He looked at me, shocked, and without speaking went below, leaving me to wrestle a helm as uncontrollable as I was.

When I had exhausted my vocal cords, I called to him, nearly hoarse, and full of remorse and shame. "We've got to talk. We've got to work it out. There's just you and me."

"What do you suggest?" he asked coldly.

"Please don't be like that," I pleaded.

He thawed slightly and said, "Look, we both need sleep. I'm exhausted. I'll take the sails down, lash the helm, and we'll lie ahull."

We went below, climbed into the berth, and slept without touching. The next day, feeling low and sorry for myself, I wrote:

Today Don is polite, distant. I don't know whether we can survive together or not. Perhaps I'm holding on to something I should have relinquished a long time ago. Am I hanging on because "to fail is the worst part"? I have to make a decision.

Despite our standoff, my morale continued to improve as my appetite did, and I began to assume more of the duties. Navigation and plotting lessons were finally beginning to stick, and I enjoyed them, but I felt like a pupil being driven by her master.

I imagine myself the study of a daguerreotype, sitting beside the master who holds a willow switch in his hand. Glaring at every figure I write down, every page I turn in the Nautical Almanac, every calculation I make, he's ready to rap my knuckles at the first error.

His lessons are peppered with: "Don't you know anything?" "Can't you understand?" "I told you that before. Can't you remember anything?"

Right brain versus left brain. I want to lash back with: "How come you can't spell?" "Why can't you learn to say 'should have gone' instead of 'should have went'?" "Can't you remember height ends with a 't,' not 'th'?"

But I don't. I am learning self-control. My defense has been to write my own succinct step-by-step procedure in "simple English" for calculating and plotting our position. I have just reduced a hypothetical sun shot in fifteen minutes flat, and the master proclaims my calculations "excellent!"

DECEMBER 23

Don's noon sun shot put us halfway to Easter Island (1,471 nautical miles from Acapulco). With sunny weather and brisk winds for two days we had been able to run with all sails, including our largest, the 550-square-foot genoa (genny). We were logging miles, but west toward the Philippines, not in the direction of Easter Island.

Concerned about our inability to head south, Don wrote:

The wind is from almost due south, and with a northwest-setting current and this broad beamy boat, we can't make headway against the wind. I curse the Ecuadorian government for not letting us call at the Galapagos—it would have made this leg of our journey a lot easier. But if the old clipper ships managed to pass close west of Easter Island on their route from San Francisco to the Horn, eventually we should be able to do as well as they did.

We had spent the day making repairs—projects that had been piling up on our fast-growing "to do" list. At home, repairs bored Don, and since I liked puttering I usually replaced toilet valves, changed faucet washers, reinstalled weights in window frames, removed old wallpaper and hung the new. It was easy. The house didn't rock and roll; the corners were all ninety-degree angles, and the surfaces were flat.

On a boat, though, where right angles don't exist, Don was challenged. For ten hours he worked as though he'd been pumped with a quart of high octane.

He dismantled the defective galley pump and exchanged it with the head pump. (We would have to take our "baths" in the galley, but I didn't care since the head wasn't my favorite part of the boat.) His challenge was intellectual and physical: to dismantle the pump he had to lie on the galley sole, wrapping his torso and legs into two distinct ninety-degree angles, or stand on his head and carefully finger the bolt he wanted to tighten but couldn't see—all this, while the boat leapt and charged. I couldn't handle that; he could.

Since we were still shipping tremendous amounts of water in the forward part of the salon, he attached a portable bilge pump to the mast, adding six feet of tubing that would stretch forward to the head sink. Now, instead of bailing with one of my cooking pots, we could pump out the water.

He cleaned and resoldered the connections in the tape-deck speakers so we had music again! He repaired the emergency strobe light and lashed it to the bottom of the boom gallows where it could be seen by another boat. He tested the shortwave transmitter (for emergencies) but couldn't get the proper amperage output. He'd have to puzzle that one for a while.

In addition to these critical repairs, he was testing ideas for singlehandling the boat. But he had begun to cut the cord and wasn't discussing his ideas with me. He had spent several hours rigging a line from inside the cabin to the steering vane at the stern, so the vane could be adjusted without going on deck. He had also made a sketch for an inside steering seat with a cupola mounted in the hatch cover, similar to Moitessier's design. He did show me the sketch, mumbling something about hiring a master carpenter on Easter Island to build it. I thought, *Good luck finding a carpenter of any kind*, but I kept quiet.

Each time Don began a repair today, I asked if he'd like my help. Each time, he replied in a sing-song tone, "No, thanks, I can do it myself." I know he's feeling lonely, but his martyr attitude has begun to annoy me. I wanted to say, "Drop the act, will you!"—but that would spark another feud. I don't want to disturb our tenuous truce.

Since our fight, we have avoided confrontation. We are friends, comrades. We talk about the boat, the weather, the books we finally have time

to read. We spend several hours in the evening making amateur radio con-
tacts. We make repairs; we cook (Don executes, I direct). We pump; we
pump. But there's no exchange of affection, no shared joy. No "God, I'm
glad you're with me!" Just the captain and his (reluctant) mate, enduring.

    What will my decision be? My unresolve depresses me. I have to make
a decision, stick to it no matter what happens, even if it severs the cord. I've
lived alone before. I can do it again.

DECEMBER 24

Just after midnight, halfway through my watch, I heard, "Holy sheeit."
Don climbed out the hatch and came toward the helm with a flashlight in
one hand.

"Take a look at this!" He flashed on the light—a flying fish, not more
than seven inches long, wriggled in his clutched hand. His voice was full
of enthusiasm, and after his attitude earlier in the day I was surprised that
he wanted to share this incident with me.

"He flew in the porthole and landed on my stomach," he said. "I
don't know which of us was more frightened. Do you want to save him
for breakfast?"

"Not unless you can get a couple dozen others to do the same trick,"
I said.

He threw the little creature back in the water, climbed down the ladder, and went back to bed.

The night sky was beautiful, and as I sat at the helm I began to mull
over the pros and cons of continuing with Don. I was getting my sea legs,
and the more weight I pulled, the better we got along. But as long as he
thought I would bail out at Easter Island, I was sure his coolness would
continue. It was a catch-22, and I couldn't expect him to melt first. But
by the end of my watch, 0300 local time, something else consumed my
thoughts. The symptoms of a bladder infection I'd been trying to ward off
hit full bore. Two weeks without proper fluids had lowered my resistance,
and my immune system finally caved in.

I went below, dug into the ammo box we used for medicine, and
pulled out the vial of Azo-Gantrisin our doctor called "horse pills." They
were huge, red, and big enough to gag a horse. I swallowed two of them
before climbing into the berth, but when Don awakened me at 0800, I
had chills, aching muscles, and a fever. And I was nauseated again.

He passed me a cup of Ovaltine. One sip and my stomach did reverse
peristalsis. I slid down from the berth, leapt forward, flung the toilet seat
up, and put my face into the head.

No gagging session this time—the vomiting went on and on and on.
Don came forward to check on me, worried by my inability to stop, and

puzzled by what had brought it on. He had the tact to wait until I was back in bed before he asked, "What did I do *this* time to make you unhappy?"

In a barely audible voice I squeaked, "It's not *you*—and I thought I was over this nausea. It's either the cystitis or the pills."

I expected him to suggest his usual remedy—drink lots of water and keep a positive attitude, but he took the *Merck Medical Manual* out of the bookcase, turned to the section on genito-urinary infections, read silently, then looked gently at me. "Maybe you'd better keep taking the pills. It says seven days here . . . You go back to sleep. I'll handle the boat."

I fell into a drugged sleep and dreamt it was midsummer. *Don and I stand ankle-deep in a green, daisy-sprinkled meadow that slopes steeply to a stream. Suddenly it begins to snow, and the meadow turns to ice. The temperature rises again, and the meadow froths and bubbles with blue water. A toddler suddenly appears, falling and tripping over her own tiny feet. We enter a house, and the baby follows us, filling her mouth with crystals of Ovaltine. Suddenly she begins choking, and when I stick my finger down her throat to dislodge whatever has caught, she goes limp, like a rag doll. I panic: Oh God, how can Don and I survive if this child dies? I scream to Don. I scream and scream and scream, but he doesn't come.*

I awoke drenched with perspiration—my fever had broken. I lay still for a moment trying to interpret the dream. *The changes in temperature are those of my own body. The toddler is our marriage. Oh God!*

I glanced at my watch—1710 hours. I had slept all day. I heard Don adjusting the jib sheet, and I realized that it was Christmas Eve. I felt better; the nausea had passed. I slipped down from the berth and gave myself an alcohol bath.

Don came below: "How do you feel?"

"Much better, but weak still."

"Would you like some supper if I cook it?"

"Just some bouillon and crackers."

"Okay, then we'll see if we can find a ham radio operator to do a phone patch to your parents."

Sailing down the coast of Baja these little flying fish had provided as much entertainment as a pod of dolphins. We frequently found six or seven of them lying around deck in the morning, but this was the first we'd seen in a while. In "flight" they reminded me of magpies swooping in for a landing. Technically they don't fly; they glide along the top of the water on birdlike pectoral fins, sometimes attaining speeds up to thirty miles an hour for as much as a thousand feet, or they launch themselves out of the water like rockets with their vibrating tail fins.

I gave him a hug, tender and prolonged. *I love him right now,* I thought. *If only he understood how much these small moments of thoughtfulness ease tension between us.*

It was 2040 hours local time when Don tuned up the radio. Palmer Station, Antarctica, boomed through in communication with the *Hero*, an American Research Vessel on its way to the Horn.[5]

Don broke in: "KC4AAB, this is K6KWS on board *le Dauphin Amical.* We're on our way to Easter Island now, but we'll be down your way in a few weeks."

"Anything we can do for you by radio, we'll be glad to," answered John, the radio engineer aboard the *Hero*.

"Appreciate that," Don said. "Our chronometer is acting up and we're having trouble getting time ticks on WWV."[6]

Palmer Station (KC4AAC) broke in and told us they monitored the air every night and offered to give us time signals when the *Hero* wasn't around.

"Are you headed for the Horn, or do you plan to go through the Strait of Magellan?"

Don told them the Horn. He didn't mention he might go solo.

John suggested we stop in Ushuaia on our way north to Punta Arenas. "We'll be there for over a month and we'd like to have you aboard if you stop there."

I thought about Ushuaia, "the southernmost town in the world." I remembered photos in *National Geographic:* bright blue and aqua frame houses that dotted the base of fog-wrapped mountains; the Beagle Canal, still and glassy, or windswept with spume; impenetrable forests; snow-capped cordillera. I asked myself if I wanted to miss the fun of a stop like that—the spontaneity, exploring the land, meeting the inhabitants. That was what excited me; that was my type of adventure. I'd miss it if I flew to Chile.

After he signed off with Palmer Station and the *Hero*, Don searched the band for a California station. Three minutes, five—the band was dead. Ten minutes later he tried again. He shook his head. "Well, Christmas Eve . . . I guess all the hams are busy with family tonight." He waited five minutes and tried again.

"This is W6MWL in San Francisco. Did I hear a Maritime Mobile Station on frequency?"

"You must be the only ham working tonight," Don said.

If I could have leapt over the airways I would have. I wanted to hug the man, wanted to hug all the hams who had helped us—all those who'd given their time so we could communicate with our family and friends. I wanted to tell the world about them, to let everyone know how wonderful they were. They were our only tie to land.

Don and I bet that Daddy's first words would be "overdrawn at the bank," and instantly I regretted having been so flip. The day we left Acapulco, I'd received a letter from Mother telling me Daddy had cancer. His back problem, which had been plaguing him for two years, had been diagnosed as a slow-growing cancer of the spine. According to the doctor he had two or three more years. I had tried not to think about it, and although I would never have let on to Don, I secretly wondered how much the shock had contributed to my drawn-out bout with seasickness.

I felt bad that I had asked him to handle our finances in the first place, but I hadn't known at the time that he was ill. He had always been my rock, and I'd never thought about his mortality. Now I prayed he would hold up until I returned home.

When we got through at last, Daddy didn't mention a word about banks, checks, overdue bills, or bills paid. It had been over three weeks since we'd talked and his joy was apparent. But, as always, he was embarrassed to think someone else might be listening. After a few sentences he passed the phone to Mother, who carried on with family news and the weather in San Francisco ("raining wildly"). She also told us she had arranged for the Salem Clock Company to send a replacement chronometer to Easter Island. She passed the phone to Sean, who was spending the holidays with them.

Up to that point nothing had made me nostalgic. Nothing on the boat or ocean resembled Christmas. But hearing Sean's voice brought up all the memories of Christmases past—candle stubs melting in a saucepan over a makeshift kitchen in the backyard, fruitcake ingredients steeping in brandy and wine, the odor of fresh redwood boughs clipped from trees in our front yard—memories and traditions put away till another generation renewed or remolded them in its own fashion.

Christmas 1974 would have been our last big Christmas together. Would . . . have been.

"I miss the kids," Don said quietly after we signed off the air.

"I do too," I said, barely able to speak.

He put his arms around me. "Let's go to bed. The boat will sail herself."

CHRISTMAS DAY

I awakened after nine hours of sleep, during which I'd been totally oblivious to Don's ups and downs during the night to check conditions and make adjustments.

I smelled smoke and burning pine. "You built a fire in the woodstove!"

Don grinned, happy he'd pleased me.

"Take a look outside," he said

I slid down from the berth, still a little weak, pulled back the hatch cover, and poked my head up. The view I would have chosen for Christmas morning—snow-covered mountains, evergreen branches weighted and heavy, poplars and elms denuded—wasn't what I saw. But it was drizzling, cold, and grey—the grey of a winter's day—and I liked it.

"I've planned the menu for dinner. I'll make it if you tell me where to find everything . . . You look a lot better. How do you feel?"

"Like I've come out of a tunnel. Like I'm finally going to live."

Making sail repairs, I felt useful again

We listened to Handel's *Messiah* as we opened Kathy and Jean's gift—a small box marked "No peeking before December 25." Inside we found tiny red and green *ojos de Dios,* a felt Christmas tree, miniature stockings filled with sticky candy canes, and a bright green tablecloth, the exact dimensions of our galley table, with napkins to match.

Don prepared dinner under my direction: turkey and gravy with chestnuts, yams glazed in sweet butter, celery hearts, plum pudding with hard sauce.

We saved our last gift until after dinner: a cassette tape made without our knowledge at a going-away party Kathy had thrown for us.

Voices glided across the tape, philosophical, warm, or teasing, like—"Hey, Don, is sex in the South Pacific everything it's cracked up to be?" (*How little they know!* I thought.) Then Kathy's voice, low and throaty, with sentimental comments about past Christmases and New Years celebrated with the "gang." When the tape ended, I looked at Don. His face was as wet as mine. Our hands met and squeezed.

Christmas Day was wonderful. I was overwhelmed by the thoughtfulness of our families and friends—the warmth that makes life worthwhile. Don was human, affectionate, natural. Nothing contrived in his behavior—no sar-

casm, no disdain or affectation these past few days. When he's like this I could go to the ends of the earth with him.

Le Dauphin was looking more and more like she had as *Liddie Mae*, before we renovated and renamed her. There had been no letup in squalls since we hit the southeast trades a week before, and she was a mess. She acted like a horse jumping hurdles, landing in black holes, and we—the jockeys —could barely hold on.

I thought of the nonsailors who'd asked us, "How are you going to get enough exercise on the boat?" and wished they could see us now, climbing up and down the ladder, adjusting the sheets, changing the sails, reefing the main, unreefing it, or raising the genny and dousing it the moment a squall passed through—all at a thirty-degree incline. In addition, we were building up our biceps—the boat was taking on more water, and we had to pump more frequently.

In fact, managing the boat was equivalent to running a 10K race twice each day. We didn't need to worry about getting fat.

During one of the midday squalls, Don rushed to the bow to douse the genny and raise the jib.

"This is purgatory," he yelled.

"You love it! You know you love it."

"Yeah! It sure cures boredom."

I felt good. I'd recovered from the cystitis and, despite the horrid beating we were taking, had no more nausea. When Don relieved me from helm duty I went below to bake Irish soda bread—a first after twenty-two days at sea.

The two of us seemed to be holding up better than our equipment. The rotor and weight on the recording log wore through its line sometime during the night

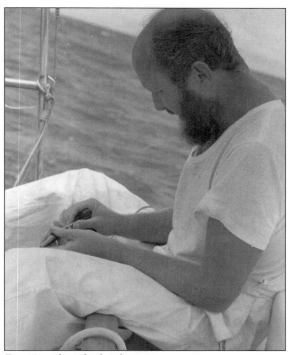

Don tries to knot the thread

and dropped off; Don had to replace them and adjust the reading. Halyards chafed through, slides and thimbles parted from the sails and fell on deck like hailstones, and by December 28 our mainsail and two headsails were out of commission.7

Saltwater had damaged tins of food stowed in the bilge; the Presto logs stowed in the "wood box" below our berth (the driest spot in the boat) soaked up bilge water and exploded into pulpy mush. Two cartons of bandages, pills, and syringes stowed on top of the Presto logs were mildewed and soggy. We spooned the wet pulp into plastic cartons to save for a sunny drying-day. I salvaged what I could of the bandages and medicines and threw the cartons and boxes overboard.

DECEMBER 28

Don's noon sun shot puts us due north of Easter Island—10°26'S, 109°30'W, with 670 miles to go, and 10 degrees latitude to gain. He says if we don't get relief from this southeast wind, we'll overshoot Easter.

Today he is discouraged and exhausted, short-tempered, headachy, and nauseated, and it's his turn to hit the bunk. I have managed not to ask stupid questions or make sarcastic remarks about the fact that he "never" gets seasick. He is human and weak, and it's my turn to take over while he rests.

I went above and engaged the steering vane so I could make sail repairs without interruption. The vane chattered and banged, objecting to the wind, but I ignored it and went forward to remove the mainsail from its track. Wedged against the mast, I began the tedious task of sewing on new slides. Rain pelted me; waves broke over the cabin. The boat galloped, jumped, twisted, rolled from port to starboard, and shuddered.

I loved it! I loved the cool air—the rain, the wind. I loved being well, being useful again! *I feel so good,* I thought. *I might even be able to handle Cape Horn.*

Repairs completed, I reinstalled the main in its track, lashed it to the boom, and went below to make myself a cup of cocoa. The boat lurched—throwing me against the galley counter—and boiling water spilled down my front.

"Dammit! Can't you do something about this boat?" came out before I could bite my tongue.

I expected instant retaliation. Instead, Don said, "Yeah, I've about had it, too. I'm not even going to raise the main; we'll let the jib drive us. Come to bed with me, and we'll stay here till we feel like getting up."

DECEMBER 29

Captain has declared this Mental Health Day. It's our first day without rain in two weeks. We slept past local noon. Don missed his midday sun-

shot and doesn't care. "No shots, no plotting today," he says.

He has been logging the number of strokes it takes each time we pump the bilge. The total for the past twenty-four hours is 1272. He figures it takes eight strokes to empty a gallon of water, so in one day we pump out 159 gallons. A lot of water!

Whenever conditions permitted Don and me to go to sleep together, we took turns pumping. At the slightest change of motion—a sound in the rigging, a difference in the cadence of the water rushing against the hull, water sloshing in the bilge—like a mother's response to a newborn baby, we were both instantly awake.

"Your turn this time," one of us would say when the sloshing got too loud to ignore. The other would roll over and go back to sleep.

With the self-steering vane behaving, we had more time during the day to read. At night, we expanded our circle of amateur radio friends. Burt in Brasilia fed us international news. Peter, who worked on a peat farm in the Falklands, wanted to know if we planned to call on "his" islands. Our ETA (estimated time of arrival) for Port Stanley was mid-April. "You must come to visit me, then," he said in a clipped British accent.

Darrell at McMurdo Sound, Antarctica, wanted to know if we were the boat bringing their "much needed supplies."

We laughed. "Hey, we're just a rowboat compared to the ship that delivers your supplies," Don said.

John, on the *Hero*, now 600 miles northwest of Cape Horn, told us the waves were getting "very big and very interesting!"

L., under house arrest in Quito, Ecuador, for violating the 200-mile fishing rights boundary, swore he hadn't.[8] While he was detained, waiting for the American government to pay the fine for his release, the soldiers "guarding" his boat stripped the deck of everything not bolted down—anchors, lines, fishing

tackle. We wondered how he had managed to save his ham radio intact, but we didn't ask. His story seemed contrived.

New Year's Eve

Don uncorked the champagne some friends had given us for the occasion, and drank by himself.

"You sure you don't want any? Just a taste?"

"Hell no!" As much as I love the bubbly lightness of champagne, I didn't want to risk even a swallow. I'd learned early on that rolling seas and alcoholic beverages were a volatile mixture for me, and the minute I headed out of port, I became an ardent teetotaler.

One bottle of champagne entirely to himself made Don giggly and amorous. He looked at my hair, frizzy and unmanageable from lack of shampooing, and ran his hand through it. "You look sexy," he said.

I had recently read about the mating habits of doves and learned that they mate only after a rain when the air is clean and they've had their bath. I figured I was a dove.

JANUARY 2

The boat was heeling forty-five degrees to starboard, but I couldn't stand my dirty hair any longer. The "sexy look" had to go.

I belted myself into the galley, stuck my head under the saltwater spigot, and pumped. At 23°C (70°F), the water seemed glacial. I squirted liquid Joy into my hair, dreaming of fragrant-smelling shampoos (which don't work in salt water), conditioners that make hair silky, and a blow dryer that gives it fluff.

The boat jerked and rammed me against the edge of the sink. (Inattention always brought trouble.) I rinsed, then decided my hair needed a second wash, since it had been three weeks.

The cap was loose, and detergent spread over my head like an oil slick, running into my eyes, my nose, my mouth. I squeezed out what I could, grabbed a dish towel to wipe my eyes, unbelted myself, groped for the ladder with my eyes still closed, pulled myself up, and shouted to Don, "Please help me!"

Back to the sink, I snapped into the belt and hung my head over it again. Don came below.

"Will you rinse my hair, please." My voice resonated against the stainless steel.

"Jesus! It looks like you've got a whole bottle of Joy in your hair."

JANUARY 4

We have just 300 miles left to landfall. More squalls during the night created havoc. Twelve more thimbles dropped off the mainsail; the steering vane sail blew out; five snap shackles parted from the genoa. So it's another repair day.

While Don adjusted the rigging, cleaned and greased fittings, I attached thimbles. My repair tools were a leather sailmaker's palm, a curved needle that looks like a halibut hook, and waxed sail twine that could suture an elephant's hide.

Don stopped what he was doing and stationed himself across from me in the cockpit where the genoa and I took up most of the space.

"It sure is taking you a long time. Can't you hurry a bit? We need the genny."

Sail repairs are no ordinary home-sewing job—they're slow, tedious, and hazardous—and I was working as fast as I could without doing a sloppy job.

"Take it easy. I don't want these slides to wear through in a week."

"Yeah, but you take forever just to thread the needle and tie a knot. You're too much of a perfectionist." His hands were fidgety; he wanted to grab the needle and show me how to do it. "How come you don't use a longer thread than that?" (Twenty-four inches.)

"Because it gets tangled if it's any longer."

"Come on, let me do it." He grabbed the thread and knife, cut off a forty-inch length, said, "Here, gimme the needle. . . . What do I do now?"

"Tie it off at one end."

"Why can't you tie it off at the needle so it doesn't pull through the eye?"

"It won't go through the sail if you do that."

He tied it at the eye, anyway. "I just want to see if I can make it work." He couldn't. "Yeah, I see what you mean." He took two turns around the thimble slide and into the sail. Wrong direction.

I saw my chance to get even. "Good grief, I thought any idiot knew how to sew. You were in the army, weren't you? Didn't you have to sew on your own patches?" His thread was too long. "No! That's not the way to do it! Don't you remember? I told you your thread would get tangled."

He lost interest, wanting to do it his way, instantly, which didn't work. He stood up and pushed the sail back on my lap.

"Oh no," I said in a stage voice. "Every good sailor should be able to do his own repairs. Keep it up; I'll just sit here and watch."

"Uh, you'd better show me again."

I repeated everything: the length of thread to cut; how to thread the needle; how to knot the thread at the end; how to anchor it securely in the hem of the sail; how to do figure-eight stitches to attach the slide to the sail.

He attached two slides properly. "There, how's that? You can take over again, if you want to."

"I don't want to. You keep at it. You've got to learn to do it right." He did one more, incorrectly. "No, that's not what I showed you. You weren't paying attention. How can you be so stupid? Even kids know how to sew."

He gave me a sheepish grin. "Okay, you've made your point. Will you please finish? My fingers aren't coordinated enough for this job."

January 5

As we headed farther south, reception on our portable short-wave radio grew increasingly weak. In order to strengthen the signal, Don had rigged a jumper cable from the shortwave antenna to the ham transmitting antenna that led to the top of the mast. We had been receiving BBC and the Voice of America. The night before, he had forgotten to disconnect the jumper, and when he tuned in for our nightly ham schedule he "fried" the shortwave.

He was already getting nervous as we approached land—he wanted the boat to be in good enough shape to receive the Chilean port captain—but his carelessness had put him in a nasty humor.

"You could have helped by reminding me," he accused.

It was true. I usually remembered those things, but I hadn't and told him I was sorry. My apology didn't help. He began to pick at me again. I knew he was feeling vulnerable, wondering if I'd catch the first flight out, but his sarcastic outbursts during the day cooled any sympathy I felt toward him. I was angry and felt my only defense was to bite my tongue to keep the peace.

One voice inside me insists, "You want to continue, you know you do. You want to test yourself—admit it. The worst is over; you feel good now, and you and Don are lovers again. You know you want to participate in the ultimate adventure."

The other voice says, "After you leave Easter Island and go back to sea you'll get seasick again. You don't want to go through that again, do you? Besides, family and friends are more important than pursuit of adventure. Life is so fragile and precarious, why spend the little time you have testing yourself? Leave while you can."

So what will I do? I don't know yet . . .

Noon log entry: "Have regained all our easting and have only 100 miles to go. Predict we'll sight Easter Island tomorrow."

I spent the morning scrubbing the cabin floor, polishing the brass lamps, cleaning the lamp chimneys, putting away books, reducing Don's sights (twice), pumping and pumping and pumping. The boat was in Bristol-shape for our official entry.

JANUARY 6

"Land! I see it!" Don yelled to me at 1030 hours. It was day thirty-two out of Acapulco.

I rushed above to look and saw a mound rising along the western horizon. Hour by hour, as we approached, the mound rose, becoming a vivid green, and except for its volcanic cones—purple and indigo—it looked like Ireland.

I hugged Don. "Pretty good, *Capitán!*"

"Not bad, huh? It's a helluva thrill to make a landfall after thirty-two days. Our navigation isn't too bad after all." He had included me in his kudos. I was surprised and pleased.

"We should be off the east end of the island by sunset. We'll try to anchor in Hotu Iti."

The chart showed Hotu Iti as a small cove open to the south and east. The *Sailing Directions for South America* read: "Provides shelter from northerly and westerly winds. Heavy swells are predominant."

At sunset—just as Don had predicted—we passed the bold, perpendicular headland of Cabo Roggeween, named for the Dutch navigator who sighted the island on Easter Sunday in 1722.

Cumulonimbus clouds, which had churned above the craters all day, opened and poured out. The sea surging against the cliffs of the cape looked menacing. Along the waterline, sea caves and blowholes ingested white foam, then spewed it out and upward along the reddish-brown rock.

The entry to Hotu Iti is so deep we had to approach within a hundred yards of its head before the echo sounder gave us a reading. Swells echoing off the sides of a cliff knocked us from side to side, from bow to stern. The squalls had extinguished the loom of Hanga Roa—the town on the opposite side of the island—and it was pitch-black by then.

Don sent me to the bowsprit to watch for rocks. A pick-up truck on shore flashed its high beams and honked its horn.

"They're welcoming us!" Don yelled from the cockpit. "What's it look like? Do you think we can anchor here?"

The headlights blinded me, and it was too dark for me to see the lay of the cove. But I could see rocks glistening in the rain thirty yards to port, and the cliff to starboard. The staysail slapped from side to side, jerking and tugging on the forestay like a wild animal under yoke. The bowsprit bucked and dipped, setting me knee-deep in foam. My arms, locked under the rail, were numb from gripping, my glasses fogged and coated with salt.

"For godssake, what's it look like?"

My answers carried forward with the east wind; Don couldn't hear a word I said. I crouched along deck, clutching the lifelines as I went aft. I should have been wearing my safety harness, but it hadn't occurred to me that it would be so rough.

"Look!" Don said pointing toward shore.

Three figures stood in front of the headlights, waving their arms. "Maybe they're trying to tell us the anchorage is safe," Don said.

"Maybe," I said. "But they could be warning us away, too. I don't like the feel of this place." I hoped Don would agree.

"I don't, either. Let's turn and run, but we'll have to tack back and forth till daylight. Are you game?"

At 0430 hours, a pale yellow streak along the eastern horizon announced day. The glow of the village was visible again over the northwest tip of the island. Exhausted from our sleepless night, we started the engine and motored west along the coast of the island. Direction—Hanga Roa.

NOTES

1. A noon sun shot is the oldest and simplest technique of celestial navigation used to determine latitude. A sextant, a nautical almanac, and some simple math are all that are required to determine latitude. However, the frequent obstruction of the sun or the horizon by clouds at midday makes noon shots somewhat difficult and unreliable in the tropics and at high latitudes.

2. The word *horny* is supposed to have originated during the days of the clipper ship passages round Cape Horn. When the Cape Hornies landed in San Francisco, they made a beeline for the nearest prostitution houses.

3. Spraying the bulkheads with Lysol and keeping books and clothing in tight zip-lock bags helped cut down the mold, but after a while I got used to the fact that everything acquired a musty odor. I even grew sentimental about it, and now that musty odor can bring back a flood of memories.

4. The *Mariner's Handbook* defines the Equator as: "An area of low pressure situated between the trade winds of the two Hemispheres. Characteristics: light and variable winds alternating with squalls, heavy rain and thunderstorms. Varies greatly in width both daily and seasonally. Average strength of the trades is Force 4." (p.70)

5. The *Hero*, a 125-foot wooden-hulled motor-sailor owned by the National Science Foundation, spent many summers transporting international scientists between Ushuaia (Argentina) and Antarctica. Although she was "retired" in 1985 and replaced with a larger, more modern ship, she still plies the waters around the Strait of Magellan.

6. Time tick: The National Bureau of Standards in Boulder, Colorado, maintains an atomic clock that is the world time standard. It broadcasts time signals ("time ticks") on clear-channel high-frequency stations in Colorado and Hawaii. During the oil crunch and electricity "brown out" of 1974/75, the radio stations WWV and WWVH reduced power as a conservation measure. They also stopped broadcasting the time interval in Morse code, which is easier to read than voice transmissions in difficult radio conditions. Without a reliable external reference to Greenwich Mean Time (now called Universal Standard Time), we had to correct our chronometer's time to what we thought the average loss or gain was since we had last adjusted it. We were experimenting with a new "quartz chronometer," which turned out not to be up to the pounding our trip was giving it. Without accurate time (from a chronometer, short wave radio, or satellite) there is no way to determine longitude.

7. Our recording log, mounted on the stern (or taffrail), consisted of a long line trailed behind the boat with a rotor at its end. Although it was more accurate than our electronic knotmeter, the line was subject to wear, and in extremely rough seas we couldn't use it.

8. Between 1953 and 1973, Ecuador seized 127 fishing vessels that refused to recognize its self-acclaimed 200-mile sovereignty. The American government reimbursed all fees, fines, and estimated losses in time to those American fishing vessels apprehended.

CHAPTER 3

Isla de Pascua—the Long Wait

JANUARY 8

1000 hours. We are anchored in Hanga Roa Bay off the only village on Easter Island, waiting for the Chilean officials to come aboard and clear us for entry. Our yellow quarantine flag and the Chilean tricolor with its lone white star flap noisily on the halyard above the cabin.

On shore, a string of brightly painted casitas dissected by red clay roads stretch along the black volcanic rock formations. To the north of the village, a row of the famous stone moai (statues) stand with their backs to us, looking inland. Rano Kao, one of the island's extinct volcanoes, rises above the village to the south. As we passed by it early this morning, we noticed that its flanks appear to plunge straight into the Pacific. Just after we anchored, a squall brought thirty minutes of heavy wind and rain and chop, and waves are still slapping against the hull.

I'm overcome by a curious mixture of emotions. Awe—to realize we are here at an archaeological treasure I've seen in picture books since I was child; an island that, until recently, could be reached only by the means

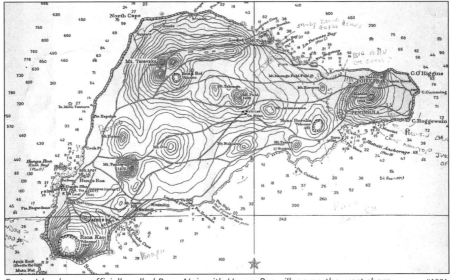

Easter Island, now officially called Rapa Nui, with Hanga Roa village on the west shore   #1281

we've chosen. Relief—to know that we made it 3,500 miles with just a sextant, the Nautical Almanac, Sight Reduction Tables, and a radio to give us time ticks. (I've always believed that Don is a good navigator, but this proves it!) Joy—to know that within hours I'll be able to walk on solid ground, touch the earth, talk with other people, read our mail (perhaps even our chronometer will have arrived). Uneasiness—wondering how we'll be received. Will the people be friendly, welcoming? If I decide to continue, or if I don't, will we be able to find someone to help crew?

We had read *Aku, Aku,*[1] Thor Heyerdahl's entertaining account of his 1955 archaeological expedition to Easter Island, and although it answered many of our questions about the historical mysteries on the island, it had left us wondering about present conditions. The only other source we had aboard—the American *Sailing Directions*—said that fuel could be obtained, but no mention was made of other facilities.

What about water? Would we have to haul our five-gallon jugs 10 kilometers to the fresh-water spring, or had wells been sunk in the twenty years since Heyerdahl's visit? Could we leave our boat at anchor and go ashore during the day without having it stripped, as previous boats had reported? Would we be able to buy fresh provisions? What about a laundry? A hot shower?

Some of our questions were about to be answered. We could see a group of men launch a wooden skiff through the surf and head out toward us.

Shortly afterward, the skiff bumped against the starboard hull, and

We anchored at Easter Island and raised our Chilean and quarantine flags

six men in muddy street shoes climbed aboard. Shyly and politely, one by one, they kissed us on each cheek, wishing us *Bienvenidos a Rapa Nui*[2] and introducing themselves. The mayor of Hanga Roa slipped shell leis around our necks. Benno Schlecter, the port captain—a tall, sandy-haired Chilean naval officer who spoke English with an impeccable British accent—sat down in the cockpit and, within ten minutes, completed our entry papers courteously and efficiently. It was the antithesis of our experience in Mexico.

Dido, one of the welcoming crew, offered to take me around the village in his jeep to change money and buy provisions. They had been expecting us, we were told.

"Everyone on the island knows about you, and the post office has a lot of mail for you," Lieutenant Schlecter said.

"Have you received a chronometer for us?" Don asked.

He hadn't heard anything about a chronometer, but he suggested we contact the governor of the island, an army colonel.

I went below to grab my *bolsa* and wallet so I could go ashore. The six men had already climbed back into the skiff, and as the port captain gave me a hand over the side of *le Dauphin*, Don blurted out, "*She* was seasick the entire thirty-two-day crossing. I need crew, and she'll need a place to stay after I leave until she can fly to the continent." I could have killed Don. Not only had he exaggerated, but his timing was all wrong. And he had called me "she" (as rude as "my old lady"). Now, we'd be

We anchored off Hanga Roa, the only village on the island

The landing beach at Hanga Roa

bombarded with "applications" the moment we set foot on shore, and the whole island would know about his poor señora.

With Grecian features, high cheekbones, tightly clipped black hair, and a pockmarked face, Dido's unsmiling manner intimidated me at first. I was surprised to find a native Pascuensan so nervous and intense, thinking the inhabitants were more laid back.

I changed my money and filled my *bolsa* with the stacks of mail waiting for us.

"Where next?" Dido asked. I asked him to take me to a market where I could buy some fruit and vegetables.

It was Wednesday, and the weekly farmers' market took place on Saturdays. Farmers didn't usually sell their produce during the week.

"But we will try. I'll drive you to Vaitea where the farmers live," Dido said.

The jeep followed a narrow dirt road lined with pineapple bushes whose bayonet-shaped leaves—green and bright from recent rains—scratched the sides of the jeep noisily. Vegetables arranged in neat patchworks outlined by stone hedgerows grew in rich, black-red soil. The odors of grasses, eucalyptus, and wet earth made me heady. Earth! I'd dreamed of it for thirty-two days!

Stopping at farms, Dido spoke in Pascuensan, a Polynesian dialect that resembles the language of Tahiti. After four farms and four rejections,

I began to catch on. No dollars: no fruits or vegetables. We tried one more.

The fifth farmer nodded, went to the center of his garden, pulled up two clumps of onions, shook the dirt off against the fender of the jeep, and said, "Four dollars" (in pesos). I gasped. Four dollars for a clump of dirty onions!

The farmer shrugged. I could take it or leave it. I took it and the farmer threw in two small pineapples.

"You found that expensive?" Dido asked as we drove away.

"Yes. Look, we're ordinary people, we don't have much money to spend. We have to be careful." I always felt a little uncomfortable when I mentioned our need to be frugal. One look at our sailboat and the natives assumed we had unlimited funds.

He was silent for a moment, then asked if we had anything to trade. I asked what he had in mind.

"Jeans, pants, T-shirts, sunglasses, parts for boats, screws, nails, nylon line . . ." His list went on and on.

I pictured all the stuff the kids had left aboard and mentioned a few items I knew we could spare. That did it—we had a deal. In exchange for clothing, his family would provide us with fruits and vegetables from their garden. Not only that—his wife would do our laundry.

Later, at their home, Dido's wife, Ana, made me a cup of coffee. Warm and friendly at first, she slowly hardened into complaints about the difficulty of life on the island. A Chilean who had grown up on the mainland, she and Dido had met and married when he was doing military service. I could understand her difficulty in adapting to Pascuensan life, but I was too tired to do more than nod my head.

I finished my coffee, and excused myself, walked to the beach, and yelled across the bay for Don. There was no answer.

Easter Island (called Rapa Nui by its native people) lies 2,500 miles due west of the coast of Chile. Its shape resembles an isosceles triangle, with its coastline totalling roughly thirty-two miles. There is no harbor or facilities for boats. Since it is farther from continental land than any other island, it has the distinction of being "the loneliest island in the world." Temperatures in this subtropical climate vary from 60°F (17°C) in winter to 75°F (23°C) in summer, and average rainfall is over a meter per month. Chile annexed the island in 1888, and during the 1900s it was administered by the Chilean navy. Two-thirds of the population of 2,100 inhabitants are of Polynesian descent. In 1984, governorship of the island was turned over to its native population who are the only inhabitants permitted to own land. Languages spoken are Pascuensan (more recently called Rapa Nui) and Spanish.

I sat down on a rock to wait till he appeared. On either side of the beach (a thirty-foot strip of red clay) clumps of jagged black lava stretched seaward like the claws of a crab. Sturdy, planked-wood fishing boats lay on the beach, secured to automobile or truck tires with decaying hemp lines. A few kids who had been gathering shells in the water approached and asked if they could make me a shell lei. A string of tall, handsome women with Polynesian features filed by to offer condolences about my seasickness. They offered the services of their husbands, too. They had already heard that Don was looking for crew.

Afternoon clouds had built up over the island's craters, casting shadows on the yellow grasses. The slopes of Rano Kao looked like fields of crushed green velvet woven with strands of blue eucalyptus. Red earth shone in bald spots amidst the green. There was a touch of the pampa, a touch of the tropics, and there was no haze, no city drone. Just clean, cool, blue air, clear turquoise water, and a light rustling of wind through the branches of the eucalyptus.

An hour later, Don poked his nude torso out of the hatch, looked toward land, waved, and shouted. He disappeared below, reappeared dressed, untied the dinghy, lifted it off the cabin, and slipped it into the water.

Kids—I counted eight—swam to the dinghy and hung on its sides, stern, and bow, giggling and laughing, then swam toward shore in a race to beat Don.

Don arrived breathless from a quarter-mile row against the wind and the youngsters. He was rested, now, and ready to come ashore.

I shouted in English, "No, no! Don't beach the dink. I want to go back to the boat!" Dead-tired and dying to take a nap, I hopped into the dinghy.

"Take me home," I said to the oarsman.

JANUARY 10

We have been anchored here now for four days and haven't been able to get any information about our chronometer. Mom's letter said it was sent air-mail from Massachusetts December 15. Two flights have come in since we arrived and we've received lots more mail, but no package from the Salem Clock Company. Don wants to leave by January 20 and he's frustrated. When we met with the military governor, he said he'll try to locate it by sending a telex to Customs in Valparaiso. Don stressed that he can't leave for Cape Horn without a chronometer, but I'm not sure that made an impression on the governor. He's shifty-eyed, and we don't know whether to trust him or not. As we were leaving, he asked Don if we'd chosen a crewman yet. He recommended Bernardo "highly."

News had spread like wildfire, as I had suspected it would. Bernardo had already cornered Don. He showed us his credentials from earlier years in the merchant marines. He looked like he was in his seventies, but he was lean, tanned, and muscular. His father, he said, had been a member of Heyerdahl's first archaeological team in 1955. Something about the dates didn't compute, but I ignored it.

"I will go with you, *Capitán*, and write a book that can be translated into English. You and I will be famous, like my father."

Each time we saw the man I became more irritated. At times he was fawning and servile; at times, angry and aggressive. Don was impressed with his credentials.

"Invite him aboard for a sail," I urged, "before you make up your mind." That night I wrote:

I can see I'm going to have to make a decision soon. Don is hot to sign Bernardo on as crew. When I told Don not to be too hasty in making a decision, he blew up at me.

Memories of the nasty moments we had on the crossing from Acapulco preyed on my mind after that. I know that the thought of rounding Cape Horn with a total stranger preys on his mind, too, and that he also feels the urgency to choose someone. But God—right away, so hastily? No! I really was beginning to think I wanted to stay on with him, but it's so hard to erase the memory of his temperamental outbursts.

I have to make a decision soon—it's either me or someone else.

Overlooking the Pacific Ocean at Rano Kao

JANUARY 12

The next day, a lengthy storm hit the island, bringing torrential rain for three and a half hours. Red clay washed down the slopes and left the water red, the beach muddy. We rowed ashore and joined Jermán and Gabriel Ika—teenage brothers who had befriended us—for a trip to the crater at Rano Kao and a visit to Orongo, the Bird Man village above the crater.[3] We trudged to their house with two inches of red goo stuck to the soles of our Adidas.

Jermán captured and muzzled two horses grazing behind the house and threw sheepskins across their backs. Although the islanders have their pick of four thousand "wild"

Birdman petroglyphs at Orongo

horses, many of which are spirited, handsome creatures destined never to be caught and broken in, these two barely blinked when Jermán approached. They were carbon copies of Don Quixote's Rocinante and had to be coaxed up the volcanic slope.

At Orongo, overlooking the Pacific, Jermán pointed out the rocks where stylized birds were etched in relief. With their long curved beaks and human hands and feet, they crouched in profile or stared face-on with huge encircled eyes: the famous Bird Men.

This is the place where, for centuries, the competitions for a ruler of the Bird Man cult took place. Once a year, in the austral spring, swimmers scrambled down the thousand-foot cliff below Rano Kao, swam the two kilometers to Motu Nui (the largest of three islets at the south end of the big island), and camped there waiting for terns to lay their first eggs of the season. The first man who could snatch a newly laid egg, swim back to Rapa Nui, and scramble up the cliff with the egg still intact won the race. His sponsor became ceremonial ruler, Bird Man, for the next twelve months.[4]

As Don and I stood atop Rano Kao, listening and watching, I was struck by the stark beauty, the quiet, and the remoteness. Aside from an occasional outboard motor, the whinnying of horses, a jeep, the only sounds were the wind whistling through the grasses, the squeak of eucalyptus branches, the shrill calls of the terns, gulls, and hawks. Standing there I knew that the mystery of Easter Island reached beyond archaeological questions, and I felt I could stay there forever.

JANUARY 13

I wrote a short note to my parents with good news:

"The governor received a telex this morning informing him that our chronometer is in Valparaiso and that Customs will forward it at once. Hooray! Thanks for your help, Mom, in arranging the replacement. This note is just a 'quickie' because we're expecting thirteen islanders (adults and children) to join us this afternoon for a sail and picnic aboard."

We had invited both Chileans and Pascuensans, without realizing we were committing a gaffe—the two "societies" didn't mix. Thirteen Pascuensans and the one resident American showed up—Dido and Ana with their four children, Paolo (Dido's eighteen-year-old nephew), Estevan and Tomasa Pakarati (who would become good friends), their daughter María, Bernardo, Jermán, Gabriel, and Mike, the *Americano*. Each one came bearing a gift—a small stone or wooden carving, a handmade shell necklace, homebaked soda bread or yeast rolls, filets of fresh tuna, homegrown tomatoes, watermelons, pineapples, potatoes, and onions.

Bernardo arrived in a swimsuit, rubber-soled shoes, a rain poncho, and sun hat. The others were starched, pressed, and polished.

We weighed anchor and sailed south toward the three islets we had passed on the morning of our arrival, the same we had sighted from Rano Kao. Our guests were excited to see their island from a different perspective, and they pointed, giggled, and argued about whether Motu Nui looked like a bird man or the profile of a *moai*.

For lunch, I served slices of canned ham and pork, sweet pickles and dills, sliced tomatoes, onions, Ritz crackers, chocolate bars, and trail mix. So polite and subdued earlier, the guests ate like animals. They grabbed, snatched, and practically inhaled the food, reminding me of the greedy hermit crabs I'd seen along the shores of Mexico.

As we reanchored at 1600 hours, everyone thanked us enthusiastically and kissed us on both cheeks. Dido and Ana were the last to go ashore.

Don asked them if Bernardo would be a good crewman.

"*Cuidado!*" Dido said. (Be careful.)

"What do you mean?"

Our friend, Estevan Pakarti

"Cuidado!" He refused to say more.

That evening I wanted to discuss with Don the possibility of my continuing to Cape Horn, but before I had a chance, he told me in an arrogant, dictatorial tone, "I want you to ask around the village about Bernardo. I need more information." That tabled any discussion about my crewing.

So we discussed Bernardo, whose behavior continued to bother me. Despite the fact that he had come "prepared" for sailing, when he took a turn at the helm he gyrated the wheel so wildly to make small corrections, it was obvious he didn't understand the relation of the wind to the sails. And at one point when a gust of wind filled the genny, he heeled the helm so hard to starboard that the rail went under—and he screamed for me, panicked. Don was below at the time and hadn't witnessed the incident.

Later, when Don asked him to let someone else have a turn at the helm, he sat silent and morose, staring transfixed into space like a stone *moai*.

I mentioned all these things. "He's a strange person. I don't trust him." I took a breath, knowing the effect my next comment would create. "Also, I will *not* ask around the village. That's foolish. I'll get as many answers as people I ask, and the whole island will know you're asking about Bernardo."

Don's eyes popped out. I got the dreaded Mongolian scowl. He hopped into the berth in a huff, turned toward the hull with his back to me, and went to sleep.

I sat up for several hours, discouraged. I wanted to awaken Don and say, "Look, can't we talk as friends instead of adversaries?" But instead I wrote in my journal.

Don expects me to be a partner and take initiative, but when I give him my opinion, he throws a tantrum. I don't understand the man.

Since I've gotten over being seasick, we've had some good times together that make me feel I can continue as a genuine partner. But then something sets him off and destroys all my loving feelings. I want a lover and a husband who cares and appreciates me for what I am. At least some of the time. I know I have to tell him whether I'll continue or not. But I'm damned if I'll wake him now—I don't like him!

JANUARY 15

The chronometer hadn't shown up on the plane two days before, but we were hopeful it would arrive on today's flight.

I was beginning to feel that our only function was to row back and forth from shore and check with the governor, do chores, or search the two small *tiendas* (stores) for provisions. We were anchored more than a quarter-mile from the beach, and it was a hefty pull every time we went ashore. To refuel, we had to transfer diesel from two fifty-gallon drums on shore to our five-gallon fuel jugs, row back to the boat, offload the jugs, empty the fuel into our tank, then row back to shore again. We had to do the same with water. Even with Paolo giving us a hand, it had taken two whole days to refuel and fill up on water.

We visited the governor again today. The same script as previous visits— Don spoke, I translated.

"Please tell him we urgently need his help."

"Tell him I need the chronometer before I leave Easter Island, that I can't leave without it."

Not only were the lines the same, but the summary lecture delivered to me afterward was the same. "Dammit, you're not forceful enough. You've got to be more assertive. You're too polite. You let others push you around." Ad infinitum.

I asked Don if he wanted me to translate for him or not. "Your pidgin Spanish gets you by in Mexico, but here it's different. If you think you can do better, dammit, take over."

He flushed and said, "I guess you'd better do it."

JANUARY 16

The next day, the wind veered to the north, leaving *le Dauphin* exposed and threatened with a lee shore. It was too risky to leave the boat; we had to be ready to weigh anchor if conditions continued to deteriorate.

Despite the motion in the anchorage, I hadn't had any recurrence of seasickness, and that morning was a real test. The bow tugged, pulled, and snapped on the anchor rode (line) like a bronco in a rodeo. The boat pitched and rolled as if we were still at sea beating into the wind—these were the conditions the *Sailing Directions* had predicted for Easter Island.

I liked the respite. I read, baked biscuits, reread letters we'd received and wrote replies. I wanted to tell my family and friends how much their letters had buoyed me, how godawful much I missed them. But instead, I wrote about Heyerdahl theories, frustrations about a chronometer that hadn't shown up, petroglyphs, and bird men. I was afraid I'd get too emotional.

When we didn't show up on shore, Bernardo motored out in a skiff with Paolo to talk about his trip with Don. As if it were settled, he asked for a one-year contract. He didn't expect pay, he said, he just wanted room and board. He promised to learn English so he and Don could communicate and said he'd carve souvenirs to sell in port for his spending money.

He showed me a small yellowed logbook—the size of a paperback. Written in minuscule, regular handwriting, it held meticulous details of his days as a merchant sailor. It appeared genuine, but quite old.

Earlier in the week, I had asked Mike, the American, about Bernardo's compulsion to be famous like his father.

"That was his *brother,*" Mike blurted out. "Not his father."

It was clear Bernardo didn't want Don to know how old he was.

It was hard to read the man. As long as Don talked directly to him, he was excited and animated, but the minute either of us talked to Paolo, he lapsed into petulant silence. I couldn't imagine spending a year with someone like that. Don would go nuts, and I certainly didn't want him around as crew if I went.

After Bernardo left, Don admitted he was coming around to my opinion and wanted to know how to handle telling him no.

Now's the time, I thought.

"Maybe you won't have to. Maybe you can just avoid him for a while and let him get the idea. Besides, I've decided I want to go on with you. That could be your excuse."

He was stunned.

"If you're kidding, that's a mean way to tease. I can't believe you're really serious."

I told him that I'd been thinking about it a lot, that I had wanted to discuss it the night he blew up and went to bed, but that his attitude had turned me off.

"You know I want you to come. But not if you say you'll come one day and change your mind the next. You were so damn unhappy on the crossing."

"Being seasick made me unhappy. I haven't been seasick since we arrived. This boat rides like a pony at anchor all the time, and if I were going to be sick again I would be already. I really do want to go with you!" I put my arms around him.

Cool and wary, he'd been guarded for so long he was afraid to let down his defenses. His hug lacked enthusiasm.

JANUARY 18

Today's mail brought a notice from Customs in Valparaiso that they have our chronometer, but no word about when they'll send it. Don is furious. How can the governor receive a telex and we receive notice—but still no chronometer? Why can't they just send the damn thing on the same airplane as the notice? Dido says, "Maybe someone sells your chronometer?" Maybe even the governor is covering up.

After we received the notice, we went to talk to him again. He was nervous, shifty-eyed, pompous, and evasive, and he answered my questions with such rapid, half-swallowed utterances that I could barely understand him. When I translated, he looked at Don, not me, as if Don were doing all the talking.

I do not like the man!

JANUARY 20

I was beginning to feel like a ventriloquist speaking through a dummy. We spent the afternoon with the director of schools, whom I had arranged to interview as part of my sabbatical research. During the entire interview (conducted in Spanish), the man directed his answers at Don.

Afterward, his wife invited us to stay for coffee and dessert, and the director asked what I thought about the status of women in the United States. Without a pause, he told Don that American women had aroused such negative feelings around the world, they had created a loss of respect for themselves.

"Chilean women feel they are liberated," he boasted. "We men treat our women with equality. We share the housework; we help raise the children. Our women don't feel the need to organize themselves—they're satisfied. They even keep their own names."

We got up to leave, and as we shook hands, the director's eyes met mine for the first time in three hours. He thanked me for comparing "pedagogical information" with him. How different, I thought, from male colleagues at home who looked at me when I talked. Men who showed spirit or anger—and who weren't threatened or shocked by mine. *Thank God Don isn't like him*, I thought.

Later we stopped at Dido's for a "party." Paolo and a friend had brought their guitars. The rest of us accompanied them with bongos, kitchen utensils, bottles, and bones while Don and I recorded it all on our cassette player. The kids checked to be sure I remembered the words to "Pae-pae, Haumarú,"[5] and they taught me the *sau-sau*, a Polynesian hula.

"You've got it! You've got it!" they applauded. "Not him, not him—he can't do it." They giggled and pointed at Don, who was trying half-heartedly to move his hips and shoulders.

Dido's three young children delighted me. We danced with each other. We laughed. They looked me in the eye. They had not yet learned adult artifice.

After the get-together at Dido and Ana's, everyone helped us down to the beach to load the dinghy. When we got to the boat and offloaded our belongings, there was no tape recorder, and no case of tapes. *Toke-toke* (thievery) had hit us, just as it had hit every recorded visitor since the eighteenth century.

We checked with Ana the next day to see if we'd left them at their house, but she swore she saw us with them before we hopped into the dinghy. We asked around and no one knew anything. Or if they did, they wouldn't admit it. The loss of the tapes—the Pascuensan songs we'd recorded—disturbed us more than the loss of our expensive machine.

JANUARY 21

We enjoyed meeting Dr. Ramón Campbell, amateur of archeology and an expert on the music of Easter Island. The night we met him, we sat in his *pae-pae* (a typical Pascuensan bamboo hut, celebrated in the popular song we'd learned at Dido's). He told us how he'd first come to Easter Island as a young naval doctor in the late 1960s and fallen in love with the place. He'd witnessed its transition from a pre-electric, no-running-water culture to an about-to-be television-bred culture that would develop its tourism industry in the decade to come. He told us with sadness, "The people were charming and simple back then, and the island was lovely."

He took us "touring" in his ambulance to visit Ahu Akivi—Platform of the Chiefs—the most famous of the restored ceremonial platforms, and the one most often photographed. [6] Standing out against a background of smooth green turf, its seven *moai*—proud, tall, disdainful—look out to sea. The platform—thirty-eight meters wide and two meters deep—was pocked by time and discolored by lichen.

The seven *moai*, which natives irreverently call *los Siete Monos* (the Seven Monkeys), are nearly five meters tall. Each statue—with its proud face tilted upward in slight disdain, its pursed lips, long flat nose, wide truncated chin, and deeply cut eye sockets—is distinctly different from the others. But the body of each one looked identical to my untrained eye: curved spine, protruding navel, elongated fingers pressing on the abdomen as if to hold up the belly.

Wild horses milled about the *ahu* behind it and on top of it. Dr. Campbell complained that they destroyed everything they came in contact with—they ruined the ceremonial terraces, pawed the earth, and ate the island's flowers and bushes.

As we stood there, two stallions on the hill bolted in unison, cast out of their group; the first revolted, kicking at the other with his hind legs and striking with his front hooves. At that moment I couldn't worry about the damage they do. I could think only of their slender muscular bodies—works of force and color in contrast to a stark, almost sterile panorama.

That afternoon we explored the caves along the north side of the island, easily identifiable by the lush thickets of fig and banana trees, mulberry bushes, and grapevines that surround their openings. Petroglyphs of stylized men, flowers, turtles, dolphins, and boats covered the rocks nearby.

Using our flashlights, we followed Dr. Campbell down its narrow passageway to interconnected chambers that were dense with moss and ferns. Two large subterranean pools rang musically with constant drips. We tasted the water—cold, quenching, like a Sierra stream. A hundred times better than the salty well water we'd been using.

Dr. Campbell saved the most impressive cave, Ana Kakenga, for last. We descended into a dark passageway that twisted, turned, and tricked us with dead-end side passages until we finally came to a large chamber that

Réanne with Dr. Ramón Campbell in his "pae-pae"

branched into two tunnels. One led deep into the island, and the other led to an open-air ledge-window, a hundred feet directly above the sea. We watched the surf as it rolled in from an unimpeded sea and sprayed high in the air, catching itself on the spectacular lava spills below us. Turning back, our batteries finally gave out, but Dr. Campbell rolled up a newspaper he'd been carrying all afternoon, lit it with a match, and led us out of Ana Kakenga by torchlight—a classical touch of drama!

JANUARY 22

We had become good friends with Paolo and were impressed with his abilities. He held the Chilean depth-record for free diving and would frequently swim the quarter-mile from shore to visit us. He was always willing to lend a hand when we needed it. He also seemed forthright and honest.

A week before, he had caught on so quickly when Don showed him how to sail the dinghy that we began to think he might be good crew. We asked him to meet us January 24 in Anakena Bay and spend several days helping us work on the boat. We made it clear that if everything went well and we got along, we'd consider signing him on as crew.

JANUARY 23

Anakena Bay, on the northeast side of the island, has a lovely white sand beach, one of only two on the entire island, and it was a quieter spot for working than Hanga Roa. Protected from all but north winds, it had less swell than the anchorage off the village. Don and I arrived a day earlier than Paolo so we could spend some time alone. We anchored close to shore and swam in translucent aquamarine water, so clear we could see our white anchor shimmering forty feet below.

It was the first time since our arrival that Don and I had truly relaxed together. We took time to explore the shore. We photographed derelict statues, earth ovens, lookout towers, made rubbings of petroglyphs, and cave entrances. Alone —no tourists, villagers, fishermen, or shepherds— we felt like children playing Robinson Crusoe, the first explorers on a deserted island. We hiked through thickets of guava, paper mulberry, fig trees, and pineapple plants; we picnicked on figs and pineapple and studied ways to weave fibers of the mulberry plant into grass skirts; we planned the reconstruction of an ancient boat-shaped hut (*hare paenga*).

JANUARY 24

The next morning, Dido brought Paolo for our "trial run." I was happy to see him. His sense of humor and good-natured attitude livened the atmosphere. He was strong, willing to work, and eager to learn.

We stressed that the two days would be a test of his willingness to work, as well as of his responsibility and honesty. If he passed, he was on. He nodded, serious, while I explained in Spanish.

The day went well. Paolo and Don fiberglassed the steering vane rudder while I mended sails, fetched tools, and cooked. For supper, Paolo speared four fish, filleted and fried them. The sea urchins he had prepared as *aperitivos* sat in a saucer, giant thistles waiting for some courageous mouth. Don declined. One bite was enough for me.

JANUARY 25

The second day, Don and Paolo scrubbed the hull, while I followed in the dinghy, keeping my eye on them for safety. Three hours of sitting finally got to me, and I asked Paolo to spell me. "Don't take your eyes off Don," I instructed as I dove in the water for a swim.

After twenty minutes, Paolo wanted to go aboard. I got out of the water and pulled myself into the dinghy. "Don't be long—we need you here to watch us."

"Okay, Señora Réanna."

Too many minutes passed, and I became suspicious. I told Don I wanted to check on Paolo, and I climbed aboard. A box of drill bits that had been left open next to the companionway was closed. I opened it. The quarter-inch drill was missing.

"What did you do with the quarter-inch drill?" I called to Don.

"I put it back in the case."

"It's not here now."

"That's strange. Maybe you'd better check with Paolo."

I called through the hatchway. "You've been gone a long time, Paolo. Will you please come back up here and watch Don."

I asked if he had seen the drill bit.

"No, I haven't," he said, climbing back in the dinghy. I went below feeling slightly nauseated with what I might discover, and disliking myself for the manner in which I had to check.

I thought about Cape Horn without a crew, just the two of us to do all the work. Paolo was our last chance. If we couldn't trust him, we would have to go it alone.

I looked into his flight bag. It was empty. *Thank God!* I thought. I picked it up and turned it over, just to doublecheck, and the drill bit fell to the floor.

Confrontation American-style did no good. Paolo "just wanted the bit" for himself. "You have a lot of them," he said. "Why should you miss just one?"

I tried to make him understand that we had no way of replacing equipment, that everything on the boat was essential. Everything! He gave me a petulant stare that meant "Don't exaggerate."

I went on, stressing that we needed to trust any crew we took aboard. Trust—an abstract concept he didn't understand, or didn't want to.

Don began a duplication of my lecture in his pidgin Spanish. Paolo's jaw hardened, his eyes narrowed. He was insulted. In his mind we were the wrongdoers. He had nothing more to say. We had nothing more to say.

He sulked in silence for two hours until Dido honked and Don rowed him ashore.

Examining the ceremonial village site of Orongo

Back on board, Don broke out a bottle of Dubonnet. "Well, I guess that leaves the two of us." He paused, suddenly looked worried, then said, "Are you sure you want to go? I could still single-hand. I was getting used to the idea."

"Yeah. I know you were. But I haven't changed my mind. I don't want you to go alone. I want to go with you."

His eyes filled. He put his arms around me and held me tight. "You know, when the chips are down, you're the only one who comes through. I should have known I could count on you. I'm sorry I've been so cold lately. I was trying to cut the cord, but that only made it harder for you to commit, didn't it?"

I nodded and nuzzled my face against his neck. *God, he's learning*, I thought.

JANUARY 25

Everything on Rapa Nui had been on hold for the Big Celebration—the arrival of President Pinochet. We were on hold, too. It was impossible to see the governor, and the post office didn't have a clue about our chronometer.

The ancient ceremonial site of Orongo

The road to the airport at Mataveri had been raked and swept clean with Yankee efficiency, and its red clay shone like tile. Banners strung across the road every hundred meters welcomed the president in Pascuensan and Spanish and thanked him for having given the island liberty and television.

It was truly an event. No matter that he was a dictator. No matter that he had *not* given them liberty. What mattered most was that under Pinochet, this very week in January 1975, television came to the island.

Everyone was excited. Sunday best was *de rigueur.* Children were scrubbed, polished, and starched, and fishermen looked out of place in their white shirts and ties. No tanned and callused bare feet were visible.

We spotted Estevan in a handsome suit. He shook hands, muttering that he couldn't wait to take off his tie. The Military Guard in dress whites, lined up at the edge of the runway, stood at attention awaiting the president's plane, their dignity slightly marred by the cut of their uniforms—tight-fitting jackets and pants too short.

The LAN-Chile jet circled overhead, then landed. At the same time, clouds cracked open and poured out, drenching Military Guard, dancers, guitarists, officials, spectators. We waited . . . five, ten, fifteen, twenty minutes . . . for the rain to stop and the plane to discharge its passengers.

No sign of let-up, but the door finally opened. President and Mrs. Pinochet stepped out, waved, walked down the ramp into the crowd, followed by their *Guardia*—black, curly-haired, heavy-set *mafiosos* whose waistlines were abnormally thick (but no guns were evident).

Banners welcomed President Pinochet

Unrestrained by the *Guardia*, people pawed and patted Pinochet's shoulders from either side of the cordon. Visibly touched, smiling and composed despite the downpour, the dictator and his wife shook hands with each person in the long line—including us.

"Do you realize I just shook the hands of a dictator?" Don said, as excited as the rest of the spectators.

"Yeah, I just hope he gets the significance of the UN flag flying from our mast."[7]

The jet took off again; the presidential party would have no means of leaving the island till the plane returned four days later. Estevan and Tomasa joked: "Do you realize your boat is the only way Pinochet could leave now if he wanted to?"

JANUARY 26

"We leave February 2, chronometer or no," Don declared. "We've got to go see the governor today. We've already delayed too long. The risk of gales increases with every day, temperatures are dropping to freezing off Cape Horn, and our window of opportunity is closing. See if you can locate the governor—somewhere."

I groaned. Don was a caged animal that morning: pacing, growling, roaring. I understood, but I still felt like the whipping boy. I was in the middle—Don to Réanne to governor, governor to Réanne to Don. Don's attitude wore on me. I wanted to get away from him, for a day, even a half-day. But it was impossible.

President Pinochet

We rowed ashore, beached the dinghy, walked uphill past the plaza, past the eucalyptus grove, and turned right toward the governor's office. Farmers were just setting up the open market. A jeep pulled up, and Pinochet and his cronies descended. The governor was among the celebrities.

"There's your chance. Go talk to him about our chronometer."

I groaned again, instantly regretting it.

Don grabbed me. "Look," he said angrily. "Do you realize how important that chronometer is to our safety? *I don't think you do.* We won't be able to determine longitude without it. Do you realize what *that* means? It means we may end up on the rocks of the worst coast in the world. So stop arguing, goddammit, and go talk to him."

I wanted to say, "He won't help and you know it. He doesn't give a damn about us or our chronometer." But I didn't.

The governor saw me approaching and his eyes steered a 180-degree course from side to side, hoping to avoid confrontation. I did the routine I knew by heart and hated. I wanted to call him a sonovabitch to his face. Instead, I was slithery and ingratiating.

Still avoiding my eyes, he looked over my left shoulder and said, "Well . . . come to my office Monday. I will see if there is anything more to be done."

"You will be there?" I asked.

"Yes."

"Seguro?" (Sure?)

"Yes."

I thought, *Fat chance,* and said, *"Gracias,"* with my teeth clenched.

An old man on horseback stopped us as we were heading back to the beach with our vegetables.

"I carve good. You come see at my *casa,*" he said in English.

I wanted to get back to the boat. "We'll have enough stuff when

Estevan finishes the carvings he's doing for us," I whispered, irritated. "Besides, we're running out of room for everything."

"Baloney. We'll make room. We'll never have another chance like this. Come on!"

I relented, and we followed the old man to a stucco pre-fab under eucalyptus trees on the hill. A "jungle" of fig trees, hibiscus, oleander, *florabunda,* and morning glories surrounded the house. He ushered us into a dimly lit room, narrow and cluttered. An iron daybed, a worn-out breakfast table, and a plastic chair filled the room.

He brought out a two-foot-long wooden carving of a *moai kava-kava*—a cadaverous, grotesque likeness of a man with an exaggerated rib cage, extended ear lobes, bulging eyes, and hooked nose. I read covetous signals in Don's eyes. The old man read them too.

"You like this, eh?"

"Yes," said Don, "but we have no money. We will trade."

"You have furniture? New kitchen table?"

Don laughed. "No. We have a little boat. We have clothes, nylon rope."

"Like this?" He pointed to a hemp bridle.

"No. Nylon rope—very strong."

The two of them began to bargain. The man's jaw, previously set, began to loosen, and the corners of his mouth relaxed. They dickered intensely, feigning and exaggerating. The old man wanted a pair of tennis shoes and offered his wood carving. Don countered with a pair of tennis shoes and thirty meters of nylon rope, asking for the wood carving, a

Negotiating for a moai kava kava

small stone statue, and a bowl. The bargaining went on for twenty minutes until both were satisfied with the deal. We stood up to leave. The old
man handed Don the *moai kava-kava*.

"Okay, then. Tonight at the beach, I come for the rope." He handed
Don a carved paddle and a crude stone carving. "Gifts for you," he said.

Don thanked him. They shook hands, the deal concluded.

That evening we put the "goods" in an old denim laundry sack and
rowed to the beach where the old man was already waiting.

"Here's the stuff," Don said, "but we had only twenty-seven meters
of nylon line, so I—"

"No! That was not our agreement!"

"Wait. Wait. I brought you seven meters of a better line, bigger diameter. See?" Don pulled out the half-inch line.

"Okay . . . Okay. And the sunglasses? They are in the sack?"

"Yes, at the bottom in a case. And there's some cloth for your wife,
some canned meat. Are we okay now?"

"Yes. No problem." The old man grabbed the sack. He and Don
shook hands a second time and he left, carrying his loot.[8]

JANUARY 27

Pinochet left, and the island resumed its natural rhythm.

The sky was dark; the wind howled through the rigging; the mast did
its heavy weather shudder; and the anchor rode tugged. It was ugly
weather. As long as the prevailing wind came from the southwest, Hanga
Roa—open to the ocean—was a satisfactory anchorage. But the wind
had already veered 45 degrees; another 45 degrees would put us in
extreme danger, smack on a lee shore.

That afternoon, as we were returning from errands on shore, we watched
from the dinghy as *le Dauphin*, bucked, plunged, reared up, yanked at the
anchor, and rolled to starboard.

"Oh Christ, I think the anchor just broke loose," Don said. "Climb
aboard and start the engine." I pulled myself up onto the deck and started
the engine. "Yeah, the chain broke, and the anchor's still down there.
Let's get out of here. We'll have to worry about it later."

He climbed aboard and tied the dinghy off at the stern. The waves
came at the stern furiously in short, high curls. The dinghy was tossed
into the air. An oarlock with its oar still attached flew out, sank, and the
oar was immediately propelled toward shore.

Don looked at it, hesitated. His impulse was to jump in and swim for it.

He turned around, jammed the throttle into forward at 3500 rpms,
full emergency power, and wheeled hard to port. Barely making headway,

we clawed off the lee shore and made our way south—clearing the point past the cliffs below Rano Kao, past the islets of Motu Kaokao, Motu Iti, and Motu Nui—running with the wind to Hotu Iti, the cove we had explored the night of our arrival, January 6.

JANUARY 28

Wind and rain raged on through the night and the next two days. We bobbed precariously at anchor in Hotu Iti. The black lava flows that encased the cove formed peaks, valleys, and plateaus. Polished by years of salt waves, they glistened under the rain. Across the bow to landward we could see Rano Raraku—the volcano whose crater held the quarry where the giant statues had been carved. Its peak was shrouded in grey; its corn-green slope was dotted with *moai* heads.[9] Hotu Iti was deserted. Only the wind and squalls disturbed us. The barren, rocky cove was the perfect hiding place for a submarine, but not a good anchorage for our underpowered sailboat. Our loss of nerve the night we sighted Easter Island had clearly been wise.

Don had become testy again, snarling at anything that got in his way. I was "anything," and I made the mistake of pointing out that the chronometer had gained ten minutes in twenty-four hours. He cursed the clock company for making defective chronometers. He cursed the governor. Cursed me for my ineffectiveness with the governor.

"Why is it so goddam hard to get anything done in life when you have to go through other people? No one understands," he raged. "Not even you."

I didn't argue. I was too tired and discouraged. I wanted to leave Rapa Nui. I wanted to be by myself. But on a stormy day I couldn't even hide on the foredeck. I was forced to share the cage.

FEBRUARY 1

"We're leaving tomorrow, with or without anchor. The window has already closed," Don declared. It would be without a chronometer, too. There was no LAN Chile flight for the next two days. He asked me to row ashore to check with the governor one last time, and I got the usual, "No information, so sorry."

Don had asked everyone he knew for help in diving for our anchor, but Paolo was the only person on the island who could dive that deep. He wanted me to go ashore again and ask him to do it.

"Nope. If you want him you'll have to handle that yourself."

Paolo accepted Don's deal to trade for a pair of made-in-France sunglasses. Then he didn't show up.

FEBRUARY 2

D-day. Paolo still had not shown up, and the CQR—our best anchor— still lay at the bottom of Hanga Roa Bay. Last-minute visitors came aboard early in the morning to say good-bye. Captain Schlecter lent us his own portable radio receiver to use as a backup. He told us to give it to Admiral Allen in Punta Arenas to return to him later.

A fisherman motored out with Jermán and Gabriel. The boys handed us an enormous yellow banana squash from their garden and a life-sized *cara lloranda* (weeping face) that Mrs. Ika had carved for us.

Estevan, Tomasa, and María rowed out in a skiff to deliver the small statues we'd commissioned Estevan to carve. They had a gift for us, too— a ninety-pound stone *moai*—"for your garden in California."

Five of us struggled to get the *moai* aboard and down the ladder. We wrapped him in Ensolite and an old bedspread, lashed him with cord, wedged him between the engine box and port quarter berth, and tied him to the floor beams.

We embraced and said good-bye. They were true, kind friends, and along with the Ika family, I would miss them.

At noon, Don snarled, "Hell, Paolo's not going to show up, I'll go look for the damn anchor myself. Will you help?"

I found the paper on which I'd written the bearings when the anchor chain broke and climbed into the dinghy. Don dove into the water with his snorkel and mask and swam toward the area where he thought the anchor was located.

Without warning, Paolo surfaced near the dinghy, startling me. "I have looked several times for your anchor, but I don't see it."

He acted as if showing up at zero hour was the natural thing to do. But Don kept his irritation concealed. "Wait, Paolo!" he said. "Follow me, I think the anchor's over here." He swam fifteen meters toward shore.

Paolo dove down and resurfaced. "I see it! Get me some rope to haul it up."

I grabbed some nylon line and threw the bitter end to Paolo, who dove down twelve meters and connected the line to the anchor. He and Don swam back to the boat, climbed aboard, secured the line to the windlass, and pulled. The anchor and chain came up.

"Now, Paolo, will you help me take the anchors and chain below?"

We had four anchors mounted on deck. Don wanted them all stowed below for safety, to lower the center of gravity for our passage to Cape Horn.

Paolo hadn't bargained for this, and I didn't like Don pushing for more than they had agreed upon. I rolled my eyes at him, hoping he would catch on. Paolo waited, wary.

"Just one more thing, Paolo . . ." Don paused—he had read my sig-nals—then smiled, showed Paolo the sunglasses, and said, "Okay?"

Paolo grinned, put them on and shook hands with Don. I rowed him ashore, and he hugged me as if nothing had ever happened. I pulled the dinghy up on the beach and ran up the road to say good-bye to Dr. Campbell.

"You will be crossing one of the most dangerous seas of the world," he said. "I will be very concerned about the two of you till I know you are safe."

I promised to write as soon as we got to Punta Arenas, hugged him, and ran back to the dinghy.

The wind freshened from the north and I had a hard pull to make headway. Three fishermen in a motorized skiff passed on their way out to sea. "Buen marinera, Señora," they shouted. Four weeks on Easter Island, and I had finally earned some praise!

NOTES

1. Thor Heyerdahl's book *Aku Aku* brought worldwide attention to Easter Island, and, in 1960, Ahu Akivi was restored, and the *moai* erected, under a program funded by UNESCO and the Chilean gov-ernment. (Orongo was restored during the same period.)

2. Easter Island has been known by other names: Te-píto-o-te-henúa—the Navel (Center) of the World; la Isla Más Lejos del Mundo—the Most Remote Island in the World. Islanders prefer the Polynesian name Rapa Nui—which, loosely translated, means Big Island—and they have recently adopted the same name for their language. The Pascuesan dictionary gives the etymology of the words in more detail.

3. Orongo, the Bird Man ceremonial site, is a series of underground interconnecting chambers. The walls and ceiling of the rooms are constructed of large, flat rocks covered with earth. The ceilings were just high enough to allow us to crawl from room to room.

4. The race has been recently reinstated for tourists.

5. Written by Dr. Ramón Campbell, "Pae-pae, Haumarú" (Tranquil Cabaña) was one of the most pop-ular songs on Rapa Nui at that time.

6. The statues on Ahu Akivi were the first to be raised in the "ancient" manner, using log levers and derricks.

7. The UN had repeatedly called for sanctions against Pinochet's government for its violations of human rights.

8. The Pascuensans were wily, tough negotiators. All our bartering experiences ended positively, with both sides giving additional gifts to show their mutual respect and appreciation. The only cash we used in our four-week stay was to purchase a barrel of diesel fuel, postage stamps, and a few provisions.

9. In 1960, a tsunami hit Hotu Iti and washed up the sides of the volcano, knocking over fifteen colossal statues that had stood on an *ahu*.

CHAPTER 4

South Pacific High

FEBRUARY 3

Me, the landbird—I'm happy to be underway. I sing and whistle again at sea, as "mysterious" Isla de Pascua grows smaller and smaller in my mind and on the horizon. I am happy to be alone—just the two of us now, relaxed and able to talk without the constant distractions of translating—to read aloud, and to be able to listen to music.

We have spent the last twenty-four hours trying to understand what went wrong. Naïve Americanos, I suppose. We expected honesty from the abogado and high performance from the governor, and got neither. Perhaps if our chronometer had arrived, Don might have been able to relax, and we would have come away with entirely different memories.

But we shall always remember the kindness of Jermán and Gabriel Ika, Estevan and Tomasa, Lieutenant Schlecter, Dr. Campbell, and Mike, the Americano.

FEBRUARY 5

We had failed to make many of our prearranged radio schedules with Tex. He couldn't always get to the "radio shack" in General Dynamics where he worked, and his antenna at home wasn't powerful enough to pick up our transmissions. During daylight hours, when we were supposed to have our regular contact, atmospheric conditions were often unfavorable. Today, we tried to get through for our schedule, but couldn't.

At night, we searched the band for anyone who could place a phone patch to California. "This is K6KWS on Maritime Mobile," Don broadcast. "Does anyone copy?"

A male voice boomed through the transceiver. "This is W6MAB, Big John, in La Crescenta, California . . . I handle all the South Pole traffic every night," he said, "and would be glad to handle yours, too."

I wanted to give him a bear hug; he was another of those selfless ham operators who spent hours in useful contacts. He dialed my parents' number in San Mateo, and our first contact in four weeks came through loud and clear.

Daddy was still valiantly slogging along with our finances. He asked when I'd be home, so I could take over. Startled by his question, I couldn't answer for a moment. "Are you there? . . . Over . . . Are you there? . . . Over," he repeated.

Big John broke in. "It's all right, Mr. Hemingway, it takes a few seconds for the answer to come back."

Again, I urged Daddy to hand the bookwork over to Don's partner, but he still insisted on "keeping it in the family."

Despite his increasing worries about his own condition and our finances, Daddy had behaved himself remarkably well in all the phone patches these past five months. Before we left, I used to dread talking to him about our trip—he always sent us the gloomiest nautical tidbits he could cull from the press: Had we read about the recent piratings in the Pacific? Had we received the article he sent about a seventy-foot wave that obliterated a freighter in the Mozambique Channel? Did we hear about the Botleys' trip to Baja? They had to shoot a whale that tried to turn their boat over. (We doubted his secondhand details.) Did we have a gun? (Yes, we did, but we never told him a .22-caliber doesn't make much impression on a whale.)

Sometimes I think his subconscious conjured up these tactics to get me to stay home. "Daddy's little girl." Looking back to my college days, he pulled the same stuff when I wanted to study in France.

Is that what I did to Sean before we left? In reverse? Trying to convince him what a marvelous trip this would be, coaxing, prodding, urging. Instead of listening to what he really wanted and helping him attain it . . . Some parents have a harder time letting go than others. Maybe I'm just like Daddy.

Mother offered to write the American Embassy in Santiago about the chronometer to ask their help in tracking it down. She'd have the letter in the mail the next day, I knew.

Don's second phone patch to our sailing friend, Will Durant, left me feeling uneasy and gloomy, like the articles Daddy used to send us. Don wanted to be sure a responsible party had all the details of our condition in case someone had to come looking for us, and he asked Will to take notes of what was wrong with *le Dauphin*.

"We have a damaged bobstay," he said. "We're taking on fifty gallons of water a day—due, perhaps, to the damage at the bobstay. We have no chronometer and just two portable radios for receiving occasional time ticks, so it may be tough to calculate our longitude precisely." He added that we were having trouble charging our batteries and hadn't located the trouble yet. As he concluded the phone patch, he said, "In case you don't hear from us, we have an eight-man Avon life raft with supplies for forty-five days. Otherwise we're in good shape for the high latitudes and not expecting any problems."

"An eight-man life raft with forty-five days' supplies." I don't like the sound of it, and I worry about Daddy. Will I make it home in time to see him again? His mind seems to be slipping—I've never heard him so irritable before. Before he took over our finances, I explained how complicated they are, but he insisted he could handle them for the whole year. That was before he learned he had cancer. We've been gone five months and it's already too much for him. I wonder if the pain in his spine is causing his irritability, or if the cancer is moving to his brain. I wish I knew how rapidly this type of cancer moves. It's so sad to think he's on his final run.

FEBRUARY 6

Don inspected the fiberglass he and Paolo had applied to the steering vane trim tab at Anakena and declared it "unshipshape." The resin hadn't cured properly. He spent the morning resanding and refiberglassing it, finishing before the sun was overhead. He hoped the two of us would be able to reinstall it in the next day or so. Since we hadn't been able to receive time ticks on WWV in the morning, we practiced tracking the noon sun. While Don took a series of sights I wrote down the sextant readings.

His journal entry, later in the day, read:

I kept on taking sights, and it seemed that any moment the zenith would be reached and the sun would start its postmeridian descent. But today it kept going up, up, up at a maddeningly slower and slower rate. I ended up taking sixty-two sights at one-minute intervals, so as not to miss the zenith. What a hassle!

That proves what lengths you have to go to when you don't know your position, or what time the meridian is likely to occur. I can't get excited about finding and knowing our exact position—it's more important to sail well and enjoy this solitude after our hectic life ashore at Rapa Nui.

Our strategy now is to expect the worst in terms of weather and seas when we reach the high latitudes and to be prepared. I just hope we can finish stowing and securing things before we hit heavy weather. Although I'm taking advantage of the wind to push beyond the South Pacific high pressure zone, I intend to take a defensive position as soon as the weather kicks up. The damage to the bobstay worries me a little, as well as the leak in the forward part of the boat. Réanne's been doing well and I'm glad she's along on this leg. I find myself yelling at her a lot for not grasping how to do something, but I'm really glad she's with me. To face this alone would be frightening—and exhausting, since so many things still remain to be done.

FEBRUARY 8
35°03'S, 110°05'W

The engine wouldn't start this morning. Don imposed a moratorium on electrical power to save the charge in the batteries and bled the system to try to eliminate air, but it still wouldn't start. After he checked everything in detail he found the problem—me. I left the fuel cut-off switch in its stop position two nights ago when the engine overheated.

Relief! The starter switch whirred, and Don ran the engine for thirty minutes to charge the batteries. I got a ripping lecture served up with a Mongolian scowl but managed not to get defensive—I deserved it. With just enough battery power for a couple more radio transmissions, the thought of rounding Cape Horn without power is like contemplating suicide.

Washing my hair in the most remote spot on Earth

After noon, we took advantage of the beautiful weather and lack of wind to reinstall the trim tab (auxiliary rudder) of the steering vane rudder. Don worked on board from the transom (edge of the stern) while I crouched on the swim step and, like a monkey hanging from a tree by one arm, steadied the shaft with my free arm until he could insert the pins securing the vane. It was another of the acrobatic feats we had to perform daily. I was on a maritime dunking stool—one minute completely out of the water, the next totally immersed. Installation time sixty minutes.

Afterward I put on my harness, tethered a line to the boat, and went swimming. I floated on my back, suspended in turquoise liquid, watching wisps of white clouds drift by on their interminable journey toward Australia. I was so hypnotized that if I hadn't been tied on, the boat would have left me slowly, slowly, as I gazed forever at the sky.

Don's voice brought me back to reality. He leaned over the rail and said, "Just think, babe, people wouldn't even be able to find our current position on a world globe. We're in the region of the ocean where the manufacturers usually put their legend—the most remote spot from land anywhere in the world."

When I'm tethered to the boat, the miles of water separating me from the ocean floor don't bother me. But whenever I swim without a harness, I become immediately uncomfortable, nervous. The boys used to tease me, "Come on, Mom. It's just like swimming in a lake." But without a shore

*for reference I need that security—the tie that assures my return to the boat.
The sea with its immense, boundless water rolling on to infinity is beautiful, but its power frightens me.*

Don decided to go overboard to check the hull, knowing that if he waited much longer the water would be too cold. After two hours of scrubbing the hull and checking the seams and fittings, he declared *le Dauphin
Amical* fit.

Afterward he wrote in his journal:

The open ocean to the south of Easter Island must be the least congested in the
world. No major shipping lanes, no local traffic of any kind. This is a solitude so
complete it defies description. As if to appease the cartographers, all forms of
life seem to stay away from this remote region. There are no dolphins, no sea
turtles, no sharks, no jellyfish. No pollution. The only thing we've seen in 900
miles since leaving Easter Island is a single barnacle-encrusted fishing float, a
handful of sea birds, and a few flying fish. That's all! I didn't see a single sign of
life in the water this afternoon.

Our bodies detected a drop in humidity. We noticed a dryness in the nose,
an ache behind the eyes, in the sinuses. Water and air temperatures were dropping, too, and a blanket over us at night began to feel good.

FEBRUARY 10

36°56'S, 112°56'W

While I was preparing lunch I detected an odor of rubber. There had
been no wind all morning, and we had been motoring. I poked my head
out the hatch and yelled to Don.

"Something's burning, smells like rubber."

"Oh yeah?" His lips curled in a sneer. He took my acute sense of
smell so lightly, I was annoyed. I resumed cooking, and the odor got
worse.

"Dammit, Don. Check the engine temperature. There's something
wrong!" Smoke was coming out of the engine box by then.

"Oh shit, you're right. It's 200 degrees."

He raced down the ladder, took off the engine cover, studied,
observed, and poked, considering aloud possible problems, possible solutions. He removed the front cover of the saltwater pump, let saltwater
flow through for a few seconds to check the flow. Slow, at first; then the
water increased to its normal flow.

"Come here. I want to show you how this works . . . See this? That's
the saltwater cooling pump . . . See this." He pointed to what looked like
an inverted toilet plunger of cast bronze. "That's the impeller." He pointed to a set of six rubber blades equally spaced, like the carpels in the
ovary of a flower. "Water flows in through this intake pipe. The impeller
turns this direction." I could see the anterior curve of the blades, indicat-

ing that they turned counterclockwise. "The water flows through the impeller and out this pipe. See these little pieces of seaweed? I think they're the culprit. If I'm right, they were blocking the impeller."

I thought of what Don had written about the absence of life—"water so clear it doesn't exist"—and wondered how minuscule pieces of seaweed could find their way into the only vessel within 5,000 miles. Where did they come from?

Don checked the fresh water in the heat exchanger, added oil to the crank case, reinstalled the motor cover, turned the starter key, and the engine roared. The deafening sound of our Perkins diesel was beginning to affect me as joyfully as Beethoven's Ninth.

0300: Wind gusts hit 30 knots at midnight, and we had to drop the main. Neither of us was sleepy afterwards, and we have been sitting at the galley table snacking on homemade paté with crackers, reading aloud from Darwin's Voyage of the Beagle. The wind has just decreased, Don has reengaged the steering vane, and we shall hit the sack.

FEBRUARY 11

My forty-second birthday, and possibly the most unusual one I've ever had since the day Don asked me to marry him eight years ago. When I awoke I found a note on my pillow: "Happy Birthday to you who choose to be here—may I long sing the praises (and show my daily appreciation) to Réanne, my love! Don—38°S, 114°W." Then he gave me another gift of true love—the day off.

My birthday always brought up good memories of the night Don proposed. He had arranged a surprise dinner date for me, enlisting the aid of a friend who was an accomplished pilot. As we sat in the rear of a four-passenger Cessna, looking down at the San Bernardino Mountains, Don began reciting a poem he'd composed asking me to marry him. The instant he had finished the last verse—"Réanne, my dear, do say Oui"—a down draft hit the plane, the stall-warning lights blinked red, the horn blared, and we dropped two thousand feet toward earth before the pilot could stabilize the plane.

While Don took over galley duty, I relaxed and finished another book on my list. The past week since we left Easter Island had been what I thought was the best leg of the entire trip. Pleasurable—like dream cruises were supposed to be.

Here, a thousand miles away from land, we have no need for clothes, no need for night watches or running lights. We set the steering vane and let the winds fill the sails and propel us smartly south. I feel as if Don and I have come out of the darkness after a long estrangement. It's been wonderful.

Don's diary filled in the rest of the day:

Morning bright and sunny, just a few clouds and almost calm seas, a perfect tribute to Réanne's birthday. Perhaps the first woman to celebrate a birthday in these parts.

Breakfast: Unsweetened grapefruit juice—to prevent scurvy. Stewed mixed fruit—for taste and an aid to elimination. Cream of Wheat Hearts with California Real Fresh whole milk and honey—for energy. Cocoa—for warmth and stimulation. Served to my Lady, in situ, at 1030 hours by a scrubbed chef in turtleneck.

Lunch for my Lady: Sweet cucumber chips and pickled cocktail onions, ripe Chilean cheese strips, sliced cooked ham on Ritz crackers, cream of chicken soup, watermelon (heart only—rest overripe), sweet cookies with vanilla frosting, apricot nectar. Served on the fan tail in sunny but nippy weather at 1400 hours.

Just where are we today? I honestly don't know. Are we lost? Not really. I feel like the boy who said, "How can you be lost when you don't care where you are?" I have neglected navigation since leaving Rapa Nui eleven days ago, and I haven't even attempted to plot a line of position. To draw all those lines and work with numbers seems out of place here in this danger-free expanse of sea. Determining latitude and longitude to five significant places, advancing lines of position, gauging intersections for indications of accuracy—the whole rigmarole seems unnecessary now. Besides, I'm lazy and enjoying the time off!

FEBRUARY 12

38°14'S, 115°00'W

Don took one look out the port this morning and said, "You might as well stay in bed today." A grey, colorless, forlorn panorama, from horizon to horizon, and a gloomy drizzle.

As we penciled our position on the chart, a quarter-inch per day—on good days a half-inch—we neared the infamous Roaring Forties—the area between latitudes 40° and 50° south where strong, prevailing winds blow from the west. (The old clipper ships rounding Cape Horn from San Francisco to Boston relied on these winds to make timely transits.) In these prevailing winds, our self-steering vane was a boon. It allowed us on days like this—when we had steady 20-knot winds behind us—to stay below if we wanted to, with an occasional trip up the ladder to check on conditions. Today we were running under small jib and staysail.

One wool blanket during the night hadn't done the trick. We snuggled in an "S" trying to stay warm. We tried two blankets. Not sufficient. It was time to unroll the Dacron comforter, and it felt great! Today, to

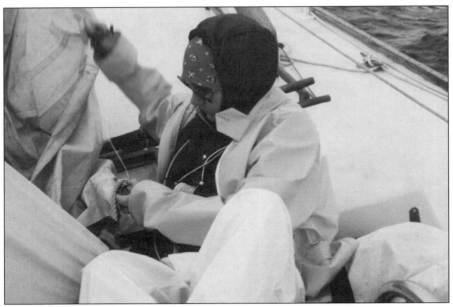

I looked like the Michelin Man prepared for action

stay warm inside the cabin, I wore sweat pants, socks, a wool pullover with a long- sleeved turtleneck underneath, a stocking cap on my head.

During the night, I had heard sail slides pinging on the cabin roof. I couldn't postpone replacing them another day because we might need the mainsail. So today I put on my down vest, down jacket, foul weather pants, and foul weather jacket (tied the hood securely around my head), and climbed up the ladder. I looked like the Michelin Man prepared for action.

I fished in the lazaret for the big green canvas tarp we kept ready for days like this, went forward, pulled the lower half of the mainsail out of its track on the mast, stationed myself against the mainmast, wrapping myself in the tarp, and began replacing the slides. Simple repairs like this took so long on a sailboat and required such care that I always got an immense feeling of accomplishment after I'd finished. I felt like a little kid receiving praise. ("Where did you go?" "Out." "What did you do?" "Replaced sail slides." "Good girl!")

FEBRUARY 13

We slept most of the day, snuggled, made love. Afterward Don wanted to know what made me feel sexy today, since I didn't usually. My answers: the boat had a nice motion to it (we weren't getting knocked from side to side); he was clean; he took time to arouse me instead of acting like a robot; he's been nice. In his "engineering tone," he suggested I just relax a little more to feel sexy. Damn, I wish he'd just shut up and enjoy the afterglow, let the romance linger instead of trying to figure out how my machine functions.

Later, Don poured comments into his own journal:

Why is Réanne so turned off, or at least annoyed, a good part of the time by my continuing and constant sex drive? For the life of me, I can't figure out if her sex drive is cyclical or aperiodic; if it's related to something physical or mental. It seems to come out of left field somewhere. If I could only find the key to her drive, I'd be a lot better off.

FEBRUARY 15

42°37'S, 113°27'W

We crossed the 40th parallel two days ago, motoring in flat seas.

"I can't believe the Roaring Forties are all they're cracked up to be," I told Don with a big kiss. "This part of the trip has been wonderful. And it helps not to be seasick!"

Southeasterly winds had prevented us from heading east, a repeat of our passage to Easter Island. We had gained four degrees in west longitude since leaving Hanga Roa Bay.

"If these southeasters continue," Don said, "we'll end up in Australia. Would you settle for Cape Leeuwin, instead of Cape Horn?"

The barograph—high at 30.50 inches—had begun a descent today, indicating a change in weather. Instead of wind from the southeast we now had a north wind behind us, and *le Dauphin* was carrying us southward, instead of west, at a respectable 5 knots.

At sunset we noticed a strange layer of yellow haze above the western horizon, like a forest fire. Something about it made me uneasy. Were we approaching the area of Slocum's "Great White Arch?"

FEBRUARY 16

The Roaring Forties! They heard my belittling remarks and took revenge by sending a full-fledged gale. We were averaging 5 to 6 knots and rolling from side to side. Swells twenty feet high rushed toward the stern, lifted it, paused as if pondering whether to engulf us or not, then burst into foam, rolled under the keel and let the stern settle back down, while another set of waves poised ready to torment us.

Le Dauphin Amical rode up, up, on each wave, shuddered a bit, rocked, shook herself off, and settled down again. She was in her element. Don was in his. I was not.

Breakfast this morning exploded all over the galley sole. I am feeling queasy again. Either from the violent motion or lack of sleep last night.

Bad news late this afternoon. The engine wouldn't start again, but this time it isn't my fault—I pushed the cut-off switch back in its correct position. We ran out of daylight before Don could figure out what's wrong. We're both discouraged, trying not to voice our worries. But thoughts I can't control flash through my mind. Like Agatha Christie's And Then There Were None. *God, the mind plays awful tricks.*

Don plotting our position in the Roaring Forties

FEBRUARY 17

Don dismantled the fuel pump and discovered air bubbles throughout the lines. He bled the system again, and the engine started and ran. I was almost afraid to write about it. We've had so many close-calls, though not anything Don couldn't solve.

But today we had some additional setbacks that were beyond our control—our portable Sony receiver went dead, and new batteries couldn't revive it. When Don took it apart he found the circuit boards all corroded—just from salt air. We were down to the port captain's portable radio now to try receiving time ticks."What ifs" were plaguing me again.

What if Don can't figure out the engine troubles? We won't have a way to charge the batteries so we can use the transceiver. That means no contact with anyone. No electricity. What if there's too much interference on Schlecter's receiver to get a time tick? That would mean I'd have no way to set my Seiko accurately, and we'd have no way to determine longitude. What if we have a problem Don can't repair? What then? If we're lucky we can rely on sails alone—Slocum didn't have an engine or batteries on Spray; *so maybe the two of us could manage.*

What if we can't contact our family and friends? Mother and Daddy will be frantic if they don't hear from us. Even worse is the thought that if something should happen to us, all my notes will be lost forever. No word will remain. I feel bad for those I love. If we were lost, lost at sea, they would never, never know what happened.

While I poured black thoughts on paper, Don wrote more pragmatic thoughts, in line with his mathematical temperament:

> If we were astronauts, thousands of scientists and technicians would be monitoring our progress, giving us constant instructions on how to solve our problems, feedback on how our systems are functioning. Here, we cope with each situation by ourselves, taxing our bodies and minds to the limit. No one, not our families, not our friends, know what we're going through out here each day. Only those who have sailed these high latitude waters can appreciate our experience.[1]

FEBRUARY 18
45°38'S, 107°15'W

Westerlies finally set in, and we were able to make our "big left turn" southeast toward Cape Horn. Don engaged the steering vane at about 2200 hours so we could catch some sleep and he left the working jib and staysail up so we could gain headway.

At 2400 hours, a sensation of the boat's being pushed sideways awakened me. I roused Don. "I think we're going to have to drop the jib."

He poked his head out the hatch. It was pitch black and raining. "Hell, yes, pass me my boots. The port rail is under water."

The boat was riding so wildly, I said a prayer asking Don not to send me forward.

"You man the sheets and helm," he shouted. "I'll go forward and drop the jib."

The rain hit my face and stung, and I thanked him silently.

The sail doused and tied off, Don readjusted the steering vane and plopped down on the cockpit settee beside me, visibly shaken. "God! Those forty feet to the bow are like going to Siberia. You don't know if you'll ever be heard from again."

I went below to prepare him a cup of hot cocoa and resurfaced.

At 0030 hours, the wind lessened. "Maybe that was premature. Maybe I should have let out on the sheets and fallen off."

Fifteen minutes later another gust hit. *Le Dauphin* rounded up

The great wandering albatross, largest of all living birds, breeds in colonies on offshore islands of the Southern Ocean. Its wings are so adapted to soaring that when the wind drops it cannot get airborne. The albatross has been the source of legends and lore for centuries.

into the wind and took off on a gallop again. "No. Maybe we're okay under mizzen and staysail."

When I could, I had been reading aloud to Don parts of H.W. Tilman's *Mischief in Patagonia*. Tilman, a remarkable British mountain climber and sailor, had made numerous high latitude voyages in both the Northern and Southern Hemispheres in his cutter, *Mischief.* He first caught sea fever in 1955 at the age of fifty-four when he bought and refitted a Bristol cutter for the express purpose of sailing to the Patagonia channels to climb the ice cap. Like the Smeetons, he was one of those who seemed oblivious to hardship. Whenever he complained about the weather, or problems with his boat and crew, he made such short shrift of it, and with such wonderful wit, that his prose hooked me. I found myself frequently copying excerpts in my diary, or saying to Don, "Listen to this . . . Let me read this to you!"

One passage compared sailing and mountaineering. It was so apt to what I felt about Don and our situation, I kept flipping back to the same dog-eared page to reread:

> Each is intimately concerned with elemental things, which . . . demand from men who practice those arts whatever self-reliance, prudence, and endurance they may have. The sea and the hills offer challenges to those who venture upon them and in the acceptance of these and in the meeting of them as best he can lies the sailor's or mountaineer's reward. An essential difference is, perhaps, that the mountaineer usually accepts the challenge on his own terms, whereas once at sea the sailor has no say in the matter and in consequence may suffer more often the salutary and humbling emotion of fear.[2]

FEBRUARY 19

This morning we sighted our first great wandering albatross, a beautiful soaring-machine with a twelve-foot wing span. He followed us for over three hours, not once flapping his wings, and neither of us can imagine how anyone could shoot these magnificent creatures. They don't even make good eating, although I suppose sailors who survived on nothing but salt pork and hardtack found their meat a welcome addition to a dreary diet.

A squall later brought hail that clattered on deck. The wind rose to gale force (35 to 40 knots). Waves hitting the stern shot thirty feet into the air, then dropped, glistening like icicles caught by a slow-motion video camera. The albatross had disappeared. Where did he go? we wondered. Above, to gain soaring power? He might be off Cape Horn by this time.

Don plotted our position—46°23'S, 106°16'W—but figured his calculations put us too far west. Without a chronometer or the ability to pick up time ticks on WWV, the errors that Don had predicted were occurring.

The sky had lost its harshness, its blinding vividness, its hard line. The sunlight, whitewashed and soft, seemed diffused with microscopic particles of ice. We had traversed Gauguin's tropical palette and were moving across a Monet canvas. It was summer still at this latitude, but the weather was winter—the winter I had longed for earlier. I inserted cassettes of Christmas music in the tape deck—Handel's Messiah, the Mormon Tabernacle Choir, the Nutcracker Suite, French carols—and played them at maximum decibels. I wrapped myself up in five layers and sat behind the helm singing at the top of my lungs. I replayed the Christmas tape Jean and Kathy had made for us.

The size of the seas, however, sobered me. Enormous, unceasing "greybeards"—the waves that turned the sailor's beard to grey—rolled eastward. I was beginning to understand what draws sailors to this Great Southern Ocean: the same excitement that ignites mountain climbers, that draws them to the Himalayas.

During our nightly radio contacts we managed to get through to Tex in California. Static was extreme; we heard just enough to know that Salem Clock had sent him another chronometer that he had been planning to forward to us in Punta Arenas. But they had sent it in a box without padding, so clock number three was *kaput*.

Burt, PT2ZBS in Brasilia, said, "Maybe you'll get a chance to buy back chronometer number two when you get to Chile."

We laughed, but his comment struck home. It hadn't occurred to us to ask what it would take to get our recorder and tapes back, or even to mention *cash* to the Governor. We had assumed the Chilean military were aboveboard. Why had we thought they would function any differently than Mexican officials?

FEBRUARY 21

0100. Under staysail, jib, and mizzen, 700 square feet of canvas (the maximum Don had attempted to leave up at night in these latitudes), we were sailing at a good 4 to 5 knots.

I wrote:

Adieu to days of sun—of warmth, of comfort, of nights of reading, of nestling in the captain's berth. We are tasting true high latitude sailing now, and catch sleep only when we can—and separately.

Don's middle-of-the-night journal entry read:

I had just warmed up the sleeping bag in the quarter berth and was marveling at how smoothly the boat was riding—like a Greyhound bus—with the bow raising her knife-edge a couple of inches now and then, as if nodding to local mermaids.

I was drowsily thinking how few hard times we've had on this leg and that Réanne has been able to say she actually was enjoying some of it. Then, suddenly, the sound of the wind in the rigging increased and I regained full consciousness. The boat heeled 10 degrees, hard over, and a galley locker flew open, sending cans careening across the floor. I glanced out the aft port. The wheel was turning by itself, as if answering some invisible powerful hand, and the wind vane oscillated madly. I climbed up to the cockpit, carrying my socks and boots, yelled to Réanne to bring me a jacket, and disengaged the steering vane before it destroyed itself.

After his noon sun shot, Don declared we were officially in the high latitudes. To reduce his shots, we had to switch to volume three of the HO Tables that covers the area from the Roaring Forties to the South Pole.

At 1600 hours he tried to start the engine in order to charge the batteries. After four tries, it coughed, sputtered, just about grabbed, then quit. Trying to keep a sense of humor, I put new words to the 1940's song, "Takin' a Chance on Love:"

Here we go again
It's the same old show again
The motor won't go again . . .

Beginning the bleed process again, Don took apart the three primary fuel filters and found air bubbles throughout the system. He tried starting the engine again. No deal—it wouldn't catch. He bled two of the four fuel injectors, and it finally started. He logged: "I discovered that I'd stripped the threads on the air bleed screw of the fuel pump—air was probably entering at that point, and heavy surging in the fuel tank must have aerated the fuel. I wound Teflon tape around the threads and hope this will remedy the problem."

Taking advantage of calm seas and a sunny afternoon, I continued preparing for the Screaming Fifties.[3] I chinked the center hatch with Ensolite (water had been pouring through it every time we took a header), and I installed thick bungee cords across the drawers in the salon to keep them in place when we heeled. Two days before, the top drawer had shot out, dumping our clothes on the floor, and the corner of the drawer broke off as it hit the salon settee, leaving ugly gashes on the wood.

FEBRUARY 23

Conditions were deteriorating. So was I. There had been no letup in jerking and rolling for two days. Don thrived on the excitement and could function on short snatches of sleep. I couldn't. If I didn't get at least three hours of uninterrupted sleep, I was no good. For forty-eight hours we had been up and down continuously, dropping sails, raising sails, reefing the main, and pumping, pumping. We had made a log entry every single hour!

I made the mistake of complaining about the motion and lack of sleep. "Can't we just leave the jib down for the night and run with the staysail?" It launched us into a ripping fight, complete with a nonstop sermon about how I didn't understand that we had to push as hard as we could, that the weather was worsening, etc., etc., etc.

All I wanted was for him to empathize, "Yeah, it's pretty bad, isn't it?" and put his arms around me, instead of flying into a fit. Just because he had such a capacity for hardship, did he have to negate my feelings?

Later that night we made contact with Big John who patched us through, first, to Kathy, then to Sean. It was wonderful to talk to them, but because of my fight with Don, I had a hard time keeping my spirits up. After we signed off, instead of being cheered up, I was depressed and overcome with longing. Lack of sleep was doing it, I knew—I hadn't even had time for dreams.

FEBRUARY 24

Our day began at 0400 when Don awakened me for a black-of-night sail change. This time, he sent me forward to drop the jib.

I snapped the carabiner of my harness onto the starboard lifeline, crawled forward along the side of the cabin, and grasped the handrail till I reached the mast. Clinging to the main mast with all the strength in my left arm, I dropped and secured the jib halyard with my right, then inched forward along the bowsprit, and lowered and tied off the jib sail. Drenched, I inched my way back to the cockpit.

"Good job!" Don said, giving me a hug. "How did you feel up there?"

My mouth was so dry I could barely answer, "Scared as hell!"

"Did you like *anything* about it?"

"Yeah, the wind in my face, and the first light of dawn," I answered, amazed that my senses had upstaged my fears. I had self-righteously accused high latitude sailors of being Pollyannas and never "telling it like it is," but as I gained experience, I realized that the sailors did have a truly unique capacity for enduring discomfort, which was the reason they underplayed bad conditions. They knew what they were in for, and followed the credo: "You get yourself into difficulty; you rescue yourself."

Cut from the same fabric as the Smeetons and Tilman were Moitessier and Hal and Margaret Roth. The Roths[4]—an American couple whose film about their circumnavigation of the North Pacific we had seen in California—were now circumnavigating South America. We followed their adventures in a small sailing publication and had learned just before our departure that their boat had been thrown ashore in a storm on Wollaston Island near Cape Horn, and her hull had been ripped below waterline. We were eager to learn whether they had been able to repair *Whisper* and continue their voyage.

The Southern Ocean—they had all sailed it, as we were now. You won't find its name on a chart, in an atlas, or in the geographical section of a dictionary, but those who have sailed here call it the Great Southern Ocean. Circling round and round Antarctica, it builds itself into limitless fetch, sweeping on with a vengeance, with nothing to block its way.

Bernard Moitessier had become our mentor. His *Cap Horn à la Voile* was one of our bibles. I had purchased a copy several years earlier in France and translated parts of it aloud to Don. Page after page, paragraph after paragraph, was underlined in black ink or highlighted in yellow, and it was so worn I had to rubberband it to keep it from falling apart. I read, reread. To myself. Out loud. Adding more highlighting at paragraphs that corresponded to our position, our conditions.

Bernard and his wife, Françoise, set out from Tahiti in late November 1965 and by mid-December reached the Roaring Forties, where gale after gale pounded them. My newest "rediscovery" shouted at me from page 194: "I had already forgotten that you don't sleep more than a few hours in a row south of the 40th parallel. But what I don't suspect at this moment is that Françoise and I haven't seen anything yet."

How had I missed that on my first reading? Perhaps I might have steeled myself sooner for what we were going through now.

The rest of the day went like a typical day 1,000 miles west of Cape Horn. My journal was beginning to read like a *real* sailor's, I thought.

0700: One hour's sleep after the sail change. I awaken, gagging from smoke. Don's trying to build a fire in the fireplace. Within five minutes I can't see the fireplace from the companionway ladder where I've taken refuge. Don goes to the forepeak to open the front hatch. "I think the wind's too strong for a fire," he says, rushing aft to get some air. We crawl out into the cockpit, coughing and laughing the smoke out of our lungs.

0800: The sun comes out momentarily. Don grabs his sextant to try a shot. We have a big argument over the time tick. I can't get an accurate tick—too much interference on the radio.

0900: We eat the oatmeal I cooked an hour ago.

0945: I hang the radio locker weather cloth I sewed yesterday.

1000: Don takes another sun shot. "You gotta get it when you can," he says. "Yeah, like sex," I reply.

1015: Doing 6 knots, the boat pounds like hell. I'm sitting below the center hatch writing. Water pours in. So much for my chinking job.

1030: Don reduces the shots today. I work on a wool muffler I'm knitting for him.

1100: Don goes back to bed. I start dinner—a casserole of canned beef, tomatoes, onions (fresh, still, from Easter Island), celery flakes, fresh garlic, spaghetti, sour cream mix, seasoned with basil and thyme and topped with black olives.

1145: Extreme heeling, suddenly. Don rushes above to check. The log line snagged itself on the steering vane release (second time this week), and the vane is going wild. Don reels in the log line and cuts the vane release. Gusts are increasing. We discuss reducing sail.

1200: We shovel a few bites of the casserole down our throats, drop the jib, then run under staysail only. The gusts are too strong—the vane won't control the boat and one of us has to remain at the helm.

1300: Don says, "Maybe we'd better reef the staysail." We drop it instead. Don curses about not being able to make speed. We're under bare poles now, no sails. The wind is too great for even a handkerchief-sized sail.

1400: I go below. Bilge water is pouring over the floorboards. I mop.

1430: Don decides to try the canvas storm jib, supposedly just the thing for extreme conditions like this. It blows out the minute he raises it. Rotten canvas. We lower it; the wind and spray catch it before I can grab it; one of its snapshackles catches on the bobstay. We pull what we can of the sail back on board, tie it down, and leave the rest of it hooked to the bobstay. Le Dauphin looks like an orphan. Under bare poles, with the vane engaged, we fly downwind. Wind, Force 7 to 8, barometer descending rapidly.

1600: We collapse into bed, get up again at 1800. Conditions horrible—the galley floor is awash; Don's tools and prize voltmeter stowed below the sink are soaked and ruined. He's devastated and writes in the log, "Things are getting serious; this isn't much fun."

Conditions weren't much fun. I was nervous and tense, but Don was so discouraged I didn't complain. I tried to cheer him up, thinking to myself, *This is the reason sailors become Pollyannas—they have to, to be able to survive these conditions.*

FEBRUARY 25
50°16'S, 94°35'W

This is the most miserable day we've had in five months. Gale force winds have screamed all day. We haven't been able to carry any sail and have made only fifty miles under bare poles. Seas break continuously over the cabin roof, and we've taken two near knockdowns. Everything below is drenched. The motion is so violent you can't sit. You can't stand without being thrown across the cabin. There's no place in the damn boat to get any relief. I ache. I'm tired. So is Don. Everything's falling apart.

Don set a reef in the staysail and raised it, thinking that would give us some stability. He tied the boom to a stanchion so it wouldn't jibe, but with the wind so violent, the staysail kept tugging. About forty-five minutes after he had raised the sail, the boom started vibrating wildly, lifted suddenly, and snapped the stanchion in two. The port lifelines that kept us from being thrown overboard now lay limp along the deck.

At night we managed radio contact with the *Hero*, and Don asked them to transmit a message to the port captain in Punta Arenas.

Before I lay down, I wrote:

Don has been irritable all day. If conditions don't let up, we'll be at each other's throats soon.

I do not understand why anyone would want to beat his body like this. Did I write that Tilman, Moitessier, the Smeetons, and the Roths have a unique capacity for discomfort? Hell, they're masochists!

Sometimes I think daily routine is harder to face than the heroic efforts that make headlines, and I wonder if these sailors could weather some of the emotional storms I've endured. Sure, the lone sailor who rounds Cape Horn or the climber who scales Everest or Denali is admirable. But it took courage, too, to divorce an alcoholic spouse who wouldn't get help for himself. To raise two kids without child support, scrape to put myself through graduate school. To get up in the morning and teach with a smile on my face at the end of a love affair. To come home to my kids at night exhausted and give them the little energy I had left. A daily routine that took endurance and guts—but not the kind that makes the front page of a newspaper. Lone parents don't make headlines for their courage; they make the obits if they throw in the towel and swallow a bottle of sleeping pills.

St. Exupéry expresses my feelings so beautifully: "To come to man's estate it is not necessary to get oneself killed round Madrid, or to fly mail planes, or to struggle wearily in the snows out of respect for the dignity of life. The man who can see the miraculous in a poem, who can take pure joy from music, who can break his bread with comrades, opens his window to the same refreshing wind off the sea."[5]

NOTES

1. Sailors that participate in sponsored long-distance races, now benefit from constant monitoring and help in distress, but the lone round-the-world sailor is still responsible for his or her own safety.

2. *Mischief in Patagonia*, pp. 4, 5.

3. The area below 50° south, where prevailing winds "scream" round Antarctica, is called the Screaming Fifties.

4. The Roths are one of America's foremost sailing couples. The author of eight books about their adventures, Hal holds the prestigious Blue Water Medal of the Cruising Club of America.

5. From *Wind, Sand and Stars*, Harcourt, Brace and Company, 1967, p. 239.

CHAPTER 5

One Week to Cape Horn

The American yacht, le Dauphin Amical, *with two persons aboard, which left Isla de Pascua on February 1, will arrive later than expected because of weather and minor equipment problems. New ETA Punta Arenas: March 10.*

—*Radio message relayed by the* Hero, *February 25, 1975, to the port captain in Punta Arenas*

FEBRUARY 26, MORNING

"One week to Cape Horn!" Don said with enthusiasm as we gulped down our morning cocoa. "Just think! We're now south of New Zealand, Australia, and Africa—everything except Cape Horn. "

My mind belched sarcastic thoughts. *God, enthusiasm is a disease with him. The more miserable it gets, the happier he is.*

His enthusiasm was short-lived. "Do you hear that clunking sound? There's something wrong with the motion of the boat." He glanced quickly at the inside compass. "The steering vane's not holding its course. I'll have a look." I watched from the partially opened hatch while he examined the steering vane. "Get your foul weather gear on, and come up and look at this."

I suited up and went above.

"Come back here," Don said, looking down over the transom. "Hang on tight to the mizzen boom gallows, and look straight down the steering vane shaft . . . What do you see?"

Hanging onto the gallows as if it were a chinning bar, I knelt and peered over the stern. I could see that the shaft was badly bent.

"It's not much good now," Don said. "It's bent at least fifteen degrees."

Not much good now . . . I knew what that meant—full-time watches in an open cockpit, around the clock, and one of us at the helm no matter what the weather—if we wanted to get to our next port on schedule.

The steering vane had been so trustworthy that we hadn't practiced much with the inside control lines Don had rigged when he thought he'd be singlehandling. When we tried them a week earlier, they had worked well, but the steering vane wasn't damaged at that time.

"I want to do one experiment before we give up on it. Let's see if we can get it to work from below." He went below, stationed himself on the middle step of the companionway ladder, and pulled alternately on the two nylon lines. Although the boat turned from one tack to the other, it wouldn't hold a straight course.

"Well, that's it, babe. You know what this means, don't you?" I nodded. I didn't have to say anything; he knew I understood. "This may change our plans," Don said.

After our last contact with John on the *Hero*, we had talked about what fun it would be to make a brief stop at Ushuaia on the Beagle Channel, to visit the *Hero* and its crew before heading north to Punta Arenas. I didn't ask what he meant about changing plans. I was too discouraged to think rationally. It terrified me to see what the power of water could do to a 2½-inch-diameter stainless steel shaft—just twist it, like I would a disposable aluminum cake pan.

AFTERNOON

Don's noon sextant reading put us just over the 50th parallel, 800 miles west northwest of Cape Horn. We have logged nearly a thousand miles since leaving Easter Island, February 2.

I volunteered to take afternoon watch so Don could snooze. The storm was building to a full gale, like the one we'd had two days before, and I knew he would need his strength for the heavy stuff to come.

An albatross that had been following us for the past twenty-four hours had now disappeared. I wondered where it went. It would have a thousand miles to go before it found land.

At noon we had doused the jib and staysail, and we were running under bare poles again. Even without sail, I had to fight to control the helm. Waves crashed continuously across the port quarter, slapping the boat at a forty-five-degree angle, dumping gallons of water into the cockpit. As I looked up from the trough of each wave I was sure we would be engulfed.

Sleet mixed with salt spray stung my eyes and found its way through my muffler and down my neck. I shivered and looked astern. The sea was a battlefield of white. Rollers moved forward like tanks; geysers piled up and exploded. White froth curled and tumbled for a thousand yards before crashing into bottomless holes. Overhead, dark clouds churned, meeting the edge of a western horizon that glowed yellow with the intensity of an uncontrolled forest fire. It was the "old familiar white arch, the terror of Cape Horn" that Joshua Slocum had described—the sign, we now knew, of hurricane force winds that made the hair on our necks stand up—this was it.

I thought of Moitessier sitting under his little turret post, inside the steel-hulled *Joshua,* instructing Françoise how to handle the wheel in seas like this.

I volumteered to take watch so Don could snooze

> See that wave coming . . . the wind's dead behind so *Joshua* keeps up speed
> and the helm [can] respond. . . . Now I turn the helm, we heel, the stern lifts
> up and just when it begins to settle, I turn the wheel to the other side. . . . If
> the helm resists when the wave passes under the boat, and if you don't let it
> go. . . . you'll [put us] broadside without any speed.[1]

I tried to do what Bernard had taught Françoise. What had she been thinking? Was she afraid? His descriptions of her made her seem imperturbable.

Don pulled open the hatch cover and climbed up into the cockpit. "You
go below now. It's getting so bad I'm going to lash the helm." I
unsnapped my safety harness from the mizzen mast traveler. "I'll be back
down in a second," he said.

I climbed below and took off my foul weather gear. The wind hitting
the rigging sounded like jet engines revving up. The mast shuddered and
reverberated. How long could it hold up against winds like these?

I watched the barograph needle as the small brass penpoint inked its
way violently down the graph paper, like a plunge on the seismograph.
It'll be off the paper if it goes any lower, I thought. At home, atmospheric
pressure followed an uncreative line, varying little over the course of a

year. But at this latitude, the pressure had dropped a full inch to 29.1 (985.44 mb) in the last 24 hours, and the rapid descent indicated serious trouble.

Don came below and lit the kerosene lamps. "This looks like a full-blown storm—the worst I've ever seen. I've lashed the wheel to starboard; everything's pretty secure. Not much more we can do, except lie ahull." He slid behind the galley table and lay down to rest on the galley settee, his head aft next to the radio locker.

The flames of the kerosene lamps cast an amber glow on the white bulkheads, the shadows flickering as the boat heaved and rolled. The gim-balled table and stove swung back and forth, each in their own tempo, tolling bass tones as they hit against the bulkhead.

Aside from the violent motion, the noise of the wind and waves, and "waterfalls" through the center hatch when a wave broke over the cabin roof, the interior seemed shipshape and safe. Above, except for the kids' surfboard and the dinghy, lashed to the cabin with nylon rope and 3-inch seat-belt webbing, the deck was clear.

I kept reviewing what we'd done since we left Easter Island, wondering what more we could possibly do to make the boat safer. We had moved the heaviest gear to the salon—the lowest point in the boat—to keep the center of gravity low and the motion less erratic. Our four anchors and the toolboxes were lashed either to the frames or to floor beams in the salon (wrapped three times with one-inch tubular nylon webbing). Heavy canned goods were stowed in the bilge. Unneeded sails were crammed into their bags and stowed in the forepeak. Anchor lines were neatly coiled and stacked in lockers under the galley seat. The bungee cords I'd installed across the face of the drawers and the string nets across the bookshelves had done their trick so far. The radio locker at the foot of the companionway ladder was protected by the canvas cover I'd made. Don's work on the engine had apparently put it in shape—we hadn't had any problems since February 21.

Was there anything more we could do? I made mental lists continuously.

The last half of the banana squash from the Ika's garden thumped and banged in the bottom of the sink whenever a wave slapped us to starboard. The thumping annoyed me, but there was nowhere else I could put the squash—it was too big.

Cooking had become a pain. I couldn't battle the galley. I asked Don if he would settle for Cup of Soup.

"Sure. Then fill the thermos with boiling water, will you? It's going to be a long night!"

We had tried to make contact with Tex and Big John earlier in the day, but there was too much interference, and we hadn't been able to rouse Palmer Station in Antarctica either.

"If I can rouse the South Pacific Net later tonight," Don said, "they may be able to get a message through to the States to let people know we're okay."

I pictured the kids standing next to Tex in the radio room. "K6KWS, K6KWS, this is W6PXQ. Do you read?" How many times had they shown up and not been able to talk to us? We hadn't talked to anyone at home in a week, and I knew Mother and Daddy would conjure up all sorts of horrible thoughts as our estimated approach to Cape Horn drew near.

Don shined the flashlight on the barograph to take a reading. He flicked his finger gently against the glass case. The needle was still descending. It read 28.55 (966mb) now.

"The bottom's falling out of the barometer!" he said. [2]

"Let's discuss emergency procedures again," I said, feeling uneasy.

The abandon-ship locker not only held our survival gear, but it had been built to strengthen the cockpit just aft of the companionway. We could release its safety latch from below by pulling out a heavy stainless steel pin, but to open the locker we had to stand on the top step of the ladder with the hatch cover open, or completely exit and stand in the cockpit.

The cover itself weighed almost forty pounds and was a struggle for me to open. How fast could I execute the maneuver in an emergency? And could I pull up the Avon which weighed more than eighty pounds? Lashed by its own ripcord to an eye bolt inside the locker, the life raft was supposed to self-inflate when you threw it overboard. This wasn't something you practiced before you needed it. You prayed that the manufacturers were reliable.

"You remember the life raft procedures, don't you?" Don asked.

Yes. I had memorized the script: Release the pin, snap your safety harness onto the lifeline on deck. Pull up the locker top and secure it to the mizzen mast traveler. Put on your life jacket. Pull the life raft out of its locker and throw it overboard, making sure you leave its line tied to the mizzen mast until it's time to abandon ship. First mate goes into the Avon, then the captain releases the snap hook, or if the pressure is too great, he cuts the line with the attached knife and jumps in.

I thought again about our phone patch with the Durants early in the month. *"In case you don't hear from us, we have an eight-man Avon life raft with forty-five days' supplies."* We never voiced it, but Don knew, and I knew, that with air and water temperatures in the thirties or forties and freezing seas washing over the life raft, we'd die of hypothermia, if the waves didn't get us first. No Coast Guard in the Great Southern Ocean, no helicopter patrols, no search planes. We were on our own.

Don climbed up the ladder, sliding the hatch cover open just enough to poke his head out. Clinging to the starboard handle at the top of the ladder to keep from being hurled down and across the galley, he studied the conditions. "It looks as bad as ever. Hand me the anemometer again, and take down the readings as I call them out." He called out the numbers at five-second intervals for three minutes: 55, 52, 40, 42, 48, 32, 51, 38, 46 . . . "Damn, those last ones pegged the meter at 65! Quick, total the figures and do an average."

Excited now, he climbed down and shut the hatch. "Wow, this qualifies as a Violent Storm with gusts at hurricane force! These are the worst conditions we've seen yet!" I was struck by Don's tone of wonder—he was truly amazed by what he'd just seen. "And don't forget we're drifting several knots down-wind and the current is with us—so add another 5 to 10 knots for the actual wind speed."

"Pass me Robb's book," I said. "I want to reread the section on survival before I go to bed."

Wedging myself into a corner on the floor below the sink, I opened the book and scanned a few chapters. I preferred Robb's book, *Handling Small Boats in Heavy Weather*, to any other sea survival book. It was short—about a hundred and thirty pages—and concise. A skipper with forty-five years of experience, most of it off the coast of South Africa, Robb was opinionated and "told it like it is."

He called what we were doing now—lying ahull—the sailor's last-ditch effort. With the helm lashed we were letting the boat assume her own position in response to the wind and waves, both of which were coming from astern. According to Robb, in these conditions it was easy to underestimate the velocity of the wind. I turned to the Beaufort Scale on page 40, ran my finger down the column of "Mean Wind Speed" to 52 knots (Storm), 60 (Violent Storm), 65 (Hurricane Force), then across to the description of sea conditions. I read the descriptions aloud.

"Which would you say?" I asked Don.

"I'd say Violent Storm matches what we're having right now. It'll be Hurricane Force if it gets any worse."

Every few pages a photograph showed either a huge cresting wave, a gigantic "geyser," or an avalanche of white water moving toward a ship. (One of the photos was the same I'd seen used in the Smeetons' book as an example of the kind of wave that had hit them.) I had opened the book to reassure myself, but kept coming across descriptions of "the exceptional" that horrified me.

I stopped reading for a moment to think about *le Dauphin's* safety features: Water tanks bolted to the oak frames. The six batteries secured with stainless steel rods. The 3-inch-diameter stainless pole at the foot of the companionway running from the galley sole to the doghouse ceiling, strengthening the cabin. In the salon, the small emergency dome light wired independently to its own series fuse in case we lost house electricity. I hadn't appreciated the value of these touches when we were rebuilding the boat and said a silent "thank you" to Don and Al Ryan.

I turned back to the book.

> Study the accounts of small boats that have been damaged or come to grief in heavy weather at sea and you will find that in a surprising number of cases if the crew had simply gone to sleep and left the boat to her own devices she would have ridden the gale unharmed.[3]

Good, I thought, *we're doing the right things.*

I had purposely tried to avoid Chapter 7, "The Ultimate Wave." But like people who read about air disasters before climbing aboard their flight, I was compelled to read on.

> The occasional freak sea, the abnormal wave, the catastrophic sea—the blame for many a lost-without-trace tragedy can be laid on them. . . . Once have I seen such a wave. . . . It rose far out, perceptibly higher than the surrounding seas, but what caught the eye was not so much the height but the shape, for the forward face of the wave appeared to be a vertical wall of water . . . falling continuously, so that it seemed like some white waterfall sweeping across the ocean at—maybe—30 knots? The speculation is inevitable—what happens to a small boat lying relatively stationary when it meets a vertical wall of water moving at 30 knots? . . . It goes against the grain to believe that a condition can exist in which no amount of skill, courage, vigilance or equipment can save a small vessel from catastrophe.[4]

I closed the book. "I wish I hadn't read that."

"Not exactly a bedtime story, is it?"

"How about getting some sleep now?" Don said. "The boat will look after herself. No reason for you to stay up. I'll wait another hour till I can check into the Maritime Mobile Net. Besides, I'll have to get up every hour or so to check things above, so I'll just doze here on the settee. If I need help later, I'll wake you."

I did a quick alcohol swab of my face, climbed up into our berth without taking off my clothes, and made a diary entry:

> *I thought the gales yesterday and the day before were bad. Nothing compared to this! It's bitterly cold, rainy, sleeting, and miserable. Fortunately, the sun shone this noon and Don was able to plot our position. We're now lying ahull facing east, taking a terrible pounding on the port quarter.*
>
> *Do we really have enough to survive in a life raft for forty-five days? Could we survive in these seas, these temperatures? Of course we couldn't, and the life raft would cartwheel across the top of the greybeards before finally being crushed under a wall of water.*

I don't want to think about it. I am uneasy. No, more than that. I'm frightened. Fright has been such a big part of my adventurous life with Don. But I have to remember that I am here because I chose to be with him. He didn't force me. I made the decision myself. I have been miserable and have hated parts of this trip, but this is no time to complain—conditions are too critical.

I feel I have become a partner. I've done what I can to prepare for whatever comes next. I am afraid, but there's nothing more I can do. Neither of us has any power over the conditions, and the only thing we can do is work together and hope for a break in the weather.

I threw my diary into the hammock above our berth and wedged myself crosswise at the foot of the bed, my feet flat against the washboard to prevent being thrown out, but I couldn't fall asleep. I couldn't even begin to relax. Tense and jumpy, I felt every motion, as *le Dauphin* fought, shuddered, groaned, leapt, and then softened as if she had no more strength and could only submit to the waves.

An hour after I lay down, I heard Don make a brief contact with Palmer Station, Antarctica. The radio operator told him he had relayed the message to the port captain in Punta Arenas giving our new ETA. When Don signed off from Palmer Station, he checked into the Maritime Mobile Net in American Samoa. Bob, the usual operator, was not on the air. His boat had been tossed aground and damaged during a hurricane the night before. Don told his alternate: "Looks like maybe we're getting the same stuff that hit you. We're riding out a Force 10 to 11 storm, and it's pretty miserable, but we don't seem to be in any immediate danger. I'll check in again tomorrow night at this same time."

I fell asleep as soon as he completed the transmission.

NOTES

1. *Cap Horn à la Voile,* p. 196 (translation mine).

2. The Lufft barograph paper was designed for seven days in 2-hour increments. The horizontal lines, indicating barometric pressure, ran between 31.00 inches at the top and 28.00 inches at the bottom.

3. *Handling Small Boats in Heavy Weather,* p. 96. [now out of print]

4. *Ibid.,* pp. 43, 44.

CHAPTER 6

Pitchpoled

NIGHT, FEBRUARY 26–FEBRUARY 27

I was dreaming that I couldn't move. I was being pushed against a bulk-head and couldn't shove away from it. My stomach was pressing against my lungs, my throat. I was doing loops and figure-eights, experiencing negative Gs, nausea? Was I in a small plane? *Oh no, I'm having the night-mare again.*

Now I was floating around the berth. There was a thunderous crash and a deafening noise, as if the lurching boat were being torn apart. Every timber groaned. I was flung out of the berth and across the salon. My shoulder hit the edge of the portside pilot berth. The boat pitched and rolled. Metal, glass, and books shot through the salon. Icy water poured in from all directions. *Oh God, this is real!*

"We're going down!" I screamed.

The kerosene lamps blew out. Then, total blackness.

I heard Don. "Sweetheart, where are you? Are you okay?"

The boat plunged, gyrated, then rolled on her side. Water gushed through the cabin. I struggled to grab hold of something and stand up.

"Okay, baby, I think we've pitchpoled." Don's voice was shot with adrenaline. "This is it—a fight for survival."

Suddenly there was silence. *Oh God, it's all over. We're totally submerged!* Without a sound, the boat reeled, tumbled, twisted, and turned over. "We're upside down, we're sinking, we're sinking," I moaned. *We're spiral-ing to the bottom of the sea. I don't want to die this way.*

"It's okay, it's okay," I heard Don say. "Turn on the light and get pumping . . . Get to the gusher pump!"

Water poured over me again. The boat stumbled, heeled to starboard, shuddered—then held. Abruptly, the roar of the wind screaming the and waves smashing against the hull began again.

"She's righting herself, she's righting herself," Don said. "The keel must have held, we're not under water now."

"I can't see anything," I whimpered.

"Turn on the emergency light, dammit!"

Dazed, drenched, oblivious, I felt for the light above the captain's berth and flicked on the switch; it crackled, arced, and fizzled.

"No, not that one!" Don shouted. "Turn it off so we don't have a fire."

He shoved me aside, reached above my head, turned on the emergency light, and grabbed me. "It's okay, we're going be okay, sweetheart." He held his face against mine, kissing me, stroking my hair. His face was wet and tasted like blood.

We're going to die, I thought. *No one will ever know.*

"It's okay, baby. Get pumping. Pump for your life. Pump!"

I crawled across a mountain of floating debris, silently repeating, *Don't let us go down this way without a trace. Don't let us go down.*

"Try the radio. Please try the radio," I urged.

I squatted in water at the foot of the radio locker. Diesel and kerosene mixed with the water. Wind rushed through the cabin—it was freezing.

Don reached over my head to grab the microphone on the transmitter. "Mayday. May . . ." he said. There was a flash. The transmitter sizzled and blew. "Shit! We could have an explosion." He jumped across the galley, reached down in the water, and turned off the master battery switch. "Okay, baby. This is it. We're really on our own, the radio's gone."

I ran my right hand along the side of the locker to locate the pump handle. It was no longer in its clip. The boat lifted and took a deep lurch to starboard. A wave hit the port quarter and rolled across the cabin top. Water poured in on both of us.

A momentary shaft of moonlight cut through the hatch, revealing chaos everywhere. "Oh no! The hatch is open," Don said. "I've got to close it."

In the brief rays of moonlight I could see the companionway ladder hanging askew at a forty-five-degree angle, its brass hinges twisted forward. Don pulled himself up, poked his head out the hatch, and looked forward across the top of the cabin.

"Oh God! The dinghy's gone. It looks like the main boom sheered off. But the masts are still standing! I can't believe it." His voice registered amazement.

I thought, *Even when he's about to die he sees the wonder in things.*

"I can't see anything out there but white foam," he said. "There's nothing but white foam. The dinghy's out there somewhere, but I can't see it."

A wave washed over the boat, knocking us abeam. Water cascaded through the hatch over Don, over me. The impact sent me face first into the edge of the radio shelf. Water gushed up the starboard bulkhead, soaking my front. My forehead stung, and I could feel blood dripping down my cheek.

"No, not again, please don't turn over again," I moaned. "Don, I can't find the pump handle."

"Oh Jesus, look for it!" he said, finally jamming the hatch in place. "I've got to find something to bail with."

How could I find anything in this mess? The pump handle could have been thrown out of the hatchway.

"Here! Here," he said. "Can you believe it! The handle's in the sink . . . with the chamber pot!"

I reached across the galley for the pump handle.

"Oh no, your face is bloody," Don said, pulling me toward him. He wiped his hand gently over my face so tenderly I wanted to sob.

I wedged myself into the space next to the pump and sat on a mattress. Water soaked into my pants. "Pump slow and easy, baby, slow and easy," he instructed.

I felt for the slot, inserted the handle, and began pulling and pushing for all I was worth. Water, diesel, kerosene sloshed over my legs—over everything piled on the galley sole.

"Slow down, sweetheart, you'll wear yourself out. Slow and easy, you're going to be pumping for a long time . . . I'm going to check for leaks first. Then I'll start bailing."

Steadily, slowly, like a robot, I pumped. I was stunned, in a trance, an abandoned child searching for her parents. *Please just let me see my family again. Don't let us vanish . . . Where is my diary?* If I could just find it, put it in a waterproof bag, someone might find it floating somewhere. Then a part of us would remain.

The boat lifted, teetered, did a deep roll to starboard. A wave crashed over the cabin, and water poured over me again. I screamed. "Don! We're going over again, we're going over."

"No we're not. No we're not! Shut up and keep pumping!"

Don's sharpness made no impression. I was too petrified, too cold and wet. *I've got to keep pumping, got to keep pumping,* I told myself with each stroke.

"I love you, Réanne."

I looked over as he made his way toward me along the starboard bulkhead, checking the hull. The side of his face was covered with blood, too. "Don, your face . . ."

"It's okay, sweetheart. Don't worry about it now. I've got to find out if the water is rising or not."

I pushed, pulled, and counted—122, 123, 124—then wondered why I was counting.

The emergency light cast a grey pall throughout the cabin. I stared numbly at the chaos. Everywhere I looked lockers had emptied. The upper locker doors in the galley swung back and forth—the plates and bowls were gone.

I looked up. A jagged piece of ketchup bottle had lodged in the galley deckhead. The carving knife—embedded in a crack above my head— quivered with every jerk of the boat. Pots, pans, spices, broken mayon- naise and mustard jars were strewn everywhere. Galley floorboards lay upside down on top of mattresses and cushions. The bilge had regurgitat- ed its contents: anchor chain, food tins, hardware, motor oil, grease cans, spools of wire. Wet sawdust, yellow squash, and ketchup were splattered all over the deckhead. The radios and barograph were missing from the forward shelf of the galley.

I watched Don lift and throw things out of his way, checking the hull for damage. Quickly, carefully—a physician probing for broken bones—he inched his way through the icy, oily water into empty lockers, worming his body into drawer spaces, running his fingers along the hull at the mast step, in the forepeak, the head, the salon, the galley, the aft quarters, giv- ing me constant feedback as he moved. "Goddam, the water's above my knees in the salon here . . ." Lying down on top of debris in the salon, his arms and shoulders under the water, he felt for the keel bolts. "I think the keel's okay. The bolts feel secure. I can't feel any water coming in . . . That's good, that's good! The hull feels smooth here in the salon. I think it's holding! I think the keel's holding."

The boat lurched to starboard, knocking me into the locker. "Oh no, not again. Not again." Water poured over me. "Oh God, not again, please stop!" I screamed.

"It's okay. It's okay, baby, we're gonna survive. We're gonna survive. As long as the keel holds we'll be okay. Keep pumping. We've got to get this water out of here. I'm almost finished checking."

Back and forth, back and forth—256, 257, 258. With each stroke I thought about our families, our friends. *The kids? They'll recover; they're young. Mother and Daddy? It'll kill them if we disappear. Oh God, they'll never know a thing. No diaries. Nothing. "Vanished without a trace," the newspapers will say.*

Water flooded over my head. "Don! Make it stop. Make it stop." Despite three layers of wool against my skin, I was beginning to shiver uncontrollably and was losing my senses. "I just want to get to land, see my family and friends. *Just get me to land!*"

"It's okay, sweetheart, it's okay. That wave was one in ten thousand. It won't happen again. I've checked as much of the hull as I can get to. It seems to be okay. I'm sure the keel's okay."

One in ten thousand . . . I wanted to believe him, but I couldn't. The waves just kept knocking us over. I looked at Don. Was the water rising? Was it over his knees? I couldn't tell. *Got to keep pumping.*

Don began bailing with the chamber pot, frantically dumping water into the sink. He began mumbling to himself, "I'm afraid it's gaining on us. The water's gaining . . . Those vibrations when the boat heels to starboard—what are they? The rigging? Keel coming loose? How can it take a pounding like this and stay fastened to the frames? I wonder if the hull's opened at the first strake? Maybe I should try to clear this junk away . . . stuff something in the crack . . . Hell no. There's no way I can see anything with water this high." He was getting panicky.

"Slow down, sweetheart," I repeated his words. "Don't panic—you'll be bailing for a long time."

"You're right. We've both got to fight panic. Smeeton was right—there's nothing like a drowning man to bail with vigor."

The boat lunged to starboard. Don looked at me and stopped bailing. "Good Lord. No wonder you're shivering. The cabin deck seam above you separated, and the portlight's blown away—that's why water keeps pouring in. Hang on and keep pumping. I'll see if I can find the emergency board to nail over the port."

I heard him mumbling, "Jesus, I told her to shut up, and she's never stopped pumping. Sitting there with water pouring over her.

"These portlights are our Achilles' heel," he said, "even as sturdy as they are. If I can find a hammer and the plywood, I'll cover that hole. The stuff should be here in the battery box."

The cover to the battery locker was a pain to open; we'd always complained about it. But it was the only one in the galley that had held.

The hammer was still tied to the bulkhead on the inside of the locker, and the boards wedged between the batteries hadn't budged. A box of 3-inch nails that had been wedged along the bottom of the batteries had spewed its contents, but Don was able to fish out enough to do the job.

"Jesus, with the force of that wave the stainless rod holding the batteries moved forward more than a half-inch. . . . Keep pumping, sweetheart . . . I'll go above and cover the hole." He opened the hatch enough to put his head through to look out and gauge conditions. "Not too bad right this minute. Now's my chance."

He pulled himself out and closed the hatch. I could see the board being flattened across the porthole and hear him trying to hammer. *My God,* I thought, *he's up there without a harness!* I quit pumping and yanked open the hatch, shrieking into the wind, "Get down here now!"

Shocked, he climbed down. "Sonovobitch. How stupid . . . I must be panicking . . . All I could do was hit my fingers—I couldn't get the damn nails started. I couldn't even hold them, my hands are so numb. I have to get these nails started where I can see what I'm doing."

He swept debris off the galley counter, laid the plywood board over it, and drove in eight nails. "Shit! I overdid it. Nailed the goddam board to the counter." He pried it loose and started for the hatch again.

"Open the abandon-ship locker and get out the extra harnesses."

"I don't want to open it right now. It's too damn risky."

"You're not going back above without a harness!" I yelled. "Find *something,* dammit . . . I think I saw a line over there somewhere." I pointed to the salon.

"Come on. There's no way I can find anything in this mess . . . By God, you're right. There's the bitter end of something . . . probably a jib sheet."

He tugged on the line. A thirty-foot length came loose. He tied a bowline around his waist, threw a couple of half-hitches around the top step of the ladder, leaving fifteen feet of slack, and opened the hatch. He paused. "The mast is flinging back and forth wildly. Especially to port. I'll have to deal with that later." He climbed out and closed the hatch.

I heard nails being pounded into the side of the doghouse. The boat lurched, hit by another wave. Water flowed over the cabin, through the seam. The hammering stopped. *Oh, God, make him hang on. That line could break. Like the dinghy webbing did.* The hammering began again. *He's okay! He's okay.*

The boat righted herself. The hatch flung open; Don jumped back down. "I nearly lost it!" he raved. "I wrapped my arms and legs around the boom gallows stanchion to hold on . . . You should see that stanchion—it's bent forward, bad."

Grabbing the potty, he started bailing again. "I think the water's emptying overboard all right," he said, although much later he would tell me he'd been sure it was rising.

"I love you, sweetheart. We're gonna make it," he said.

I shook uncontrollably. *I'm so cold, so cold. The wind. I wish the wind would stop.* But it just kept on and on, shrieking in the rigging. *The noise is awful. God, I'm cold . . . Got to keep pumping . . . keep pumping.*

Suddenly I thought about my diary again. Where was it? I had to find it. If we went down, it would be the only thing left to tell our story. With each stroke of the pump I became more obsessed with finding it. If only daylight would come so I could search.

Don dumped potty after potty of water into the sink. "We're doing all we can. The water's holding steady."

"I hope so," I stuttered.

"It's time to get out some emergency supplies. Let me get the abandon-ship locker opened. Then I'll take over the pumping."

He climbed the ladder and clung to it with his legs, quickly opened the hatch, released the stainless pin, and opened the locker. "Here, catch this bag," he said.

I opened a moldy nylon ditty bag and rifled through its contents for Hershey's Tropical Chocolate bars. I dug out a handful and stared at them. The wrappers were blue with mold.

"Come on, babe. Eat one. You need some calories." Closing the hatch, he crawled down the ladder and took over at the pump.

I tore off one of the wrappers with my teeth and stuck the bar in my mouth. I couldn't swallow any of it. The pieces stuck to my molars. I had no saliva to wash them down my throat.

Watching Don's power strokes I suddenly realized how tired I was, and how slow I'd become. When I tried to stand up pain surged through my body. Soaked, cold, and cramped from crouching so long in cold water, I could barely unwind. How long had I been pumping? I looked down at my feet—I couldn't feel them. "The water's going down," I said expressionless. "It's at my ankles now."

"Yeah, by God, we're gaining! Give me a chocolate bar, sweetie, and try to find something dry to put on."

I crawled aft to the port quarter berth. "The *moai's* still here!" I said. "It hasn't budged."

"Good. That baby could have crushed one of us. But find some dry clothes, for godsake."

The two large duffels I'd stuffed with emergency clothing and army blankets were still at the foot of the berth. The quarter births were like small caverns and the duffels had flown round and round inside. I unzipped one of them and pawed through its contents. I found sweaters, an army blanket, and a couple of pairs of wool air force pants my brother Tom had given us. *Tom. We haven't talked to him for so long . . . Please, Tom, help Mother and Daddy survive if we don't.* I pushed the duffels aside and lay down. It felt so good to rest that I started to doze.

"What the hell are you doing back there?"

I shook myself. "Lying down . . ."

"Dammit. Take off your wet stuff and put on some dry clothes—now! You're going hypothermic."

I unpeeled the wet layers, in slow motion. Every movement seemed to take forever. *It feels so good to get out of these wet things, put something dry on . . . If only it would get light. It's horrid not to be able to see.* Two dry wool sweaters, fishnet long johns, air force pants, hiking socks. I crawled out of the berth, warmer.

Don was still pumping strongly. I didn't know how he could keep going at such a pace.

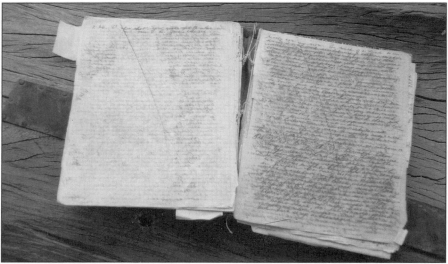

My diary was smeared and almost illegible

"I'll take over again if you want me to."

"Not yet. See if you can find your foul weather gear and put that over your dry clothes. You'll need everything you can find."

I crawled across the galley. My dry socks immediately soaked up water from the soggy mattresses and cushions piled on the floor. Such an unbelievable mess! Every locker, bookshelf, and drawer in the salon had emptied. The drawers I'd secured with ⅜-inch bungee cord had shot out, dumped their contents, and resettled halfway back. They swung up and down, cracking each time a wave hit the boat. I shoved, pushed, closed. They were badly splintered and chipped.

Clothes were strewn about in soggy lumps. The small down pillow I'd used as a child was a clump of wet feathers. I picked it up by a corner and looked at it. Mother had found it as she was cleaning out cupboards and had sent it to me, knowing I didn't like heavy pillows. It would have to be chucked.

Waterlogged paperbacks and charts clung to the mattresses. I peeled off one of the charts. My diary was underneath.

My diary! The pages were soaked and stuck together, the ink was smeared and hardly legible, but I didn't care. *I've rescued our story,* I thought. The waterproof pouch with the ship's papers lay nearby. I stuffed the diary in with them. In my daze I didn't consider that the pouch might circle Antarctica for months, years, or decades, and my diary would finally disintegrate, unseen and unread.

"I can see the floorboards now," Don said slowly. "The gusher just started sucking air . . . I think we'd better rest now. Till dawn, when it's light. Then we'll figure out what to do next."

Tired, cold, our forces totally spent, we lay down on the crumple of sailbags and mattresses in the salon. I wrapped the wet army blanket around us, thankful for the wool. Each time a wave crashed over the dog-house roof, the boat heeled to starboard and water poured through the leaky skylight above us.

"Please make it stop. Please!" I whimpered, my teeth chattering. Don tugged at a cushion and pulled it over us. It was heavy with saltwater, but at least it would insulate us.

We clung to each other, Don stroking my face, my hair. "We've done all we can for now, sweetheart."

There was nothing more we could do but wait—wait through the dreadful darkness till dawn.

I never have held death in contempt, though in the course of my explorations I have oftentimes felt that to meet one's fate on a noble mountain, or in the heart of a glacier, would be blessed as compared with death from disease, or from some shabby lowland accident. But the best death, quick and crystal-pure is hard enough to face, even though we feel gratefully sure that we have already had happiness enough for a dozen lives.

—John Muir, *Stickeen*

CHAPTER 7

The Morning After

FEBRUARY 28 (?)

Last known position: 49°52'S, 89°01'W

Impossible to sleep. Waves continued to pound the boat, to knock her on her starboard beam. The mast reverberated like a body in convulsions, shaking from its head, fifty-five feet above, to its foot in the mast step next to us. Would it hold?

Please, I pleaded silently. *Let it get light.*

To whom was I pleading? I didn't know. I don't pray, but perhaps I was praying. I thought of the childhood bedtime prayer: *Now I lay me down to sleep . . .* I was exhausted, but fought falling asleep. Not being able to see, not knowing what it was like outside, was the worst part. *If I should die before I wake . . .*

"We're going over again, Don! We're going over!" I screamed.

He tightened his arms around me. "We'll be all right. I told you, that wave was one in ten thousand. Get a hold of yourself."

One in ten thousand. How many waves had knocked us on our beam since the Big One? Fifteen? Twenty?

"Ten percent chance of Force 10 winds" . . . Don in Mexico, so casual, assuring Jeff and me, "Only ten percent . . ."

Suddenly angry with Don for telling me to get hold of myself, for lying to me about conditions down here. Angry with myself for losing control. I snapped at him, "Look, just hold me. I'll be all right as soon as it's light. I'll be strong then. Just hold me now and let me be a baby."

Like the vibrating mast, Don shivered uncontrollably, his shoulders and torso trembling, his legs jerking. *Hypothermia. He has hypothermia,* I thought. *Wet, cold, wind-chilled. Numbness . . . that's why he couldn't hit the nails! Now the shivering. He was so concerned about my putting on dry clothes, but he's still wearing his wet ones. People die of hypothermia. "Exposure," say the headlines. "Exposed to the elements." Got to keep holding each other. Don't fall asleep. Don't let Don fall asleep. He might not wake up—hypothermia does that.*

I listened carefully to his breathing. He wasn't sleeping. "Animal stalkers," he'd once told me, "hold their breath and breathe shallowly through their mouth so they can hear better." His grip on me tightened

with every quiver of his body. I knew that like a stalker Don was alert to
every sound. I could almost hear him thinking: *That clunking noise when
the boat rolls to starboard—what is it? Are the keel bolts loose? No. Maybe it's
something inside a locker hitting a cross beam . . . No. It's hitting the hull . . .*
But caught in my own terror, I didn't break this silence.

Dawn. Grey, dismal light filled the cabin. A war zone was revealed. *How
will I ever find anything? Like people poking through embers after their house has
burned. How can I even begin? There's too much to do.* Water sloshed heavily
against the inside hull—like a siren warning us to man the gusher pump. I
leapt up, terrified.

Don yanked on the hatch, pulled it partially open to check conditions, and stared at the seas. Sleet stung his face. The waves were still violent and heaping, skyscraper waves. "I've never seen anything like this . . .
We'd better stay up—it's light enough now. I'm going up to see how bad
the damage is on deck."

"Change into some dry clothes first," I urged.

I pawed frantically through the emergency duffel. I remembered how I'd complained about all the extra gear and clothing Don insisted on bringing for emergencies. "We don't have room," I'd said about each extra item he brought aboard. "We'll never find a place for all this junk—there's not even room for six *people!*" I would never complain again about what he had brought along. If only we could find more.

I insisted Don open the abandon-ship lock-er and get out the extra harnesses.

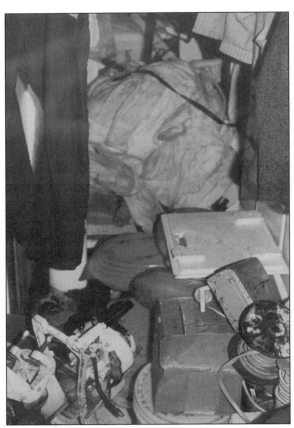

Daylight revealed a war zone

"You're not going anywhere unless you're snapped on." I pulled myself up to look in the locker. It was organized, reassuring. I grabbed the supplies I'd loaded the night before—pouches of cocoa and tea, foil packets of freeze-dried food, the first aid kit, waterproof matches, three hospital blankets, a waterproof flashlight, an extra rotor and line for the recording log. I put in the waterproof pouch that held the ship's papers and my diary. We hadn't found the logbook yet.

Grim. It was grim. Assessing damages, searching for missing gear. Was it last night I had sat on the galley sole reading Robb and discussing survival techniques with Don? The sole had gleamed under the light of the kerosene lamp. Now everything was grim and disorienting. I didn't know where to begin.

Don made a quick observation tour of the deck. As he'd suspected, the main boom had sheered off and was held only by the mainsail. The main and mizzen masts were cracked along the lines of lamination but were still standing.

"Well, we can't use the main, and I don't know what kind of load the mizzen mast will be able to carry under these conditions," he said.

The mizzen and staysail booms were fractured, but still attached. The main mast starboard spreader had been carried away, along with the deck light. All the mast tangs—where the shrouds attached—were twisted. Their through-bolts had held, but they had been shoved downward about three inches, badly tearing the wood of the mast. "I can't believe the mast could sustain this much damage without being carried away. We must have been dropped upside down, nearly vertically," Don said. The main and mizzen boom gallows were bent forward. Gone were one of the lightboards and the radio antenna. Also gone was the man-overboard pole with its attached xenon light. The deck had been swept clean. Hours earlier, we had realized that the dinghy was missing, but now we knew what that meant—even if we did get to land, we would have no way to get off the boat.

The warp line that was attached to the car tire ready to use as a drogue to slow the boat down had wrapped itself around the mizzen boom. Like a hangman's noose, the tire swung over the cockpit on two feet of loose warp.

Below, the damage seemed worse than above. Even with all my preparations—nothing, nothing had stayed in place. The anchors, the dinghy motor, lines, sheets—they were all down there in the salon somewhere. Someplace under the mess. Thank God we had stowed them below.

I stood dazed. Everything I needed was missing. Where were the stove elements? How could they have come unscrewed like that? The kerosene lamps were upside down, askew—mantels and globes missing, even their elements had come unscrewed. Radios, barograph—missing, too.

The galley sole was layered with cushions and mattresses, so heavy with water, kerosene, and diesel I couldn't budge them.

It seemed as if we were in an arctic elevator, riding up the face of each wave, down the back. Never stopping, never slowing.

Don's first thoughts were to put the boat in better shape, to help her cope with the punishing seas. He shoved the hatch open and

Artist's rendition of our pitchpoling

peered down at me. "In a strange way it's good to be on deck again," he said. "I don't feel good below. At least up here I can see what's going on. I'm going to stay at the helm and drive us east with bare poles. I don't dare leave the boat to herself any longer."

Later, he wrote:

First thing was to stabilize the gyrating mast. The starboard spreader, sheared off at both ends, dangled overboard, held only by the nylon signal halyards. The upper shroud was so loose it didn't restrain the top of the mast.

Using two lengths of nylon webbing I made a tourniquet of sorts between the upper shroud, two lower stays, and the mast itself. With the spreader stub, I twisted the tourniquet over and over until I could get all possible tension into the upper shroud. This partially cuts down the gyration of the mast and the awful vibrations of the hull. I'm so happy to have both masts standing, to have a fighting chance to save ourselves. Completing this small task, in this wild environment, is deeply gratifying.

With the major safety items secured, I went to the helm, turned the boat from beam to the waves, to a course due east. Straight down the greybeards toward land.

I want to get near land as quickly as possible. The Horn and the lee channels to Ushuaia are about 750 miles to the southeast. Cabo Pilar and the entrance to the Strait of Magellan are about 600 miles east southeast. The rugged coast of Patagonia, the closest land, lies about 500 miles due east, and Valparaiso is more than 1,000 miles, clear across the Roaring Forties to the northeast. Until we can determine the boat's damage and weigh our options, the only thing to do is sail due east as fast as possible.

The more I think about it, the more convinced I am—no more lying ahull. No more staying below, wondering and worrying. We will drive this boat with all we have. As long as we have it.

I worried about Don in the cockpit. Could he keep his body core temperature high enough, with the icy seas breaking over the cockpit and cabin continuously? I kept shoving chocolate bars to him out the hatch. I had always snubbed them on backpacking trips—they were so dry I could barely digest them. *It's funny what you complain about at home,* I thought. I promised myself not to complain anymore.

I didn't know how long Don had been at the helm. With no wristwatch minutes seemed to crawl. *How are we going to keep track of where we are now? How will we know what day it is?* I guessed that it took about sixty minutes for the bilge to overflow, and that I'd pumped at least three times since dawn. *Three times. Maybe three hours since light? It must be about 0830.*

I forced myself to eat a chocolate bar. My salivary glands were still running at half speed, but I knew I had to keep myself going. Keep Don going, too.

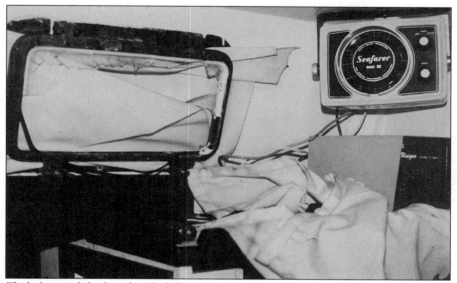

The broken port light above the radio locker

I, who had longed for winter, now had more than I'd wished for. Grey, cold sleet and hail fell ceaselessly. Stinging, bitterly cold water kept pouring into the cabin through the opened starboard deck seam. There was no way to get warm. No kerosene stove. No kerosene lamps. No Presto logs for the fireplace.

What had I thought a sub-arctic marine landscape would be? Carpets of crystals sparkling white in the sun? Wind devils blowing banners into a sapphire sky? A study in chiaroscuro?. How poorly we visualize the unknown.

I remembered the snow-survival courses Don used to lead in the mountains. "Be prepared for survival," he always stressed to his students. We would trudge through snow, find a level spot, and trample the snow. Carve ice blocks and stack them row upon row, fitting each block like proud masons, chinking the spaces, the holes. I loved the feeling of accomplishment as we placed the final icy keystone. I loved sleeping in those igloos, toasting a long day's work with champagne chilled in a snow bank. Loved the marvelous stillness that enclosed us as we lay inside, cozy in our sleeping bags, overwhelmed by the brilliance of our snow cathedral whose altar glowed with candles. Who would have guessed then that something like this could happen?

I could see my breath inside the cabin. My feet were still numb. I was freezing. *I have to find the parts for the stove. We need hot cocoa or soup to warm our insides. Got to get some warmth into this cabin. Where can those stove parts be? Did I put replacements in one of the ammo boxes? Where are those boxes? The last time I saw them they were stowed under Sean's berth* [the starboard quarter berth]. *Maybe they're still there.*

I lay on my belly, facing aft. The cover to the stowage area, a sliding door of quarter-inch plywood, had swollen and jammed. I couldn't get it open. I turned over on my back, inched my way aft over the cross beams until my right leg was even with the door, then kicked with all my strength. The door smashed and splintered.

Four ammo boxes. A jackpot: extra mantles for the kerosene lamps, flashlight batteries, medical supplies, our cameras, a spare logbook, a small looseleaf binder. Good finds. But no stove elements.

Water washed up the hull, inundating the cabin sole, soaking the seat of my air force pants. I cursed. *I've been swearing a lot,* I thought. *So what!*

The water "siren" again. Time to pump. Squatting at the foot of the radio locker, I pumped and stared forward at the chronometer mounted on the bulkhead above the salon step. *There's something odd about it,* I thought. Its second hand pulsated in place. Its rhythm hypnotized me. *It's like a heart in fibrillation.* Frozen at 0110 for the last four weeks, it now read 2250.

In a trance, still, I surveyed the cabin. What had looked so nautical, so handsome, a few days before now resembled a marine dump. I kept spotting weird things. Screws and knives wedged into bulkhead seams. Pieces of glass stuck so firmly I couldn't dislodge them. And books all over the place. Paperback classics—over a hundred of them—ruined. *Did we really think we'd have time to read all these? Maybe, if we'd had more crew. But if the boys had stayed—oh God—one of them would have been on watch and washed overboard.* A wave of nausea rolled over me as I recalled the nightmare that had haunted me . . . Too awful to think about. *Think about something else.* I pumped and drifted back to a happier time.

"What color do you want to paint the interior?" Don had asked me when *Liddie Mae* was being transformed into *le Dauphin Amical.*

"White. Pure white. *Glossy* white."

"Why white?"

"I want the interior light and airy. So we can *see.*"

"And the upholstery?"

"Yellow. Not nautical blue. Not green. We'll see blue and green all day in the cockpit. I want a contrast."

So bright and cheery before, the bulkheads were now nicked and blackened with oil, shot full of shrapnel. The yellow tweed cushions were dulled with kerosene, diesel, and bilge water. *What a shame. Poor ole Liddie Mae! Maybe the man was right. Maybe we shouldn't have changed her name.*

I came out of my trance as the gusher sucked air—140 strokes this time. The hatch cover flung open, Don jumped down. "I want to see if the motor will run. Maybe we can get some heat in this cabin." He turned the key. The engine growled. "Wow, what a great sound! I didn't think it would start . . . I'll just leave it in neutral to get some heat into the cabin. In this storm we don't need any more speed than we have right now under bare poles."

Maybe we have a chance to get to land now without going all the way to Cape Horn. But how, I don't know. There's no way to tell longitude, no ham radio, no VF radio, no way to get time ticks. Please, Don, head for the Strait of Magellan instead of Cape Horn.

My feet wet and numb, I squished across the mattresses searching for the stove parts and my boots. Instead I spotted my Timex. I had fastened the strap around the rail of the barograph shelf—it was still hanging there! An inexpensive analog model I'd paid only fifteen dollars for, I had worn the Timex on board in place of my good Seiko. It was—amazingly—still running. I read 1030. Cautiously, I rewound it. I couldn't allow it to stop.

I knelt on the galley bench and felt along the starboard shelf for the box of navigation tools where we kept my Seiko. (It was the only time-piece that kept consistent time, and Don had been using it for naviga-tion.) A six-inch-high rail of teak ran along the entire length of the galley settee, and since the bulkhead curved inward, it was impossible to peer into the shelf itself. *Let me find it. Please let me find it intact.*

No box, no watch, no navigation tools. Everything gone. Then my finger touched a metal object. I tugged; something was wedged into the wood at the corner of the shelf. It loosened and came out.

Excited, I shoved the hatch open and shouted: "I found a stove ele-ment! It's bent, but the threads look good. I'll try to get the stove going and boil some water."

Don looked horrible. "Are you okay?" I asked.

He nodded grimly. He'd been at the helm since dawn in glacial con-ditions. *Chocolate bars alone won't keep his core temperature up,* I thought. *I have to get the stove going quickly.*

"If I can get the stove going, I'll make you some cocoa. Then I'll spell you at the helm."

He shook his head. The words came slowly, "No. I want to make as much easting today as possible. I don't want you up here in these conditions."

Frozen. He can hardly talk. I've got to get the stove going. Please let the stove work. Please . . .

Utterly drained of energy, I craved sleep, but I had to stay alert. *How can Don hang on the way he does? I'm so tired. But I know he's exhausted. He's been speaking so slowly. Please, please give us a break. Don't let this go on forever. He needs to sleep. I need to sleep. My eyes feel like sandpaper . . . I can barely keep them open. Stop this, Réanne! Stop thinking about how tired you are. You have to hang on.*

I screwed the element into its base. The gas jet tipped at an angle. I didn't care. Questions raced through my mind: Is the kerosene tank still attached? Is there enough fuel in it? The copper tubing from the tank to the stove—had it held? Was it intact, or had it been crushed? Had water gotten into the tubing?

I knelt on the mattress and peered into the narrow locker directly below the stove. There was fuel in the bilge. Was the tank leaking?

I twisted the intake cap. I couldn't budge it—my fingers were too weak. I pulled my denim shirt out of my trousers, wrapped the front flap around the cap, and twisted again. It broke loose. I stuck my index finger through the opening to verify the level of fuel. An oily line came to the wrinkles of my knuckle. I calculated: *About two inches of air space at the head; the tank about six inches deep. Must be two-thirds full.* My hands were filthy and they ached. I wiped them on my trousers. *The bicycle pump. Have to look for the bicycle pump.*

Where would I find the pump? Still mounted on the port side of the engine box? As I worked my way aft, my feet suddenly slid out from under me. Grabbing hold of the ladder, I looked down. The flooring was coated with a bubbly film of fuel and liquid soap. I pulled at a quarter berth cushion and dumped it on the floor to use as a non-skid. I would have to deal with the coating on the floor later.

Amazingly, the two straps around the pump had held tight. I undid them, tucked the pump under my chin to leave my hands free, and moved cautiously from motor box to aft galley locker and ladder, to the mattress in front of the stove. I knelt again.

Would the tank hold pressure? If it didn't, we were lost. There would be no way to boil water, no way to get a little open flame going so we could warm our hands. I unscrewed the valve cap, stood up, wedged the base of the pump under my foot, and pumped. The boat took a roll to starboard and I fell back. I hadn't fastened the safety belt around me.

The belt hung at the side of the sink, and the eye-bolt connecting it had been bent downward. *Would it hold me?* I wondered. I hooked in and restarted the process. Up and down, counting, till the gauge read 16 pounds.

The plastic bottle of alcohol floated in the bilge below the tank. I picked it up, wiped it on my leg. *Paper towels. I wish I had some paper towels. Rags. Anything. There's nothing to wipe off the diesel with. It's such a mess. Now, let's see if I can get the stove primed.*

Waterproof matches. A package of ten small boxes. For emergency. All dry in a shrink-wrapped package. The label on top of the little box read: "The 45 wooden matches in each pocket-sized box must be struck on the waterproof striker surface to light." *Ten boxes of 45 each. Just 450 matches. Have to be careful with these.*

I tore open the shrink-wrap with my teeth and took out one box, carefully putting the remaining nine boxes back in the waterproof emergency pouch. I poured alcohol into the cup at the base of the burner. Bent and tipped, it would hold only a partial fill. I struck a match to the alcohol. The jets in the stove element had to heat enough so that the kerosene would vaporize.

I checked the gauge. The needle still pointed at 16. The alcohol burned off with the sickeningly sweet odor I disliked. *At least I'm not gagging and vomiting now,* I thought. I tried lighting the element. Black smoke hissed out—the jets weren't hot enough yet.

Five more refills with alcohol. Five more matches. Five more tries with the burner. On the sixth try, jets of yellow sputtered out of the burner's tiny holes, then blue, then yellow again, and threatening to die. Blue jets forced themselves back to life and burned. Hot blue! Hot blue.

I, the medical technician racing against time, had revived this heart-stove. I was ecstatic. But next I had to feed the human stoves.

The teakettle. I think I saw it on the port pilot berth. Yes. There it is! Battered and dented, its top had staved in.

I pulled on the handle of the water pump. No water came out. I tried again. It sucked air. *Oh no! Could the tanks have split and the water leaked out? Could the hoses be broken?* I looked under the sink to check the tubing. Everything was connected. I tried the pump a third time. Air, nothing but air. Panic.

Wait! I'd seen the spigot of a three-gallon water container poking through the mess in the salon. I wrestled it out and filled the teakettle with Los Angeles Municipal Harbor water, dated October 10. If we couldn't get the freshwater pump going, how long would our supply of water jugs last? I couldn't remember how many extras we had, nor where we'd stowed them all.

Did the saltwater pump work? I tried it. Saltwater sputtered up, then flowed. At least we could wash our hands—but we'd have to ration drinking water very carefully.

Steam began rising from the teakettle spout. But there were no utensils, no cups—the galley lockers were empty. I pulled up one of the sail bags in the salon and looked underneath. Nothing. I climbed up on the captain's berth and found a spoon wedged in a seam, two cups, and the logbook, damp but usuable.

I opened the portlight to the cockpit and yelled to Don, "Hot cocoa, sweetheart!" and passed him the cup. "How does it feel in your belly?"

I could barely hear him. It seemed like a big effort for him to get his words out. "It's good . . ." he said slowly. "Can you find a packet of soup?"

"No, you come down here yourself and take a break," I insisted. "The packets are in the emergency bag."

He unsnapped his harness and climbed below. "Put all my gear on before you go up," he said. "And be careful. The deck's extremely icy."

"Don't turn off the burner," I instructed. "It might die."

I took my position behind the wheel, snapping my harness to the mainsail traveller. Its ¾-inch stainless bar was now bent skyward, and I wondered how strong it would be.[1]

Hail stung me awake, reviving my adrenal glands. I wrestled the helm, maneuvering the roller coaster down one wave, up another. Grey rollers swept on and on. The wind had extinguished life. No albatross roamed these struggling seas today. He knew better.

I stared at the water washing along the cockpit deck. As the boat rolled from side to side, the water gurgled out the starboard scupper (drain hole), then the port scupper, then frothed back up again into the cockpit. I wondered if the drains were plugged. I had always thought the two little drain holes were too tiny to let anything through. On the other hand, if they had been any larger they would have allowed the cockpit to inundate. *God, everything on a boat is a trade-off.*

I thought about the ham radio operators who had been following our progress—Big John in California, Tex, John on the *Hero*, Burt in Brasilia, the men at Palmer Station, Antarctica. Would any of them suspect what had happened? The only ham who knew the weather conditions and our position was the alternate in American Samoa. Would he contact anyone? "I'll check in tomorrow night," Don had told him. *I'm confused. Was that last night? If so, no one will suspect anything yet. We've missed so many schedules with Tex, he'll just chalk it up to atmospheric conditions or forgetfulness.*

I was suddenly angry with Tex. He'd gotten touchy with us once or twice when we'd missed a scheduled radio contact. Sure, he was an angel to volunteer as our regular contact, but trying to match our two schedules hadn't worked once we'd reached the Southern Hemisphere. He could talk only on his lunch hour—1600 hours our time, when atmospheric conditions were the least favorable. So either weather conditions weren't quite right or we were in the midst of a sail change or some little crisis when we were supposed to crank up the radio. He didn't have a clue what we were going through. Nobody did. Nobody could, except people who'd been in these seas.

The trouble with being at the helm . . . I think too much. I don't want to think of Mother and Daddy and the kids, my relatives, my friends. I can't think about them; it's too painful. I just want to think about getting to land. Just keep thinking about getting to safety. We'll make it. We'll make it. We've got to.

The hatch pushed open and Don's head popped up. "I got a good snooze."

He couldn't have slept more than an hour. But that was like him. A short nap and he was ready to go again. How could he do it? He was made for this stuff. He hadn't bargained for something this rough, but put him in this kind of situation, give him a little sleep, and not only did he thrive, he saw the marvelous again. This quality of his had always irritated me. It irritated others, too. When we complained about the miles we had to cover on a hike or the mosquitoes we had to combat, he just ignored us. Or, he chalked up our attitude to "mental illness," as he did my seasickness. But his ability to see things differently was a quality I had admired when I first met him; he didn't behave like "normal" people.

He's a wild animal, untamed, uncomfortable in "civilization." He senses nature intuitively. Are all mountaineers and cruising sailors like this? There is

something wonderful about that quality. Thank God, I'm not with someone I con-
sider "normal" now: no normal person could survive in a situation like this.

"I'm going to check some of the equipment down here and look for
the radios. The wind seems to be lessening somewhat. It doesn't look as
bad as it did earlier this morning. Can you manage the helm a little
longer?"

"Sure. Have you pumped lately?"

"Yeah. I just finished 200 strokes."

He disappeared below. He was right about the wind and sea conditions. I was having less trouble with the helm, and *le Dauphin* was riding
more easily now.

Maybe we'd be able to get some canvas up this afternoon. I wondered
how far we were from land, how much easting we had made since our
last calculated position. The entrance to the Strait of Magellan was about
74° west longitude, and the last position we had logged was 89°W. We
were still about 600 miles from the coast of Chile the night we pitchpoled. What kind of speed were we making now without sails?

The sky was lightening. The sun was trying to make an appearance. I
pulled off my gloves and glanced at my Timex. 1145 hours. I unsnapped
my harness from the mizzen traveller, resnapped it to the port lifeline,
crawled to the hatch, and pushed it open.

"The sun's trying to come out. Maybe you can get a noon shot."

The look on Don's face told me things weren't going well below. "I
found all the radios, but not one of them works. I found your Seiko, but I
don't know if it's right or not. Found my watch, but it's smashed . . . I
cleaned up the radios with fresh water from the three-gallon bottle and
put new batteries in, but that didn't do a thing. The port captain's radio
seems to work, but it's weak—we're too far away to get time ticks." He'd
been so happy after he awakened. Now he was completely discouraged.
"Saltwater might as well be hydrochloric acid," he said.

"Look up!" I said, pointing to the sky. "I think you'll have a chance
to get some shots. Have you checked to see if your sextant is okay?"
Stowed in the icebox, the sextant had been surrounded by heavy canned
goods and dried foods (most of which had ejected), but it had remained
in place. Packed in foam in its original wooden box, it was in good shape.

Don found a pen and passed me the logbook so I could write down
his sightings. I resumed my position at the helm with the logbook and
pen in hand. He wedged himself in the companionway on a step of the
cockeyed ladder and took six different sights, calling out each one as he
took it. "46°50', 47°41', 47°41', 47°39', 47°37', 46°50'." My hand was so
cold, I could barely scrawl a digit.

"Great! We caught it just right. The sun's on its way to the other side now. What luck! Hang on a minute." He closed the hatch, did his calculations, pulled the hatch open again and yelled, "It looks like we're right on the 50th parallel—I get 50°07'S. What's the taffrail log read?" I turned aft and read 237. "Let me do a little more figuring." The hatch shut again for a few minutes, then reopened, and Don's head poked up. "I estimate we're at 87°20' west. . . . You come below now and get some rest. I'll take over," he said, climbing above.

"Try to dry yourself and get some warmth into your bones. With the engine still idling, it's starting to warm up a little."

I went below, took off Don's jacket, pants, and boots and passed them back out to him. I squatted at the pump, stroked 80 times, and recorded it in the logbook. I noticed that his entries were becoming illegible.

If I could only find my boots, I thought, then I suddenly remembered that Michael and Sean had left their boots aboard, and I had stowed them in a garbage bag aft of the port quarter berth. My feet would float in them, but two pair of socks would do the trick. I wormed my way to the end of the berth. Stuffed tightly in so small a space, the bag hadn't budged. I took out one pair of boots and wedged the others back in place. I rummaged through the duffels and found two pair of wool socks. The cotton socks I had on were sticking to my feet like glue. I peeled them off and put the wool over my wet feet. I might as well have been putting on a pair of down booties. Warmth, wonderful warmth!

Before I lay down to rest I glanced quickly around the salon. Stuck in the seam at the side of our berth I found a little address card with the previous owner's name. On the back of the card was printed, "Smile, God loves you."

NOTES

1. The mainsail traveller, a three-quarter-inch bar of stainless steel attached to the mizzen mast, allowed the mainsail sheet block to "travel" freely from port to starboard.

CHAPTER 8

Oil on the Water & Towing Warps

MARCH 1

I listened for the whir of the starter as Don tried the engine. No sound, not even a click.

"It's dead now, like everything else," he said.

Don stood staring at the engine. He looked horrible. Dark semicircles hung under his eyes. He'd stayed at the helm for eight hours through the night, refusing to let me take watches, insisting I get some sleep. Between pumping and keeping him supplied with hot chocolate and Hershey bars I'd managed to doze enough to renew my energy.

I didn't speak. Replies ran through my mind: *Maybe you should bleed the system. Maybe there's kelp in the saltwater pump. Maybe you should change the oil filter.* Instead, I said, "We're alive, sweetheart."

Secretly, I was frightened. No engine to power against the wind; no mainsail to give us drive. This could mean that we'd *have* to head for Cape Horn, to avoid the dangerous lee shore of Patagonia till we were downwind of the Horn. We couldn't approach the Strait of Magellan without an engine. ("Rocks five to ten miles offshore," the *Pilot* read. "Gales blowing toward land, heavy seas, low visibility with rain, snow.") And the Strait was our only chance of getting help from the Chilean navy.

Without control my mind wrestled negatives and positives. *Cape Horn, oh God, not Cape Horn. The boat won't hold up that long in these seas— no, we'll make it. We'll make it . . . Maybe we could try the Strait. Joshua Slocum made it a hundred years ago singlehanded, without an engine, without electronics. Maybe we could, too. . . Not Cape Horn. Please not Cape Horn.*

"Maybe it's Battery 1 that's no good." Don switched to Battery 2 and tried the starter again. Again no juice, no click. Nothing. "None of the gauges registers. The control panel's filled with water. The saltwater's ruined everything. Even the depth sounder." Saltwater. The hydrochloric acid of sailors.

I thought, *No depth sounder to pick up the contours along the coast, to warn us of underlying rocks.* The "indestructible" depth sounder. (Billed as the best on the market—with a water-tight rubber gasket guaranteed to keep the circuits dry—its warranty had hooked us.) Don took it apart, sure he'd find a solution to its malfunction, but when he unscrewed the back to examine it, a cupful of water spilled out.

I put my arms around him. "Why don't you try to get some sleep right now? Let me take the helm, I'm feeling better."

"No. No. I've just got to keep driving this thing east. We've got to make as much easting as possible. Besides, the barometer's falling again."

We were using a small wall-model barometer I'd found in one of the ammunition boxes, another of Don's many backups. It was mounted in rosewood, with *"Stormy," "Rain," "Change," "Fair,"* and *"Very Dry"* painted in Old English type around the face of its gilt frame. We questioned its accuracy because when I flicked the glass with my forefinger, the needle jumped. But at least it gave us an idea of atmospheric changes.

"I'm going back up to take the helm," Don said. "You stay down here and keep giving me hot chocolate or tea."

Pumping, keeping hot water simmering, and checking on Don were taking most of my time. But little by little, I was able to determine what foods we could still use and what would have to be discarded.

Most of our dried food had been stowed in four 5-gallon plastic buckets. I had stashed three of the buckets at the stern under Carl's berth (the port quarter berth); their tops were so difficult to open that I literally needed a crowbar. The fourth bucket, stowed in the forepeak, had flown aft into the salon, ejecting all its contents. Packets of Quaker Oats, cream of rice, Bran Buds, and granola, and small tins of dried basil, thyme, parsley, and cinnamon were glued to mattresses or plastered on the bulkheads along with the smashed squash and sawdust.

I peered under Carl's berth. The three buckets were still jammed where I had stowed them. I tugged on the one marked "mashed potato mix, sour cream mix, dried milk packets." I had an idea for dinner—the first indication that my energy was returning.

I scooped up the wet packets of cereals and the corroded tins of herbs and spices and dumped them in a garbage pile at the foot of the ladder. I picked up pieces of glass and cracked bottles. Some of the cans were so badly rusted that their ends bulged; they'd have to be deep-sixed also.

Paperbacks went into the pile: Conrad, Mark Twain, Dickens, Steinbeck, Pagnol, Robert Louis Stevenson, Alan Paton, Rostand, Solzenitzin, Maya Angelou, Henry Miller, Sartre, Saint-Exupéry. Books from the kids' reading list, books we'd planned to read, books we loved. Friends, old friends, lay wet and lifeless, awaiting burial at sea.

I gathered up Don's charts. The series we'd stowed in the teak slats above the pilot berth were the ones we needed for the Strait of Magellan and Cape Horn. Printed on heavy paper, they hadn't dissolved like the paperbacks; they were wet and still rolled. Somehow we needed to figure out how to dry them.

I shoved open the hatch and began transferring the refuse to the deck. I set aside the soggy copy of Saint-Exupéry's *Vol de Nuit*—the story of the first postal flights on the east coast of South America in the early 1930s. The aviators of those small planes were my heroes. Long before radar was invented they had flown through Patagonian storms as bad as the ones we were encountering, and some hadn't made it back. I picked it up carefully and examined it as I would have a very old book. Its cover was wrinkled and lumpy, and the gloss had peeled off. I couldn't bear to part with it.

Don stared at me from the helm, expressionless, which snapped me back to the present. "The smallest task totally exhausts me," he said slowly. "I sure wish I could park this thing for a few hours, then resume the battle."

Again I tried to convince him to let me take over the helm so he could rest, and finally he agreed. But he wanted me to help raise the mizzen staysail before he went below.

With the damage done to the main spars and the starboard spreader we couldn't use the mainsail, and Don didn't want to risk raising a head-sail. The mizzen staysail was a beautiful old cotton sail that he had bought secondhand at a good price. It was a great sail to use when the wind was abeam or from behind, and we'd used it several times in the tropics with good results. With the wind coming across our port quarter now, he felt it would help us gain speed. Although it was lighter in weight than the mainsail, it was a pain to raise because it didn't have a sail track; and to raise it one of us had to hold the luff while the other hanked the head onto the stay, then hauled in on its sheet.

I wrapped myself from feet to waist in a canvas tarp, tied the hood of my foul weather jacket so tightly I almost choked, hooked my safety harness onto the lifeline, and settled down at the helm to try to keep the boat on a course of 070° magnetic, as Don had instructed.

A northwest wind drove across the port beam, filling the mizzen stay-sail and the staysail and propelling us eastward. Droplets of ice fell from a toneless grey sky and pinged on the deck. I did my best to keep *le Dauphin* on course, but I was having difficulty following the compass. Don had explained that because we were approaching the south magnetic pole, there was a lessening of tangential force on the compass needle that caused it to respond more slowly, and with less reliability. Although I thought I understood the concept, I didn't quite have the hang of keeping the helm on course.

I glanced repeatedly at the horrible, fascinating seas behind me.

Before Don turned in to rest he wrote:

> The seas are colossal—as high as the masthead—40 feet on the average. But this morning, off to the side of the boat, I saw four or five giant sea-swell combinations that I guessed to be 70 or 80 feet high. The wave's entire upper portion surged forward like a slab-avalanche, rolling and churning, while the back side of the avalanche erupted, sending forth 20-foot vertical geysers. The aftermath is pure white foam, the size of a football field. There appears to be no consistency or reason behind the sudden appearance of these monsters—it's pure statistical chance.
>
> It must have been a wave this big, or bigger, that hit us. In surveying all the damage, it's my opinion that we fell vertically, landing with the deck flat upside-down. The evidence: the way the spreader lightboard and the three booms broke; the way the main and mizzen boom gallows were bent forward—as if the boat were going backwards when it fell; and the way the fittings, the through-bolts, and the screws were forced downward.

I struggled repeatedly trying to turn to port or starboard. The wind was rising to gale force again, and the helm wouldn't respond to my touch; it was time to douse the mizzen staysail. I beat my feet against the cockpit floor, hoping Don would hear.

The hatch shot open instantaneously and his bald head popped up. "What's the matter?" One glance told him. "Shit, we've got to drop the mizzen staysail."

Le Dauphin slid down another wave, threatening to broach this time. Don jumped out on deck, without hat, gloves, or foul weather gear. He grabbed for the halyard, loosened it, and started to drop the sail. The wind caught it, and it filled again. "Fall off!" he yelled.

The stern rose on another wave; the bow turned to port. "I can't," I screamed, trying to bring the boat around to starboard. "The helm won't come around."

"Fall off, dammit. The sail's caught on the stanchions."

I tried again to force the helm over. It wasn't ready to yield, and I couldn't fight it. By the time it began to give, the sail had torn. Without waiting for me to try bringing the boat around so the sail would backwind and blow on deck, Don let out more halyard and tried to clear it from the stanchion. The sail continued to balloon and the rip lengthened.

"Sonovabitch! Bring the stern through the eye of the wind."

"I can't. She's overpowered!"

The boat raced down the wave at hull speed. The stern rose on the next wave, perched, and threatened to rise higher.

"We're going to broach if I fall off any more!" I screamed.

"Let the sheet out," he yelled.

I jumped up, pressed my hip against a spoke of the wheel to try to control it, and reached over to the starboard winch to release the sheet. The clew of the sail flew downwind over the water; its sheet was still attached and flailed like an angry snake. The boat gave and began to respond to the helm.

Don watched the sail flapping off the starboard bow. As it disintegrated he turned toward me, wild-eyed, and raged, "Goddammit, if that's the best you can do in high performance we'll *never* save ourselves. That was the only large sail we could fly from the mizzen mast—the only one that could give us real drive."

I flinched. Was it really my fault, or was he so distraught he had to rail at me just to vent his anger? I felt terrible about the sail, but I didn't think either of us was to blame. Conditions were too violent, and Don was trying to get us to the coast faster than the boat could handle. I wanted to say, "Look, just ease off and we'll do what we can. You're driving yourself and the boat crazy." But I didn't dare open my mouth.

He stopped raging, went forward, tugged at the sail, and gathered in the sad, shredded bundle. Unhooking the head and tack, he opened the forward hatch and stuffed it below. He came aft and climbed down the companionway without a word. I could see tears in his eyes.

We were crawling now—the recording log had registered only ten nautical miles since we ruined the mizzen staysail—and at this rate, with these seas, it might take another three weeks to get to the coast.

The wind continued to build. The sleet had let up, but it was drizzling now. My shoulder blades and arms ached from the cold. My nose dripped constantly, and my mouth had congealed into a rigid line.

The hatch opened an hour later and Don climbed up slowly, carrying a cup of cocoa and a chocolate bar for me.

"Did you sleep?" I asked.

"A little. But I'm too discouraged to relax. That sail was our only hope for getting out of a tight situation . . . Besides, I get too spooked to sleep—it's ten times worse below than up here. I relive the nightmare a hundred times down there. I spent most of the time looking for reserves and making a list of things to do to keep my mind off things."

I drank the cocoa and stuffed the chocolate bar in my mouth.

"I'll take over now," he said. "But first let's talk a little about our options."

The options were south to Cape Horn, east to the Strait of Magellan, or north to Valparaiso. Without an engine or depth sounder, Cape Horn was "the logical route" for avoiding the rocky coast.

"I'm worried that the boat won't hold together to get us around the Horn or even to Valparaiso," Don said. "There are too many strange sounds, and the boat jerks like something's loose. I feel uneasy . . . What do you think we ought to do?"

I felt the same way and was glad he'd said it aloud. "I'd rather give the Strait a try. Valparaiso is over 1,200 miles north—that could take us another month. How long do you think it would take us to reach Cabo Pilar?"[1]

"Well . . ." He leaned across the stern to read the recording log. "This indicates we've gone 160 miles in the last 48 hours. We've probably done another 30 due to current. But we're at the mercy of the winds, and I don't know how many miles we've really done. I'd guess we're still somewhere near the 50th parallel and maybe 85°W, so it might take us another week."

"I vote for the Strait," I said.

"Okay. Let's prepare for the Strait, then."

We had a lot to do to prepare for a landfall. Don ran through the list: try to hand crank the engine; connect a spotlight directly to the battery; repair a leak in the fuel pump; dry out the charts; fix the binnacle light; dig the International Distress flag and flare kit out of the abandon-ship locker. We would have to bring the anchors topside and connect them to their chains; figure a way to get drinking water out of the tanks; refill the kerosene stove tank; somehow strengthen the mizzen and staysail booms. But with the seas as violent as they were, until we got a break in the weather, we couldn't do anything.

I suddenly recalled that John on the *Hero* had warned us that the navigational light at the northwest entrance to the Strait was not functioning, and the weather had been too stormy for the Chilean navy to service it. I mentioned it.

"Yeah. I remember that now. We'll have to try and hit it during the day, or stand offshore. I'll take the helm now, but I'm getting hungry. Will you go fix us something to eat?"

I went below and pumped, recording 77 strokes in the logbook. I glanced at the numbers for the last ten hours, making a rough estimate. Over 700 strokes. I couldn't remember how Don had figured the amount pumped out with each stroke—but 700 strokes was a lot of water.

Don had filled the entire page of the logbook with problems and lists, but I could barely read his handwriting. I did notice, however, a badly scrawled sentence at the bottom of the page: "Réanne's been such a great help and support, my love and admiration for her have deepened through this tragic situation." I tried to decipher what he'd accomplished while he was supposed to be resting, but my eyes filled and I couldn't.

MARCH 2, MORNING

I awoke with a start and glanced at my Timex. 0600 hours. *God! Two hours since I pumped!* I jumped up and pushed open the hatch cover. "Sweetheart," I yelled. "Why didn't you call me to relieve you?"

"You needed your sleep," he hollared back. "Besides, I wanted to make as much time as possible, and I can handle the helm better than you can in these conditions . . . The wind's increasing again. Take a look at the barometer, will you, then come up and take the helm so I can drop the jib."

I opened the ice box and peered in at the barometer: 28.88 inches (975 mb). I flicked the glass. The needle jumped and resettled in the same position.

I climbed above and took over the helm as Don unsnapped his safety harness and started forward.

"Snap on to the safety line!" I screamed above the wind.

"No! It takes too long."

"Snap on, dammit!"

The wind was so intense he could be blown overboard. *Don't let anything happen to him. Please. Without him . . .* A wave of nausea swept over me, and I felt feverish. It was fear. *Get a hold of yourself, Réanne.*

As I glanced at the size of the seas and the yellow glow on the western horizon, dark thoughts buried for two days surged forth. *If it happens again it'll be all over.* Conditions were identical to those the evening we pitchpoled. *The boat won't survive.*

Don doused the jib, leaving the staysail up, and ordered me below as black clouds opened and sent a storm of sleet. I lay down again on the crumpled sails in the salon repeating my mantra—*we'll make it, we'll make it*—to get rid of the negative thoughts. I had begun to doze when water sloshing above the floorboards disturbed me—I'd forgotten to pump! I got up, made my way aft, and pumped: 111 strokes. I prepared a cup of cocoa for Don, then flopped back down on the sails. The motion of the boat was as violent as the night we pitchpoled, but I tried not to think about it. Exhausted, I dozed again, awoke from anxiety, then dozed again. I felt bad for Don. He was taking long watches so I wouldn't have to be up there in the black of night. *How long can he take this? I've got to get enough rest so I can relieve him.*

The water above the floorboards awakened me again. I looked at my Timex. 0800. The motion of the boat was wild. The mast worked back and forth in its step. Its awful groan reminded me of a film I'd once seen of an elephant tearing up the roots of a tree. I hoped to God the mast wouldn't break. I jerked my way to the pump and did 91 strokes.

I put the teakettle on the "eternal" flame—our only source of heat now—and screwed the sea rails around it to keep it from flying off the stove. The sea rails had come unscrewed from the stove the night of the pitchpole, ending up at the foot of the starboard quarter berth. We were finding things in the strangest places.

Noon. I prepared mashed potatoes: reconstituted dried milk, dehydrated potatoes, a half packet of sour cream mix, water, and a bacon bar crumbled over the top. I ate in the cockpit with Don, sharing the one bowl we'd found. Afterwards I climbed down to the galley, put the bowl in the sink, and pumped.

I opened the ice box and looked at the barometer. It hadn't budged since morning. I flicked it. No change.

I poked my head out the hatch to shout encouragement to Don. He looked shell-shocked; his eyes were glassy, and he was shivering.

"Let me take over now. You need to rest."

"All right," he said in a monotone. "But before I do, I'm going to try some oil on the water."

Oil on the water. He's losing his mind, I thought. Oil spread on the water was supposed to have a calming effect by increasing surface tension like an invisible membrane. Intuitively, I knew that leaking oil onto waters like these would have no effect. I thought of what I'd read in Robb and other sources—that it would take a "devil of a lot of oil." An oil tanker leaking thousands of gallons might calm them, but I doubted it. How could *anything* have an effect on waves that had their inception thousands of miles away?

I recalled an argument we'd had at the dock in Los Angeles. Don was draining waste engine oil into half-gallon containers to stow in the lazaret for the trip, and I said self-righteously, "That's dumb! We can't carry enough oil to calm heavy seas. You don't believe that stuff, do you?" My comments had exiled me for the rest of the day; Don had thrown me his Mongolian scowl and continued to fill the containers. His bible, Bowditch's *American Practical Navigator,* suggested that oil proved effective "if the vessel drifts or runs slowly before the wind."

He's grasping at straws now. He's losing it. I had to let him try, though; ridicule would put him over the edge.

He looked aft at the seas. "Now. I think I can get the oil out now," he said, half to himself. "Before the next big one comes." He unlatched the lazaret, lifted up the cover, and let himself down into the hole. His head disappeared for a minute as he dug for the containers.

"Here," he said. "Set these in the cockpit." Four containers. I set them at my feet while Don pulled himself back up, closed the cover, and secured the lock. He grabbed one bottle and started forward on the port deck.

"Snap your harness on the lifeline!" I screamed over the wind.

He turned around and looked at me as if he didn't understand. Then it registered, and I could see him mouth, "Oh yeah," as he snapped on. He inched forward toward the mast. A wave picked up the stern, setting the bow to starboard. He grabbed for the mast as the wave rolled under the boat. The boat settled back down, he unscrewed the cap, and poured oil over the windward rail. The wind blew the oil forward, spraying the port bow with ribbons of black.

"Goddammit, wind. Ease off!" He clenched his fist and raised his arm to the sky, then fell back and collapsed on the edge of the doghouse. His face looked ashen. He slumped on the doghouse roof for a few seconds, then straightened his back, stood up, worked his way aft to the cockpit, picked up another bottle, and muttered that he was going to pour the oil down the toilet and pump it out. (He'd read a suggestion in Bowditch that oil could be discharged from "waste pipes.")

A few minutes later he poked his head out the hatch and yelled, "Do you see any change?"

Almost afraid to say anything, I just shook my head, hoping he'd stop and lie down. Instead he climbed back up and lifted the two remaining bottles onto the cockpit seat. He opened his Swiss army knife, which hung on a lanyard from his harness. He jabbed the tops full of holes, snapped his harness onto the port lifeline, and went forward again. He tied a nylon cord to each bottle, secured them to the cathead, and suspended them over the port rail. Like jumping jacks the bottles hit the water, flung upward, hit the water and bounced up again, splattering oil over the port bow a second time.

He was at the end of his own cord.

Holding onto the handrails of the doghouse, he crept aft and looked straight through me. His head shook as if he were palsied. "It's gonna get us. We're not going to make it. It's more powerful than we are," he said.

"Dammit, shut up. You shut up and don't *ever* talk like that again. Go below and get some sleep. I'll stay at the helm."

My rock had shattered. It was my turn now to be the rock.

I tucked the canvas cloth around my legs and under my fanny and tightened the strings of my hood. It was bitterly cold.

I looked astern. The yellow glow on the western horizon had intensified. We now knew that meant we were in for cyclonic winds. Black storm clouds raced toward the stern, trying to grab us, enfold us.

The greybeards and breaking seas continued to build, crest and break into white foam. The boat slid into a trough. The seas towering above

I couldn't control the helm and I was terrified

our 50-foot mast had to be more than 70 feet high. I was terrified but, at the same time, hypnotized by the sight. One moment I was on top of a mountain looking across a great blue desert of peaks and valleys, then suddenly in a canyon surrounded by moving white walls.

These were the colossal seas Don had described in the log; the same seas that Robb had described. *Oh God, the sea must have looked like this the night of our accident. Don't let it get us. Wind, please ease. Please.*

The helm didn't want to respond. I remembered Moitessier's Golden Rule: take each wave at a 15- to 20-degree angle, then let the helm respond freely without trying to force it over.

I practiced. Down one wave to starboard at an angle no more than 15 degrees. Up the next, to port, at the same angle. Let the wheel do what it wants for a second or two when it's too hard to control. Then grip again—which I did with all my strength till my hands were numb.

Suddenly I noticed that we were going in circles. The wind kept shifting. From northwest to west to southeast, a full 180-degree shift . . . *Oh God, we're in the eye of the storm!* We were caught in the dangerous semicircle described in Bowditch.[2]

The bow headed directly into the wind, and the seas came from every direction, breaking first across the starboard bow, then the port quarter. I looked aft just in time to see a huge wave racing down toward the stern. The wave crashed over my back and into the cockpit. Foam swirled around my boots.

"Don," I screamed. "I can't control the helm!"

The hatch shot open. Don took one look and yelled, "Oh God, we're surfing. Hang on, babe. I'll put out the warps.[3] I want to try something new."

He wrapped his legs around the mizzen boom gallows stanchion and the opened the lazarette. He pulled up two bundles of badly tangled nylon line and began untangling then; first a 300-foot length, then a second.

"I can't control the helm any longer. Can't you hurry or just take over for me."

"You're doing fine, Sweetheart. Just be patient."

He attached the lines to each of the small automobile tires he'd wrapped with 20 feet of anchor chain and slowly, carefully, first off the port stern, then off the starboard, he paid out 50, 100, 150, 200, 250, 300 feet of line.

"The trick is to let out enough so that the tires are one and a quarter wave lengths behind us," he explained. Watch."

We surfed down a wave. The lines tightened and pulled. The boat slowed. The helm began to respond and I no longer had to fight it.

"The boat's responding well now. I'm going back to sleep." Don smiled.

"How can you do that to me?" I yelled. My shoulders ached from tension. The small of my back ached. My hands hurt. Water had worked its way inside my foul weather jacket.

"You're doing great!" he hollered, crawling back down the hatch.

"But I need moral support!" My mouth was bone dry.

Already an hour of sleep had restored his good humor, but he needed more to repair his body. I didn't protest any further.

One hour: down one wave, up another. *Keep the bow at a 15-degree angle. Let the helm respond. Don't force it. Up. Down. Let her do her own thing. The warps seem to be doing their trick. We'll make it, we'll make it.* "Stop this wind!" I screamed to the sky. "Stop this wind!"

Don's head popped out of the hatch.

"You didn't sleep very long this time."

"I know. It's too exciting!" He began shooting photographs.

"How the hell can you take pictures at a time like this?"

"You're doing just fine!"

"I'm scared!" I tried to wet my lips.

"I'll take over now. I've had a good sleep, and I feel much better. You go below now. You did a great job, sweetheart! "

I went down, washed my face with alcohol for the first time in four days, and flopped onto the sails utterly exhausted, my foul weather gear still on.

NOTES

1. Cabo Pilar is located off the north entrance to the Strait of Magellan.

2. "The dangerous semicircle . . . is considered dangerous because (1) the actual wind speed is greater than that due to the pressure gradient alone, since it is augmented by the forward motion of the storm, and (2) the direction of the wind and sea is such as to carry a vessel into the path of the storm (in the forward part of the semicircle)." The American Practical Navigator [Bowditch], p. 516

3. Warps or drogues are large lines towed behind a vessel to slow it down and hold the stern into the wind or seas. If a boat is running under bare poles, and still threatens to broach (turn sideways and capsize) or surf down the leading edge of a steep wave, a skipper must tow warps to help keep the vessel under control. The moderating effect of these warps was immediate and substantial, and we towed them several times after our pitchpole when the winds and seas became excessive.

CHAPTER 9

Decision

MARCH 2, EVENING

"I've lashed the helm," Don said as he came below. "It's too cold to stay up there anymore."

I panicked. "No! I don't want to lie ahull again."

"Sweetheart, we can't stay in the cockpit all night in this weather. The storm's passed, and the seas are going down. The boat will take care of us."

The boat couldn't take care of us—she couldn't do it the night we pitchpoled. As damaged as she was now, she would totally disintegrate if we turned over again. One more time and it would be all over.

Don took off his foul weather gear for the first time in three days and made a log entry: "1830 hours local time. Barometer 29.48 inches (998.31 mb)—rising. Wind SW, Force 6. Distance logged in 24 hours: 57 nautical miles. Position unknown. Very cold with bitter south wind. Rudder still has a bumping sound that concerns me. Balanced and lashed tiller, so we don't have to be at helm. First time in many hours we don't have to stand watch. Signs of exhaustion are setting in, and we need rest and warmth. Just to show us who's boss, Neptune sent a rogue sea over the cabin and water came through the closed hatches. Everything wet and muggy. I got the Optimus kerosene light going and hung it from its hand grip. Heat and light most welcome (not using battery power). Also got a wood fire going which helps, but we're running low on Presto logs. I spoon-fed as much wet sawdust into the fireplace as possible, but it smothered the fire."

Don lay down on the sails. I sat at the galley table writing my journal on a pad of dry paper I'd found at the bottom of our clothes drawer. I got up every ten minutes to check the compass heading and peek out the hatch. He heard me opening and closing the hatch. "Sweetheart, come and lie down. You need your rest."

"I can't. I'll stay here in the galley and keep checking above."

An hour later I told Don, "I'm going above. I'm nervous about leaving the helm unmanned."

"Okay. Be sure to snap on."

I was wearing fishnet long johns (not warm!), a man's T-shirt, long-sleeved thermal top, long-sleeved cotton turtleneck, wool pullover, acrylic pullover, down vest, and wool air force pants (still damp in the seat). They were the same clothes I'd worn for the last four days. I added my down jacket (still damp and lumpy), foul weather jacket and pants, mittens, and a muffler that I wrapped once around my head over my stocking cap and twice around my neck. I could barely move.

Hooking my harness to the main traveller, I wrapped up in the canvas tarp. The wheel was still lashed and caring for itself; I had nothing to do but gaze around. Gusts of wind and squalls swept across the water, washing spray over the stern quarter. The boat flew downwind to port, giving me momentary fits of panic.

I looked up. The sky was beautiful. For the first time in over a week I could see stars twinkling around the horizon. And overhead, the moon back-lighted constantly changing clouds that resembled protozoa whose cilia and flagella floated and spread, stretching and retracting across an indigo sky. The sting of the night air told me the humidity had dropped. Snowy memories of childhood drifted through my mind.

I am five years old. Mother and I are driving to my grandmother's in Wisconsin for Christmas. Snow begins to fall heavily on an already blanketed landscape and soon turns into a raging blizzard. Suddenly, the car skids off the road and lands in a ditch. There is no way to get it out.

"What are we going to do, Mommy?" I ask.

"We'll look for a farmhouse and call Daddy."

There is no touch of panic in Mother's voice, nothing to indicate I should be afraid. We are dressed warmly, and there is enough light to walk a half-mile to the nearest farmhouse, where a kind elderly couple puts us up for the night.

"Let's go get a chocolate shake," Daddy suggests on the evening of my seventh birthday. "I'll pull you on the sled."

Bundled in a snowsuit and boots, I grip the slats of my sled with mittened hands as Daddy pulls me to town. The metal runners whine over the snow, the cold makes my nostrils stick, forcing me to breathe through my mouth. Ribbons of clouds float across the night sky, opening and closing my view of the moon and stars. *This is fun!* I think.

Sixteen years old. Dad takes me to the high school parking lot for a driving lesson. The icy pavement is covered with a layer of snow. "If you start to skid," he instructs, "turn the steering wheel in the direction of the skid. Don't try to turn it in the opposite direction until you have the car under control."

I step on the gas. The car skids to the left. I jerk the wheel to the right.

"No. That's not it!" Dad's voice is stern, not what I'm used to. "Do it again."

I repeat the steps, letting the steering wheel turn into the skid until the car slows, then turning it back to the center. We practice for an hour, until I master the concept. I don't understand the physics, but I can handle the mechanics.

Dad's instructions were like Moitessier's: "Let the helm do what it wants, then turn . . . " I started to sob. Hot salty tears fell on my raw face as my brain continued to unload, dumping out more memories, then thoughts about Don and me. And feelings of guilt about how we treated each other.

Silently I spoke to him. *I know I've ridiculed you—your interminable enthusiasm, your driving ambition, your demanding ways, but if this had to happen, there's no one else I'd rather be with.* At that moment, I wished I could give him the appreciation he so desperately craved. But his need for this, like everything else about him, seemed so exaggerated. I went on: *But I know you can't be any other way. I can't be any other way, either. Will we be able to resolve our life together? Will you be able to accept that I am made differently? Can we follow our separate passions and still be together?*

I hadn't thought about us recently and didn't want to now. Not now. I had to stop crying. I had to concentrate on just getting to land. That was all that mattered. That, and getting word to my parents. I drew in a long breath, held it for twenty counts and exhaled. My tears subsided. Too cold, I had to go below. Besides, idleness had brought on too many memories, too many thoughts.

Climbing below, I checked my Timex in the dim light of the Optimus lamp. It was 0030; I'd been at the helm for an hour and a half. I opened the icebox and checked the barometer. It had risen to 29.72 inches (1006.44 mb).

> *Le Dauphin is holding her own. Nothing more I can do above, but I'm so tense I don't know if I'll be able to sleep. Before we pitchpoled, I accepted the knocks and the waves over the cabin as annoying and miserable. But now I panic. Each time the stern rises to a huge wave I wonder if we'll make it down this wave and up the other side, wonder if the boat will hold together or if something else will go wrong. We've both had diarrhea and nausea since the accident—nerves, I'm sure.*

I lay down on the sails and fell asleep snuggling against Don.

MARCH 3, MORNING

Log: "Barometer still on the rise: 29.97 (1014.90 mb). Wind S, Force 4. Outside air temperature 45.5°F (7.5°C). Except for pumping the bilge hourly and quick checks outside during the night we both got some good sleep."

The sun shone. The sky, a steel blue, hurt our eyes. I had begun to think the sun no longer existed. Seven days of hell. One of heaven. Who knew what was in store for the rest of the day, or tomorrow?

Don's morale was improving. "Gotta make hay while the sun shines," he said cheerily. "Maybe we can get some things accomplished."

With the helm lashed and well balanced, le Dauphin loped along on course all morning, allowing us to finish tasks on the list Don had logged two days earlier. He'd already completed two-thirds of what needed to be done, and had added his comments in parentheses:

Take flare kit and distress flag out of abandon-ship locker
Try freshwater bath/alcohol rinse on radios (tried—unsuccessful)
Try to hand crank engine (no good)
Plug leak on fuel pump (half-assed job)
Fix binnacle light
Find Seiko watch (found—but there's a discrepancy between Timex and
    Seiko—can't tell which is more reliable)
Repair mizzen boom (another half-assed job; completed with 2-inch adhe-
    sive tape)
Tighten rigging
Refill kerosene stove
Repair leaky intake valve on stove (found copper tubing and connectors at
    tank damaged—another Band-aid approach—hope it holds)
Find kerosene lamps and get them going (got one going; can't find parts to
    the two others; did get Optimus going)

Still to be done:
Ready anchor gear
Rig pump and siphon drinking water from the tanks to the 5-gallon con-
    tainers
Repair mizzen sail. Sew hanks on working jib; mizzen sail torn
Dry out charts and choose what we need for the coast

Don lit a fire in the fireplace while I gathered up the charts that lay about the salon and separated those we needed from those we didn't. We had only two small-scale charts that covered the coast. One covered the area from *Golfo de Peñas* (Gulf of Rocks) at 47°20'S to the south side of Canal Trinidad at 50°S. The second, and most critical for our approach to the Strait of Magellan, covered the 150 miles between Canal Trinidad and the Strait. Both charts were inadequate for pinpointing dangers or locating small anchorages.

I opened the second chart and studied it carefully. "Look at this. See how large the entrance to Canal Trinidad is? And it's right smack on the 50th parallel! Maybe that's a possibility. I'll finish rolling the charts and see if I can find the British *Pilot.*" Since our copy of the American *Sailing Directions* was wet and ruined, it would have to be chucked. I hoped our British *South America Pilot* had survived.

I counted sixty-two charts and stacked them in piles near the fireplace. Damp and fragile, they began to dry from the heat of the fire. The once-crisp white paper now resembled antique parchment.

Our large, hardcover resource books and editions of nautical literature were stowed in a tight locker underneath the bookshelves: treasures such as Don's *Bowditch*—the bible of seamen; a copy of *Chapman Piloting* that he'd given me as a birthday present; the *American Heritage Dictionary*; a Spanish-English dictionary; the Pascuensan dictionary; *Petit Larousse*; Slocum's *Sailing Alone Around the World*; Moitessier's *Cap Horn à la Voile*. Located along the port bulkhead next to the fireplace at the deepest part of the boat, the locker—we called it the "safe"—held our valuables and hard-core medical supplies like syringes, sutures, and painkillers. Its cover was built to stay closed, and it had.

I pried it open with a long screwdriver and hung my head over it to survey its contents. The medical supplies at the bottom looked like candidates for jetsam, but the books had survived rather well. They were warm to the touch from the heat of the fireplace. I located the hardbound *South America Pilot*.

"Look up what it says about the Strait, will you?" Don said. I turned to the chapters on Estrecho de Magallanes and began reading: "The difficulties and dangers in navigating the strait . . . are accentuated by the prevalence of bad weather, especially towards the W end, and by the generally foul and rocky character of the anchorages. Violent and unpredictable squalls are frequent all over the strait, making boatwork dangerous."[1]

Paragraph after paragraph was filled with descriptions of groups of rocky islands off the northwest entrance to the strait, with phrases such as, "surrounded by rocks," "tidal streams set toward the rocks," "area should be avoided," "exposed to the force of the Pacific Ocean."

Don frowned. "Without radar or a depth sounder that approach sounds horrible. Remember, the Evangelistas Islands lie about 24 miles northwest of Cabo Pilar, and with no way to determine longitude we could end up on one of those rocks in the middle of the night. I don't like it . . . Read what it says about Canal Trinidad."

I continued: "The weather and sea experienced in Canal Trinidad and Golfo Trinidad being 150 miles N of the W entrance to Estrecho de Magallanes, are generally more moderate than that farther S; hence it offers a favourable alternative route to that through the NW end of Estrecho de Magallanes. Golfo Trinidad and Canal Trinidad should not be entered from the Pacific Ocean at night or in thick weather when it is not possible to identify the high land [since] there are many off-lying rocks and shoals [and] the sea sometimes breaks 4 miles from the land."2

"Generally more moderate" sounded more promising than what we'd read about the entrance to the Strait of Magellan. But "the sea sometimes breaks 4 miles from the land" sounded menacing. Canal Trinidad was closer, though, and we might stand a better chance of entering there, rather than trying to hang on till the Strait.

I knew that the Chilean coast south of the 47th parallel was an archipelago of mountainous, tightly forested islands and deep fjords that stretched all the way to Cape Horn at 55°S, and that the Canales Patagónicos (Patagonia Channels)—a series of intricate channels connecting Golfo de Peñas to the Strait of Magellan—were used by commercial ships wanting to avoid that 300-mile stretch of open sea. However, I was unaware of the extreme dangers and difficulties facing vessels that navigate those inner waters. To leave these frightening greybeards behind, reach one of those channels, tuck behind an island, and anchor was all I could think of. Maybe then we'd be able to evaluate our chances of continuing, or at least prepare to abandon ship *on land.*

"I vote for Canal Trinidad," I said. "I don't want any more of these seas."

"Yeah. I think it's our only hope under the circumstances. We don't even know if we're still on the 50th parallel, and I'm concerned about trying to head south without knowing our longitude. If the sun keeps shining today, maybe I can get a noon shot. Otherwise, if we deviate the slightest bit from due east, I'm afraid we'll become totally lost."

The *Pilot* warned not to proceed east of 76°W until latitude 49°58'S had been reached, so while the weather was good, it was imperative that Don get noon sightings to determine our latitude. Although my Seiko had been the better timekeeper, the difference between it and the Timex bothered us. Since the Timex was a known quantity, however, we decided to use it. I glanced nervously at my watch all morning knowing Don wanted to start taking shots at 1100 hours.

In the meantime, I began the job of siphoning water out of the water tanks into the five-gallon jugs. I sucked the water as far as it would go into a twenty-inch length of half-inch tubing, pinched it off with my fingers, then quickly transferred it to the five-gallon container.

After thirty minutes I had transferred just a half-gallon. *At this rate,* I thought, *I'll never get any repairs done. It will take me twenty-four hours to complete the siphoning.*

Don came below for a few minutes. "What the hell are you doing?"

"Siphoning. Like you asked me to."

"Haven't you ever siphoned before?"

"Not since high school chemistry."

"Look, you're making it complicated. Here's all you have to do."

His manner was so patient and gentle I burst into tears.

"What's the matter? Was I being sarcastic?"

"No," I blubbered. "You're being so nice I feel like crying." I sobbed into his shoulder for a few minutes as he stroked my back and my head. My morale was on a downward spiral. Thank God, I had held up when he was low.

I removed the floorboards and placed the jugs in the bilge below the level of the main tanks so I could siphon correctly. An uncapped bottle of Joy was floating in the bilge. That and the leaking kerosene had been coating the cabin sole.

After filling the jugs, I pulled the mattresses aside, tied a scarf over my nose, and dumped half a quart of ammonia on the floor. I mopped, rinsed the mop in saltwater, mopped again, rinsed again, and poured out the remaining half of the ammonia. I mopped and rinsed until the floor was finally clean. I glanced at my watch, winding it cautiously for the third time in six hours.

"Don't you think you should start taking some sights pretty soon?" I hollered through the aft port.

"What time is it?"

"1100 hours by the Timex."

"Yeah. We'd better get ready. The sun's still climbing, but I don't know when the zenith will occur, so we'll start a series of shots. Pass me up the sextant, will you?"

I lifted the sextant case carefully out of the icebox and passed it up. Grabbing a pen, the logbook, and the Seiko as a backup, I climbed above.

Don lifted the sextant out of its wooden box, attached the telescope to the sextant, and secured the sextant cord around his neck. Steadying himself at the main boom gallows with his legs, he raised the telescope to his right eye with his left hand, rocking the sextant from side to side, and adjusted the index arm and micrometer with his right hand. The trick was to adjust the sextant so the sun just touched the horizon in the telescope at the very moment the boat hit the peak of a swell. All that, while the boat rolled and pitched.

It was a procedure I'd never mastered. If I had tried after my seasickness disappeared I might have learned. But with just the two of us handling the boat, it seemed I never had the time to practice.

"Get ready. Mark!" Don called out.

I wrote down the time while he read the index arm and micrometer for the altitude of the sun, then called it out for me to record. He had

Leaving Los Angeles Harbor, Columbus Day, October 12, 1974

Trade wind sailing at last!

Don at the helm in trade winds.

Replacing more sail slides—a never-ending task—en route to Easter Island

Sighting Easter Island after thirty-two days at sea

Breaking surf off the village of Hanga Roa

*Happy kids followed us everywhere
we went at Easter Island*

Réanne with Jermán on "wild" horse

Our first view of the moai

For some islanders, this was their first view of Rapa Nui from offshore

View of rugged coast from cave window

Ahu Akivi surrounded by wild horses

María Pakarati among her father's carvings

The slopes of Rano Raraku were dotted with moai heads

Réanne studying the moai

Local entertainment for President Pinochet's visit

*Small wild pineapples
grow at Anakena*

We make petroglyph rubbings near Anakena

An elderly friend

*We explored caves
with Dr. Campbell*

More sail repairs in the Roaring forties

*I pecked away
at my typewriter
in the cockpit*

Dismantling the steering vane in Dársena Aid

Don ties the bow to the Bendoran

Paso Shoal—the most impressive wreck we'd seen in the canals

Réanne falls asleep studying her Spanish verbs.

Our "home" at the pier in Punta Arenas

Hand-built fishing boats ply the Strait

The happy navigator off Cape Horn

An even happier Don signs the register at the top of Horn Island

The curious
Magellanic penguins

Two decades later we visited beautiful Paine National Park

already taken four sights when I looked at my Timex to start the fifth. The minute hand wasn't moving.

"This thing stopped," I said.

"Oh for christsake."

I felt guilty and wondered if, in my anxiety, I had wound it too much, or if it had just died a natural death. Hoping Don wouldn't blow up at me, I said quickly, "Look, we'll start over using the Seiko. It's the only thing we can do."

We restarted the procedure and continued for nearly an hour. Don took one sun sight after another at intervals of one to three minutes until the sun appeared to reach its zenith (46°52'). To be sure he'd caught the peak, he took six additional sights. His last reading (46°39') verified that the sun had begun its arc to the west.

"Get out the *Nautical Almanac*," he said, unscrewing the telescope and replacing the sextant in its box.

I climbed below, put away the box, then opened the soggy *Almanac*, looked up the sun corrections for the date, and read them to Don. His calculations put us at 49°58'S, just two miles north of the 50th parallel. He figured our longitude (82°15'W) might vary about 2 degrees.

I grabbed the *Pilot* and thumbed back to the descriptions I'd read earlier about Canal Trinidad. "Do not proceed E of the Meridian 76°W until latitude 49°58'S has been reached."

I called up to Don: "You're right on the button!"

"Yeah, it seems a bit weird to hit it like that. I hope our calculations are okay. Canal Trinidad sounds like our only chance. I figure we're 120 to 150 miles offshore now, and it'll be a good three days or more before we make a landfall. If we can keep a course due east, we should be able to head right into Golfo Trinidad."

He logged: "Estimated longitude 81° to 83°W." Then, pointing to the logbook, he said, "When we've finished all the things on the list, we'll study the chart for Canal Trinidad, and you can read me the instructions for entering and finding an anchorage. Right now I've got to finish attaching the hanks to the jib."

"You're doing that? I thought you wanted me to do it."

"I did, but you have so much to do down here, I thought I'd finish it and get it raised. I want to get this vessel moving." I was impressed. My sewing lessons had apparently sunk in.

I thought about his words: "A good three days or more before we make a landfall." Land—we were finally going to make it! Anything necessary to prepare for a landfall seemed easy. I ignored the dangers. All I cared about was escaping the horrid seas.

Don's journal, however, guarded worries he hadn't mentioned to me:

Every day the circle representing our possible position gets bigger and bigger. We face such serious offshore dangers that, starting today, I'm assuming for safety's sake that we're at the extreme eastern point of that circle. Tonight will be our last night of sailing blindly due east. I've purposely understated our progress because I don't want Réanne to get despondent if it takes longer than I've estimated. Another worry: south of the 47th parallel, the current of the Southern Ocean runs roughly east, then divides into two branches as it approaches the continent. One branch heads north toward the Galapagos; the other heads south to Cape Horn. Since we have no way to calculate drift or current it's possible we're either farther north or farther south than my calculations indicate. Could we be trapped in one current or the other?

AFTERNOON

At 1500 hours I put on my foul weather gear and harness and climbed above to do some repairs of my own. The sun was still shining, and except for clouds building along the eastern horizon, the sky was clear. It was beautiful! Although the seas were lumpy and uncomfortable, they were not the monstrosities that had been attacking us.

I snapped my harness onto the starboard lifeline and went forward to the deck locker. The padlock had kept the locker cover secure, but inside it was a mess. I pawed through its contents, found two cans of *Poxy Putty*, and mixed up a batch.

I lay down on the starboard deck and examined the seam where the doghouse had separated from the deck. Half-inch lengths of the through-bolts were exposed, but none had pulled loose. I figured that if I could spread the epoxy thick enough it would decrease the amount of water that poured in over the galley settee every time a wave broke over the doghouse. I couldn't believe how lucky we had been. We wouldn't have survived if the doghouse had sheered off the way it had on the Smeetons' *Tsu Hang*.

By the time I had filled the seam, the sun was low on the horizon. Wet and cold, I went below and pumped (173 strokes), then tried to tidy the salon. Although the cabin sole was clean now, the mattresses still lay on the floor, so waterlogged we hadn't attempted to lift them up onto the berths. We had been using them as stepping stones instead.

Don's late afternoon log entry read: "Things are looking up a bit today. I got a little rest, and good weather really helps, but everything is so damned damp or wet. Ceiling still covered with droplets of water; so are the bulkheads, floor, and portlights, etc. Back cushion for the galley seat weighs about eighty pounds because of the water it contains.

"I'm still worried about the current. How accurately can we continue heading due east? How can we tackle approaching the coast without engine and depth sounder? What kind of steerage will we have? No way to tell tides or currents.

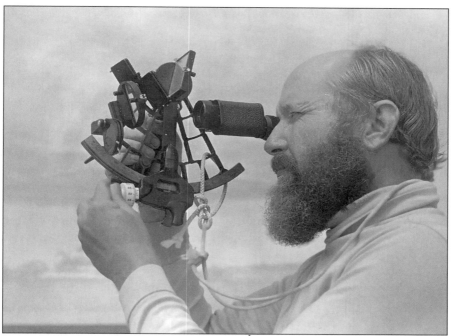

Don took one sun shot after another

"Our hands are a mass of blisters, rope burns, scratches. Our fingers tingle constantly, and I can barely read my own scrawl. Still haven't found the can opener, so I've been using a screwdriver to pound holes. I took a can of V-8 above this afternoon, and a rogue wave pooped the cockpit— it was super-salty V-8."

That night, before flopping onto the pilot berth for a rest, I complained:

Nothing dries on this boat. We've kept a fire going most of the day, but our sweaters and long johns are just as wet as they were after we pitchpoled. Just a while ago, we finally managed to lift the mattress onto our berth. It's still sopping, but who cares? We never take off our foul weather gear anyway. Got a lot of things accomplished today, but I'm so tired I'm weepy and falling apart. Don's been great today.

After supper, he took out his Swiss army knife and began cleaning his nails. I asked how the hell he could take time for that now. He just grinned and said, "I'm doing it!" I'd like to do the same, but I don't feel I can spare the time for myself. My hands look like a cowboy's, and I haven't even brushed my teeth or changed my underpants since the accident.

Slowly, slowly we're making it toward land. Land! I know that once we get to land I can take care of myself. Out here, no. If anything were to

happen to Don, I don't know what I would do. I could not handle this
boat. God, what a horrid thought.

MARCH 4

A dreary day with drizzle and rain. Grey stretched over the entire sky, and
I wrote: *I admire artists and poets who can find beauty in this dullness.* Don
said, "Yesterday was unusual, I guess. We're back to normal today."

The seas were choppy, shooting their tops off as squall after squall hit
from the northwest. The barometer remained high and steady (30.00
inches [1015.92mb), but the eastern horizon looked strangely threatening. Since storms usually came from the west, the weather conditions
puzzled me.

"We won't be able to verify our latitude today unless there's a break
in the clouds," Don said. "Read again what it says about entering Canal
Trinidad."

I reread the instructions.

"Okay. Now read the landmarks again. I want to etch those details in
my mind."

I read:

> The coast S from the W entrance . . . is fronted by Rocas Vidette, consisting of
> many low islets and rocks, some of which lie nearly 3 miles offshore.
> Numerous breakers have been observed extending 3 miles NW of Cabo
> Rugged. . . . The S shore of Canal Trinidad is bordered by high hills and
> mountains. . . . Monte Tres Picos, the NE of Picos Orientales, rises abruptly
> from the S shore, to an elevation of 603 m (1,978 ft), 1 mile W of Cabo
> Cardinal; it is wooded nearly to the summit, which is of dark and bare rock
> with three distinct peaks, the N peak being lower than the other two. These
> prominent peaks form an excellent mark, and can be clearly distinguished . . .
> from seaward.
>
> On the N side of the entrance Monte Nares is the highest land, backing
> Puerto Alert; when seen from W of Península Corso, bearing 099°, it appears
> as a truncated conical mountain.
>
> Monte Catedral is a prominent peak . . . 11 miles NNE of the entrance; it
> is 1,169 m (3,836 ft) high, resembling at a distance the spire and roof of a
> church, but is usually hidden by clouds. In clear weather it is visible from Golfo
> Trinidad.[3]

Silently I read the descriptions of two possible anchorages inside Canal
Trinidad. The recommended anchorage, Puerto Alert—an inlet on the
north side—extended four and a half miles north northwest, and depths
were so great I figured only freighters could find anchorage there. Puerto
Henry, listed as suitable only in fine weather, was located on the south
side. A series of landmarks listed in the *Pilot* weren't even identified on
our small-scale chart. Even a small miscalculation in plotting our position

from these charts could mean a significant error—a hazardous proposition along this coast.

I described the two anchorages to Don. "Hmm," he said. "Our ability to anchor is going to depend on wind and current, and how well we can sail and steer this boat when we get into Golfo Trinidad. Keep reading, though, and retain as much as you can."

Le Dauphin had held her own all day, propelling us eastward at 3 knots under the staysail and working jib, and we had been able to work below, checking the inside compass frequently and going topsides to make adjustments in the helm and jib sheet.

The anchor chain that we'd stowed in the salon bilge after leaving Easter Island was tangled and wedged under the frames. We worked together, locating the bitter end of the chain, untangling it, and dragging it forward to the forepeak to restow in the chain locker—its stowage place under normal conditions. Rusty saltwater dripped off each link of its 300 feet, depositing ugly stains on the vinyl floor covering.

I looked around the forepeak. The workbench where Don wanted to stow the anchor lines was speckled with globs of rust. The toolbox lashed to the table had spewed all its contents. Nuts, bolts, screws, and nails were jammed in every crevice I could see. A chisel was embedded in the hull; a keyhole saw that was stuck between the hull and floorboards quivered with every lurch of the boat. Trying to pick anything out was impossible—everything seemed wedged in for eternity. Thinking I'd do Don a favor by cleaning the table, I wiped it with a rag. The rust spread like peanut butter, covering the once grey paint with a gooey orange.

The previous afternoon Don had worked on deck, untangling the anchor lines that we'd used for warps and checking them for chafe. He brought them below now, coiled them up on the workbench, then went back to the salon and flopped belly-down on the pile of sails below our berth. He reached into the space below our berth where the CQR, the two Danforths, and the yachtsman were stowed, and unlashed them. He looked up at me, serious, and said, "Good thing this nylon webbing held. Otherwise you would have been pulverized when we pitchpoled."

Together, we manhandled the 60-pound CQR to the forepeak and laid it at the foot of the chain locker. I recalled how much work we'd done to clear the decks after we left Easter Island, and how tired we had been. But lowering these 60- and 65-pound hulks through the forward hatch had required a lot less effort than raising them would.

"You climb out the forward hatch," Don instructed. "I'll lift the CQR up. You reach down, grab the flukes, and try to hold it steady till I climb out the rear hatch and come forward. Don't try to lift it! I'll pull it the rest of the way up . . . As soon as we get the CQR up, come back down and help me move the Danforth to the forepeak—we'll lift it out the same way."

I climbed out the hatch, sat on its teak frame, and wedged my feet across the opposite side. Don passed the CQR part way up; I leaned over, grabbed hold of the flukes, and held on. When Don came forward he grabbed the flukes, and we both lifted the anchor up and out of the hatch. He moved it to the end of the bowsprit by himself, inserted it in the bow roller, and tied it down.

We repeated the process with the Danforth. I could feel the muscles of my right forearm stretching while I held the flukes of the 65-pound Danforth. We had been working so fast all day we had nearly exceeded our strength. "We can't do much more of this," I said, immediately sorry for being negative. We had to do "much more," and I couldn't allow myself to listen to my pains. "Maybe this is the answer to rehabilitating juvenile delinquents," I told Don. "We could bring them down here."

"No thanks. It's hard enough with just the two of us."

I broke into tears.

"You just thought about the kids, didn't you?" he said.

"Yeah, but they wouldn't be very happy," I said, laughing and crying at the same time, "if they knew 'juvenile delinquents' had triggered my thinking about them."

"I'm so glad they weren't with us," Don said, fitting the Danforth in its chocks. "One of the kids would have been on watch . . . We'd have lost someone—I don't even want to think about it."

I didn't either. An image from my recurring nightmare appeared before my mind's eye: Sean thrown out and lost when we turned over.

"Let's not talk about it anymore," I said.

We continued down our list of tasks: Feeding 300 feet of nylon anchor line up through the hatch, then down through the hawse pipe, carefully coiling it in the upper chain locker. Passing 300 feet of chain up through the hatch, attaching it to the eye at the end of the CQR shank. Feeding the remaining 290 feet down the hawse pipe—first tying off the bitter end to a beam at the bottom of the chain locker, then laying it carefully in the locker without letting it kink.

The last time we'd gone through this routine, we were docked in Los Angeles Harbor and the boat didn't budge. Now, every movement was an acrobatic feat, and I was feeling a bit queasy. All I wanted to do was sit down and rest. I began to complain to myself again. *Can't these things wait a bit? Why does Don drive himself so?*

Exhausted and aching when we finally finished, we flopped down on the cockpit seats to rest and sat without speaking. It was 1630 hours.

"I know you'll laugh at me," I said, breaking the silence. "But all afternoon I've been thinking I smelled land. There's something different about the air. It doesn't smell like the ocean. It smells like earth."

"Oh come on. Your damn nose plays silly tricks on you."

I didn't argue. *Maybe he's right,* I thought. *Maybe I want to smell land so much my nose has manufactured its own perfume.* But I was edgy. My nose didn't usually fail me.

We ate supper. Freeze-dried noodles and chicken. Neither of us had much appetite. The noodles were a sticky mess. The chicken bits were chewy. I should have ignored the try at variety. The ready-mix mashed potato and bacon bits recipe seemed to hit the spot more than anything else.

After we'd eaten, Don went above to douse the working jib. The wind had increased to a light gale, and it was time to run with bare poles again.

"You get some rest," he told me. "I'll take the helm till you wake up."

I lay down on berth with the *Pilot*. I was exhausted, but the book fascinated me so much I kept thumbing through its pages to read sections about the area we were approaching. Compared to the dry American *Sailing Directions*, it was full of data on the climate, descriptions of the land, even observations made by vessels as far back as 1828—the first voyage of the *Beagle* under Captain Pringle Stokes. It held such an interesting combination of nautical directions and history that I couldn't put it down.

I studied the climatic table for the Evangelistas Islands off the Strait of Magellan. The number of cloudy days in the vicinity was over twenty-one for February; more than twenty-six for March. One sunny day a month seemed to be about normal—and we'd been issued our fill.

The band of dark clouds hanging over the eastern horizon still puzzled me. Were we headed for fog, or was I seeing rain squalls? I checked the index for fog and turned to chapter one. *Sea fog is not frequent in any part of the area covered by this volume, but the lowest clouds often lie only a few hundred feet above sea level and sometimes have their bases on the sea surface; the identification even of nearby landmarks may then become very difficult."* [4]

I couldn't sleep. I was nervous and kept wondering about conditions. The seas weren't normal. They were choppy, unlike anything we'd seen since the Roaring Forties, and there was something strange about the sky.

I got up to pump for the twelfth time in twelve hours, ruminating about the weather with each stroke. I pushed open the hatch cover and turned to look forward across the bow. The black band to the east was still there.

"That looks like fog ahead," I told Don. "But the *Pilot* says there's less than a 5 percent chance of sea fog at this time of the year."

"Don't be ridiculous. Do you believe everything you read? Just because you read that sea fog isn't frequent doesn't mean we won't encounter any."

"Dammit, Don. Something's weird ahead. I swear I smell land. *Stand up and take a look.*"

He stood up, reluctantly. "Oh Christ! You may be right. I think I see mountains. Weird shapes. Get the binocs quick, and the hand bearing compass."

I jumped off the ladder, pulled open the icebox, grabbed the glasses, and passed them up the hatch to Don. He looked across the bow, adjusting the binoculars.

"By God, it is land, babe! Wait . . . No. Maybe it's just layers of clouds . . . "

My chest pounded. *It's land,* I thought. *I know we're near land. I can smell it!*

"No," Don kept on. "I think those really are peaks. Gimme the compass. Write down the bearings as I read them. Hurry. It's almost dark."

I grabbed the logbook and scribbled: "074° to a possible islet. 076° to a mountain peak. 112° to the tip of a possible island. Land roughly from 080° to 100°. Possible entrance 108°. More land through 115°."

My hand trembled, and I could barely read my own numbers.

"Yeah. Yeah. I'm sure it's land. But it's hard to tell how far off we are. Things don't quite add up . . . You take the helm and keep a course due east. I'll check the chart and try to make sense of the bearings." He disappeared below.

Five minutes. Ten. An eternity. Then his head popped back up.

"Okay babe, I have a vague idea of where we might be. We'll have to stand off all night and see how it looks in the morning. We've got a lot to do and we'll have to stay alert. This is a different ballgame."

I didn't care what kind of ballgame it was or how much work we had to do. This was land. Land! After all we'd been through, I could do anything. No more horrid seas. Yes, we might have to abandon ship; but we'd survive on land. I knew we could.

The last glimmer of twilight faded in the west. Fog closed in from the east, and a long sleepless night began.

NOTES

1. p. 108

2. pp. 193, 198

3. p. 198, 199

4. p. 9

CHAPTER 10

Patagonia—the Lee Shore

MARCH 4, NIGHT

Discharging clouds and wind attacked us with horizontal sheets of flak, invisible against the blackness. Imperceptible except to our stinging faces. We raised the mizzen to give *le Dauphin* some stability, and hove to in the dark.

This was Golfo Trinidad. It had to be; I felt it in my gut. We had no proof, and Don would have sneered if I'd said, "I know this is it." But I had faith in his navigational abilities, his innate sense of reading the land.

It was a different ballgame, as he said—the most dangerous time since our accident: near-gale-force winds from the west, a lee shore—the most perilous of South America, perhaps of the world—and no engine. Phrases from the *Pilot* were imprinted on my brain: "A ridge [bar] extends across Golfo Trinidad, at the W entrance . . . [that] has not been thoroughly examined . . . rocks which lie nearly 3 miles offshore, numerous breakers extending 3 miles NW of Cabo Rugged. . . . Some rocks remain yet to be charted, uncharted islets, offshore reefs, heavy breaking surf . . . the sea sometimes breaks 4 miles from the land." No way to determine our position, the depth of the water; no tide or current tables; no way to maneuver quickly without an engine; no mainsail; crippled mizzen and staysail booms; and no detailed charts—just two small-scale charts for the entire Patagonia coastline.

"We may have to abandon ship, so think of everything we could use on shore. Anything to help us live like Robinson Crusoe. Get those things ready to load in the cockpit."

Don's warnings stabbed at my gut. This was a high-performance ballgame with lousy odds. Fear, shock, and euphoria simmered, each trying to overpower the other. Euphoria took command—we were in Golfo Trinidad; I knew it.

"Don't count on getting any sleep. We'll have to tack back and forth all night, and I'll need your help."

I was so exhausted I felt nauseated, but somehow I had to hold on.

"Another thing I want you to do is study the *Pilot* well. If we get a chance to enter Canal Trinidad in the morning, I'll rely on you to read

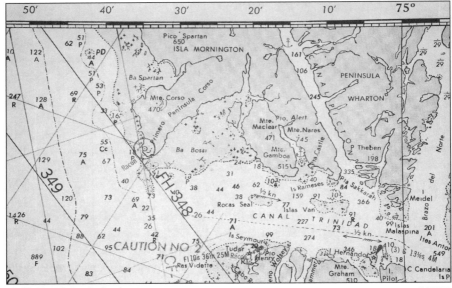

Golfo Trinidad—the lee shore   #22390

me those directions. Later tonight, when we've readied everything, we'll read the directions again and discuss strategy for the various scenarios. Okay?"

His voice raised in a question, but it was an *order* to understand. I nodded.

"Open the locker underneath our berth and untie the other two anchors. We'll need those big ones on the stern in case we have to kedge[1] off a reef. Don't try to move them by yourself, I'll do that. Then take the flashlight and get the spare coiled lines out of the lazaret. I need them as anchor rodes."

I removed the locker cover below our berth, lay on the sails, worked my head and shoulders into the space, and untied the nylon webbing. I climbed above, snapped my harness to the starboard lifeline, and felt my way along the cockpit to the lazaret.

Driving rain had diminished to heavy drizzle, and the beam of the flashlight bounced off the foggy blackness. I undid the lazaret latch and lifted the cover with what strength I had left. Bending into the opening, I spotted the anchor lines in the port corner. I was sure I could pull them out without crawling into the "dungeon." I reached over, my fanny pointing toward the sky and my torso at a forty-five-degree angle, grabbed one of the coiled lines, and pulled at it. Suddenly, a wave pounded across the port quarter, the boat jerked, the stern lifted, and the lazaret cover crashed down on my head. The pain was so intense, I thought I'd vomit. I collapsed on top of the lazaret cover and blacked out.

"What the hell's taking you so long?"

I groaned. "Please come here."

"Shine the light so I can see you."

"I can't. I need help."

"What's going on? What happened?" His hands groped for me as I explained. "Let me take off your cap and check your head."

"Oh, please don't touch it." I tried sitting up. Waves of nausea and vertigo swept over me. "Let me lie down again." I slid into the cockpit and lay on the bench. Supporting my neck with one hand, Don pulled my cap off with the other and palpated the back of my head. "Oh, God! Don't touch it."

"Sweetie, I've got to. I'll be careful . . . You've got a great big knob back here, and your hair's damp so I think the skin's broken. We'll have to watch it and make sure you're okay. Let me get you below so I can see what's going on."

Pain fanned into a burning ache. "I think I'll be okay. But I'm cold." My teeth chattered, and I had begun to shiver uncontrollably. "Can I go lie down?" *Shock,* I thought. "Get me below. I'm think I'm going to pass out again."

"Sweetheart, I hate to wake you . . ." Don rubbed my shoulders and arms gently. "But I need your help." He raised my eyelids. "I just want to check your eyes . . . Your pupils look normal. Boy, you really gave me a scare. You've been asleep for two hours. It's 2200 hours."

I raised myself on one arm. My whole body ached, and I couldn't tell which hurt most, my head, my joints, or my muscles. I stretched, trying to ease the tension, and sat up slowly. I touched the bump on my head. It was large and terribly tender, and I could feel a cut just above the base of my skull. My hair felt like dried shellac.

"Do you feel faint? Are you okay, sitting up like that?"

I felt weak, but the vertigo and nausea had passed. "Yeah. I think I'll be okay . . . What do you want me to do?"

A couple of snap shackles had dropped off the jib in the afternoon, and Don asked if I would sew them on now since we might need the jib in the morning.

The small nylon sewing bag and its contents were soggy. The needles were rusty, the rivets on the leather palm were corroding, and the leather was stiff. I pulled the sail up and spread it around my lap. Don had unhanked it and stuffed it down the front hatch while I was asleep. I wondered how he had managed alone and in the dark.

I finished the repairs, opened the hatch, and reported to the captain. "The jib's ready—I've stuffed it back in the forepeak."

Sail shackles have been dropping off like flies at the first sign of winter. The jib was new when we left California, but constant flapping on the luff slices the waxed twine like a scalpel. Just now, as I sat enveloped in yards of dirty sailcloth, grunting and straining to push the curved needle and twine through the heavy Dacron, I laughed, recalling the sewing lesson I gave Don after we left Easter Island. (He's a little more patient now that he understands what's involved in these jobs.) I recall, also, a night on our passage from Acapulco to Easter when I thought I heard hail and rushed on deck thinking I was out of my mind. What I heard were mainsail slides raining on deck. How many slides and shackles have I replaced in these past five months? Must be hundreds.

"I'm going to wear around now and head south," Don shouted. "We may be getting too far north."

Tudor Light at the tip of Isla Madre de Dios (Mother of God Island) north of Cabo Rugged was listed in the *Pilot*. If we could spot it we might be able to get a fix on our position.

The wind veered to the northwest and freshened, and gravelly drops pelted the doghouse roof. In a safe anchorage, I loved the sound of rain on the deck, but now it beat a primitive rhythm: *danger, no visibility, danger.*

We tacked back and forth, waiting for daylight and trying to spot Tudor Light. But nothing was visible. *Le Dauphin* was encased in black.

We wore around again and headed north. Short, nasty chop piled up preventing us from making headway. We rolled and wallowed, barely able to maintain steerage. Leaving the staysail up to steady the boat, Don doused the mizzen, lashed the helm, and came below.

"It's grim above. Blowing like hell. We'll heave to for a while so we can study the charts. I'd like you to reread about the anchorages inside Canal Trinidad." He unrolled the two charts and compared them. "Here, reroll this one. Chart 22390 shows the approach from the north better." We bent over the galley table and examined the chart. "I would guess we're somewhere near here." His index finger pointed to the opening of the channel inside 76° west. "See all these reefs and rocks?"

Even on this small-scale chart, numerous dangers were apparent. But as I tried to study it, fatigue overpowered me. Sinking into a stupor, I couldn't focus—the hypnotist conquered and sent me into a trance. The chart became an abstract watercolor painting: a shoal became a small bead of turquoise encircling the words "8 fathoms"; other words—"heavy swell," "breaks, "rocky"—were sprinkled among fine squiggles that resembled a Matisse pen-and-ink doodle; a blue amoeba, marked "Rocas Seal (5 ft.) (breaks heavily)," had ingested several black crosses and dots. *Five feet, five feet, five feet.* Something was trying to warn me.

I shook my head, took a breath, and tried to concentrate on the chart. "Five feet! Oh shit—the *recommended track* for entering the channel passes just inside those five-foot rocks and the eight-fathom shoal."

"You got the picture, babe! Now read what it says about the anchorage on the south shore."

We had already rejected Puerto Alert on the north side of Canal Trinidad. The anchorage was almost fourteen miles from the entrance, and too deep for a boat of our size. According to the *Pilot*, Puerto Henry, the first inlet east of Cabo Rugged, just inside Canal Trinidad, was "the only safe anchorage on the S shore of Canal Trinidad. . . . [but] exposed to squalls which blow with extreme violence in bad weather." Despite the foul weather and our inability to maneuver quickly, Puerto Henry was our only hope.

I read aloud from the *Pilot:*

Puerto Henry is entered between Islotes Seymour and Islote Low, the E islet of Islotes Arragón. . . . On its E shore, the white sand between Punta Maple, 4 cables SE, and Punta Parr, 4 1/2 cables SSE, respectively, of Islote Low, is also prominent; it is the first sandy beach seen on the E shore after entering the channel, and is backed by a low sandy cliff, with a round, rocky and wooded mound at its SW end. A good mark for a vessel off the entrance is Picos Organ Pipes, a sharply serrated ridge, 700 m (2,397 ft) high, 1 mile SSW of the head of Dársena Aid.[2]

Neither the Arragon Islets nor Puntas Maple and Parr appeared on the chart—the scale was too small. Just one of the Seymour Islets was marked. The only other markings were Tudor Light at the tip of Isla Madre de Dios and a series of crosses which indicated rocks, extending three-quarters of a mile northeast of the point.

"Hell, what's the length of a cable? Look it up, will you?"[3]

I fumbled through the *Pilot* looking for a glossary or notes on British terminology. Americans had dropped *cable* from their nautical vocabulary decades earlier. "I can't find a thing."

"Damn. How the hell can we figure out the distances if we don't know the length of a cable? Read it again."

I reread it, and we tried to visualize the layout of the area.

Nervous, Don opened the hatch periodically to look for a flashing light. "If only we could see Tudor Light, but there's nothing! It's pitch black. I

can't see any foam or detect any wave patterns. God, it's nerve-racking."
His thoughts kept spilling out. "Maybe we're too far north, near those
horrible rocks." He leaned over, stared at the chart again, and pointed.
"This shows foul ground three to four miles out from Cabo Primero." He
closed his eyes, trying to comprehend. "Christ, if we're too far south, we
may be caught in the Cape Horn current. We could be blown right on
by Canal Trinidad and Cabo Rugged." His eyes shot open.

He was thinking aloud and didn't need a response, but I nodded to let
him know I was listening.

"I wish I could tell what the tide's doing. If we're where I think we
are in Golfo Trinidad, trying to cross that bar in gale force winds could be
suicide. I wonder how good our last noon shot was." He groaned.
"Suppose we made a mistake in our calculations. I wonder if we've been
using the proper compass deviation." He stared through me. "I'm trying
to think of anything we might have missed. Any clue—any clue at all.
Maybe our minds are playing tricks on us. If we're near the entrance, why
the hell don't we see Tudor Light? The chart indicates it's visible for
eleven miles."

His thoughts played out, he climbed above to resume watch, leaving
me to gather up emergency gear—and make the cocoa he'd asked for half
an hour earlier.

I hadn't mentioned that the light at the west entrance to the Strait
wasn't functioning and maybe Tudor Light wasn't either.

MARCH 5

Don's head appeared through the hatch a while later. "We're starting to
get some light. Get out the life jackets, and put yours on right away. I'm
going to raise the mizzen and staysail and turn due east to have a look."

Blackness faded into a monotonous grey. Squalls blew horizontal
sheets of rain across the cabin top; spume blew off the waves. One
minute, zero visibility. The next minute the squall would pass, and an
opening in the clouds would tease us with a brief glimpse of land. Then
fog would close in again.

I stood on the ladder, staring without seeing. A short phrase from
Heart of Darkness flashed through my mind: "The sea and sky were weld-
ed together without a joint . . ." Conrad's bleak London sky could have
been the very tableau I was facing.

The wind dropped, and the curtain raised briefly again. "It's clearing!
I see land!" Don shouted. "Write down these bearings . . ."

I scribbled nervously, trying to catch all the details. "A high peak to
the north bears 345°; smaller twin peaks bear 035°; rugged cliff bearing
130°; land 135°. Rocks and a low spit between 300° and 335°, and a

small possible channel bearing 000°." I checked my watch; it read 0640. As Don came below to triangulate the bearings, I dashed above to take the helm and hold our course. The night had been so miserable I hadn't given much thought to what daylight would bring. It was gloomy and frightening. I was exhausted and would have made a pact with the devil for eight hours of sleep. But the word *land* burned in my brain like hot coal, refueling my furnace.

Don stuck his head out the companionway to report his calculations. "The bearings indicate we're in the middle of the entrance to Canal Trinidad, about six miles northwest of Cabo Rugged. Near the eight-fathom shoal. *If* our latitude is correct . . . I sure wish we could see Tudor Light to give us a positive check."

"Here comes another squall!" I yelled.

The wind slammed against the masts and booms. "We'd better douse the mizzen," Don said.

I reached forward with my left hand and uncleated the mizzen halyard, keeping my right hand on the wheel. The sail flapped wildly as it descended, and I glanced up at the crack in the mast, praying it would hold through all this violence.

Don tied down the mizzen and went forward to lower the staysail. His log entry afterwards read: "We're inside Canal Trinidad somewhere, lying ahull, bare poles. Visibility zero. Wind NW Force 7. Seas boiling. 35 strokes on the pump."

The squall passed east within thirty minutes, and Don climbed above again to raise the sails we'd just doused. We tacked back and forth for another twenty minutes holding our position as well as we could, then turned east to take another look, hoping the fog would lift again so we could see land.

Don wheeled the helm till the compass read 070°, and we headed in. Surf cracked against the port hull; waves heaped up, cresting, then breaking; foam shot 200 feet horizontally toward an invisible shore. We had turned too soon.

"Shit! We're over that reef!" he said, wheeling the helm around and pointing the bow southeast.

Le Dauphin seemed like a young badger, recently turned out on its own—sniffing the air, poking its nose into unknown water; jumping ashore in time to evade a wide-mouthed reptile waiting to snatch it; continuing on its way, testing, probing; each time venturing a little farther. Would it survive to see a second season?

"Maybe we should hold off farther out in open water," Don muttered. "So if we can't make it in here we can head south to the Strait or the Horn if we need to."

No, no, I prayed. *There's got to be a break in the weather. Please don't make me go back out there.*

0800. Don doused the mizzen and staysail; we lay ahull again to finish preparations in case there was a break in the weather.

"Let's get those stern anchors on deck. I want them ready to let go on a second's notice."

I wondered how could I muster the strength. *You don't have a choice, woman,* I told myself.

A frantic race began. Lift the anchors on deck; shackle the chain and coil onto the line; prepare the lead line. Pass the jib up the forward hatch; hank it to the forestay; run the sheets aft. Like prisoners preparing an escape, we couldn't rest, pause, or make an error. Despite arms like putty, heads aching, hands scratched and raw, rain stinging and smarting our faces, we continued our race.

Short, high seas built up as the wind increased again. *Le Dauphin* leapt from side to side. We raised the mizzen and staysail to stabilize her, and once more Don headed east. "We have to close the coast soon. In this weather we can't identify any landmarks from way out here."

He made a log entry at 1000 hours: "Wind NW, Force 8. Very rough seas. Spooky. Squalls hitting at full gale force. A grim scenario that keeps repeating and repeating itself." A minute later, the rain stopped, the fog lifted to a thirty-foot ceiling—and for the first time we had a brief glimpse of the south side of the channel. We were still two or three miles offshore, and nearing the reefs off Cabo Rugged.

We tacked north again. Grey mist descended over the land, hiding all the peaks, rocks, ridges, and islets. *Zero visibility.* My salivary glands shut down.

"Find me a pencil and paper and read about Puerto Henry again," Don said. "I'll make a crude map."

I dashed below, tore a plotting sheet in half, grabbed the *Pilot*, rushed back up to the cockpit, and reread the directions. Once, twice, three times I read them. Trying to visualize the features, Don made a sketch of Cabo Boleyn, the Seymour Islets, and the rocks and reefs listed.

I could have recited the details from memory. But to what good when we couldn't see any landmarks? We could have been smashed against the rocks while I reeled off the directions.

If we didn't get a break, we'd have to tack back and forth all day. Then what? The answer sank in my gut like a lead line: turn south and run toward Cape Horn or the Strait—*if* we can turn.

"Damn, I wish we knew how long a cable is," Don kept repeating. "How can I tell where the Arragon Islets are, and Punta Maple and Punta Parr? I can't put the puzzle together—I don't have enough information. Sooner or later we should get a view of something. Then I hope we can figure out where the hell we are."

As we huddled in the cockpit, Don studied the clouds and the action of the waves, and the streaks of foam blowing downwind. His head rotated like a radar antenna, searching the entire dull horizon. "The weather's probably a local phenomenon," he explained. "This seems to be a series of gale-strength squalls, not a major storm. Maybe this is as good as it ever gets." He tightened the hood on his foul weather jacket. "Get the jib up," he ordered.

"In this wind?"

"You heard me. We've got to test this bucket and see what she's capable of. I don't know how well she'll perform with no engine and just three small sails. We'll put a bone in her teeth and find out."

Clichés were sprouting. "Test this bucket." "Bone in her teeth." Captain had regained his passion. He was poised, like a jockey waiting for the gun to go off, to push his filly for all she was worth.

The jib filled, and *le Dauphin* shot to the north with a fury. "Tighten the sheets!" Don yelled, pointing the boat higher and higher into the wind. I raced back to the cockpit and cranked on the jib winch.

"Tighten the mizzen now!" *Le Dauphin* heeled to starboard, knifing through the choppy seas with a clean edge. "We're doing hull speed— look at her!"

I moved to the high side of the cockpit and planted my feet against the starboard bench.

"No! No! Stay by the jib winch so you can tighten the sheet some more. I want to see how high she can point." His cheeks flushed, he looked better than he had for hours—like a jockey bringing his winning horse down the home stretch.

"You love this, don't you?"

"Yeah. It feels good to be sailing," he shouted above the wind. "To find the limits of this broken rig. This is the edge, babe, and it may be the finest sailing I've ever done in my life."

The edge, I thought. *He loves it. But he's not doing it now for love of risk or to test how far or how fast we can go—he's doing it because he has to.*

Layers of fog alternated—sometimes heavy, dark, and undulating, hiding the entrance to Canal Trinidad; other times, like chiffon curtains billowing against the north shore, giving us fleeting glimpses of the off-lying dangers.

"Tighten the sheet all the way," Don ordered. "I'm going to point higher and see what kind of heading we can maintain." *Le Dauphin* heeled menacingly; the rail was awash. I jammed my legs under the starboard bench to keep from falling over. "It looks like 010° true is all we can hold. We lose ground on each tack."

I heard pots crashing onto the galley floor and could feel the thumping of the gimballed table resonating through the hull. We were carrying too much sail for these conditions.

"Here we go!" Don hollered. "The test." He put the helm to port to bring us into the wind and the bow crashed into the waves. *Le Dauphin* slowed and stalled out. "Damn! We can't come about. Ease the sheets. We'll try again."

As we gained momentum I tightened the jib sheet. Don brought the helm hard over again. The bow wouldn't come within 20 degrees of the wind.

He clenched his teeth. "One more try. This time we'll start with greater speed and fall off to a broad reach. When we attain hull speed, I'll start a turn to port again. Not too fast, not too slow. Keep maximum tension on that sheet. When we come into the wind, draw it in. The moment we approach the eye of the wind, you take the helm and I'll run forward to backwind the staysail. We'll see if we can force the bow over. Timing is critical. We're too near shore to mess around."

We'd been working well together, and I could tell Don was pleased.

"Without a mainsail to drive us to windward, she may not come around at all . . . Take her!"

Don slid from the helm, ran forward, uncleated the staysail sheet, and pushed the damaged boom out to starboard as quickly and carefully as he could. I put the helm hard over to port. *Le Dauphin* slowed, the mizzen started to luff, but we still couldn't bring her into the wind—the backwinded staysail wasn't enough. She wouldn't come about, and we were too close to the north shore to try again.

Out of breath and red-faced, Don came aft yelling, "Fucking boat! Helm hard to starboard! We've got to wear around. Quick! We'll get caught in irons. Stand by the sheets."

I had the helm hard to port. How the hell was I supposed to turn the wheel and manage the sheets at the same time?

"Move! I'll take the helm," he said, reading my face.

Regaining steerage, we began a controlled jibe directly downwind toward the lee shore. Carefully, Don brought the stern through the eye of the wind, ducking his head while he nursed the damaged mizzen boom to port. I let out the starboard jib sheet and took in on the port sheet. The staysail boom flapped wildly but held. I flopped on the cockpit bench, exhausted.

Don kept glancing over the stern, then back at the compass. "Hell— 165 degrees is all we can do! And we lost a good 300 yards to leeward with that maneuver." He went on in his engineering voice. "We're dealing with two really bad limits. This baby won't sail against the wind, and we can't come about."

We had pushed the mare as far as she could go, but like the old square-riggers, without an engine she would sail downwind only. "We're lucky we didn't get caught in irons back there—you did a great job on the winch and the helm!"

I was giving it everything I had and was totally wiped out. It was heartening to have a compliment.

"She wanted to sail," Don continued, dejected. "But she's just too damaged. She's like us, she doesn't have much more to give . . . Anything downwind—any rock, islet, reef, or shoal—is a danger. Without the drive of the mainsail, we simply can't claw our way off anything . . . And if we have to change tack"—he paused—"we'll be heading directly downwind. Since the radius of our turn is nearly a quarter of a mile, we'll hit anything within 1,000 feet to leeward!"

I swallowed. *1,000 foot radius!* We couldn't even see that far downwind most of the time!

"Before we commit to heading in," Don said gently, "I want you to know how proud I am of you. We've accomplished a lot together." He continued, "We don't know what lies ahead. We have to steel ourselves against panic—we can't give in. As long as there's one second remaining to do something, we have to do it right. We have only *one* chance. Do you understand?"

I nodded.

"Okay. Listen to me. I'll stay at the helm. You go to the end of the bowsprit and point to any obstacles you see. Keep pointing until I yell okay. If worse comes to worst, I'll sail this hulk right up onto a beach—if we can find one. If it looks like we have to beach her, jump and swim for shore when I give you the order. But only when I say so. Get out of the surf as fast as you can. I'll follow with whatever gear I can muster."

1100 hours. The fog ahead lifted slightly, and I could make out a rough coastline to the south. "Is that Cabo Rugged?" I asked.

"I think it might be." The wind decreased and we tightened the sheets to pick up speed. "If that *is* Cabo Rugged, this is our last chance to head in. We're too close to the breakers to mess around any longer. You realize the hazards, don't you? There's no turning back once we start in. Do you want to give it a try?"

I knew the hazards. For the past twenty-four hours they had pounded in my brain, like the waves against the hull. Did he want me to recite them? *No depth sounder. Inadequate charts. Unmarked dangers. Rocks and reefs. Numerous breakers. No engine. No way to come about or maneuver quickly. The boat could be smashed to pieces. We could be flung on the rocks and crushed or drowned. No one would ever know what happened.*

"We have to," I said. "It's our only chance." It was this, or the 150 miles of open sea to the Strait of Magellan.

"Okay. You go to the bow now and watch for rocks and breaking surf. If you see anything that looks dangerous, *anything*, yell. And keep pointing. Don't assume I've seen the hazard. Understand?"

"Yes, Captain, I understand." I leaned over, kissed him, and whispered, "I love you."

I went forward, knelt on the bowsprit, and clung to the stanchion without snapping my safety harness to the lifeline. I had to be ready to move fast. I untied my life vest, pulled the straps as tight as I could, and retied them. An inch of kapok encased me. If I had to jump and swim, that one inch could add five minutes before hypothermia got me.

Le Dauphin wore around, and we headed downwind. I strained to see. Foam and breaking crests flew across the water and shot into the air. Was I seeing whitecaps or rocks? I couldn't tell.

This is it, I thought. *The final commitment.*

I saw a line of solid white foam between some rocks—were those reefs? A cape came into view—a headland fronted with rocks and islets that jutted into the foaming surf.

"Tudor Light!" I screamed, pointing at a rusty, antique structure—the light wasn't functioning, but it identified Cabo Boleyn.

"Can you identify any of those islands?"

The wind carried Don's yell forward, but I couldn't give him an answer. Nothing made sense. Arragon Islets, Seymour Islets, Low Islet. All of them were low-lying. *Which is which, for godssake?* I turned around quickly to give him the shrug sign.

Something about him struck me as I saw him standing beside the helm, barely touching it, his sensors receiving all stimuli. A memory flashed—the first time I'd driven his jeep. "You've got the mark of a good driver," he said. "A light touch on the steering wheel." *He has the mark of a good navigator,* I thought now. *My God, he is a good navigator!*

The swells began to smooth, the chop lessened, and the fog lifted slightly. Conditions were changing. Had the tide turned? Had we crossed the bar?

"Keep looking! Does it make any sense to you?"

"I can't tell," I yelled.

We were skirting the southern shore of Trinidad, just close enough to keep it in sight. *God! If we could just get a glimpse of Picos Organ Pipes,* I thought, *we could identify the entrance to Puerto Henry.*

Don came forward momentarily to the main mast and uncleated the jib halyard. I reached over my head, yanked the jib down the forestay, gathered it in, and put one foot on its head to keep it from blowing overboard. I couldn't risk taking my eyes off the water to tie it down.

With the jib dropped, the boat slowed. "Do you see any signs of a reef or a shoal to starboard?"

"No!" I shouted back. There was a lot of foam, but I couldn't see any reefs or shoals.

"We may be inside that first line of reefs and islets. Do you see any kind of bay to the south?"

"Yeah." I pointed. "It looks protected in there."

"That may be Puerto Henry. I'm going to turn right and head farther in."

The swells had gradually disappeared. The water was calm now. The boat glided gently, and I was able to stand up.

"Don't worry if we pass some rocks close to starboard; I want to keep as much room between us and the lee shore as possible."

I nodded okay.

"Do you think those are the Seymour Islets to port?" It was so quiet Don didn't have to holler.

But I didn't answer. I was overcome by the odor of damp earth, by the sight of green, by the silence. We had entered a sanctuary, dark and mysterious, of breathtaking beauty. Flat-topped, wind-crippled cypress, long tufts of golden grasses, ferns, and bushes with tiny white flowers grew to the very edge of the water. It was so beautiful, my eyes filled with tears.

This must be Puerto Henry, I thought. But nothing made sense yet. I couldn't see the landmarks—a white beach or a low, sandy cliff with a round, rocky, wooded mound. There were mountains to the south, but fog enshrouded their peaks.

The wind dropped to nothing, and *le Dauphin* moved silently through the water, the mizzen and staysail barely drawing her forward. We continued toward a small island. The channel on either side had narrowed, and Don was steering a slow zigzag course. *He's doing that to avoid dangers,* I thought.

"Is it clear ahead? Do you see anything underwater?"

I hated to answer. To break the silence. "No, it's clear as far as I can see. Where do you think the anchorage is?"

"I don't know. We may have passed it."

Suddenly a second channel, no wider than a hundred feet, opened to the southwest. Gulls—thirty, forty, fifty—sat in neat equidistant lines—

facing into the north wind like a squadron of fighter planes ready for takeoff. They parted lines, lazily, to let us pass through, as if the sight of a sailboat were an everyday occurrence. We glided on through the channel, the land so close I wanted to reach out and touch it. To touch the earth, the trees, the grass, the tiny flowers.

A magical current seemed to be carrying us in; we couldn't stop. Hypnotized by the silence, by the beauty, neither of us spoke. The channel opened into a narrow basin, rimmed on its western shore by a sheer granite wall, and on the south by steep grassy slopes. A long, gently contoured island guarded the eastern side of the basin. We were in a landlocked basin!

"This must be Dársena Aid," I said, recalling the information in the *Pilot:* "Dársena Aid [Aid Basin], at the head of Puerto Henry, is completely landlocked and only accessible to small vessels. . . . There is little to be gained by entering, as it is impossible to judge the weather outside; it often rains heavily here when it is fine and clear in Puerto Henry."

"We've passed Puerto Henry," Don said. I didn't care that we'd passed the recommended anchorage, or that it was impossible to judge the weather outside. All I cared about was finding a place to anchor. To rest, recuperate, regain our strength. God, how I longed for sleep!

"Réanne! Come back and take the helm."

I jumped, thinking I'd done something wrong; Don rarely used my name unless he was angry.

"We'll drop anchor here."

"Shall I tie off the jib first?"

"No, leave it for now. Hurry!"

I stood beside the wheel and waited for orders. "I'll drop the staysail," he said, "then hand-maneuver the mizzen, and try to get us facing into the wind so we can drop anchor. As soon as I'm ready you put the helm hard over to port.—Now!" he shouted as he ran forward to drop the CQR.

Metal and chain clanked and grated over the bow into the water, then the anchor line paid out. I watched Don wrap a loop of line around the Samson post, while he waited for the wind to blow us back so the anchor could grab. He turned his head constantly, watching and checking, before he let out more line. So assured earlier, now he looked like an animal that had been stalked for weeks, not knowing which way to turn or which way to run. His adrenaline seemed to have run out, and I noticed how gaunt he looked.

A gust of wind shrieked across the spit at the north end of the basin, blowing streamers of spray along the top of the water as it headed toward us. The calm had been short-lived. The squalls had resumed.

The boat backed down, and the anchor grabbed. Don let out more line, took a loop around the Samson post, and the boat jerked to a stop.

"Halleluia! It's set."

"Hurray!" I shouted back.

I glanced to starboard to take a bearing and screamed. The boat had come to rest twenty feet from the eastern island. Six feet from the starboard quarter there were three huge jagged rocks. *We made it this far. Now we're going to lose it on those rocks.*

Don ran back to the cockpit, raised the mizzen, and pushed the boom to port. *Le Dauphin* turned west, toward the granite wall. The stern backed toward the rocky shore.

"Take the helm. We'll have to sail off the anchor!"

He's crazy, I thought. *We'll never be able to sail off the anchor!*

"Sailing off the anchor" meant using the wind to maneuver the boat and help retrieve the anchor. Since the bow tethered into the wind, we had to sail over the anchor by tacking back and forth, using the momentum of the boat to break the anchor loose. Sure, we'd done it dozens of times before—California, Mexico, even Easter Island—but under better conditions. "Sailing off the anchor is the ultimate test of seamanship" was one of Don's favorite sayings. He prided himself in testing the boat in tight, tiny coves, under almost impossible conditions—at times, even with a bad lee shore—while the boys and I would roll our eyes at each other. And he had always pulled it off. But then we had an engine we could start in an emergency.

We didn't have a choice now. It was sail off the anchor—or *le Dauphin* on the rocks.

"Get with it!" Don screamed. "Helm hard to port. Let go the starboard jib sheet. Get to the . . ." His commands trailed away in the wind, and he motioned me angrily to the foredeck. "Didn't you hear me yelling, dammit? We've gotta get this anchor up and get out of here. Raise the jib, quick!"

Nervous and shaken, I ran to the starboard side of the main mast and uncleated the main halyard.

"What the hell are you doing? The jib halyard, you idiot!"

I felt as if a plug had opened in my brain and my memory had drained out. What the hell *was* I doing? Instantly I stepped around to the port side of the mast, uncleated the jib halyard, and pulled.

"Come here and hold the anchor rode tight around the Samson post while I push out the jib. We'll see if we can make this baby fall off to port."

I squatted by the Samson post to make sure the anchor rode didn't give way while Don was pushing the jib out. The bow began to fall off.

"Get behind me and pull. We've got to pull in as much scope as possible . . . Pull when the wind stops—rest when it blows. D'you understand?

"Now! Pull, dammit, pull!" he hollered.

I wanted to scream, *I can't! My arms are coming out of their sockets.* But I pulled harder.

Short thirty-second blasts of wind and sleet blinded us to everything except the rhythm of "pull, rest, pull, rest." Twenty tons of boat against wind and current, until we'd hauled in more than a hundred feet of line.

"Here comes another gust!" Don said, looping the line around the Samson post. "Push the staysail boom to starboard!" I did as I was told while he leaned into the jib, trying to get it backwinded. We had just one chance, and he didn't need to tell me. If the boat backed down any more, we'd be aground on those three rocks in less than two minutes.

The bow began drifting to port, slowly coming through the eye of the wind.

"Go back to the cockpit," Don yelled. "Stand by the jib sheet and make sure the helm is hard over." He stood on the bowsprit until the jib was backwinded. "Clear the starboard sheet, then winch in on the port sheet."

The jib began to draw, and *le Dauphin* slowly gained way to the west. I winched in the jib sheet, sheeted the mizzen, and straightened the helm. Don handed in anchor line as fast as he could. We were sailing! When we were directly downwind of the anchor, he threw three loops around the Samson post, wedged his back against the main mast for support, and yelled, "Hang on!" The anchor line snapped tight; the bow buckled to starboard like a filly on her knees, then raised.

"The anchor broke loose! Tighten the sheets and let's get the hell away from these rocks!"

"Do you want help getting the anchor up?" I yelled.

"No. We'll just drag it."

The jib filled, and the boat headed toward the western shore, picking up speed with each gust.

"Let out the jib sheet," Don yelled. "Slow this baby down."

White seasmoke rushed across the basin. *My God,* I thought as a gust hit, *it must be blowing 50 to 60 knots!* The boat heeled to port, and we shot straight toward the granite wall on the western shore.

Don began paying out anchor line so fast I knew he'd have rope burns. "Release the jib sheet. Put the helm hard to starboard. We've got to give the hook a chance to catch."

"Please let it hold," I shouted to the wind as we raced toward the granite face.

"It's biting!" Don shouted. He continued to let out line, and the boat headed slightly into the wind, the wall just a hundred feet from our port beam.

"We're going to hit!" I screamed.

"No, no! It's okay. But I can't snub the line yet. The anchor might pull out." The boat slowed, stopped just short of the wall, and began to drift slowly downwind. Don came aft.

"My God, that was close!" I said.

"Yeah, it took a long time to set the anchor. It must be deeper than hell here."

"This isn't much better than the rocky side—we're less than a boat's length from the wall."

"Yeah, but as long as the wind comes from the northwest we're okay. Besides, do you want to try and sail off anchor again?" He sat down for a minute and spread his palms out on his thighs. His hands looked like raw sausages. They were swollen, cracked, and ready to pop open. "When the next gust hits, see if you can line up a feature on the wall and tell if the anchor's dragging or not."

I spotted ferns spilling out of a ledge on the vertical face and lined them up with the main boom gallows.

"Get ready," he said. "Here comes another gust!"

I kept my eye on the ledge across from the boom gallows. The anchor seemed to be holding.

"Can we go below now and get some rest?" I asked.

"Are you kidding? We've got to prepare for evacuation!"

"Oh God. Can't we go below and rest just for a while?"

Don's face turned red instantly, his nostrils flared, and his eyes bore into me. I'd said the wrong thing, waved a red flag. "Oh for christsake, you're not thinking!" His chest ballooned, his lips parted in a sarcastic grin. "We might still end up on the rocks."

The delivery was so caustic, it seemed to have been fermenting for months. I knew how exhausted he was, how much he'd been taxed. He was at the end of his rope, but I was exhausted, too, and I didn't deserve this. The knob on my head was throbbing. What I wanted to hear was, "Well done!" A hug would have been wonderful.

I climbed below trying desperately to control my tears. I grabbed every piece of dry clothing I could find to stuff in the emergency duffels, then anger and self-pity tore down the dam, and I broke into sobs. Tugging and jerking at the genoa bag lying in the salon, I dragged it inch by inch aft to the ladder. "Goddamn ladder," I muttered between sobs. "How'm I gonna get this damn sail up that thing at that angle?" Anger fed my muscles. Step by step I pushed the bag up, until I could get my head underneath it and shove it the rest of the way out the hatch.

Rain was falling in torrents. Don had dropped his two sweaters and jacket on deck, and they were already soaked. I thought, *Maybe he's getting hypothermic*—but at that moment I was too angry to care. I turned around, kicked the genoa bag into the cockpit, and felt immediately ashamed, as if I'd kicked the family dog. The genoa had been our faithful mattress for so long.

I talked to myself: "Keep your morale up. Don't let Don's remarks get you down. He's feeling as bad as you are. Keep a good attitude." The more I talked to myself, the more I sobbed. Barely able to see through my tears, I kept searching and grabbing—for anything, anything we could use if we had to abandon ship. *The other sails,* I thought. *I've got to get those on deck. We can use them for shelter.*

I opened the forward hatch, lifted one of the twin headsails onto the workbench, climbed out, and pulled the bag up, kicking it along the deck and into the cockpit. I repeated the steps with the second sail, kicking it into the cockpit as if it had attacked me. *Good Lord, what's happening to you, Réanne? Get hold of yourself!* I was becoming a mess, mentally and physically. *Pull yourself together, for godssake.*

Don lifted himself out of the lazaret where he'd been unloading spare lines, water, and kerosene jugs. I turned my face so he couldn't see it and climbed below. Leaning over the sink, I held the faucet extension tube against my face and pumped with my foot. The cold saltwater took my breath away. I stood up and wiped my hand across my face and over my eyes. The salt from the water and my tears stung. I stopped crying, took a long breath, and snapped at myself, *That's enough!*

I lay on my belly, reached into the locker under Carl's berth, and pulled out the three ammo boxes that contained our cameras, ship's papers, batteries, and matches, then I wiggled my way back out of the narrow space.

I dragged the plastic food containers up the ladder to the cockpit. I filled damp stuff sacks with canned foods whose labels had disappeared into the bilge. I added packets of freeze-dried foods that could be mixed with cold water. Everything went up the ladder into the cockpit ready to throw onto the rocks at the first crash.

"Watch this one." Don nodded to windward. "Here comes another williwaw." He headed to the foredeck to check the anchor line.

Froth steamed toward us, and the wind slammed across the boat. *Le Dauphin* rocked and yielded a few yards. I jumped up on the doghouse, stood by the main boom gallows, and lined up the ledge. We hadn't changed position. The nylon anchor line stretched and held. Then the wind let up as quickly as it had come, and the boat pulled forward a few yards.

"Good news!" Don shot me a weak smile, his peace offering. "The boat stayed feathered into the wind, like those low bushes and cypress on shore. We haven't moved an inch closer to that wall. As long as the prevailing wind blows parallel to the wall, the anchor should hold. If the wind shifts to the east or south, we'll be in trouble." Slowly, almost inaudibly, he said, "We've got to get some sleep now. We'll do more later." He collapsed on top of a sail in the cockpit and looked straight through me, his face white. He was totally spent. He'd gotten us to land, and now his systems were shutting down.

I looked across at the wall, where a stream of water was trickling over the ferns. Everything was mottled grey and exquisitely green.

I pulled at his sleeve, "You got us here, Captain. You promised me you would, and it's so beautiful I could cry. Come on. Let's go below and have some cocoa." I reached for his hands to pull him up. He winced and I saw with horror how bloody his fingers were.

He pulled himself up, put one arm around me, and balanced against the mizzen mast with his other. "We did a great job together, sweetheart. I couldn't have done it alone. You're a good partner."

NOTES

1. Kedge is a maneuver that involves dropping an anchor, letting it go, then winching the boat in to the anchor.

2. p. 196

3. A cable equals 600 feet.

CHAPTER 11

Dársena Aid

MARCH 5 (?), EVENING
To sleep. To be able to sleep more than an hour or two. To sleep without having to worry about being slammed against the bulkhead or thrown out of the berth. That was all I could think of as we lay down fully clothed on our damp mattress and covered ourselves with the sleeping bag. But as desperately as I longed for sleep, craved it, it wouldn't come.

Don fell asleep immediately, but he turned frequently, groaning with pain each time he did. His body consumed the entire space, and I couldn't stretch out. Our berth (a nautical double) measured forty-three inches wide at the head, thirty-six at the foot. In a conventional double bed, lying shoulder to shoulder on our backs, our combined torsos mea-

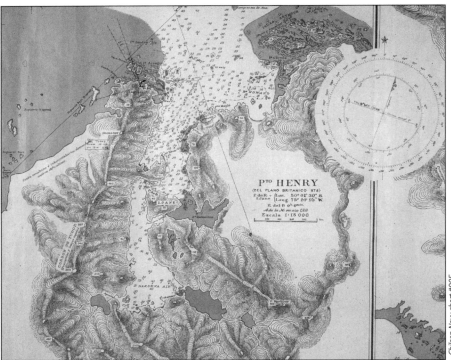

Puerto Henry and Dársena Aid, anchor site was along west shore across from Isla Jane.

Chilean Navy chart #905

sured forty-eight inches across. In the berth, snuggling usually made up for lack of space. But tonight, with Don sprawled flat on his back, I had to sleep on my side like a two-by-four, my knees bent and hanging out over the edge of the berth. In this awkward position, I couldn't relieve the aching in my joints enough to relax, but I didn't want to nudge Don. He needed his sleep too badly, and whenever I bumped him he moaned.

Finally, I slipped down from our berth and climbed up on the pilot berth on the other side. I lay on my stomach and joined my hands behind my back, stretching and arching my body to release tension. I turned over and began relaxation therapy—tensing, then relaxing each muscle, from my toes up to my head. But my mind refused to relax.

Every noise, every motion made me tense—the tick, tick, tick of the main halyard against the mast, the howl of the wind in the rigging, reverberations of the mast, the creak of the anchor rode as it tugged against the Samson post and rubbed across the bowsprit; the blitzing rain on the doghouse roof, the slap of windwaves against the bow, and awkward jerkings of the boat. My mind was filled with questions: Would the anchor hold? Would we be able to abandon ship in the dark if we had to? How could we set up camp on a shore with an incline of forty-five degrees? I couldn't relax; it was useless to try.

I stared out the porthole. It was only 1740 hours and still light. The granite face stared back. *Oh, my God. We're going to hit!* I thought.

I grabbed my foul weather jacket, jamming my arms into the sleeves as I raced up the ladder. Sleet coated the deck, and the wind hit with such force I had to crouch to keep my balance. I shuffled forward, grasping the lifeline. Was this another full-blown storm from outside? Or were these the williwaws we'd read about—the cold, violent, short-lived winds that sweep down the mountains at velocities of 100 knots or more?

The anchor line was as taut as a violin string. I knelt, wondering if I should wake Don. We had 400 feet of line out; 200 more to go. With so much force on the line, the anchor was sure to drag.

My answer came with a shove.

"Move, dammit!"

Startled, I screamed.

"See how close to the cliff we are!" Don said angrily.

What the hell did he think I was doing? I thought. *I can't believe it—he's like a crazy man.*

He bent over to test the line, straightened up, and looked in all directions to check our position. A short calm between gusts gave momentary relief to the tension on the line. The anchor didn't appear to have dragged. It was okay for now.

"If the anchor rode chafes through, or the anchor breaks loose, we'll ricochet down the side of this cliff and land on the rocks at the end of the basin," he said. "We may need the yachtsman anchor before long." He told me to get the lead line and test for depth.

I dropped the lead line over the stern. As the line sank into the water, I counted the knots. Each one indicated a fathom (6 feet). At the tenth knot—the bitter end—the lead still hadn't touched.

"Damn, it's deep! No way we could wade ashore here," he said.

Wet and shivering, we went below. "Please come back to bed with me," Don begged. "I want to hold you." He reminded me of a nursing baby. One minute, angrily pushing his mother away; the next, clinging to her tit for all he was worth.

I couldn't flip-flop emotionally the way he did, and climbed back in the berth with him reluctantly. As my body warmed his, he relaxed, spread out, and began to snore. Forced back into the two-by-four slot, I slipped down and crossed again to the pilot berth. I covered myself with an army blanket, closed my eyes, and tried to sleep.

But my mind wrote lists: honey, powdered milk, nuts, deviled ham, raisins, cocoa, meat bars—items I wanted to add to the abandon-ship bags; Mother and Daddy's last letter to Easter Island; Sean's letter. A momentary twinge of self-pity shot through me. We hadn't received any mail in Rapa Nui from the other kids. I hadn't heard from my older son, Chris, for over four months. *They don't care,* I thought. I threw off the blanket and slid down. *Nonsense! Quit feeling sorry for yourself. They're just normal teenagers.*

I lit the kerosene lamp next to our berth and the Optimus tied above the galley table. It would be dark soon, and the heat would feel good.

I opened the top of the icebox and took out the binoculars, sextant box, and hand-bearing compass. I set them on the galley table, ready for off-loading. I knelt, opened the center section of the locker, inserted my left shoulder into the opening. Stretching my arm as far I could, I managed to pull out the remaining packages of dried foods. I wrote myself a reminder to remove the meat and chocolate bars I'd put in the abandon-ship locker.

Two weird souvenirs I had found in the bilge went into my abandon-ship pile also; they were treasures I couldn't bear to part with. Before he left Acapulco, Jeff had given us a little gag gift—a rubber statuette of two children leaning against a tree. A little girl with her eyes closed was planting a firm kiss on a boy's cheek; his round black eyes were opened wide, and a smile covered half his face. The base of the statuette was inscribed, *We Need Each Other.*

The second treasure, a gift from a student of mine, was a small, hand-carved, wooden gnome with a pointed head, ears of a fox, a single white tooth, and piercing green eyes. I could barely pronounce his name, *Knorgolwoggle*, but he delighted me. Intricately carved, he looked like he'd come straight out of an underground hideaway in the Black Forest. "If you carry this with you," my student had promised, "you'll never have bad luck." And so far the little creature had done his trick. Although bilge water had discolored his features, his iridescent eyes still glowed.

I climbed back onto the pilot berth. But it was no good; my mind filled again. I got up and wrote:

> *Where would we be now if we hadn't pitchpoled? Somewhere in the South Atlantic between the Falkland Islands and Tristan da Cunha? Or maybe still in the Falklands? We were due to be in Madagascar in July—I think about Elise, how I would have loved to see her. Instead, we'll continue to correspond as we've done since our student days in Grenoble. Such faraway dreams, these islands seem now. It's strange, but aside from not seeing Elise and meeting her children and husband, I don't feel any regret. My disappointment is abstract, intellectual. The only thing I feel now is the will to survive and see my family again. Dear God, just don't let them give up hope for us.*

The sky darkened. Although the rain let up, the wind still howled, the granite cliff still hovered above our port rail. I put my pad of paper under the mattress, climbed back onto the pilot berth wondering if I should check the anchor line again, and fell asleep.

> *I'm walking through store after store searching for warm pants and heavy shoes. I paw through racks full of cotton dresses, cotton skirts, cotton pants. There isn't a single item of wool in any store. "I want something warm!" I scream at the top of my lungs. A sneering clerk tells me, "Don't be ridiculous. You can't buy wool in California." As I continue wandering, I bump into acquaintances who tells me I don't need to worry. "We'll notify the authorities. You won't have any problems."*

A low roar and the mast vibrating awakened me. I lay still for a moment trying to interpret the sound. Was it a jet overhead? Could it be searching for us? Then I realized it was the sound of the wind in the rigging.

I thought about the dream. Such simple answers occurred during sleep—*You won't have any problems.* I hoped my subconscious was right.

My conscious mind took over again, remembering a watertight container of alfalfa seeds stowed in the icebox. *The wire shelf in the oven—that will come in handy, too, as a fire grill.* I got up and set them both near the ladder.

Before climbing back on the pilot berth, I patted Don's back gently. "I love you, sweetheart."

He stirred and moaned, "Hmm."

MARCH 6 (?), MORNING

My Seiko read 1000 hours. Don had slept over sixteen hours. I had slept twelve. I turned on my side and looked across at him. He was awake, staring at the ceiling.

"How do you feel?" I asked.

"I think every single bone in my body aches. And my hands tingle— they keep falling asleep—and I can barely bend my fingers. I think I may have broken a rib, too . . ." Then he looked at me penetratingly. "How come you didn't sleep with me?"

His question made me laugh. It was typical of him to gloss over his aches and pains and ask why I hadn't slept with him. I suggested he rest all day and let me keep an eye on things above.

"Good idea. But you need your rest, too."

I would rest, also, when my mind let me. But for now it was impossible—there was still too much to prepare in case we had to abandon ship.

"Okay, you go through the food stores. But first let me get up and build a fire so we can begin drying this cabin out—then I'll go back to bed."

His spirits were up. He'd hit bottom the night before, and I admired his ability to bounce back.

I had been having desert-island fantasies ever since we got to Dársena Aid. Playing Robinson Crusoe was my favorite game as a child. One summer at our cottage on Lake Michigan I appropriated a wooden shipping crate that had held a new refrigerator and I set up camp in our backyard. I nailed an old blanket over the crate and stocked it with emergency gear I'd need to survive on my "island." My father, a tidy man, disliked having a shack on the property, and when can openers, spoons, plates, and bowls began to disappear from the kitchen, as well as screwdrivers, pliers, rope, and inner tubes from the garage, he decreed that the crate had to go. I was crushed. He promised to build me a bunkhouse by the water where I could sleep and play "for real," but it was never as much fun as the hut I had built with my own hands.

I was sure we could survive in Dársena Aid if we had to winter on shore. I could probably make our remaining food supplies stretch; we could use the sails for shelter; we had a small hatchet with which we could clear brush. But Don refused to let me become overly optimistic.

Evacuating the boat is no game, as Don keeps reminding me. However, the idea of trying to survive on a muskeg hillside is far more appealing to me than spending one more day on the Southern Ocean. On land, I know how to take care of myself. "Out there" I'm totally dependent on him, the boat, and dreadful unknown forces.

Insisting that I don't understand the realities we would face on shore, Don went on and on about how I'm not thinking clearly: that if the boat were thrust against the cliff, the hull could be pierced or crushed; that there's no beach here; that we might not have time to get all the essential stuff out of the cockpit, let alone out of the rest of the boat; that because it's over sixty feet deep here the boat could sink in place, just settle down, and we wouldn't even see the top of the mast; that it won't be a helluva lot of fun if we can't find wood for a fire; that Robinson Crusoe was in a much warmer climate than we are; ad infinitum. I felt the way I did when Daddy tore my hut down. Hell, maybe I don't understand all of what's involved here, but he could give me a chance to prove myself. I stopped him when I asked, "Did you understand the realities of sailing down here when you planned this trip?"

With the wood fire, the kerosene lamps, and a steady flame under a pot of Dinty Moore stew, the cabin was toasty. And we actually had fun. We pretended the boat was a northwoods cabin where we were waiting out a raging winter storm; if our "logs" held out, and the cabin stayed anchored to its foundation, we'd pull through.

The storm had continued relentlessly throughout the night, and rain found every crevice in the boat. It seeped through the salon hatch, then down the bulkheads in the salon; through the deck seams into the galley, the quarter berths, and the forepeak. I gave up trying to catch the drips. The fresh rainwater would rinse away the salt; it might even wash the mattresses and cushions we'd set out on the doghouse roof.

Our clothes began to dry from the heat in the cabin, and we had to open the ports for air. What a difference it made to be anchored near land; for a change, we were warm.

The granite wall thirty feet from the port rail, the intensity of the wind, the whine of the anchor rode tugging, the bouncing of the boat as shallow, choppy waves hit the bow were all reminders of looming dangers. But as long as the anchor held, pressure to evacuate seemed remote in my mind.

Don crouched down and pumped the bilge. "What's the date today?"

I couldn't remember. Although each page in the logbook was dated, we didn't know if we'd missed a day. We had lost track of time. We sat at the galley table, with rain dripping on our shoulders, and checked the log page by page, trying to verify the date. We figured it was March 6.

"We were supposed to show up in Punta Arenas in four more days. Do you think anyone's notified the authorities yet?"

Don shrugged his shoulders. "Maybe our families."

"What about Tex? We've missed a lot of schedules. Do you think he's notified the authorities?"

"I doubt it. He's probably been calling on schedule—and who knows how many kilowatt hours he's expended futilely calling K6KWS. But he may think we're too busy to answer, or that atmospheric conditions aren't right, or that the time of day isn't. "

"Do you think the Chilean navy will start looking for us?"

"Hell, what are they going to do? They'll probably wait at least a week before putting out a radio bulletin. Then it could be the end of March before anyone gets off their duff and starts looking."

I started to weep, thinking of my parents. I felt such sorrow for them. It was early February when we last talked with them, and although we knew Big John in California had relayed our messages to them, our silence since February 27 would make them frantic.

Don stroked my hair, massaging my shoulders and back. "You've been so great. You were so nice to me last night, even when I was nasty. It's your turn, sweetheart. Go ahead and cry. We're alive—just think about that. We'll figure something out."

"Figuring something out" suddenly became urgent. I stopped weeping. "Let's discuss alternatives," I said, wanting an immediate solution. I was beginning to seesaw between utter despair and adrenaline-charged activity and wondered if I were losing my mind. Maybe we were both going crazy!

"Well, as I see it," Don said, "we have several possibilities. If we can figure out some way to get ashore, we could hike out to Tudor Light on Cabo Boleyn, leave a message and hope that the navy comes to service the broken light sometime soon. But from the looks of it, that could be years."

I wondered how Don thought we could get ashore without a dinghy. And even if we could, how could we leave the boat alone? That would be courting disaster, the way the weather changed so brusquely. And I certainly didn't like the idea of his going alone. It could take more than a day to push through that brush, and if something happened to him he wouldn't be able to get word to me.

"We could display the International Distress flag on deck," Don said. "If the weather ever improves so the navy can fly this far north, they might discover us."

I liked that idea and suggested we remove the mainsail, lay the boom on deck, and stretch the flag across the doghouse roof. That way the flag would be visible from a plane.

"Any other ideas?" I asked.

"Well, again, it depends on getting ashore . . . We could hike over to Puerto Henry, set up camp, and stand watches to monitor the outer channel. When a ship comes by, we can try to signal it. Or . . . " He paused, smiling almost imperceptibly.

"Or what?"

"We can rescue ourselves."

"What do you mean?"

"We figure out how to sail the boat south through the channels until we find a fishing boat or freighter that can help us."

With no detailed charts, no tide or current tables, no depth sounder? I told him he was nuts. The only direction we could sail was downwind. We hadn't been able to make the boat come about or tack to windward when we had entered Canal Trinidad, so how could we expect to get through the rest of the channels? One williwaw against a lee shore and we'd be beached and holed. The *Pilot* warned that any vessel without power should not attempt to enter these channels. Not only did we lack an engine, we didn't even have a full set of sails! *We'd be better off in a rowboat,* I thought. And I said so.

"Look," Don said, irritated. "I don't like waiting for someone to rescue us. There's got to be a way we can do it ourselves. But before we can do anything, we have to let our bodies and minds recover and get the boat back in shape. Hell, I still can't hold a pencil or screwdriver in my hands very well. In the meantime, we're highly vulnerable anchored here. If the boat should hit that wall, our first priority is to get everything on shore as fast as possible."

He was unaware of everything I'd accomplished while he'd slept. "Come on deck and let me show you what I've done," I said.

MARCH 7

I pushed the hatch partially open and looked out. We'd had intermittent showers all night, and it was raining lightly at the moment. The wind had decreased, and the boat had swung around and was now facing toward shore. At midnight we'd had to get up and drop the yachtsman off the stern to keep us offshore.

Although the peaks to the south were still masked by fog, I could see to the far end of the basin for the first time in forty-eight hours. The boat was stable. I closed the hatch and climbed back into the berth with Don.

Picos Organ Pipes—we could see the south end of Dáarsena Aid for the first time

"Massage my hands, will you?—carefully," he said. "I don't think they'll ever recover."

"You didn't sleep well after we put the yachtsman out, did you?"

"No. My fingers kept tingling."

"And you were thinking about alternatives, too, weren't you?"

Later in the day I completed an inventory of our food stores and separated the good tins from the bad. Our situation was looking up.

My boat inventory was contained in a three-ring loose-leaf notebook strapped together with a bungee cord. It had survived in the lower book locker, but its pages were mildewed and speckled with rust. I flipped through twelve of the narrow-ruled pages marked "Galley Stores," checking what remained. We still had plenty of desserts stowed in the buckets, but we were low on cereal, mashed potato mix, and powdered sour cream.

We had started the trip with a total of 588 tins of meat—ham, corned beef, pork loin, mini-ribs, roast turkey, tamales, chili, beef stew, Spam, deviled ham, and beef hash—enough to feed six people for six months. By the time the boys jumped ship, we had used several cartons of turkey, tamales, deviled ham, and chili. We still had a good supply of the other meats, a few tins of tuna, and about twenty cans each of fruits and vegetables. Other than the few I'd had to chuck, most of the shellacked cans had come through the accident in fair shape. I wiped them off, re-stowing them in the stern quarter.

I thumbed further, scanning correspondence I'd received from manufacturers, and a letter from the Del Monte Corporation made me smile: "Care should be taken to prevent excessive banging, crushing, or dropping, as this could result in damage to the exterior of the can."

Although our food stores appear to be adequate, we're down to barely thirty gallons of water. Don says if the rain ever lets up, we'll have to figure out how to get ashore to fill the jugs from the stream.

Our clothing situation is looking up. I found another stash of sweaters and some wool hospital blankets wrapped up in plastic garbage sacks. All dry!

I fight thinking about home, but today when I found the blankets I suddenly saw Mom and Dad's neighbor, Al Nieman, beaming above the stack he brought to us before we left. We're surrounded by so many objects family, friends, neighbors, and students gave us that it's hard not to think of home. Each time I look at the ship's clock I think of Daddy—his birthday gift to Don. Then there's the set of stainless bowls from Mother which came through the accident with just a few dings; a set of Danish plastic bowls with nonskid rings from Jean and Joel; and books—so many books.

The memories overwhelm me, and to stop thinking of home, I have to repeat my mantra: We'll make it. We're alive. We'll make it. That's all that matters.

Don maneuvered the bow around so we could get ashore

Filling the jugs with water

MARCH 8

The sun rose, casting an exquisite persimmon glow on the rugged granite domes and peaks to the south. It was our first view of the Picos Organ Pipes we'd read about. On the grassy slopes above us, flat-topped cypress leaned toward the peaks, their crooked, wind-blown branches pointing toward the rosy spires. The boat sat motionless in the water. Not a ripple disturbed its reflection.

We sat on the doghouse roof staring spellbound. The abominable weather—the rain, hail, sleet, wind, and fog—had vanished. Dársena Aid, a blue sky, a rising sun, calm waters, mountains, and trees were truly a gift.

"Who could be depressed with a view like this from their balcony?" I said softly, hoping I could sit all day, still and silent, just reading or writing. But Don yanked me back to reality.

"Okay. Let's take advantage of this weather—try to get ashore and fill the water jugs. I have an idea of how we can do it, so get yourself ready."

Grumbling and annoyed, I went below, put on a pair of shorts, a long-sleeved jersey, and a stocking cap. This wasn't going to be an easy job, I knew. We were sitting in more than sixty feet of water, and the edge of the shore plunged abruptly.

"Pay attention," Don said. "I want to explain what we have to do. First, I'll work the boat as close to shore as I can. Then, I'll have to swim or wade ashore carrying a line. I'll loop the line around a rock on shore and throw the bitter end up to you so you can pull the bow around." He shackled an extra 200 feet of line to the bow anchor, ran aft and forward, alternately letting out on the bow line, then easing the yachtsman off the stern. I hung over the port rail and, grasping our lone dinghy oar with both hands, paddled as forcefully as I could to help move the boat. After thirty minutes we had worked the stern to shore, but couldn't get the bow to come around.

Carrying a nylon line, Don jumped off onto a submerged rock and waded ashore in icy, waist-deep water. He looped the line around a rock and flung the bitter end up to me. I pulled the bow around till the bowsprit hung directly over the shore and we could crawl up and down the bobstay and jump off without getting wet.

I threw the water jugs to Don, then lowered myself onto shore. The ground, soft and spongy, gave under my weight. "Oh God, it feels good to be on land!" I said, kneeling down to touch it. Ferns drooped gracefully everywhere, and shoots of cypress poked through the moss-covered ground. I wanted just to sit there on the damp earth, look out across Dársena Aid, and let the sun warm my bare legs. "This is wonderful!" I said quietly.

"Come on, let's get going," Don said. "We don't have time to fool around—the weather could change any minute. I've found a place about fifty yards uphill where we can fill the jugs."

I followed Don up a crack in the granite ledge for fifty yards to where the stream tumbled over a shaft of rock. I got down on my knees and cupped my hands to drink—cold refreshing mountain water, tea-colored with microscopic traces of roots and mosses. Compared to the salty-tasting water we'd taken on at Easter Island, this was wonderful—it quenched my thirst.

For four hours we made round trips with the jugs

For four hours, we made round trips with the jugs; up the crack to fill the jugs; then down to the boat where, periodically, I climbed aboard, hauled them up on a line, carried them aft, slid them down the ladder, then transferred the water into the tanks.

But the rock was so slippery that each trip was a struggle, and after a couple of hours I began to slow down. I asked Don when we could quit. Instead of answering he gave me a dirty look and began his fake-sweet routine. With every step I took he would make some comment—such as, "Keep your center of gravity over your feet!" followed by "TER-RIII-FIC!" in a sickly sweet tone that pissed me off even more. I finally told him to shut the hell up.

When Carl left the boat in Mexico, he had given me a small plaque inscribed in memory of his favorite aunt and uncle. He asked me to stake it "in a beautiful place in Patagonia" and photograph it for his dad and him.

On one of our rounds to fill the jugs, I took his plaque with me. I crossed the stream to a slope where tufts of golden-green grasses hung over the rocks like the coat of a mountain sheep. I stooped to examine some low-growing bushes with tiny white flowers and glossy leaves—like the mountain laurel in the Sierra Nevada.

Don knelt on the damp moss and staked the plaque while I shot a couple of photos. I felt as if I were attending a graveside memorial service, and I bowed my head. From a nearby tree, a bird warbled, her call answered by a mate higher up the slope. A hummingbird buzzed past and put his tiny beak into one of the small white flowers. *This is truly a beautiful place in Patagonia. Carl will be happy.*

A breeze blew up from the southeast. "Come on. Hurry!" Don said. "The boat's going to get caught against the shore . . . You climb aboard, watch the bow and shore lines and keep them from fouling. When I shove the bow off," he instructed, "you start pulling in the outside lines. Then I'll come aboard and take over."

He pushed on the bow, leapt for the bobstay, and hand over hand pulled himself up the chain till he could reach the bowsprit. The bow was still facing toward shore, and we had to get it turned around heading north. Soaked and exhausted, Don took over and continued pulling in on the stern lines to back us offshore.

"Shit! The bow line's fouled around something. Do you see what you've done, dammit? You didn't keep the line taut. If the wind came up right now the bow would be crushed against the rocks. Now one of us has to go into the water."

Feeling guilty, I volunteered.

"No, no. I'll go in. Go get the face mask out of the deck locker." Wearing just undershorts and a T-shirt he jumped in, fumbled with the mask, trying to get it sealed around his face as he treaded water. "Aiee! I'm caught in kelp," he yelled.

I hesitated, unsure whether to keep my eyes on him or run back to the cockpit for a life jacket. He flailed his arms up and down, panicky, then disappeared under water. I ran back to the cockpit for a life jacket, trying to keep track of where he'd gone under. He resurfaced near shore, half crawling, groping his way along the rocks, pulling at different angles on the anchor line, and shuddering visibly from the cold.

"The wind's picking up," he yelled. "We're going to lose it for sure if we don't get out of here. Pull on the bow line now, and see if it'll come."

I tugged, and the line came freely. Don gave a hard shove to the bowsprit; the boat swung off before he could grab the bobstay, and he had to dive back in, swim to the boat, and pull himself up.

I ran for an army blanket to wrap around him. As he climbed down the ladder, exhausted and shivering, he pointed up at the sky through the open hatch, stuttering, "Look!" A large condor, with a small reddish head and long trailing wing feathers, was circling overhead. "Watch him—he's just waiting to pick our bones!"

While Don slept, the williwaws increased. I went above to check the anchor rode. It was taut but it wasn't tugging. We were about twenty-five feet from the granite wall, but the boat was well tethered into the wind, and there didn't appear to be any danger. I climbed back down the ladder and closed the hatch cover. The noise awakened Don, and he jumped down from the berth as if chased by a ghost. "We've got to put out another anchor!" he yelled. "See how close to shore we are?"

"Wait a minute. I've just checked everything. It's not that critical." He ignored me, and started pulling his pants on. "Look, you're pushing yourself to the edge. We'll be all right for a few more minutes. Finish getting dressed and have a bowl of soup."

He slumped onto the galley settee. "Yeah, I guess you're right. Maybe we can wait a few minutes."

We dropped the Danforth over, and Don motioned to me, "Come here and see what I'm doing. I want you to understand this."

Uh oh, I'm in for another lecture, I thought.

"Watch me—I pull away from shore by letting out on the shore line, then I pull in on the kedge anchor and let out on the bow line. Now if we're blown either way, it'll be toward a spot where we can get ashore . . . Do you understand?"

I understood his words. But I didn't think I'd *ever* understand the dynamics of the wind and the boat and why he cleated the lines where he did. *"Physics—why didn't you study physics?"* I'd heard the accusation dozens of times.

Over supper, he asked if I wanted to talk about what happened earlier in the day.

"Not if you're going to lecture me about it again. I think I understand what I did wrong."

"Can we discuss the steps again? I want to make sure you get it."

I got what I dreaded—the full lecture on physics, when all I wanted was a *simple* explanation. When Don had run out of steam, I asked if we could discuss another problem. He agreed, not realizing I had my own lecture in mind, about the difference between life-and-death emergencies and just plain urgent situations.

"You're still calling *Mayday* when you should be calling *Pan, Pan*. Was this afternoon a real survival situation?" I wouldn't let him answer. "I don't think so." The more I talked, the more heated I became. I had held in my anger too long. "I don't understand why everything we do has to be in high performance, like we'll die on the spot if we hesitate . . . I think you're hooked on crises. You don't know how to operate in any other mode, and if we didn't have a crisis you'd invent one. Was it *really* that critical?" I raised my voice. "Well, was it?"

He was silent, and I expected him to lash back at any moment. But he was pensive. "I guess you're right. I do act like that a lot. It's my engineering background, maybe, or my business experience. I don't know what makes me like that."

MARCH 9

Another beautiful, sunny day. The barometer remained high at 30.40 inches (1029.47 mb), the winds light. We left the hatches and ports open to dry the interior and ate our meals above so we could watch the birds and gaze at Picos Organ Pipes at the end of the basin.

I sang and whistled for the first time since we hit the Roaring Forties. Don hugged me. "The land bird sings today—I like to hear you happy!"

The galley cushions and mattresses began to dry. While he worked on deck—testing, checking, tightening, rechecking—I continued scrubbing, organizing, and doing laundry. My hands came clean, but they were still numb and impervious to the boiling saltwater.

"What would you say about trying to sail south in the channels?" Don asked as we ate lunch. He'd already forgotten my initial reaction days earlier. I repeated that I didn't like the idea.

"Slocum sailed through the Strait eighty years ago without a motor. Don't you think we can?" Don asked.

I reminded him that Slocum had had tremendous problems trying to maneuver against the williwaws. We had only a mizzen and a staysail. Although we might be able to use the working jib, with the bobstay and bowsprit loose, we didn't know how long the forestay would hold. "I don't see how we can make way under these winds. What happens on a day like yesterday when there's no wind at all?"

"We anchor then," Don said. "We'll sail on and off the anchor."

I could see the program: a crisis a day—with his screaming at me, and my dissolving into tears or screaming back.

"How do you think Slocum did it?" he asked sarcastically.

"He wasn't this far north," I said. "And he kept seeing other ships. The navy knew his whereabouts and kept an eye out for him while he was in the Strait."

Irritated by my response, he ignored it and said, "Well, if my hands recover, maybe I can figure out what's wrong with the engine. Otherwise, we sail. We'll study the chart and *Pilot* later and see what it looks like."

Each day in Dársena Aid brings surprises. Before sundown this evening, waves of vivid red krill swirled through the basin. They swept alongside the boat doing figure-eights, zeros, reversals—every movement so precise it seemed as if they had practiced a ballet just for us.

A while later, a flock of Brent geese flew into the basin, honking raucously as they swooped down to land on the water. Don's voice echoed off the far shore, "Honk if you're horny!" The geese turned their heads and looked toward us as if to say, "What's that idiot doing?"

I leaned over the mizzen boom gallows and gazed across the basin. The boat was already in the shadows of the ridge above us, but Picos Organ Pipes still gleamed in the late afternoon sun. "Glorious! It's glorious!" I hollered.

The geese took off and headed toward the sunny peaks.

Don had been relaxed most of the day, his good spirits showing in his own journal entry:

Without wind we can see small vortices on the water's surface—the mixing action of fresh and saltwater—that look like rivulets on top of the water, due undoubtedly to the waterfall sixty yards upstream. The water is a deep brown color with vertical visibility only to about five or six feet.

Sometimes we hear noises that sound like goat or pigs, but maybe it's the geese mating on Jane Island across from us. There's such tranquillity here, time seems to stop. But this fifty-foot cliff, just twenty-five feet away, hangs over our head and makes me wonder if we'll be smashed against it by the backwash of a williwaw. Fear seems so out of place right now, my mind tells

I began a letter to my parents describing our accident

me to face that in due time—not to rush things, just enjoy the quiet of the moment and let tomorrow take care of itself.

MARCH 10

Slowly Don regained strength in his fingers, hands, and arms. And the aching in our joints began to subside.

The weather continued lovely and warm. The clothes I'd washed and hung on lifelines and shrouds dried within hours and smelled wonderfully sweet. The mattresses and cushions dried to a bearable dampness, and we put them back in place.

While Don poked around the engine to see why it didn't work, I pecked away at my typewriter in the cockpit. (My small manual typewriter, which had been stowed under Carl's berth when we pitchpoled, was protected by its thick vinyl case and had survived intact.)

I had rigged a typing stool by placing a cushion on top of one of the buckets; my desk was the companionway washboard set on top of a second bucket. Facing to port I could see the stream, or look up at the hanging garden on the granite face. I began what would become a twenty-page letter to my parents describing our accident and fight to get to land.

Don interrupted my typing. "I have an idea. Can you come help me?" He explained that all the switches and controls were fouled from saltwater and the banging they'd received. "I may be able to get the engine running if I can bypass all the electrical control circuits.

"Hand me the long screwdriver. I'm going to try to short the starter solenoid." He bent over the starter motor, passed the shaft of the screwdriver across the solenoid terminal, and touched the engine block with its tip. The engine grunted and turned over. I held my breath, afraid to show any emotion; it might be premature. "There's a chance!" Don said slowly. "But maybe only one—the battery charge is too low to try it more than once."

He knelt and stuck his head inside the locker under Carl's berth. "I think there might be a can of ether under here that I can use to prime the engine. You go up and put the throttle in full forward. If it catches, pull back immediately so you don't over-rev the engine."

I climbed out to the cockpit and waited. The engine turned over, caught, and raced to full rpms. Quickly I pulled the throttle back to fast idle.

"Wahooo! It sounds great!" Don said, dashing up to look over the stern. "The cooling water's going out the exhaust. It looks okay." He glanced at the amp meter. The needle hadn't budged. "The batteries aren't charging . . . I have another idea. Wait here."

Yelling through the aft porthole, he gave me a running account of what he was doing: "I found a salt-encrusted switch that appears to be the problem. I think I can bypass the switch with a jumper wire and get the alternator system working." We tried a couple of experiments, and soon the engine slowed, indicating a heavy alternator load. The system was working!

"Now put the throttle in forward," he yelled.

I jammed it full forward and the boat pulled against the stern anchor.

"Great. Now reverse!"

I pulled back on the throttle and the boat moved aft straining the bow anchor.

"Ter-riii-fic! The engine sounds great, everything seems to be working." He appeared at the top of the ladder, grinning, and gave me the cut-the-engine sign. "Do you s'pose you could you find some plastic wrap? The air bleed screw's leaking badly again."

I climbed below, euphoric, and gave him a big hug. "Captain, you are great!" I felt like jumping up and down and screaming with joy. Now we could move on without worrying about having to sail in and out of an anchorage. Now maybe we'd find help when we got to the main channels.

I rummaged in the icebox for our last roll of Saran wrap. The box had disintegrated long ago, and drops of salt clung to the wrap. I thought back to the Roaring Forties when we had tried the same trick, and I sang, "Here we go again . . . "

That night, I scribbled "HAPPY DAY" in four-inch-high letters across my journal, then:

Don wants to leave Dársena Aid within three days, at the new moon. We'll have to ration our fuel very carefully—we have just enough to run the engine to enter and exit anchorages and will have to sail as much as possible during the day. Tonight we transferred our last five gallons of diesel to the fuel tank, adding five gallons of cooking kerosene; that leaves us fifteen for the lamps and stove.

Today was to have been our ETA in Punta Arenas; tomorrow we'll be officially overdue. Just knowing we can move on, that we will get to Punta Arenas, that we won't have to winter over here thrills me. This is the best news since we found Dársena Aid!

I've had such a terrible craving for carbohydrates and sugar since we got to land that tonight I opened a can of vanilla frosting and spooned half of it into my mouth—a minimum of 800 calories, I'm sure.

The next morning I wrote:

Last night before bed I heated up a couple pots of saltwater to fill the sink, and we both took a "bath." Don scrubbed my back, then I sat on the galley counter with my legs in the sink, washing from the waist down. A hot shower couldn't have felt better at that moment! We went to bed nude for the first time since . . . I can't remember when. Don's skin against mine felt marvelous, and we were like young lovers discovering new secrets about one another. How wonderful to feel desire again! I didn't realize how much pent-up emotion I had until I climaxed and broke into spontaneous, uncontrollable sobbing, repeating, "We're alive, we're alive, we're alive!"

Don wrote:

Both R. and I have lost more than fifteen pounds. We simply weren't aware of hunger after the accident. We existed on hot mush in the morning and a cup of soup in the evening, but mostly chocolate bars and hot chocolate. We've had diarrhea, too, caused by stress I'm sure . . .

I've read that sex is one of the first basic drives a person loses during periods of exhaustion or starvation, and the last to return. I had my first involuntary erection last night when we slept skin to skin, which proves I'm slowly beginning to recover.

MARCH 12

We spent the next 48 hours preparing to move on. Everything we had loaded into the cockpit for evacuation had to be carried back down and restowed—anchor lines, tarps, sails, distress flag, buckets of food, bags of clothing, cloth, and tools. We tied the yachtsman and fisherman (kedge) anchors on the stern to have ready for emergencies. Although the cockpit was empty and neat, the deck itself still looked distressed. The main boom lay diagonally across the doghouse roof, attached to the mast only

by the mainsail. The starboard spreader still hung
limp from the shroud; the
main boom gallows looked
like a humpback; the lifelines were a mess; and the
lightboards were still askew.

We decided to disman-
tle the self-steering vane
and its rudder. Ever since it
had been bent, it put a
brake on our speed. While
Don crouched on the swim
step, contorting his body so
he could unscrew the lower
bracket step of the steering
vane, I stood above him on
the stern, holding the shaft
in place to prevent it from
dropping overboard. The
shaft and vane rudder
weighed about a hundred
pounds. Getting it aboard

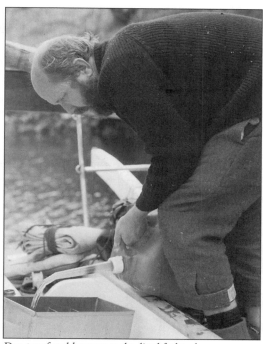

Don transferred kerosene to the diesel fuel tank

the stern, lifting it over the mizzen boom, and carrying it forward to the
doghouse roof nearly did us in.

I was pleased with what I had accomplished. The cabin—as clean as I
could get it in these conditions—looked cozy and organized.

Whenever I cleaned, I discovered lost items in odd places. When a
can of green chilies turned up under the floorboards, Don asked me to
concoct a Mexican dish for supper. I had already pulled a packet of
freeze-dried stroganoff from our emergency supplies, but the squares of
beef sat in a bowl of water trying to soak up liquid without succeeding,
and the noodles were rubbery after a half-hour of boiling. I pitched the
whole mess into the water, opened a can of corned beef hash, and added
the chilies to Don's half.

MARCH 13

Early in the morning, Don shorted the solenoid, jumpered the alternator,
and the engine turned over. It was time to leave Dársena Aid.

With me on the bow, leadline in hand and watching for rocks, we
motored briefly south to have a look at the end of the basin. Two stun-

ning glacier-cut valleys came into view directly below Picos Organ Pipes, and we spotted a lake surrounded by low-lying rocks and scrubby green vegetation. How I wished we could anchor *le Dauphin* in safety and go ashore, but those four hours carrying water from the stream would have to be our only allotment of time on land.

As we turned and motored out through the channel past Puerto Henry I felt a touch of sadness. We'd had some frightening experiences in Dársena Aid—torrential rains, williwaws that had threatened to smash us against the granite cliff or send us flying to the end of the basin—but nothing, nothing like the nightmare of 60 seas. Aid Basin, so aptly named by British explorers, had been our haven. She had sheltered and protected us, given us water, sun, mountains, and trees when we thought fog, sleet, and monumental grey seas were all we would ever see.

CHAPTER 12

Rescue Be Damned

While we were struggling to raise the anchors in Dársena Aid, I thought of a question Don had asked the night before. Excited with the prospect of moving on, he was talkative and wanting to speculate.

I was exhausted and wanted to go to bed, but his question—"What do you suppose people at home are saying about us right now?"—had piqued my interest.

I suspected what *certain* people would be saying and told him. "Those who don't like us will say, 'Douglass only did this for publicity. You wait and see, he'll show up.' Or, 'Dumb fools, they should have known better. They were foolish to try a trip like this.'"

I could picture these certain people—our cocktail party "friends." (I'd always preferred the French distinction between *amis* and *connaissances*; we Americans seemed to call everyone "friend.") I recalled a farewell party my parents had held in our honor a few weeks before we sailed. Don didn't have time to attend, so Sean and I flew to San Francisco for a short visit, loaded with slides of our trip preparation to show at the party. One of the guests—a "friend" who owned a sailboat himself—cornered me in the dining room and launched into a sermon about everything that could possibly go wrong. Treating me as if I were hard of hearing, he raised his voice, "You don't know what you're getting into!"

I cut him short, asking in a falsely good-natured tone, "And shall we cancel our plans immediately on your recommendation?"

My slide talk was peppered with another friend's sarcastically witty comments delivered in a Boston accent. "It's a fact, Rene," the man said to my father, "a man of action is *never* a man of thought . . ."

Sean was furious. "Mom, he was talking about Dad! So what if Dad isn't a philosopher? What's Roland ever done that's so great? At least Dad has goals and accomplishes them!"

My journal had continued the train of thought:

I would take a stand in Don's defense against anyone calling him a fool. There will always be people who consider taking risks foolish. Don weighed the chances—15 percent chance of storm-force winds in February.

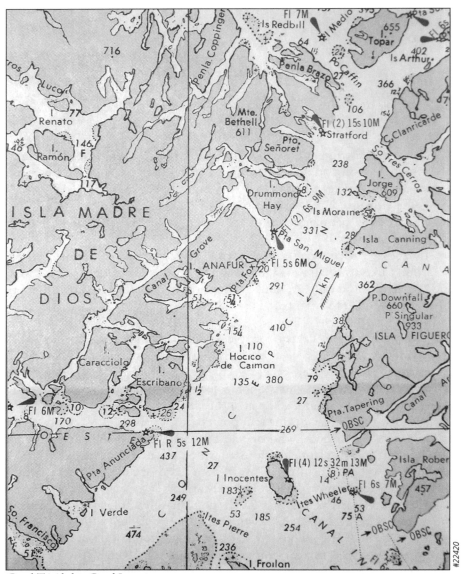

Canal Trinidad to Canal Inocentes
(Note: most of the navigational aids shown on the area charts did not exist in 1975)

Not bad odds in my opinion, but we rolled the dice and lost—like the Smeetons did in 1957.

Perhaps in a boat like Moitessier's *Joshua*—with her steel hull, flush deck, and inside steering station (where he or Françoise huddled under the cupola at the companionway, protected from the waves washing across the *deck)—we might have had less damage. But it's hard to say. Every sailor studies the literature of those who have "done it." And even our hero, who nearly pitchpoled once and was set on his beam on another occasion in the Roaring Forties, doubted Joshua's ability to ride out the seas. He said only "real boats" have the right to sail in these high latitudes.*

What did he mean by "real boats?" Wasn't his steel hull enough of a real boat? What kind of boat can survive these conditions? From everything I've read it's a matter of luck, skill, and a well-found boat.

Maybe luck wasn't with us at 50°S, 89°W. But she certainly was with us the day we entered Canal Trinidad and found our way to Dársena Aid.

Heading out to Canal Trinidad now, we glanced back toward Dársena Aid and couldn't see its entrance—it was completely hidden. And we were still unable to identify some of the islands listed in the *Pilot*.

We spotted a whale carcass stretched along the beach in Puerto Henry, and as we approached to have a look, large dull-grey gulls that were crouched on the carcass pecking away at blubber began to caw raucously, spreading their wings to assert their territorial rights.

Heading into the main channel, a chill northeast wind greeted us, and scudding clouds that played hide and seek with the sun sent us flying for our heavy jackets and caps. The barometer remained high, and I wondered:

Where is all the horrible weather the Pilot mentions for this region? Aside from our first few days in Dársena Aid, it's been beautiful. But perhaps it's building up for another big blast and I should keep quiet.

Every direction holds breathtaking views. To the east, the snow-covered, serrated peaks of the southern cordillera glisten in the sun. Mountains of blue-grey rise to the north of Canal Trinidad. On the south shore, a magnificent waterfall cascades out of a high, hanging valley, then gushes down a vertical incline and pours into the saltwater. Beech trees hang tenaciously above the waterline giving their first hint of fall colors.

I took the helm, so Don could go below to use the head. When he came back above, he said, "By the way"—pausing for effect—"do you realize we're out of toilet paper? And there's just one box of dry Kleenex. Maybe we shouldn't have chucked all those wet rolls overboard."

"They were soaked with salt water; they never would have dried."

"Well, wet t.p. is better than nothing!" He paused again and gave me a funny grin. "Are there any paperbacks left you're willing to sacrifice?"

"Yeah! *The Exorcist.* I found it wedged under Sean's berth the other day."

"Great! You can have the Kleenex. I'll take *The Exorcist.*"

"You're not going to use *that* in the head?"

He grinned. "No. Don't worry."[1]

Don raised the jib and we cut the engine. "God, it's great to turn off the engine and know we'll be able to turn it on again," he said.

His words rang in my ears a few hours later as we were nearing the east end of Canal Trinidad. We planned to find anchorage behind Isla Pilot, the largest island on the south shore, and when we were nearing it, Don asked me to manage the throttle while he shorted the solenoid. The minute he shouted, "Throw the throttle in neutral," I realized I'd forgotten to disengage the gearbox when we'd cut the engine earlier. The knob had become corroded, and because my fingers were so swollen I didn't have the strength to pull it out now.

"I can't budge it!"

"Shit!" he yelled, dashing up to the cockpit and pulling the knob out himself.

I hoped his searing lecture would make an imprint on my brain. (I'd made the same blunder with the engine cutoff switch in the Roaring Forties.)

"Can we leave a pair of pliers out here?" I asked. "That would help me remember, and I'd have an easier time pulling out the switch."

He agreed, but his cassette hadn't quite run out, and he reminded me that we didn't have enough fuel to waste, that we could lose the boat at the drop of a hat, that being inside the channels didn't decrease the dangers. "With all these rocks and reefs, the hazards in these channels are worse than they were outside. In here, we may have just one chance, and with any kind of error we can lose it and end up on the rocks."

I clammed up, inwardly pouting and storing his tone, not his words, in my memory bank. Neither one of us had recovered physically, and chances were we had a tougher pull ahead than I had realized. I talked myself into a good attitude.

After we anchored, we worked on deck reattaching smaller (narrower diameter) and more manageable chains to the CQR and Danforth. The heavy chains were getting to be too much for Don's swollen hands.

Isla Pilot rose high above the water, and our bow pointed toward a waterfall that tumbled forty feet from a polished granite cliff at the head of our cove. As the sun disappeared behind the island, the wind funneled through a cleft above the falls, sending harsh gusts across the deck. Hundreds of blue-eyed shags watched from their perches along the diagonal, moss-traced cracks of the rock face. With their black "dinner jackets," white bellies, and odd stance, they resembled the small Magellanic penguins we'd seen in photographs.

While we were eating supper, *le Dauphin* began rocking up and down, the motion characteristic of a ship's wake. "It's a ship!" we yelled simultaneously, bounding on deck in time to see eighteen-inch swells slap against the stern quarter. It was definitely the wake of a ship. But there was no ship in sight. Twenty minutes earlier, when we'd been working on the anchors, we hadn't sighted a thing. How could a vessel have come and gone between then and now?

"If it *was* a ship, they sure weren't on the lookout for us." Don remarked. "We're visible to the channel, and if they'd been looking, they'd have spotted us."

I teetered between disappointment and elation—at least there were ships in these waters; perhaps another day we would encounter our savior.

After supper, I asked about jumping the starter, so I didn't louse up if I had to start the engine. Don had explained everything carefully the day before, but with the way things had gone today, I wanted a repeat explanation. I asked which of the terminals I was supposed to touch the screwdriver to, thinking all the little metal Ys were terminals.

"That's not it—it's the place *where* they terminate." He exploded. "You don't understand a goddam thing! I explained that already. . . . You can't conceptualize, can you? But at least you should be able to listen."

The more he raged, the more silent I became. I didn't know which was worse—to quit talking or scream back. He detested silence, but screaming showed "lack of control." I resolved to shut up, but as his biting remarks spewed out like grapeshot, my resolve quickly disintegrated. To escape I gave him a dirty look and hopped on the pilot berth with my journal, furious.

He can damn well sleep by himself tonight. I'm fed up with his attacks on my intelligence and my physical weaknesses. I can't conceptualize. Bullshit! Maybe I don't understand physics, but SO WHAT!

"You're overly sensitive," he tells me. "Most sailors are like me." So? Even if most sailors are like he is, does that make him easier to live with? His sarcasm comes and goes like fireworks on the Fourth of July. I'm never quite sure when the next flare will go off, or what will ignite it. And I hate myself when I try to outdo him in it, but once I get started I can't quit.

This nastiness is what drove the boys away, not the hard work. And every time we have one of these blowups, it diminishes my feeling for him. I've been a good partner, and he has no call to be so impatient. What is it with him? If he could only say afterward, "I'm sorry, I didn't mean to be so hard." But he never does.

I wish to God he could have some other female on board for three months—God, he'd find out in a hurry that I'm not as stupid or inept as he thinks . . . And he wonders why I don't want to crawl in bed with him. Crap. He may be able to turn sex on and off like a light bulb, but I can't.

I wonder if Bernard and Françoise Moitessier ever quarreled. If, as Don says, all sailors are the same, I'd like to hear Françoise's side of the story. But I don't suppose I ever will.

Don's log entry for the day held a cursory comment in the margin:

Argument this p.m. with R. about pulling the throttle out of gear.

When I awoke the next morning, Don was standing beside the pilot berth, running his hand across my fanny, a slight grin on his face. "I'm sorry. Can't we be friends today? Please come to bed with me. It's 0600, but we're socked in by fog, so we can't move right now."

MARCH 14

Chart 22400 was acquiring neat pencil lines that plotted our progress and noted our positions in local time. We had been streaming the recording log off the stern, and by the time we had reached Península Brazo—the northeast point of Isla Madre de Dios—it registered 27.2 nautical miles.

The northern entrance to Canal Concepción is open to the Pacific, and as we rounded the point, boiling whitecaps whipped up the channel. Don had wanted to continue another ten miles, but after one look at the seas he said, "I don't feel like butting heads with that wind; we'll consume too much fuel. Get out the lead line and be prepared to lower it— we'll anchor off Isla Gort."

On the chart, Gort Island looked like a microscopic pen mark on the west side of Canal Trinidad, and its name didn't even appear. There was no mention of an anchorage in the *Pilot*. Nervously, I kept eyeing the *Cautions* written on the chart:

1. The area covered by this chart has not been completely surveyed. Mariners are warned to exercise great caution when navigating in sparsely sounded waters.

2. Detailed information has been omitted or generalized in areas covered by larger scale charts.

The view of the seas in Canal Concepción sobered me. Don's lecture made sense now. He was right: one false move and we could lose it. *Constant vigilance, his pet phrase,* I thought. *That's the only way we'll make it to Punta Arenas.*

Checking the shore of Isla Gort through the binoculars, we could see a clear-cut area, a ring of charred wood, a piece of bright blue material, and what looked like a bed. Our imaginations cranked. The refuge of a stranded crew? An old fisherman's camp? Pieces of a shipwreck? Maybe soon we'd come across another camp with live people.

After dark, Don lit the anchor light for the first time since we'd left Mexico. At 2045 hours we sighted a ship in the main channel. Excited, I ran for the spotlight. Don signaled an SOS. There was no response. Sixty minutes later we felt the ship's wake. Sixty minutes. So that first night we felt a wake, the ship had probably already passed by before we'd even anchored!

"Other than the outboard skiffs at Rapa Nui, it's been roughly a hundred days since we've seen another boat," Don remarked. "It seems strange that we've covered so many miles and seen so little activity."

After supper I logged: "Repairs accomplished today: 1. Lashed the ends of the port spinnaker pole line, and the end of the staysail sheet—both were coming unraveled. 2. Repaired the mizzen sail track so we'll be able to use the mizzen sail now. Total time for repairs, 1½ hours. Good dinner tonight: spaghetti and tomato sauce, made with crumbled meat bar, oregano, bay leaves, and red wine (our only unbroken bottle); tapioca for dessert.

My journal read more positively than it had the night before:

Today was better. We worked well together! We had fun! A simple "Thanks!" or "You did a good job!" or "I'm sorry" means so much to me. If Don could only cultivate those seeds, our life would be so much smoother. Under all his bravado and arrogance, his soft side keeps me tethered. How many times have I written these thoughts? Scores. But perhaps this trip will be the turning point—perhaps he's mellowing.

MARCH 15

Don logged: "For a touch of aesthetics, we sailed off anchor at 0845 without using the engine. But alas, we were becalmed behind Gort Island and had to start the engine at 0910. Clear, unlimited visibility; barometer steady at 30.52 inches (1033 mb). Made turn southward into Canal Concepción but wind too much to buck, so to get out of the wind we fell off and dropped the CQR in 90 feet of water off the southern shore of Seno Molyneux. Not a good place if the wind should reverse. Distance for the day: 16.2 nautical miles (cumulative total: 43.4—slow going!)"

The *Pilot* listed Seno Molyneux as one of only two good anchorages in the twenty-three-mile-long Canal Concepción, and the light on Punta San Miguel across the sound was the first functioning navigational aid we'd seen since Acapulco.

That night Don wrote in his journal:

Tonight we set the anchor light again, and I've been looking outside every twenty minutes or so to check for a vessel. Disappointed there were no boats today—not even a fishing boat—now that we're in the regular channel, and especially here in Seno Molyneux, which is supposed to be one of the better anchorages. Two buoys that mark dangers on the northern shore add to the foreboding feeling of this place: One marks Roca Fawn, on which the HMS Fawn struck in 1870. There's also the wreck of a large steamship. The Pilot says that heavy squalls come down Molyneux Sound and strike a vessel with full force, and that when the USS Pinto rode out a heavy gale here, winds varied from Force 4 to 11! [No date given.]

I'm feeling a little depressed tonight. I just spent several hours studying both the *Pilot* and the chart and have put together a plan calling for daily moves of about twenty-five miles each. Several anchorages will be marginal. In fact, even making it safely to Punta Arenas seems marginal with just two of us: no mainsail; a shortage of fuel; no electronics; no large-scale charts till we hit the Strait; and *le Dauphin* leaking several hundred strokes a day. I think she'd sink in a week if we didn't attend to her like a ritual. I tried to get the ham radio going this afternoon, but couldn't get any sign of output. Both R.'s hands and my own are still swollen and clumsy; hope they improve soon. Beautiful flying weather. Why no airplanes?

H. W. Tilman and his crew had tried to anchor *Mischief* in this same spot back in 1956, but at night during a williwaw their anchor fouled, and they had to move out into the middle of the sound and heave to until dawn.

Before that, while Tilman and two of his crew were completing their traverse of the Patagonian Ice Cap, *Mischief* had been run aground. Her propeller had been damaged, leaving the engine useless and forcing them to rely on sail power to navigate the channels. Their charging engine had broken down too, and like us, they couldn't charge the batteries in order to get radio time signals. Determined to get away from the coast as quickly as possible, Tilman had to choose between Canal Trinidad and Canal Concepción as entrances into the Pacific. He chose the latter.

The forty-mile-length of Canal Trinidad is open to the Pacific and since it trends north of west the prevailing wind would raise a big enough sea to make beating out against it a wearing business. . . . Since [Canal Concepción] . . . runs west of south we should be sheltered from the Pacific swell by the islands of Madre de Dios and the Duke of York. . . . The distance to the open sea was shorter this way, but we should enter it a degree further south in lat. 52° S.[2]

Gale force winds hit *Mischief* full on as they entered the Southern Ocean and tried to turn north. Tilman proposed heading back to England via Cape Horn, passing up supplies that awaited them in Valparaiso, but his crew didn't like the idea, and after struggling three or four days they were finally able to turn north.

Thinking about what Tilman had done with *four men* to help him, I felt good about what just two of us had been able to accomplish. But a good morale didn't help me fight a virus.

1815 hours. Slept three hours this afternoon after we anchored. I'm exhausted and have a sore throat and chills. I can't figure out why these symptoms have come on. Aside from the bladder infection I had on the crossing to Easter, caused by insufficient liquid, we've both been quite healthy. No contact with humans proves that the virus is activated by my rundown condition; I think I've hit the wall.

After my nap, I rearranged the stuff in the ammo boxes: one box for camera gear and film, one for medical and personal hygiene, one for Don's precision equipment, one for my essentials (diaries, etc.). I finished the stocking cap I started knitting for Don six weeks ago. He likes it!

MARCH 17

0400 hours: This has been as miserable a night as mischief experienced. Williwaws have funneled down Seno Molyneux all night, and we've snatched only forty-five minutes of sleep. Le Dauphin has been bucking and straining the whole time.

By daylight the wind had backed to the southeast and eased, and we left in good visibility. I took watch while Don tried to nap, and at 0920 hours, six miles south of Seno Molyneux, I spotted a ship. Excited, I shouted, "Come up on deck. Ship headed our way!" He shot out the hatch and took over while I ran below to grab the messages I'd typed for his partner, P.J., and the port captain in Punta Arenas.

"What luck!" Don exclaimed. "We're going to get help at last!" He set a collision course, increased rpms, and headed into the center of the channel to intersect the ship. I hanked on the International Distress flag and raised it. We dug our fenders out of the lazaret, and put them on the

The SS Anaconda Valley *sped past at full speed*

Canal Inocentes to Canal Sarmiento

port rail ready to come alongside the ship. I jammed the messages in a waterproof pouch and stuck the pouch inside my pants, thinking how ecstatic my parents would be when they heard we were okay. Then we watched and waited like kids at a circus.

When the ship was about a half-mile away, Don idled back and made a tight circle in front of her bow. Then, just seventy-five yards away from

Scorned by two giants, we watched the freighter Cheun On *chug past*

us, she altered course and sped past.

Don grabbed the binoculars. "There's gotta be a mistake." Focusing on the bridge, he said, "Damn, I can see three guys looking straight at us through binoculars. What's going on?" He cupped his hands around the corners of his mouth to imitate a megaphone. But the freighter continued at full speed, the name on her stern, SS *Anaconda Valley* of Stockholm, growing smaller and smaller. We remained dead in the water for several minutes, hoping they would get the idea. But there was no reaction.

"I can't believe it," I said. "What do they think we're doing—taking a Sunday cruise? There can't be more than one or two sailboats in these channels in an entire year, if that. But maybe they'll radio a message to Punta Arenas."

Don put the throttle in forward and we headed south. "Yeah. That's really strange . . . Don't feel bad, sweetheart. We'll make it on our own," he said.

I didn't feel bad for myself. I felt bad for my parents, waiting so long. It had been over six weeks since we'd talked to them. And almost four since we'd had radio contact with anyone.

The beauty of the scenery soothed us. It was as if we were sailing down the center of Yosemite Valley—glacier-cut valleys and massive granite domes bordered both sides of the five-mile-wide channel. Some slopes were so slick and precipitous that little vegetation could grow on their

Our International Distress flag was ignored

flanks. On other slopes, cypress, laurel, beech, ferns, and mosses grew so thick that no human could penetrate. Sometimes the sides plunged so steeply into the water that we could have taken *le Dauphin* right up to the vertical walls and tied the stern to a tree hung with streamers of bright yellow or orange fungus.

Charles Darwin, during his voyage in this area on the *Beagle*, wrote of the "grand, solid, abrupt masses of granite, which appeared as if they had been coeval with the beginning of the world. . . . The complicated and lofty ranges bore a noble aspect of durability—equally profitless, however, to man and to all other animals. Granite to the geologist is classic ground: from its wide-spread limits, and its beautiful and compact texture, few rocks have been more anciently recognized. . . . We know it is the deepest layer in the crust of this globe to which man has penetrated."[3]

We changed course, and began our turn southeast into Canal Inocentes. After noon, we sighted a second ship, this one a tanker.

This one will stop, I told myself.

Don flung open the lazaret cover, hung into the hole, and pulled out an orange, diesel-coated megaphone. Dousing the staysail, we circled three times in midchannel. Don held up the megaphone, ready to shout a message while I ran forward to the main mast, flailed my arms, and pointed to the distress flag flying above me.

There was no response from her bridge. Like the *Anaconda Valley*, she chugged past, so close we could see her Asian crew lining the upper deck, grinning, and waving.

What was going on? We'd been scorned by two giants. Were International Distress Rules taken so lightly here? Vessels are obligated to follow the International Rules—stop and give aid. But what could we do? I went below and logged: "The *Cheun On* of Panama has just ignored us." I looked at my watch—1335 hours—and climbed above again.

"Waves and smiles. Well, that's one step above the *Anaconda Valley*," I said.

Don gestured toward the underwear and socks drying on the lifelines. "Maybe we don't look distressed enough."

"But we're flying the distress flag," I said, angry.

"Yeah, that's got to be the ultimate insult—to see a distress flag and choose to ignore it. I don't understand it. Whoever they are, I hope their captains choke on their filet mignon tonight. Well, one of the crew is bound to feel guilty and let out word that the overdue American yacht is heading south in the channels."[4]

Bahía Wide, our anchorage for the day, was on the "not recommended" list, but compared to Seno Molyneux it was a paradise. We spotted its dangers easily as we glided in and anchored. Sheltered from the wind by low-lying islands, the cove was sunny and warm.

Don stripped and lay in the cockpit to sunbathe. I stripped from the waist down and shaved my legs for the first time in over a month.

"How come you're shaving? You look really sexy with hairy legs." (He loved the European look—the "natural look," he called it.)

My legs looked like a Patagonian forest, and under my long johns the hair pulled and itched. I didn't bother to explain.

As the late afternoon chill set in, we dressed and unhanded (removed) the mainsail, the two of us struggling to shove it down the forward hatch and into the forepeak. We tied the main boom alongside the steering vane on the doghouse roof.

"There. Without a main boom, we certainly look distressed," Don said. "But I'll be damned if I'll let anyone rescue us now. To hell with them. If we can't get ourselves out of our own mess, at least we'll make a damned noble effort!"

We sat in the cockpit watching baby geese take flying lessons. Some, starting to solo, flapped their wings just above the waterline in awkward, irregular strokes, and it was so quiet we could hear the whine of their wings against the air. The goslings competed for our attention with the *patos vapor* (steamer ducks).

The ducks were as entertaining as the flying fish off the coast of Mexico had been. They resembled wind-up mechanical birds whose

wings flapped round and round like side-mounted paddle wheelers.
Tilman's description of them delighted me:

> Their wings are too small and weak for flight but they scuttle over the water at
> an astonishing pace half swimming and half running, flapping the water with
> their wings and making so much splash and fuss about it all that the whole
> business is extremely comical. . . . On the approach of the strange sea monster
> Mischief they would begin swimming in uncertain circles. Then, becoming a lit-
> tle more agitated, the whole party would gather together and increase speed
> on what was thought to be a safe course. Faster and faster they went until at
> last the retreat became a rout when with one accord the whole flock broke into
> frenzied flight, wings and legs going like pistons, each bird half lost in a cloud of
> spray. When really worked up their estimated speed is from 15 to 20 knots.[5]

After supper we broke out our last can of eggnog and laced it with the
only hard liquor that had survived our pitchpole—a bottle of Mexican
rum. We sang cowboy songs, Italian songs, Irish songs. The rum made me
melancholy, and the Irish songs made me think of my parents, of Daddy
playing the piano and singing the old Irish tunes he'd learned as a boy.

I started to sing "The Shoogy Shoo" (the Swing), one of his favorites,
and began to weep. The song brought up too many memories.

"How come you're crying now?" Don asked in his engineering
voice. "You didn't cry after those two ships ignored us."

His tone of voice irritated me, and I stopped weeping. I was silent for
a moment while I considered his question. Then I answered, "It's personal things that cause my sadness or depression: the death of someone I love,
confrontations with you, put-downs or unfair attacks; extreme frustration
where I feel I have no control over a situation." Seeing an elderly man slip
and fall on the sidewalk could bring tears to my eyes. I could weep over a
valentine in a Hallmark store, or when I thought of my first love affair. I
could cry when I said something mean to my own kids.

"But how could you not be affected?" he probed. "It seemed so
unfair."

"Because it was *impersonal*. I was disappointed and angry, but I wasn't
touched personally. I'm just being philosophical about it, I guess."

He poured himself a straight cup of rum. "Philosophical! God
almighty. We haven't seen a ship since Acapulco, and you say you aren't
touched personally when they don't stop."

"I think I chalked it up as one more bitter pill. Sure I was stunned
and let down. But things are looking up for us. The engine works; we're
moving south. We don't need to be rescued. I just wish they had stopped
so we could get word to our family. I feel bad for them, not for me."

My answer puzzled him. He shook his head. "I can't believe you didn't
feel more than that." He wanted to press down into the depths of my psyche, but the rum in the eggnog made me sleepy and I had to turn in.

Don stayed up emptying the bottle of rum. I heard him plunking the strings of the mandolin he'd discovered earlier in the day safe and dry at the foot of Carl's berth. As he strummed away, he made up nasty songs that cursed the *Anaconda Valley* and *Cheun On*. With each sip of rum he became increasingly melodramatic, reciting aloud "Invictus," "Sea Fever," and passages from *Macbeth*.

After he'd swallowed the last drop of rum, he hopped into the berth, snuggled up beside me, covering me with amorous kisses, and a minute later, he was snoring.

In the morning he would discover that he'd covered eight pages of his journal with comments about what he'd gained from our experience: "We shouldn't waste time complaining—life hangs by a thin thread and is precious—constant vigilance is the cost of staying alive—love makes it all worthwhile—things must be shared with others to have their full meaning—it's great to be alive and have a second chance—the problems we face can best be conquered one step at a time—this dream of mine was pretty ridiculous." His last point, written in capital letters—PATIENCE —was barely decipherable.

NOTES

1. As a reminder to landlubbers who come aboard, many boaters install a plaque above the head indicating that nothing other than what has been chewed and digested (and small amounts of toilet paper) may be put down the plumbing. Using pages from a book could bring immediate disaster, and anyone who's ever owned a boat, knows that taking the head apart is an appalling task.

2. *Mischief in Patagonia*, p. 153.

3. *The Voyage of the Beagle,* p. 285

4. We had read that it costs between $10,000 and $20,000 an hour to run a ship. The costs go up, of course, if the ship stops en route. Any commercial ship using these channels must hire a Chilean pilot. Giving the benefit of the doubt to the ships that passed us, we speculated that the pilots might be docked for any delay. However, when we relayed the details later to Admiral Eduardo Allen (head of the Magellan Naval Region at the time), he was shocked to learn that neither ship had stopped, and he told us he would cite both ships for blatant violation of the International Rules of the Road.

5. *Mischief in Patagonia*, p. 92.

CHAPTER 13

Good Friday Encounter

MARCH 18

Two rejections in one day and an empty booze locker had given Don a shot in the arm: he had cursed, drunk, written away his frustrations, and was roaring to go. He kept repeating, "Screw the ships! We'll get ourselves to Punta Arenas! We'll sail this baby the whole way." and he spent hours refiguring and recalculating until he came up with an optimistic itinerary that would get us to Punta Arenas within two weeks. His new plan to average thirty to 35 miles a day was based on the favorable weather we'd been having. Clear skies and low humidity had settled into our brains as if we were sailing up the coast of California.

But higher powers had other ideas, and Don's plans suddenly went awry. Normal Patagonia weather returned with a vengeance—the temperatures dropped; gales brought an incessant onslaught of the dreary rain and the dismal, chilling cold that I'd thought was behind us. Something was jogging me out of my complacency, warning me not to get my hopes up, not to fall in love with this miserable place.

Our planned passages and anchorages for the next few days would take us through Angostura Guía (Guía Narrows), then down through Canal Sarmiento, the longest single channel between Canal Trinidad and the Strait of Magellan. For 67 miles this channel heads south-southeast, following an almost unwavering dotted line on the chart. Along the way, glacier-polished granite monoliths rise vertically over two thousand feet, and ribbons of waterfalls spill down snow-covered ridges.

We were headed first to Puerto Bueno, a quarter of the way down Canal Sarmiento, then to Puerto Mayne, another 20 miles south. Beyond that, safe anchorages would be difficult to find.

The weather worsened. Short, violent, confused chop built up, causing *le Dauphin* to pitch, yaw, and roll her way through the channel. The fact that I could see land a mile away did not reassure me. Conditions were everything I'd read about—bad!

I had difficulty managing the helm, and Don assumed more of the watches. At first, gale force winds were a boon; we flew toward Puerto

Bueno with the mizzen and staysail filled. But at Fiordo Peel,[1] which intersects the northern entrance to Canal Sarmiento at almost right angles from the east, icy winds that funnel down the fjord's tourmaline glaciers hit with unexpected intensity. According to the *Pilot*, drifting icebergs had been sighted in the area, "rendering navigation hazardous . . . in poor visibility."[2]

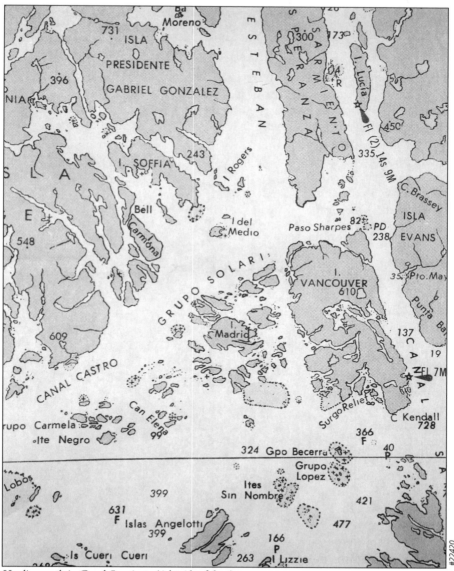

Heading south in Canal Sarmiento (right side of chart)

Don loved the challenge, comparing it to the thrill he felt the first time he went through Deception Pass—a narrow, hazardous passage in Puget Sound known for its strong currents and whirlpools. He wrote:

> The currents here in Angostura Guía reportedly reach 8 knots at times and the *Pilot* warns that a cross-current can set a boat on the southern shore. We have no tide tables, but we were lucky and hit it right today. There was heavy chop, but we roared through the narrows with the current, and I could barely maintain steerage. With Réanne on the bowsprit as lookout, the whole experience was extremely satisfying to me. Gusty, heavy winds continued, and we sailed the entire way through this channel, which looks like a flooded Yosemite Valley.

I had stretched our canvas tarp over the cockpit so we could steer without getting wet. Temperatures now hovered in the midforties, but we ate meals snuggled under the tarp, an army blanket covering our legs. The tarp setup was short-lived; williwaws struck, threatening to tear it apart, along with everything it was attached to.

Rain leaked continuously into the cabin, and I had soon used up all my cooking pots to catch the drips. In the galley and salon, high-pitched plinking tones, like plucked violins, competed with the howling woodwinds outside.

Someone had aptly named Puerto Bueno (Good Harbor). Its grassy banks lined with cedars and shrubs looked more like a groomed country club lawn than a wild Patagonia landscape. In the evening, like a good omen, the sun pierced the

Don kept looking over his shoulder to make sure that no one was there

dark clouds and a rainbow appeared southeast of us; although the noise and shudder of horrendous williwaws prevented our sleeping, we didn't feel threatened. If I could have been set down in any anchorage of my choice, it would have been this one. As much as I had liked Dársena Aid and the other beautiful anchorages we would see, Puerto Bueno offered the safest shelter we would ever find.

Torrential rains prevented visibility the morning of March 18, and when Don suggested we take a layover day I was delighted. I'd been fighting aches, chills, and a sore throat for two days, and the thought of moving on in such foul weather didn't thrill me. I spent the day in bed. That night I wrote:

The rain has poured, poured all day; the wind has screeched. But we're safely anchored here on one hook, and it's a wonderful day for sleeping!

I don't know whether it's the weather or my physical state, but I'm losing drive. There's so much high tension when we're under way—keeping a lookout for rocks, maneuvering against currents, checking the strain on the stays and booms—that I can't get excited about accomplishing anything when we finally anchor.

I'm trying to put on a good front for Don so he doesn't get discouraged, but I'm in limbo; my mind and my senses are dulled. I miss the news, the programs on the BBC, talking with other hams; I miss being able to communicate with my French friends; I miss exchanging ideas with people—the quick repartee with certain colleagues, the jokes we play on each other, the banter. Whether my flu-like symptoms are the cause of my lethargy, or whether lethargy caused the symptoms, I don't know. This morning I realized I haven't even dreamed for over a week.

Don is stimulated by the changes in weather, by the currents and williwaws; he calculates our progress, jots down ideas for articles, plans our next day's itinerary. He wouldn't understand my need for outside stimulation. Thank goodness our ups and downs never seem to coincide!

Despite Don's belief that my flu was "mental illness," my outward attitude nevertheless made an impression on him. He wrote: "R. has had such a good attitude today. She spent most of the day in bed, but she got up tonight and baked Irish soda bread while I kept the fire going."

I was beginning to wonder if my inability to shake the sore throat was related to a lack of iron. I had developed such an addiction for spinach and beets that I could open a small can and wolf down the contents like Popeye—straight, no seasoning. We were down to our last few cans of each, and I hadn't shaken my craving yet. In addition, I was still tossing off half a can of frosting each day. My body was sending me signals, and all I could do was try to feed it what it wanted.

MARCH 19

Continuous gale force winds had compensations. Visibility increased, and the winds propelled us down a raging, frothy Canal Sarmiento after we left Puerto Bueno, bound for Puerto Mayne. I was still aching and my throat was gravelly, so Don took the four-hour helm duty, loving every minute of it, writing afterwards:

> It's hard to believe how moody a place like this can be, and how the moods change so quickly and completely. Right now, it's terribly somber. Mountains and ridges fade in and out of view; waves heap up in response to each burst of wind, and the rest of the time the raindrops just fall, fall, fall.
>
> Is this a natural ritual to retire the old and make way for the new, or a show of strength between rival forces of pressure? No wonder Darwin's visits here in the 1830s fueled his imagination.
>
> I answered nature's call this afternoon in the rain and couldn't help wondering what the Chilean navy would think if they saw me squatting bare-assed on the stern. As I tore off sheets of the *Exorcist,* I kept looking over my shoulder to make sure nobody was there.

Puerto Mayne marked the halfway point of the 150 miles to the Strait of Magellan. We were still nearly 360 miles from Punta Arenas, and it looked like miserable weather had set in for good. The anchorage was not well protected, and within an hour of arriving, the anchor dragged and we had to reset it. By dark the wind was blowing more than 40 knots from the north, and we had to set an additional two anchors off the starboard and port stern to keep from blowing ashore.

At 2000 hours there was a sudden lull, and I went above to see what the silence was about. Lighted by an almost full moon, clouds formed a coronet around the horizon. Above us was a midnight-blue dome. The silence was the eye of the storm.

"Why can't the storm ever pass to the side of us?" Don lamented. "We're always caught in the middle. These are the same conditions we had two days after we pitchpoled, and I've had about all the excitement I want!"

The barometer continued to drop, and noise like kettledrums replaced the silence. The wind veered 180 degrees and screamed through the rigging, shaking the masts, swinging the boat round and round, and wrapping the three anchor lines around one another like macramé.

MARCH 20

At 0200, Don wrote:

> Williwaws have been so fierce we don't dare sleep. But we can't stay up any longer—we're too exhausted. I've just checked the anchors, but it's so black outside with the blowing rain that there's no reference point to see how we're

doing. It frightens me, but there's nothing we can do; the anchors will just have to take care of themselves while we try to sleep. God, I'm glad we decided to come in here and anchor, instead of continuing south: we would have been smashed to smithereens by now. It makes me sick to think of it.

We had a helluva time entering Puerto Mayne. We had to turn into the wind, and even with the engine at full speed, I could barely make headway. Then I remembered the technique my Uncle Phil used during his canoe trip up the Inside Passage to Alaska. "When the currents are contrary, head into shore where the back eddies help you go upwind." So that's what I did. R. nearly had a hemorrhage because we were so close to shore, but it was the only way we could make it.

At 0600, he got up to check the weather. A thick veil of rain surrounded us, and he couldn't see more than ten feet. "I think we'd better stay here another day. What do you think?"

I poked my head out the hatch and looked forward. A small albatross was hunkered down on the unbroken spreader, his talons hooked on for dear life. I closed the hatch and shook the rain from my hair. "Yeah, I think so too."

All color was gone from Don's face. The enthusiasm that had fired him for two days was gone. "I think I'm losing my nerve," he told me. "I'm having a hard time holding back a panicky feeling that we should make a run for it, just keep going till we get somewhere—at just twenty miles a day it seems like we're crawling."

He looked as if he were about to faint. I suggested he go back to bed. "Yeah? I don't feel very well. I think I will."

That evening he wrote:

I stayed in bed all day with a headache and aches. It's mental, I'm sure. Sometimes I just feel like giving in, and I guess I did today. There's so much to do—fill the kerosene bottles and lamps; pump out several hundred gallons of bilge water per day; check the barometer and the bearings; read the *Pilot;* study the chart—so much to worry about that I probably made myself sick. I worry about the anchor—if it will hold, if we'll be able to get it up in the morning. And every little task—pumping the boat out, preparing a meal, filling the thermos—takes so much time that we're just tuckered out. The boat leaks about 600 double strokes a day, which amounts to 300 gallons or more.

Réanne felt better today, and she's been pounding at the typewriter and singing. It sure makes me feel better to see her like that. Maybe we'll make it yet. We didn't have any heat yesterday or today. Have to conserve it for when we're wet. R. sits on the settee wearing three sweaters and one wool blanket as she writes letters, using only the skylight or the kerosene lamps for light. She sure is putting up with a lot without complaining.

We had been working well as partners for days and hadn't had any outbursts. I wondered if Don's mellowness was attributable to his "loss of nerve." Perhaps a certain amount of humility had begun to creep into his psyche. Perhaps he really was "learning," as he'd written earlier in his drunken state. Whatever the reason, I liked him this way, and it gave me hope for our future.

MARCH 21

"No more indulgence for now," Don declared as we left Puerto Mayne. It was Good Friday. The sky was somber, but visibility was good. Both of us had shaken our mental and physical symptoms, and Don wanted to try our luck with the wind to see if we could make eighty miles in one day.

Before noon, the sun peeked through the clouds, and Don tried to take a noon shot to double-check our latitude, but the sun disappeared. Shortly afterward, the barometer began to drop, the wind increased, and it started to rain again. The seas in Canal Sarmiento built up into four-foot breaking crests.

The staysail jibed violently from side to side, the prop freewheeled and whirred, the helm fought me. The motion of the boat didn't feel right, and I was becoming alarmed. Suddenly, the knot meter pegged at 8, and the boat surfed down a huge, white breaker. I lost control of the helm and screamed for Don to take over.

"This is as bad as those greybeards," I wailed. "We're never going to be safe. Never!" I went below to batten things down, swearing as I tried to catch the pots that flew from side to side. I could hear the staysail jibing and prayed it would hold. Just as I finished stowing things, Don called me to take the helm so he could put a preventer on the staysail.

He had just settled at the helm again when the staysail boom cracked in two and began thrashing like a tethered colt. "Go lower the staysail," he told me.

I ran forward and dropped the halyard. The boat yawed, Don lost steerage, and we went broadside to the wind. The boat raced toward shore, the staysail filling with every gust of wind, and the pieces of broken boom flapped uncontrollably. I couldn't grab hold of either section to tie it down.

"Come back here and drop the mizzen!" Don yelled.

I wrapped the halyard quickly around the sail to keep it from flying and scrambled aft. I dropped the mizzen, furled it, and tied it down.

"Godalmighty, I can't leave the helm long enough to start the engine. For godsake, get that staysail tied down so you can take over for me."

I ran back to the foredeck. The staysail halyard had come loose and everything was out of control. I grasped a section of broken boom.

"Tie it down before it kills you!" Don yelled.

I grabbed the sail and wrapped it around the broken pieces, jamming the whole bundle between my legs. The boat slowed, but we lay broadside

Bendoran *makes a lee for us*

to the channel, and the wind kept pushing us toward shore. *We're done for,* I thought. *We're going to be crushed against that granite wall.* I looked up and glanced across the spray-streaked channel just in time to spot a ship poking its bow around the corner of Paso Farquar into Canal Sarmiento.

"A ship, a ship!" I screamed, pointing.

Don turned and glanced rapidly to the south. His mouth tightened into a sarcastic grimace. "So what! Tie the goddam staysail down. That ship's not going to stop!"

My fingers were so cold from the freezing rain I kept fumbling and couldn't get the ties around the sail. Don's tone of voice implied that I was dragging my feet.

"Look, look! They're slowing down! Should I get out the distress flag?"

The ship made its full ninety-degree turn into the channel, and I was sure they had sighted us. We didn't need a distress flag to call attention to our condition. We were lying ahull, broadside to the channel, and it was obvious we were in distress.

"We've got more to worry about than a fucking freighter," he yelled. "See that granite wall at the end of the channel? If we don't get this boat under control, we've had it."

I shut up, finished tying down the staysail, then turned to watch the freighter again, risking more wrath.

"Don, dammit, look! It *is* slowing."

He was coiling a line and ignored me. When he had it secured, he turned to look at the ship while I ran below for the binoculars.

"Take a look." I jammed the binoculars into his hands.

"By God, I think you're right. There's someone on the third deck with a megaphone. No, they're not stopping," he sneered. "They're just trying to get out of our way . . . No. Wait! Look at their prop—they *are* stopping."

The wash from the freighter's propeller had gone down, and it had begun a 180-degree turn to provide a lee for us.

Don ties the bow to the Bendoran

Don ran below to short the solenoid and start the engine, then dashed back up to the helm and tried to bring the boat into the wind. No response. He jammed the throttle all the way forward. It seemed an eternity before the boat responded, and when it did, the gale caught the bow and sent us flying toward the opposite shore. Five minutes to get the bow into the wind, with the throttle still at full rpms. Finally the bow began inching its way around, the propeller losing its bite as we turned. Swells lifted up the stern, the prop came out of the water, and the engine raced.

"God, I hope I can get this thing around before the engine blows apart," Don hollered.

When the ship was within fifty yards, a crewman leaned over the railing and shouted through the megaphone in English, "Do you need help?" I spotted a British Union Jack flying above the pilot house. Don leapt onto the cabin roof and raised a couple of empty five-gallon fuel jugs over his head, and we saw the man with the megaphone run up the stairs to the bridge.

"Go below and get the messages you prepared two weeks ago."

My heart pounding, I jumped below, grabbed the messages, and scrawled on a sheet of paper, WE PITCHPOLED AT 50°S, 89°W, HAVE MUCH DAMAGE, AND NEED FUEL. I shoved everything inside a plastic film protector bag.

"Quick, get out the fenders and tie them on the starboard side. I can't come around to port."

By then, the ship had completely stopped and lay ahull to windward of us, making a lee and creating a calming effect on the seas. Somehow, we had to get those messages up the side of that monster. A rope ladder was dropped over the side of the ship and flapped out of control in the wind. As I fumbled with the fenders, I looked up and saw a seaman standing by the top of the ladder. He was wearing a life jacket, and I wondered if he planned to climb down.

"Get a life vest on. You'll have to go up that ladder," Don said. "And hang on tight, we may hit hard as we come alongside."

I looked up again and tried to swallow. I would have to climb higher than our mast to reach the top of the ladder. And the giant steel hulk was heeling toward us in the wind —I would have to free-climb without anything solid to brace my feet against.

Réanne went up the laddr at the right

As Don wheeled the helm over to bring our starboard side along the ship, I expected the mast to crash and shatter against it. But with the spreader broken, the mast slipped right under the third deck. The crew were able to reach over and push it away before it cracked against their hull.

The crew dropped two lines—one for the bow, one for the stern— and Don began securing them.

Trembling, I stuffed the notes into my pocket, snapped the two five-gallon jugs into a carabiner that I'd lashed to a line around my waist, and started up the rope ladder. I was going over the lip again. The memory of Don's words on our first date drove me upward. *You can do it . . . you can always do more than you think you can.*

The wind whipped round the stern of the ship, and the ladder swung freely. I stopped climbing and clung to the rope. The wind stopped, and I continued up, cautiously. The steel hull was a rounded monolith in the California desert, a limestone cliff above the Grand Canyon, the granite needles of Mount Whitney. The rope ladder was my only belay. *One step after another. Keep your feet on the outside of the ladder so it stays vertical. Don't take your eyes off your feet, or your hands off the rope. One step at a time. Don't look down.*

Hands pulled me and the 5-gallon jugs up over the railing onto the third deck. I felt faint.

Someone asked, "Do you need gas-oil or marine diesel?"

Hanging my head toward my knees to keep from passing out, I said, "Ask my husband." When the lightheadedness passed I stood up and unhooked the jugs.

"Are you all right?"

I recognized the crewman who had shouted to us, and I nodded.

"I'll take you to the captain."

I panted behind him as he sprinted up another two decks and into the captain's apartment, where he introduced me to Captain and Mrs. Adam Addison of the cargo liner *Bendoran*.[3]

Don wrote later:

> I was really proud of Réanne for heading up that ladder—physically and mentally no mean feat. There was nothing she could push her feet against and the ladder went out in front of her, leaving her hanging with all her weight on her hands. I don't know how she did it, but she did, and never looked back. As I saw the seamen pull her over the railing, I had the irrational fear that it would be the last time I'd see her for months.
>
> A seaman with a German accent poked his head over the railing of a lower deck. "Do you need anything else, Captain? Water? Food?"
>
> I answered that we were desperate for diesel and that we had run out of toilet paper a few weeks ago and if they had any to spare we could sure use it. I could hear a bunch of them laughing and chattering in Spanish, Filipino, English, and German. A few minutes later down came a plastic duffel filled with toilet paper; then a rope bag with a big pot of soup in it. No fuel yet, and I began to wonder what was happening, but told myself it wasn't just a matter of opening a spigot.

Gasping for breath, and with my heart still pounding wildly, I handed the packet of messages to the captain and briefly described our pitchpoling. I asked if they could radio our families, as well as the port captain in Punta Arenas. He excused himself and immediately went to look for his radio engineer.

It was warm in the apartment, and I was so excited I began to perspire under my life jacket and foul weather gear.

"Would you like some Scottish scones and tea?" Mrs. Addison asked, urging me to take off my jacket. *Fresh scones and tea!* I nodded, "Yes!" It sounded wonderful!

Captain Addison returned quickly and apologized. "I'm sorry, my engineer is down helping your husband with fuel right now, but we'll radio your messages as soon as we get under way." He also explained that the *Bendoran* had received a broadcast early that morning alerting all ships to be on the lookout for an overdue yacht. It had been four weeks since our accident, and it was ten days beyond our ETA—and as Don had predicted, the authorities had waited over a week before putting out a notice. No airplanes would have been looking for us, I realized now.[4]

I described our shocking experiences with the *Cheun On* and *Acaconda Valley*. "That's inexcusable behavior," Captain Addison said. "You were flying an International Distress flag and they should have stopped to give you aid."

Mrs. Addison reappeared carrying a large silver tray with a pot of hot tea, a pitcher of milk, and a plate of fresh, warm scones. There were three white porcelain cups and butter plates with slices of sweet butter and dollops of raspberry jam. It was such a contrast to our situation that I felt like a pauper sitting in Buckingham Palace.

The porcelain and silver made me think of Mother—she was the last of a generation that would polish silver and use her best china for a tea. I pushed her from my mind—by midnight she would know we were alive and okay. I couldn't let myself think about her or Daddy; I was already on the verge of tears from the Addisons' kindness, and I was afraid I'd break down in front of them.

Mrs. Addison plied me with questions about our trip. I gave them a quick run-down of our passage from Los Angeles to Acapulco, the kids' defections, our trip to Easter Island, the problem with the chronometer, our pitchpoling, and the four weeks it had taken us to get this far. I suddenly ran out of breath again.

"Excuse me, but I'm so excited to be able talk to someone I'm talking too fast." I took a breath and tried to slow down, then went on about how concerned I was about my parents, how I had felt the kids would survive on their own if we disappeared, but that it would kill my parents.

"Yes, it's always harder on old people," Mrs. Addison replied.

"When we spotted your sailboat a while ago," Captain Addison said, "we worried that someone aboard might need medical attention. We don't have a doctor on board, but we could take you to Valparaiso."

Valparaiso on a freighter. Comfortable accommodations, good food, hot water for showers, someone to talk to. At some other time I might have accepted. But we had to get to port now and repair the boat.

"We're in fine shape physically," I said, "and I'd love to stay aboard, but I couldn't leave my husband alone."

He smiled and nodded, then asked what had prompted us to come to the region.

"It's been my husband's life dream to round Cape Horn," I said. "But it hasn't worked out the way he planned."

"It's my husband's dream, too," Mrs. Addison said.

"Big boat or little?" I asked.

"Either!" The captain smiled.

"Why don't you climb down and talk to my husband?" I said.

Captain Addison left again to check on the fuel transfer, and when he returned he asked, "Do you drink?"

I didn't know whether to answer like a prude, "No, never!" or say, "Of course, and we're all out of booze." Seeing my hesitation, he asked if we would like a bottle of Scotch.

Mrs. Addison kept asking if there was anything else we could use. My mind went blank—and all I could think of was paprika! I learned later that Don had the presence of mind to ask for large-scale charts and toilet paper.

I'd been on board for over an hour when Captain Addison glanced at his watch, looked anxiously out the window, and hurried out to check on how things were progressing.

While I was enjoying the warm scones and hot tea, our fuel jugs were going up the line empty, and down filled with bunker oil. Don would write:

Just when I was getting nervous, with no sign of Réanne, and no fuel, the first 5-gallon jug came down. I opened it and poured out the thickest, blackest oil I'd ever seen in my life. It looked like the last few drops of oil from a car that had run over 150,000 miles without a change. It was so viscous in the low temperatures that it took forever to drain out. I was worried it might not flow through our three-stage fuel filter. *Here goes,* I thought. *Our documentation certificate calls* le Dauphin *an oil screw, and this is about as basic as you can get.*

The parade of jugs began coming down the hand line, but nothing could speed the way the oil drained. It was pouring rain by now, and I was getting worried that water might mix with the fuel.

I began to shake, partly from excitement, partly from the cold. The wind blew fuel all over my yellow slickers and into the cockpit, but I couldn't have cared less. I glanced to leeward. The granite wall was getting closer, and we'd blown well past the light marking the end of Canal Sarmiento. How gutsy of the captain, I thought, and he's got a damned good crew. I just prayed they'd keep those jugs coming as fast as possible.

The fuel jugs went down the line . . .

Captain Addison returned momentarily. "I say," he said in his clipped Scottish brogue, "I don't want to rush you, but the wind has increased and we're drifting toward shore."

I stood up to leave, and Mrs. Addison handed me a small datebook and a calendar, both imprinted with the crest of the *Bendoran.* My eyes filled. Everyone had been so helpful and considerate, I realized once again how much I missed human companionship.

The engineer poked his head around the door, smiled, and asked, "Ready?"

As I climbed over the railing and placed my feet on the rope ladder, he said, "You'll think twice before making a trip like this again, won't you?" I heard the crew cheering as I made my way down the swinging ladder.

In the 60 minutes I'd been aboard the *Bendoran,* the wind had increased and I had to shout to Don when I touched deck. "The captain thinks we should get going."

He had just finished draining 35 gallons of bunker oil and wanted to fill one more jug, but he yelled to the engineer, "Conditions are deteriorating, we'd better cast off the lines and get going!"

"Send up that last container. I'll get it filled."

"That's great! That last container will bring us up to a little more than half a tank. . . . Damn, what a crew! They have big balls as well as compassion! And look, they won't have turning room in another few minutes."

Tying down our jugs Don said, "How the hell do you pull away from a steel ship that's pushing you sideways and downwind? This'll take some doing." He started the engine and listened. "It sounds okay," he said. "I was afraid the engine wouldn't run on that stuff, but I guess a good diesel can run on just about any kind of oil."

I studied him for a moment. His yellow slicker and pants were covered with black oil. Beginning to shiver, he stuttered, "Cast off the lines."

I moved the fenders aft to the starboard quarter. Don put the helm hard to port, gunned the engine, and tried to get up some speed. The fenders took a rubbing, and we moved a few inches away from the freighter. He brought the helm to center and we gained speed, banging occasionally into the steel hull. Then we flew along its stern.

As we approached the *Bendoran's* huge flared fantail, Don gave it full throttle—and we just missed their starboard propeller. They had put their rudder hard to port, waiting for us to clear it.

"That captain is a gentleman and an artist!" Don said.

Without their lee now, the gale hit with its full fury, and we rolled into the confused seas that bounced off a vertical rock wall a hundred yards away. The *Bendoran* gunned its engines, pushing a wall of white water behind us. We did a 180-degree turn, squeezing just between the ship and the rock wall.

I opened up our abandon-ship locker, took out our Union Jack flag, hanked it to our port signal halyard, and ran it up and down in salute to Captain Addison and his crew. When the *Bendoran* had steerage and was finally out of danger, her crew lined up along the railing, waving and shouting and snapping photos of us. Laughing and crying, Don and I shot photos of them, our shouts of thanks flying to the wind. We waved, they waved, until we had lost sight of each other.

Our troubles aren't over yet—the storm rages on, it's getting darker and wilder by the moment. The temperature has plummeted, and the rain's turning to hail. The channel looks like a white shag carpet. But God, do we feel better! Knowing we have half a tank of fuel, that our family and friends will soon have word that we're alive, that human kindness still does exist.

We'll push for Columbine Cove, Don says. It has bad holding ground, according to the Pilot, and furious squalls descend the steep mountainside, but it's our only chance right now. This has truly been a Good Friday!⁵

NOTES

1. This is the fjord into which Tilman took *Mischief* to begin his traverse of the icecap. When he and his crew entered the fjord, they were so excited by the sight of the ice floes that they went out of their way to photograph them " . . . much as some ignorant clown might greet the first few ranging shots of a hostile battery. It is ridiculous to think that we went out of our way to photograph these feeble harbingers of the coming hordes." (p. 100).

2. Since 1990, all vessels are required to sound their horn when they begin entry to Canal Sarmiento and to broadcast their estimated time of arrival at ten-minute intervals. There was no way we could have done either.

3. It was our good luck that the *Bendoran*—a 12,000-ton container ship belonging to the cargo fleet of the Scottish Ben Line—had been chartered for twelve months by a German company to pick up wool in Punta Arenas and deliver it to Europe; their usual run was the Orient. This was their initial passage in the area. They had come through the Panama Canal, down the west coast of South America, and were returning the same way.

4. Later, we would learn that all planes in the region had been grounded for almost a month because of the miserable weather and storm-force winds.

5. Several months later, we discovered that we had made an error in dates: Good Friday was actually a week later.

CHAPTER 14

Strait of Magellan Ahead

MARCH 21, EVENING

Large-scale charts to get us to the Strait, fuel, toilet paper, a bottle of Scotch, and the knowledge that our families and friends would soon receive word that we were alive. We were filled with gratitude, and high as horses heading for the corral at the end of a long day.

It was still nearly three hundred miles to Punta Arenas, and the worst weather we would encounter in the Patagonian Channels was yet to come, but we didn't know that—we thought we were about to cross the finish line.

Our rendezvous with the *Bendoran* had taken more than two hours. But in our excitement neither of us had paid attention to the time, and as we rounded Paso Farquhar and headed south along the eastern shore of Isla Newton in Estrecho Collingwood, it was already dark.

Anchorages for small vessels are few in this part of the channels. Two minuscule anchors printed on the chart were the only possibilities for Isla Newton. The first, about two-thirds of the way down the island, was Caleta Columbine (Columbine Cove). The *Pilot* mentioned that furious squalls sometimes descended the steep mountainside and that it was reported to be a bad anchorage even in normal weather. The second anchorage was too deep for *le Dauphin,* so we didn't have much choice, but we decided we'd forget about Caleta Columbine if we could find an uncharted cove that looked safe. A navigation light on the northeast side of the island flashed reassuringly at us—at least some of the navigational aids were functioning.[1]

We hugged the lee shore of Isla Newton, trying to get some protection against the wind. Spotting a small indention, Don gave me orders to head in.

"Wait a minute. No . . . Head back out—it's too small."

I turned slowly to port.

"Wait. Maybe it'll go," he said. "Let's try it."

I turned the helm back to starboard, straightened it out, and headed back in.

"I'll go to the bow," he said. "You follow my instructions."

Within seconds I heard: "Head out, head out! Quick!"

Frantic, I jammed the throttle full forward and wheeled the helm around. The northwest wind caught the boat and propelled us back into the channel.

Don came aft and plopped down beside me. "God, will this ever end? Everything we do is an emergency. That cove was full of rocks. If the *Bendoran* hadn't stopped, we'd really be low on fuel by now."

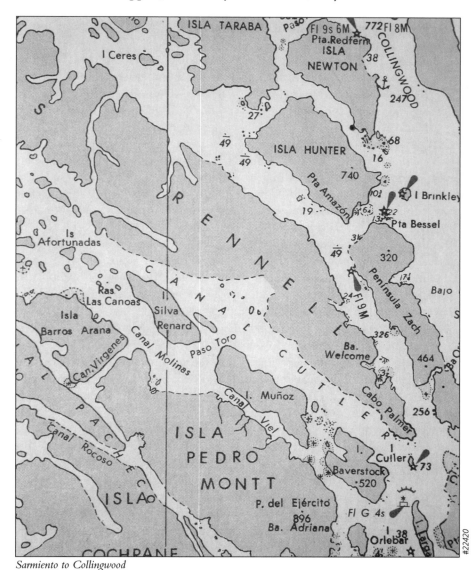

Sarmiento to Collingwood

We continued motoring south, and within an hour Don detected a small dark knob at the end of a low spit. The lay of the land fit the description of the entrance to Caleta Columbine. To me, everything looked like a massive blob of black ink. Without lights or reference points, my depth perception at night was nil.

Don shouted directions from the bow while I maneuvered the boat. "Turn to starboard. A little to port. Keep her straight. Hard right. Straight. Good, hold her there!"

I might as well have been sightless, trying to cross a New York City street—I was totally dependent on his directions, as he was on my ability to follow them.

"Okay. That's good. Neutral."

I heard the anchor chain rattling over the bow and waited for him to call "Reverse" to set the anchor. But the wind was so strong it blew us back down, setting the anchor for us.

"Okay, sweetie, you go down and fix us some supper. I'll do the rest."

I went below and noticed a huge stainless pot on the stove. I recalled hearing someone yell something about soup as I had crawled down the *Bendoran*'s ladder, but it hadn't made sense to me, so I'd ignored it. We were supposed to transfer the soup and send the pot back, but Don had forgotten to tell me about it.

I lifted the lid, peered in, and sniffed. It was real soup—a thick, creamy potage of puréed fresh vegetables, with tiny strips of carrots and zucchini. I took a taste. Cream and butter coated the inside of my mouth. No dried milk, no Butter Buds, no canned veggies in this one. It was the closest we'd come to a four-star dinner in months.

I lit the stove and heated up the soup. Don came below, broke out the bottle of Scotch, and sipped while he logged: "1930 hours: The wind is so strong tonight, I let out the full 600 feet of line. With stretch on the line, we're now the equivalent of one and a half football fields from the CQR! That should do it. But to be sure it holds, and to give us a reference point in the dark, I motored forward 200 feet, set the small Danforth, and we fell back to our original position, keeping the second line somewhat loose. If the strain on the Danforth increases greatly, I'll know the CQR is dragging."

Neither of us had ever been Scotch drinkers. Amateur connoisseurs of good wine, a foreign beer now and then, and once in a while a gin and tonic. But Scotch, never! I let a sip slide down my throat. "Sip it slowly. Savor it," my Scotch-drinking friends always urged me, "you'll love it." I took another sip and let it cauterize my throat; it did have an unusual taste. Maybe I could force myself to like it—Don didn't seem to be having a problem.

We gorged on soup. There were quarts of it, but at the rate we were inhaling it, we'd have the pot licked by the next day.

The Scotch didn't make us sleepy; our springs were too wound up. We jabbered on and on excitedly, recalling everything that had happened during the *Bendoran's* stop.

Don could hardly take a breath between sentences. "Leave it to the British. I should have known they'd stop. You knew they would, didn't you? But I was so sure they wouldn't, I was really pissed at you. Sorry if I was nasty, but if you hadn't gotten that staysail tied down we'd be on the rocks right now.

"Damn, the British are superb. The crew of the *Bendoran* are superb! Screw those other ships. Let's drink a toast to the British—they've got the best navy in the world. Those guys are my heroes. Let's drink to Captain Addison. What a captain—making a lee for us, holding that ship there with the current pushing her toward the rocks. He's on my list with Cook and Vancouver now."

Sleepy or not, it was clear by midnight that we wouldn't have a chance to close our eyes even if we wanted to. Williwaws kept us up, and by 0100 we had four anchors out. We spent the remainder of the night listening to the howl, checking conditions, verifying that the anchors were holding, and writing in our journals and log.

As we sit here on the galley settee under the kerosene lamp, I think of our first forty-eight hours in Dársena Aid. I'd been so sure that what I heard was the roar of jet planes searching for us. Listening to the williwaws tonight, I begin to think it's impossible for anything to equal the noise of these winds. It's another high-adrenaline show, and I wonder how long our glands can keep pumping out the fluid. Do they ever reach a point where they say, "Hey, I don't have anymore to give"? We have stressed everything possible in our bodies—our glands, our muscles, our joints, our brains. And still, on nights like this, we go on being stretched and tested; the human body is amazing.[2]

MARCH 22

At the first sign of dawn, conditions began to stabilize, and we lay down to rest. Our springs unwound, and we slept till noon. By then the barometer had risen and the curtain of dark clouds was lifting above the mountains.

On deck to raise the anchors, Don began with the small Danforth. A mess of line came up, hopelessly entangled. He let go of it and sat down on the cabin roof, his teeth clenched. "Christ, it's going to take hours to

In Bahía Isthmus, we had our first view of the mainland South America

get this stuff untangled. This is going to take some thought. I hope *you* have patience, because I may not."

Using the sheet winch, we pulled on the first line, tied it off while we unfouled the next line; winched some more; tied it off till the next line could be passed under or over. We kept winching, tying off, unfouling, forcing the boat opposite the direction it had swung all night, until we could pass the bitter end of one line over another. Two hours later we were finally able to raise the anchors themselves. The bow anchor could be lifted with the winch, and the twenty-five pound Danforth was no problem. The fifty-pound kedge and fifty-pound yachtsman were a different story—they had been dropped straight over the toe rail and hung straight down.

"I can't handle many more of these jobs," Don said. "We sure can't afford to leave either an anchor or a line, but I'm sorely tempted right now."

A curious creature that resembled an intricate hand-crocheted doily diverted our attention; it had wrapped its lacy arms around one of the flukes of the kedge anchor. I pried it off carefully to study it, hoping it wouldn't grab me next. I tried to lay it on deck, but it wouldn't cooperate, and without its sea environment, it quickly expired. I marvelled at it: five main arms grew out of a half-dollar-sized center disk, dividing into hundreds of smaller, more delicate branches. Although I was never able to fully extend its arms, I estimated they would have reached nearly two feet in diameter. Later, I discovered its name: basket star. Several days after, one of its relatives—a feather star—made its appearance in the same manner.

Although it was after 1400 hours and late to be moving, neither of us wanted to spend another night in Caleta Columbine. So, with a following north wind behind us, we took off sailing and covered twenty-one miles in four hours.

1800 hours: We are anchored in Bahía Isthmus on the east side of Canal Smyth. We face Peninsula Muñoz Gamero, which is part of the mainland. It sounds strange, finally, to be able to say "mainland" after we've navigated so many miles through island after island. Don claims this is his favorite spot to date. After last night's dreadful experience it looks like heaven to me.

From here we look northeast across a narrow isthmus that leads to Seno Union. The mountains across the sound glow with the last pink of the setting sun, and near their summits translucent tourmaline glaciers lay packed in carved cirques, their snouts spilling down to the saltwater in undulating waves. Trees and shrubs, now smaller and more stunted, grow along the shores to a maximum elevation of 200 feet—an indication, along with lowering temperatures, that the latitude is increasing. I called Don's attention to a blackened hill to the southeast that looks like it's been struck by fire. He thinks it's disease, but the ground appears charred to me. It seems incredible that a fire could start out here. Perhaps it was caused by man?

During the night Don and I awoke simultaneously, aware that there was no noise. Used to a constant parade of stimuli, our senses had grown alert at the eerie calm. No waves lapped against the hull; nothing rocked the boat. It was as if the boat had been lifted onto a bed of concrete.

We got up to look outside. A half-moon reflected on motionless water. The humidity had dropped, and not a cloud was visible on the dusky slate horizon. Beautiful and secure, *le Dauphin* was a painted ship upon a painted ocean.

I fell asleep again immediately, but Don lay awake thinking of the problems Joshua Slocum had had with the natives—they had pilfered everything from the *Spray* they could get their hands on. Slocum had been given a bag of carpet-tacks to use as a defense against them, and one night, when he was particularly tired, he sprinkled the tacks on deck. A few hours later he was awakened by the howl of "savages."

Most of the natives had been wiped out by white man's diseases in the early 1900s, but that didn't prevent Don's brain from conjuring up a similar scenario:

It's been so quiet. I lay here listening intently for any small sound or noise outside. My heart raced. What is it? I pictured a band of natives crossing that little isthmus and stripping our boat dry. What could they possibly want with our small sailboat? one side of my brain reasoned. Plenty, the other half replied—sails, food, clothes, nylon line, metal. I imagined that the burned spot on shore was caused by a native fire. What if the natives have been watching us and know there are only two of us aboard? What

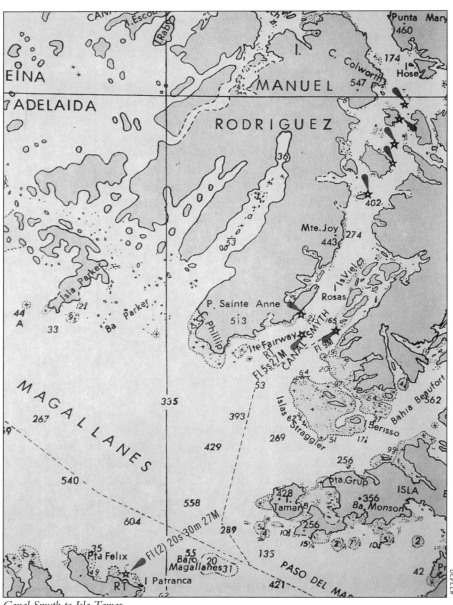

Canal Smyth to Isla Tamar

if we don't appear outside tomorrow and they think we're weak and easy victims? Slocum said they could paddle alongside silently at night, crawl on board, and you might not even know it.

At that point, I got up, inserted the washboard in the companionway, jammed it closed, and checked the screws in the skylight. Réanne woke up and asked what I was doing. I answered, "Nothing." I didn't want to let on about my overactive imagination.

MARCH 23

2000 hours. Today was a great layover day. I feel renewed. We stayed in bed till 1100 hours—eighteen hours of sleep—what a luxury! I heated a big pot of water, stripped, washed my hair, and scrubbed my whole body with hot water and soap. I washed some clothes and hung them outside, and they dried within hours, proof of lowered humidity today. I cut apart my miserable grey pants with the worn-out seat and used them as a pattern for a new pair cut out of a navy blanket. I had to double-stitch each seam by hand, which was a nuisance, but it's the only way they'll ever hold together.

Today was also Jeff's birthday—a good excuse to bake a cake. So I dug into one of the buckets and found a package of yellow cake mix, and when the cake came out of the oven, we sang "Happy Birthday." I wonder what his response will be when he hears what happened to us. The last time we talked he said he still planned to fly to Punta Arenas to join us. If we get the boat repaired there, will we be able to count on him? Or will he say, "Sorry, I have other plans"? I'm not placing any bets.

So much depended on what would happen when we arrived in Punta Arenas that, for the time being, we had tabled discussion of future plans. We were blithely assuming that Punta Arenas would have facilities to repair the boat and that if our insurance claim were handled quickly, it could be accomplished in a reasonable amount of time.

Now that we were confident our family knew we were alive, Don had begun to mellow. He was less intense and hadn't flashed me his Mongolian scowl for ages. Our layover in Bahía Isthmus seemed like another holiday.

That night, with a few sips of Scotch relaxing his tongue, he said, "We'll just take one step at a time. Whenever conditions are good enough, we'll move. Otherwise, we'll stay put and hope our anchors hold." He paused for a moment, his eyes widened slightly, his mouth curled in a smile, and I could tell he was about to spring something on me. "Suppose we can get the boat repaired in Punta Arenas. How do you feel about continuing with our original itinerary to the Falklands, then Cape Town and Madagascar?"

Making plans meant he was recovering. But I wasn't ready yet for plans. Thoughts sputtered through my brain, instantaneous and erratic. *The boat's too much for the two of us to handle. We need crew. We're exhausted most of the time—our muscles and joints never stop hurting. I want to do something other than just survive. We've been doing the boat thing for five years—I'm tired of doing "Don's thing." I want to move on. I want to do my thing!* My motor raced uncontrollably; I forced myself to breathe deeply. *I have to handle this one delicately,* I thought, *or we'll have a ripping fight.*

I mentioned the few points I dared, then added, "Besides, my sabbatical ends in September, and I've got to get home in time to teach."

"Won't you consider asking for a leave of absence next year?"

My stomach tightened. Before I'd applied for my sabbatical, we'd gone round and round about the whole issue, Don asking constantly why I couldn't apply for an unpaid leave for the second year.

I would explain. Either I had to return to my teaching job in September or pay back my entire sabbatical stipend. We couldn't afford my taking an unpaid leave of absence—he knew that. Furthermore, I'd written a new program combining literature, politics, and culture for my advanced students, and I was eager to test it. But Don would keep pushing. If I didn't go, he told me, he might find someone else, insinuating that it might not be a man. I'd stood my ground, and we had finally arrived at a compromise that my school district approved: during major holidays the second year I would fly to meet him at pre-arranged ports,

Paso Shoal—a tricky passage whose dangers became apparent

adding on a few extra weeks of unpaid leave. That way, he could avoid long stretches without me.

My mind did its usual flip-flops: *Think of it. You've wanted to visit the Falklands and Madagascar. You'll never get there otherwise.* But, like sparks of a forest fire that keep igniting weeks after the flames are out, a voice inside me refused to be extinguished. It asked, *Is that what you really want?*

But now was not the time to go to the wall. "We can't afford that," I said quietly. "Especially now."

"Yeah. I suppose you're right. I guess we do have to wait till we get to Punta Arenas before we can make any decisions about next year."

Why did he bring this up tonight? He's pushing again. He'll push till I get angry. Dammit. I know his "needs"—he'll tell me he can't live without a woman—but every time we talk about being apart, my old fears surface, and I feel as if he's blackmailing me. One way or another, I have to come to terms with this issue. I've survived this edge-of-life trip; it's time to deal with psychological risk now.

MARCH 24

The day dawned as one of the most beautiful days we'd had since Dársena Aid. The sky, brilliant turquoise above, had the muted blue of high latitudes along the horizon. Autumn air stung our nostrils, and a few deciduous trees showed touches of orange among the evergreens—proof that summer had ended.

A dozen dolphins surrounded *our* dolphin as we left Bahía Isthmus. Then a score appeared, then hundreds—small black dolphins with white bellies and pointed noses. Like chorus girls taking their bows, they leapt, dove, and careened in continuous lines, scratching their backs along the dolphin striker. The water erupted, bubbled, foamed, and spouted with geysers. It was so clear, we could watch their movements underwater and see their heads darting from side to side at split-second intervals. Their movements appeared effortless; only their horizontal double-end fins seemed to move. Never had we seen so many dolphins gathered in one place at one time. Don wrote:

Sometimes we applaud or yell "bravo" at their acrobatic achievements, and they seem to like such attention. Rather than frightening them, it seems to encourage them. To see them take three leaps in a row, completely clear of the water, is not uncommon. Sometimes a larger senior dolphin nuzzles up to the stem of the boat, moves in just inches away from the bow, and stays there motionlessly for several seconds, though we're doing 5 knots or more and cutting a good bow wake. At other times, they actually surface below the bobstay and hit the dolphin striker with a gentle blow. When they do hit, they usually dive deep immediately, perhaps to test their depth perception and to see how close they can come, or perhaps they really want to make contact. They are so alive and so much fun we can't help but enjoy life a little more with them along.

Other than a few birds, krill, and the basket star clinging to our anchor, we had seen so little animal life that this was a marvelous treat.

Continuing southward, we entered Paso Shoal, a tricky, narrow passage whose dangers soon became apparent. Along the eastern shore a large ship lay tilted on its starboard hull, the bow pointing out toward the fairway. Green and white smoke stacks leaned toward the rocks on which the ship had gone aground, and its beautiful bronze propeller, high and dry, was green from oxidation. This was the third and most impressive wreck we had seen that day. And within ten minutes, we would spot yet another submerged hull.[3]

"How can *we* hope to get through safely if these steel hulks can't?"

"It's not the strength of a ship, babe, that's at fault. It's inattention to duty, lack of vigilance."

We glided closer to take photographs. The water, perfectly still a few minutes before, began to churn with ripples and upwellings.

"I think I understand what happens here," Don said. "See these rip tides? The *Pilot* doesn't say a thing about those. If a ship rounds that point in a stiff wind, one false move of the helm and the tidal stream carries it right on the rocks."

Instead of heading directly south, which would have put us smack in the open waters of the Strait of Magellan, Don laid a course that would take us southeast, inside Isla Tamar, a small island off the mainland.

About noon he asked if I wanted to try and make Caleta Rachas by evening. Although the *Pilot* said the cove was "well sheltered with good holding ground," its name translated in English had a chilling ring—Williwaws Cove.

"Yes, let's keep going," I said, "as long as the weather's good. We've only logged twenty-five miles so far."

By late afternoon we sighted the lighthouse on Isla Fairway. According to the *Pilot* this one and the one on the Evangelistas were the only two manned lighthouses at the western entrance to the Strait.

I stood on top of the hatch cover and focused the binoculars. "I think I see somebody . . . I do! There are two sailors on the hill near the lighthouse. They're waving to us." Quickly, I passed the glasses to Don.

"Do you want to go in and have a look?"

Lighthouse at Isla Fairway

Did I want to have a look? Did he have to ask? He could see how excited I was. These were the first Chileans we'd seen since Easter Island!

I watched as the sailors raced downhill to shore, pointing and beckoning to a small channel, no more than sixty feet wide, between Isla Fairway and another islet. The scale on the chart was too small to give us any idea what to expect. Don made a ninety-degree right turn and brought the throttle back to neutral—the current was drawing us in. As we drifted toward Isla Fairway, the sailors followed *le Dauphin* along the shore. A small dog ran wildly behind them, turning circles and lifting his head toward the sky as he barked excitedly. When we were close enough to shout, I told the sailors our names.

"Yes, we already know," one shouted back in Spanish. "We've been waiting for you."

A week earlier they had received an official notice to be on the look-out for the American yacht, *le Dauphin Amical*. They had also heard the *Bendoran's* contact with Punta Arenas giving a report about us. They wanted to know if we were all right. If we could come ashore and have dinner with them. If we needed anything. Flour? Sugar? Supplies? Did we want a shower? Could we spend the night? They could see we had no dinghy, or perhaps they'd already heard. Pointing to a motorized skiff on shore, they offered to pick us up.

Dinner in a warm house, a shower, a land bed, companionship, the chance to speak Spanish again and hear about their life on this lonely island—it all sounded wonderful. The channel, fairly well protected between the two islets, looked inviting, but there was no dock, no buoy, just a narrow channel where the current rushed through at several knots.

Don looked at the sky. It was still clear, but menacing dark clouds hung low over the mountains on the south side of the Strait. He surveyed the cove. "See what's happening—the current is pushing us toward shore. This isn't good. There's not much swinging room here, either, if the wind increases." He looked again at the sky, like an animal sniffing the air for a scent of danger, then again at the cove. "What do you think?"

My excitement sank like our lead line. I was longing for human contact, and this seemed the perfect place—an hour on the *Bendoran* hadn't begun to satisfy my craving. But I knew he was right. I knew how rapidly conditions could change in these channels. I could see we were being set toward shore and there wasn't enough room to turn around; there wasn't even enough swinging room if we anchored and the wind increased during the night. Don's "constant vigilance" had kept us safe so far; there was no use chancing it. I answered reluctantly, "I suppose we'd better not."

I turned to the sailors, made the hand signal "iffy," pointed toward the other side of the Strait, and said, "It's better that we don't remain."

They both glanced southward. "Sí. Too bad. We understand."

"Please radio Punta Arenas that we expect to arrive March 30. We'll continue to Isla Tamar now."

"*Buen viaje. Buena suerte! Good luck!*" they shouted and headed back up the slope, the yappy dog following at their heels. It was hard to tell who'd been more excited—we, or they, or the mutt.

Pushed by the current, the boat slipped effortlessly through the little channel and out to the west. Don put the throttle in forward, and we turned south past the end of Isla Fairway. We looked back toward the lighthouse. Up on the hill, the sailors were dipping the Chilean flag in our honor. Don opened the abandon-ship locker, grabbed our Chilean flag, and hanked it onto the flag halyard, raising and lowering it in response.

The young men climbed to the top of the lighthouse, took off their shirts, and waved them above their heads till we were out of sight. My throat thickened. Don had tears in his eyes.

NOTES

1. Navigational aids in the *established* shipping channels were fairly well serviced. Lights on the outer islands and infrequently used channels were more difficult to service and were not always functioning.

2. I had stressed the tendons in my right arm so much that I would never be able to play tennis again. The first three fingers of Don's right hand never fully recovered either.

3. Between 1815 and 1925 seventy-seven shipwrecks were recorded in the Magallanes zone. Fourteen of those carried the U.S. flag; twenty-nine carried the Union Jack of Great Britain. By 1984 when I returned to the Canales of Patagonia, the beautiful bronze propeller had been removed from the wreckage.

CHAPTER 15

Pacific Winds, Atlantic Tides

MARCH 24

The Strait of Magellan, like Antarctica, was one of those places I learned about in grade school. I found it at the bottom of the world when I tipped the classroom globe upside down, never dreaming I'd visit it someday. We had technically reached the end of the landlocked Canales de Patagonia and were now about to enter the strait that Ferdinand Magellan discovered in 1520.

We could already feel what Slocum called "the throb of the great ocean"—swells rolling east into the Strait from the Southern Ocean. Despite the somber, awesome aspect of the land, we were excited. To "turn left" and head downwind for over 200 miles to Punta Arenas sounded easy after all we'd been through.

On a chart, the Strait looks like a stylized V. From its westernmost entrance at Cabo Pilar, it tends southeast for 147 miles to Cabo Froward, the tip of the South American continent, then turns almost due north and heads 113 miles to Punta Arenas. The final flourish of the V continues another 60 miles east to the Atlantic. Near Cabo Froward, in the cradle of the V, the Pacific and Atlantic oceans meet and thrash out their differences in tidal overfalls, back eddies, riptides, and confused seas.

The course Don had laid out to take us inside Isla Tamar is preferred by small vessels that want to avoid the heavy seas rolling in from the Pacific. The route, however, led through rocky, kelp-infested waters, and the waves that broke over the rocks and shot into the air made me shiver. I was glad we'd left Isla Fairway with enough daylight to spot the dangers.

By the time we anchored in Caleta Rachas we had completed 52 nautical miles—a record for one day since we'd entered the channels. Could we be in Punta Arenas in five days? We had high hopes!

We set two anchors for the night—the CQR off the bow and the small Danforth off the stern. "Before we get too relaxed," Don said, "we'd better get prepared in case we have to make a fast getaway. Read what the *Pilot* says."

Paso Roda, the narrow passage to the east, was full of breaking rocks on either side which narrowed our margin of safety. The center channel had a depth of six fathoms (thirty-six feet).

I leaned over the galley table to study the chart the *Bendoran* had given us. The exquisitely drawn artwork was dated 1941. Delicate curved lines, resembling the concentric ribs of a fine Venus clamshell, became increasingly tight, indicating sharp peaks on the island and mainland. Ridges looked like skinny caterpillars weaving their way across the land, their "tails" dividing or hooking up with the Venus shells. Evenly spaced dashes showed the recommended course. Uneven dashes meant unknown shorelines or unsurveyed areas—and there were many of them. Updates through 1969 had been inked by hand in purple. It was obvious the Chilean navy didn't sell masses of these charts.

"If we have to leave here, and it's impossible to make a run down the Strait," Don said, "we'll have to go into Puerto Tamar."

The small bay of Puerto Tamar lies on the south shore of Peninsula Tamar, and whoever named it had used the term *puerto* loosely. (We had long since given up the idea that a port was a place where we'd at least spot a fishing boat.) I had to squint to see the tiny anchor printed at the northwest side of the bay. Crosses, dashed lines, long streamers of kelp, blue shoal areas, and minuscule islets covered the bay on paper. A reef that extended southwest off the tip of Cabo Tamar looked particularly menacing. I didn't understand how any vessel could possibly find safety there. The *Pilot* said the holding ground was good, but it didn't recommend Puerto Tamar as an anchorage.

I noticed a purple blot near the course line at the south end of Paso Roda and wondered if the cartographer's pen had leaked. I studied the enlarged inset and found a three-sided cross—what did that mean? We'd have to avoid all those dangers. But maybe we'd be lucky and be able to avoid Puerto Tamar.

Don laid out the bearings for Puerto Tamar in the logbook: "0.4 mile (nautical) to clear the rocks in Caleta Rachas; 0.5 mile to the center of Paso Roda; 180° for 0.85 mile; 220° for 0.76 mile; 190° for one mile; 090° for 1.5 mile, 040° for 0.9 mile, then a turn to 315° to take us into the anchorage."

I gasped. Eight different turns to get us into Puerto Tamar, and we had no way to compute mileage.

"Yeah, that's it, and those bearings assume I can compensate for current and windage." He didn't mention that his bearings also assumed we could see some landmarks.

We'd had to dismantle the recording log since leaving Canal Sarmiento because the rocks and reefs in the shorter channels could have

Don treated us to a fire after supper

snagged the line. Paso Roda was no exception. We had to hope that when we headed through the passage, we'd have enough visibility.

MARCH 25

1750 hours: We've had a layover day. Not by choice. This one enforced by the weather: squalls, fog, mist, rain all day, and another extra-tropical cyclone with winds that have swung us around like a gyroscope all day. Don has spent the day stowing charts we no longer need and organizing those for the Strait. He's reading the Pilot now and making plans for the remainder of our run to Punta Arenas. Temperature inside is 42°F—about four degrees higher than outside. We've had a tough time keeping warm. I finally finished my "blanket" pants and am wearing them now—the first time in weeks my legs have felt warm.

Don treated us to a small fire after supper. The gentle crackling of the wood, the storm, our cold hands and noses, and dwindling daylight made me think of Christmas. "Let's try the cassette deck. I'd really like to hear the Christmas tape again."

Don laughed. "There's not a chance in hell it's going to work. None of the other electronics worked after we pitchpoled—even with the fresh water and alcohol rinses we gave them."

"But it's the only piece of equipment we haven't tried."

He shrugged. "It won't hurt to try."

I crawled under Carl's berth and dug out the ammo box that held our cassettes. The latch was congealed by rust. I pried it open with a pair of pliers, found the contents inside dry, pulled out the cassette, and inserted it in the player.

> *Kathy's voice came alive, booming out of the port speaker with even better fidelity than we'd had in the tropics, and this time it seems like a real Christmas. I'm happy, I'm thankful, and it's winter! But if we hadn't gotten word out with the Bendoran, I couldn't bear to listen to this tape.*
>
> *I fixed pálicinta (Hungarian dessert pancakes) while we listened to Beethoven's Third. We're now listening to the Fifth. Low battery voltage is beginning to affect it, but we've been deprived so long we hardly care! What a great anchorage this is!*[1]

MARCH 26

Weather the second day forced another holiday in Caleta Rachas. Although we dressed and were ready to weigh anchor by 0600, fog and rain closed in, so we stayed put. While I was making drop biscuits with the last of our Bisquick, Don gave me a running account of conditions:

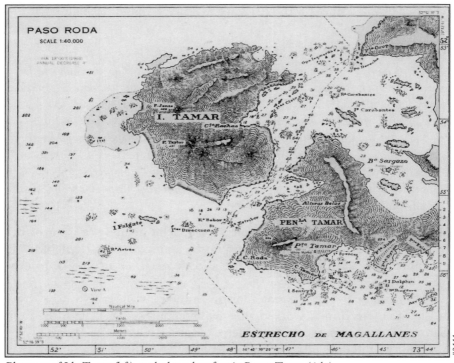

Blown out of Isla Tamar (left), we had to take refuge in Puerto Tamar (right)

Our first view of the strait

"It looks a little brighter to the east. Maybe we should leave and head up the Strait . . . No, maybe not. The fog keeps moving in and out. Those rocks to the east look bad—I can see waves breaking over them." He flicked the barometer frequently. "The pressure keeps dropping. It still looks bad out there. Well, I guess we're well sheltered here. No point in moving."

He finally settled on the salon settee to read, dressed in his Peter Storm sweater, his foul weather overalls, heavy wool socks, and red stocking cap pulled tightly over his ears. Seeing him bundled up like that made me think of a remark he'd made during the night. I wore so many clothes to bed in order to keep warm, he told me, "Good grief, woman, getting to you nowadays is like trying to get to the gold inside Fort Knox. I want to feel your skin!"

In late afternoon I had "stripped" to my sweats and was bundled up in an army blanket reading aloud from Alan Villier's *Captain James Cook* when the boat jerked suddenly and violently, once, like a mustang bucking its trainer.

"Shit! The bow anchor just broke loose. We've got to get out of here!"

Pelted by hail, we hauled in the CQR while the boat hung precariously on the small Danforth. Don kept looking at the rocks to port. They seemed to be heading straight for us.

"Take the helm and keep the bow into the wind while I raise the stern anchor," he instructed.

The bow had other ideas. It wanted to blow straight down toward the rocks. I was the driver of a semi without brakes, trying to stay in control on a dangerous incline. *Wheel to the left, center, to the right. Give it some rpms if it doesn't want to do what you want. To the left again. Steady. Don't let the wheel overpower you. Jockey it around. Show it who's boss.*

"Good show, babe!" Don climbed back into the cockpit. Gunning the engine to gain steerage, he told me to go to the bow and point if I saw any dangers. "With this goddamn rain and wind, don't try to shout; I'll never hear you."

We headed out through the rocks toward Paso Roda. I knelt on the bowsprit, my arms wrapped tightly around the stanchions to prevent my being flung overboard. The bow pitched, alternately dunking and lifting me. I tightened my grip, my fingers numbed from the cold and the pressure of grasping.

Neither of us had had time to put on our foul weather gear, and diagonal sheets of hail mixed with sleet stung my eyes and soaked my sweatshirt and pants, drenching me to the skin. My cheeks felt raw; I could hardly move my jaws. I couldn't see beyond thirty feet. I searched for rocks with the binoculars, and patterns of liquid floated across the lenses. Curtains of grey met my 360-degree gaze. I prayed that Don had memorized the bearings.

Suddenly, the boat began to roll. *We've hit the Strait,* I thought. Swells, confused seas. The motion increased, the boat pitched forward and aft, rolling from port to starboard, starboard to port. I felt a twinge of nausea. We hadn't experienced seas like this since Golfo Trinidad.

Don made the last turn, and we entered Puerto Tamar.

"Rock," I screamed. "Islet!" I stood up, gesturing wildly.

"I see! I see!" Don yelled. "Come here."

I dashed back to the cockpit and took the helm. "I'm going to drop just the CQR. We'll hang on one hook for the time being, but let's get the big Danforth and yachtsman ready for an emergency."

It was dark by the time we went below and peeled off our wet clothing. Even our underwear dripped.

"It's so deep here we'll have to keep an eye on the line. I think the anchor broke loose in Caleta Rachas because I didn't have enough scope out." He paused and said, "I'm really proud of you. You've turned into a real sailor. You ought to feel good about yourself! Do you?"

Scenes flashed across my mind. I really had come a long way. Particularly in attitude. I no longer asked "why" at every turn. I knew what had to be done, and I did it. I had become an equal partner. I thought about how frightened I had been when Don asked me to douse the staysail in a squall before we hit Easter Island and how angry I was that he had "forced" me to do it. I remembered feeling exhilarated by the wind in my face and the beauty of the moon peeking through dark clouds, and yet not wanting to let on that I had felt pleasure "under duress." Yes, I felt good about myself. I felt good, but I still had moments of terror, and Puerto Tamar provided a barrelful.

After no sleep, I wrote at 0200, March 27:

Gales, gales, gales since we dropped anchor. Slocum wrote "Great Boreas! a tree would need to be all roots to hold on against such a furious wind." Now I know what he meant. Is this wind worse than Dársena Aid, or is my memory hazy?

I have just come off anchor watch. It's Don's turn now. He tells me to get some sleep, but I can't. I'm too nervous and tense. I feel like we're bivouacking under a 42-foot overhang, suspended in black mist. The lines of our "hammock" stretch and groan. The bitter end hangs on one giant piton driven into unknown marrow. The wind strikes, flinging us up, down, and sideways against this vault. Will the line hold? will the piton hold? we ask, voiceless. We are nothings, waiting. Waiting for dawn. How many hours? How many days?

Don's middle-of-the-night journal entry read:

It's been over a month since our pitchpole. What a scary way to spend the anniversary. When will this treadmill stop and let us off? These past two days have been one frightening experience after another. I told R. how pleased I am by the way we worked together so quickly and correctly tonight, but she didn't find much comfort in my saying so. This trip has got to end for her. She's put up with so much.

MARCH 27–28

How many days had we estimated to Punta Arenas? Five! And we had already used up three and had no idea when we'd be able to move again. What a dream, what optimists we were—"just turn left" and bomb up the Strait to Punta Arenas! The Strait of Magellan—had we totally ignored its reputation, the literature we'd read?

I began to feel that the descriptions of the Strait in the *Pilot* suffered from British understatement: "The difficulties and dangers in navigating the Strait . . . are accentuated by the prevalence of bad weather, especially toward the W end . . . [where] the squalls frequently blow with such violence and from different directions as to make the anchorage untenable." On the other hand, how could anyone believe how bad it could be before experiencing it?

When Slocum found shelter for a night in Puerto Tamar during his long ordeal trying to exit the Strait, he wrote: "There was an unfinished newness all about the land. On the hill back of Port Tamar a small beacon had been thrown up, showing that some man had been there. But how could one tell but that he had died of loneliness and grief? In a bleak land is not [Sic] the place to enjoy solitude."[2]

Our post-accident habit resumed—we wore foul weather gear day and night and rested fully clothed at all times. Wind varied all over the map—light to moderate, near gale to full gale, full-blown storm—then veered abruptly, clockwise in its usual manner.[3]

One hour at a time, we alternated anchor watch, sitting in the cockpit. Wind penetrated my five layers of clothing—yellow slicker with its hood pulled tight around my face, Irish wool sweater (which had finally dried after three weeks), sweatshirt, turtleneck, long-sleeved wool underwear. And after twenty minutes in 34°F (with wind chill factor near 0°), my mouth froze in position, my hands went numb, my forehead and eyes ached. Waves of sleet and snow blew across the deck. It was like a Midwest winter, but I had never before been forced to sit outside in a blizzard!

Pain spasmed across my shoulders, snapping muscles. I stomped my feet, I did isometrics with my hands and fingers, rocked myself with my arms wrapped across my chest. A twinge of nausea, from the cold or the ache, crept up through my abdomen. At last my watch was up, and it was Don's turn.

MARCH 29

It is 0410 hours, in the dead of night, and I have just come off watch. Did I think last night was wretched? Nothing compared to tonight. After midnight, when gusts hit a peak of 60 knots, Don had to start the engine and run it for three hours at 1,000 rpms—in forward—to take the strain off the anchor. Like a horse harnessed to a giant treadmill set at the highest notch, le Dauphin has been working to her maximum, going nowhere.

I think of what I told the sailors on Isla Fairway: "Notify the port captain that we'll be in Punta Arenas March 30." Hell! We've been riding out gales for five days now. Punta Arenas seems like a dream.

At least we knew the Chilean navy was monitoring our whereabouts. We had spotted the lights of a ship in the channel thirty minutes before the storm hit. We were hoping they had spotted us on their radar.

Don's ability to drive himself continued. He made a logbook entry for *every* hour of the three days we spent in Puerto Tamar.

I can picture Don in medieval times undergoing torture on the rack. He winces every time they tighten it. He moans, but doesn't give in. They tighten the rack again. He passes out, comes to. They tighten it again. He'll die before he talks. Thank God, he's never had to face the ultimate test of torture, but I think he would endure if he had to—his ability to hang on in a crisis is extraordinary.

Before dawn the wind finally eased its pull on the anchor rode, and we were able to turn off the engine. I lay on our berth listening, waiting, expecting Don to rouse me at any moment, expecting the mast to start quivering and shaking again. But I fell asleep, finally, praying, *Please let the anchor hold, please let it hold . . . please.*

At 0530, Don climbed into the berth and slept, clutching me like a baby as if I, too, might break away. An hour later we got up, ready to make a dash, then waited for visibility to improve.

At 1000 I logged: "Cabo Providencia, 12 miles to the east, and Cabo Upright, 18 miles away on the south shore, are visible." It looked perfect for departure.

"Shall we try it?" Don asked.

"Let's wait a while and see what develops."

We waited. An hour. Providencia and Upright disappeared again in fog. Don opened the hatch slightly, put his head out, and said, "Oh God, here we go again!" He hopped off the ladder and slammed the cover shut. "If we had an echo sounder, radar, and tide tables, we might give it a try. But if visibility goes sour, we could end up like a lost spaceship without a chance of returning alive." Arrows of sleet pummeled the deck. Williwaws knocked us to starboard. Don climbed back in the berth. "Probably best we stay here where the unknowns are a little less unknown. Come to bed with me."

"I'm too nervous. You sleep, I'll keep watch." I craved sleep, too, but the wind-bull was raging again and someone had to stay in the ring. I was experiencing heartburn and nervous stomach.

I can't imagine why! I wrote. *But I do have one thing in common with a "great": Allan Villier's book describes Cook's stomach problems—the curse of mariners.*

An hour later, Don hopped down from the berth. "I feel better!" He flicked the small barometer. "Pressure's rising a bit. What's it look like outside?"

I opened the hatch and poked my head up. The wind still roared, but visibility had improved, and I could see the mountains across the Strait. Don stepped up beside me to take a look. "Wow. Look at that water."

Streamers of white blew eastward down the channel. A snow shower moved in and out of grey ravines, then crossed the Strait, like a ghost with its arms outstretched, moving slowly and unsurely. "We'd better make a run for it while there's visibility."

Oh God, where next? I thought. Where would "the run" take us? Neither of us knew, but we agreed we had to try. We weighed anchor and headed into the Strait.

The distance between Peninsula Tamar and the south shore of Paso del Mar (the western length of the Strait) is about seven miles—long enough for fetch to build up. The combination of wind and swells, plus the velocity of the flood tide, can send a small vessel screaming down the channel like a toy boat on a raging river. Or it can shove a wall of water in the teeth of a boat as it meets the outgoing tide.

Without tide tables we couldn't predict the best times for navigating this formidable body of water; we had to throw in our lot with the wind and weather. Don wasn't sure that even tide tables could help us at this point. He'd been trying to study the water level along the shoreline in order to predict flood and ebb currents, but he was having more and more difficulty understanding the effects of tide as we approached the meeting of the Atlantic and Pacific oceans.

We had our first 360-degree view of the Strait. It was overpowering. The Strait was immense and formidable. Knobs and hummocks of grey and silver granite, piled one on top of another, rose more than 1,500 feet to snowfields, ice caps, and peaks recently dusted with snow. (I shivered at the thought that below us lay equally deep walls.) The granite, incised vertically, horizontally, and diagonally, was stripped raw. No trees could find a hold in that rock. Glacier-rivers wound their way to the saltwater. Just above shoreline, bands of yellow lichen, dwarf cypress, and moss painted the rock. There was no gentle beauty in Magellan's Strait.

Mist hung above the glaciers. A blue diamond suddenly cut through the clouds, altering the mood for a second. I rushed for the camera. One photo, and the clouds moved in again; the summits resumed their dark scowl.

Snow flurries brushed across the deck. The gale pushed from behind, and we made good time to the end of Paso del Mar, then into Paso Largo. *Le Dauphin* genuflected with every blast, trying hard not to trip. Tops streamed off short, steep waves. It was anything but *pacífico*.

A Chilean navy ship passed abeam heading seaward and signaled with spotlights. What was their message? Perhaps "Welcome." Sailors on the bridge deck waved. It made us feel better.

I took watch after lunch. The barometer dropped; squalls, rain, and hail intensified. The south shore faded, then the north shore. Row upon row of white lines whipped across the water, like thousands of white horses racing down the channel, jumping and bucking, leaping fifteen or twenty feet into the air. Waves curled nastily into rollers, lifting the stern, and setting *le Dauphin* sharply to starboard. She began to surf, fighting my efforts to control the helm.

Why does this always happen to me when Don's taking a rest? I thought. The boat heeled, the bow dug in—we were going to broach, I was sure. *Please don't go over. Not again! Please don't.* I wished Don were there, but I couldn't leave the helm for even a second to call him.

The hatch opened suddenly and his head appeared. "Did you call me? It's getting pretty rolly, isn't it?" It was uncanny. He always seemed to sense when I was in trouble.

He glanced at the roiling water. "I wanted to get farther along, but we'd better look for shelter in Caleta Notch. It's a tricky entrance, though—are you game?"

"Yes, anything to get out of this!" I exclaimed.

I'd read what the *Pilot* had to say about Caleta Notch and had studied the chart. It was the only completely landlocked cove in the Strait, and it had been used by numerous explorers and transiting vessels. Slocum had anchored there, and I was curious about it. It sounded like a good place.

I had a pretty good idea of the lay of the cove. Its configuration intrigued me. There was an inner and outer basin, the inner one completely landlocked. Creeks flowed into both basins from all sides, and a river drained the head of the inner cove. Instructions for entering Caleta Notch presumed that prominent landmarks were visible and could be used as bearings.

Don signaled to turn north. Wild seas hit the port beam and shot over the cabin into the cockpit. I didn't like the way the boat was handling and glanced aft to make sure the stern quarter would clear a wave. Translucent emerald water peaked up and surged after us. "Shoal water!" I screamed, reeling the wheel to starboard.

Don turned around to look. "No, no, it's okay! Resume course." (He explained later that with the wind behind and the current against us, the waves heaped up in huge, strange configurations, and what I had taken for shoal was a momentary ray of sunlight shining through the water.)

We hit the entrance—a narrow passage guarded on either side by rocky spits that looked like claws ready to snap shut and ensnare us. Islets and half-submerged pinnacles perched inside the claws waiting for one false move from the navigator. It looked like we were headed for a suicide mission. But within minutes we slid into a circular basin where the swells flattened. A magical curtain of snow-mist fell around us, obscuring the hilltops and mounds. All we could see were small islets off the port beam as *le Dauphin* slowly worked her way in.

"I think that's Punta Maunder to starboard," Don said. "The best anchorage is supposed to be about 900 feet from the point."

We set anchor in the recommended spot, took bearings off the east and west shores, and went below to fill in the log. Within minutes, we heard hail on the roof, then gentle rain. Don wrote: "45 nautical miles today. This is a perfect anchorage! Very secure. Only brief williwaws to indicate what's happening outside."

He looked up at me from the galley settee, a whimsical expression on his face. "I was beginning to get . . . not a little . . . but *damn* frightened out there."

NOTES

1. Both the player and the port speaker were mounted underneath a shelf of the bookcase. We surmised that the books had absorbed all the water when we turned over, protecting that particular wiring. The starboard speaker was ruined.

2. *Sailing Alone Around the World*, p. 127

3. Storm winds in the Southern Hemisphere follow a clockwise pattern. In the Northern Hemisphere, their normal pattern is counterclockwise.

CHAPTER 16

End of a Nightmare

MARCH 29, EVENING
Caleta Notch—what a wonderful place!—even lovelier than Puerto Bueno. Nature had surely chosen its best designers when it was created. Tucked inside the very southwest corner of the South American continent, it was completely hidden from the Strait by an icicle-shaped peninsula ridged by a steep and narrow spine of snowy peaks. Slender glaciers lay in bowls among the ridges, and streams poured down clefts in the rock. To the east, where a river drained the land, there was a small delta and the slopes were gentle. Slocum had gone ashore there to load up on water and wood.

I had been so intent on handling the helm as we entered the basin that the details had escaped me. We spread the chart on the galley table and studied the inset for Caleta Notch, walking through each step we'd taken. Don traced our route with his forefinger, and when I studied the entrance I couldn't believe we'd managed to get through.

"This is a world-class anchorage!" he said. "Let's celebrate this lucky find with a fire. We're near enough our goal so we can afford to use the rest of our wood."

We talked about what we would do when we arrived in Punta Arenas. First priority: calling our families. Other things were less pressing, but things we dreamed about nevertheless. To take a walk, a real walk—not just forty-two feet from stern to bowsprit, but a mile stretch, or two or three. To smell the earth up close, be able to finger the leaves or needles of a tree. To buy fresh vegetables—a real potato, not flakes out of a package; onions; garlic.

"A big thick steak," Don said. "Fresh fruit and some ice cream." He added quickly: "Although I haven't had any complaints about your cooking. You create the most wonderful concoctions from a handful of ingredients. But I think the thing I crave most of all is a full night's sleep without interruptions. No wind, no anchor watch—nothing to awaken me."

We were both eager to know what was going on at home and in the rest of the world. Had President Ford pardoned Nixon? Was the country starting to recover from the economic recession? How had the gasoline

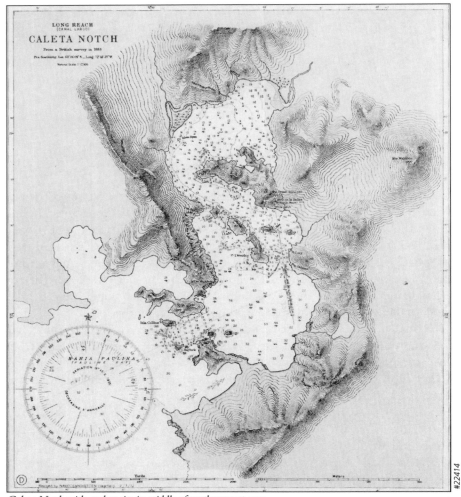

Caleta Notch with anchor site in middle of northernmost cove

shortage affected our business? Had the lengthy postal strike in France been settled, and had my letters finally gotten through?

We were curious, too, about the political situation in Chile. Easter Island hadn't been affected by Pinochet's crackdown. But we had heard stories from university students who had come to the island on holiday about conditions on the mainland: curfews imposed, military presence everywhere, and rumors of *desaparacidos* (people who had disappeared). Dawson Island, south of the Strait, was said to have a concentration camp where political prisoners were sent. With Don's penchant for blurting out whatever he was thinking, we'd have to be careful in Punta Arenas. We were going to be "guests" in a military dictatorship, and it could be tricky.

We went to bed after the fire had burned out, snuggling up for a full night's sleep. I slept like a baby, only vaguely aware when Don crawled over me several times, whispering, "I'm just going to adjust the anchor line," and then, "Everything's okay," when he climbed back in the berth.

Sometime during the night I dreamt that jet planes were taking off overhead: *The planes are lower than usual and can't seem to get airborne. The noise is deafening, and a man in the control tower looks out the window to see what the commotion is.*

The roar awakened me—*my God, those are williwaws!*

The boat lurched to port, and I was flung out of the berth, Don and the mattress tumbling on top of me.

"Oh Christ," he muttered. "Not again!"

The rail went under. Pots and pans thumped and crashed against the bulkhead. Chain in the bilge clanked like cobblestone ballast being dumped into a ship. "I can't believe this," I said with clenched teeth.

The boat righted herself. I jammed on my boots, grabbed my foul weather jacket, and followed Don up the ladder.

"Holy sheeit. A knockdown at anchor!" he said. "We must have dragged." He had already let out 500 feet of anchor line, and we had only a hundred to go. He bent over and tested the line. "I don't know what the hell's going on—it seems to be holding . . . Hmm, maybe I do know. Look at the sky."

Low clouds scudded east across a luminous slate. Somewhere behind the clouds was a full moon. As I looked at the sky, I thought of Moitessier. One night when he had been preparing telltales to hang on his shrouds, he became aware that the sky wasn't black. It was so light, in fact, that white telltales wouldn't show up against it, and he had to use dark fabric instead.[1]

"Tell me—" Don said in the professorial tone he used when he wanted to test me.

I thought, *Here it comes. In the middle of the night when we've just had a knockdown, he's going to pull his why-didn't-you-study-physics routine.*

"—what you see."

Trying to keep my wits, I answered, "I see that the prevailing wind is from the west—it's carrying the clouds east."

"Yeah! But the williwaw that knocked us on our beam was from the south. And look which way we're facing now—east." He continued on his own; I was off the hook. "I think the current from all that fresh water feeding into this basin set us broadside to the gusts."

I recalled a passage in the *Pilot* about williwaws: "During the strongest williwaws, which occur most often westward of Cabo Froward . . . the wind almost certainly exceeds 100 knots. The squall may not last more than a few minutes, but for a time visibility may become very bad because of cold rain, sleet or snow, and it may suddenly become dark, even when the sun has been shining brightly." We could have added a few comments of our own at that point, but the only printable one would have been that williwaws whip up such violent froth along the water that visibility can be reduced to zero.

"A knockdown at anchor! I can't believe the strength of these williwaws." Don kept shaking his head in wonder. "This is a great landlocked bowl, but those cyclonic winds just scream down these high peaks."

The air quieted for the moment, and we went below, so nervous and tense that sleep was out of the question. "Well, there's some consolation," he said. "We're in a landlocked cove, and the worst that can happen is getting blown ashore. It's not like Dársena Aid, where we would have had to climb a rocky cliff if the boat foundered. Here, we'd just plow into the grass and wade ashore."

Violent gusts plagued us for the next few hours. *Le Dauphin* spun like a child's top in every direction. Mizzen sail ties came undone, the rigging and the mast shook, wind whistled through the cracks. The mast itself seemed to be having convulsions. Was it my imagination, or was the whole boat being racked? I mentioned it.

"Yeah. The forestay and shrouds worry me. They're all that keep the main from cracking completely. If they part, we'll lose the mast for sure."

MARCH 30

At dawn we climbed back in the berth and dozed uneasily.

At 1100 hours williwaws made a second offensive, attacking from every direction, strafing the deck, dropping explosives in the water. We got up and dressed quickly. Don wedged in behind the galley table to study the chart. I primed the stove. A gust roared through the aft port and extinguished the flame. I opened the container of alcohol to give the burner a second dose. "Let's get out of this miserable place as soon as we eat!"

Then I heard a roar, like the roar of a steam engine. The stove tipped toward the floor, and I was hurled across the galley into the radio locker. The bottle of alcohol flew at Don, spraying its contents over the galley.

"Jesus, the mast just hit the water!" Don tried to get out from behind the table, but he was flattened against the starboard bulkhead and couldn't move.

Water gushed through the crack in the cabin deck joint, spraying both of us. When *le Dauphin* righted herself, we struggled to stand up.

Don grabbed the screwdriver to short the solenoid. "Get outside and put the throttle in gear! We've dragged this time, I can tell."

Cabo Crosstide—where the Atlantic and Pacific tides meet

#22414

Please, don't let another williwaw hit while I'm in the cockpit, I prayed. Sure, I could swim to shore or climb back aboard if I were thrown off— but God, in that cold water?

"Take her up to 2000 rpms," Don shouted rushing to the bow. Punta Maunder was just 50 feet away; the anchor had dragged more than 300 feet. As he began winching in the line, I watched for his signals. He snubbed it down and pointed to the center of the cove. I brought the boat around, pulling the anchor alongside. When Don gave me the signal to stop, I pulled the throttle back to neutral and waited while he let out the line, tested it, then snubbed it down.

"Reverse!" he yelled, wanting to put strain on the line. "Okay, neutral," he shouted coming aft. "I think we're okay now. We've got a total of 400 feet out." A gust swept down from the ridge to the northwest. Snow flurries swirled across the water, whipping up spray. "Let's go below and eat—we need some calories. We can talk about where to head next."

I flicked the barometer. "It doesn't look good! It's been on the descent for over 24 hours."

"Well . . . do you want to try and leave after lunch?" he asked. "These williwaws may just be local. Maybe it's not blowing as bad outside."

"Yes, let's try. It *can't* be any worse!"

We ate a cold lunch. I didn't want to battle the stove again.

We raised anchor and started a reverse S-curve to exit. It was 1400 hours. The wind had gone full circle and was screaming down the flanks of the peninsula to the west. The basin looked like a gigantic Jacuzzi. Wind funneled through the bottleneck entrance, hitting the bow smack in her teeth. We couldn't make headway, even with the engine at full throttle.

"The mist is starting to close in," I said. "Do you want me to get a reverse bearing in case we have to come back in here?"

"Good idea!" Don answered. "I don't dare take my hands off this wheel."

I ran below, grabbed the hand-bearing compass, took bearings and wrote them nervously in the log. We were being set toward the reefs. Swells gushed through the entrance, over the rocks, and into the passage. Heavy, dark spray and rain from the southwest met our gaze.

"I hate it, I hate it!" I screamed. "It's wretched, abominable, vile weather."

"Do you want to go back? Do you want to go back?" Don shouted.

I kept looking toward shore. Kelp writhed up, down, and sideways, as if the reefs below waterline were being torpedoed. Within seconds we would lose all options for turning around. "Yes! Yes! Let's go back!"

Don spun the helm to port. The boat pitched and rolled. "Would you bet your life on the bearings you just took?" he asked, serious.

I burst into tears. "No . . . but I think they're okay."

The wind died for a few seconds—enough to let us clear the rocks by barely 30 feet. We worked our way back along the outer basin, lining up our beam with the white patch on the rocks before we made our way past the islets and into the inner basin. Tucking in again behind Punta Maunder, we reset the anchor.

"Godalmighty, I'll take the williwaws over that stuff out there any day," Don said.

I understood then what Slocum meant when he wrote: "An instance of Magellan weather was afforded when the *Huemel,* a well-appointed gunboat of great power, after attempting on the following day to proceed on her voyage, was obliged by sheer force of the wind to return [to Caleta Notch] and take up anchorage and remain till the gale abated; and lucky she was to get back!"[2]

If a gunboat couldn't make it out of this place, how could we?

All afternoon, williwaws whipped down the ridges, from north, northwest, west. Exhausted and tense, I hit bottom, sobbing, "We'll never get there. Never." Despair hung on me like the moss on Punta Maunder's trees. I became morose. I peeled apart the stiff yellow pages in our waterlogged *Book of Famous Poetry* and read aloud from Poe's "The City in the Sea."

Resignedly beneath the sky

The melancholy waters lie.

So blend the turrets and shadows there

That all seem pendulous in air,

While from a proud tower in the town

Death looks gigantically down.

Don laughed. Then, trying to cheer me, he rattled off a list of what we'd accomplished the last 24 hours. "Look how well we worked together. Look how fast you responded—you didn't panic; you did everything right. You ought to feel proud—not discouraged."

"I know," I whimpered. "But that's like telling a kid who just broke her leg that she should think about all the unfortunate people in the world who are permanently crippled." Tears ran down my face again. "I'll be all right. It's just that we've spent seven days in this horrible strait and have made only 40 miles. When will we be able to move on? Our family's probably worried sick again. We were supposed to be in Punta Arenas by now. We're trapped here—we'll never get out."

"Yes, we will . . . we will. Look." He flicked the barometer. "The pressure's already gone up a tenth of an inch. Tomorrow will be clear."

It was dusk by then, and I opened the hatch to look out, hoping he was right. In the west, the clouds had partially cleared. A carnelian glow slipped up the ridge above Punta Florence and dissolved into purple-grey. *Red sky at night, sailor's delight,* I thought. But if the barometer rose too abruptly, it would be no delight—we'd have high-pressure winds again.

"Remember, we're fairly safe here," Don tried to reassure me. "This is a landlocked harbor. Even if we're knocked on our beam ends again, the boat can't be seriously damaged."

My ears fixed on "knocked on our beam ends again," obliterating everything else he'd said. I refused to go to bed. Instead I lay on the galley settee, conjuring up all the injuries I might incur if we had another knockdown.

If the boat's thrown on its starboard beam again, I'll be flattened against the back of the settee—that won't be too bad. But if she's thrown on her port beam, I'll be mashed against the table. I could split open my head, break a shoulder or collarbone. Or my neck.

Come on, Réanne, think about something positive. Like how to prevent being thrown against the cabin . . . Hmm, I could lash myself to the helm like the old Cape Horners used to do. Or to the mast. But the way the mast shudders, I'd break my tailbone . . . Oh, for godssake, quit this morbidity and focus on something else!

I picked up Villiers' book and finished the last few chapters. Reading about Cook's untimely and gruesome murder in the Hawaiian Islands took my thoughts away from my own possible demise. By the time I'd finished the book, my eyes were closing. It was 2200 hours. I climbed into our berth, snuggled against Don, and fell sound asleep.

MARCH 31, EARLY MORNING

It was still dark when he shook me. "Get your foul weather gear on, quick. The anchor's dragged. We're only 50 feet from Punta Maunder again. I need you at the helm while I pull in some line. We'll have to reset the anchor."

The basin was white with spray—again. The barometer had shot up; the strength of the wind, too, as I suspected it would. But Don's prediction was coming true: the sky was clearing. Above, the moon looked like a murre's egg caught in the weft of delicately spun clouds.

The barometer rose steadily the next hour, and before the moon had set, we slipped out of Caleta Notch.

Westerlies blew a "reasonable" 25 knots. In the same conditions off the coast of California, small craft stay at dock.

Rain squalls funneled one after another through Paso Largo, thrusting us southeastward to the end of passage. It *was* a miserable place!—even the *Pilot* intimated it had the worst weather of the Strait. But at last we were making progress.

We began seeing tide rips and overfalls along the southwest shore. Wavelets heaped up in short white peaks, momentarily caught the sun, and glistened like thousands of white gulls bobbing on the surface. We turned east into Paso Tortuoso (Torturous Passage), a nine-mile channel connecting Paso Largo to Paso Inglés (English Narrows). "This is it! This is it, babe." Don grabbed me and gave me a hug. "That's Cabo Crosstide." He pointed toward a massive headland on the north shore. "This is where the Atlantic meets the Pacific. Two of the biggest forces on earth come head to head here."

Two great oceans coming together are enough to disturb the waters. But at Cabo Crosstide, an additional body of water empties and fills the same area, creating even more havoc. To the north, Seno Otway—one of the largest inland sounds in the Magallanes zone—is linked to the Strait by Canal Jerónimo where tidal streams run from 6 to 8 knots. Add to those the 2- to 4-knot currents that flow through Paso Inglés, and we had our answer to the white waters on the south shore.

As we were about to enter the unstable Paso Inglés, luck descended: squalls ceased, and the current carried *le Dauphin Amical* through the passage like a whitewater raft. We motored past the anchorage where Don had planned to spend the night. He was pushing for all he was worth, and there was no sense in stopping while the weather was good. By late afternoon, when we anchored in Bahía Snug, we had logged 60 nautical miles.

Although we had yet to turn "the corner"—Cabo Froward was still five miles away—the drop in humidity and the absence of cypress and evergreen beech told us we were approaching the Patagonian plains. Wheat-green grasses covered cleared, timberless slopes. Someone had stripped the land, but there was no sign of human life.

MARCH 31

2000 hours: Sixty miles seems such a small distance compared to what we can do on the ocean with the sails flying. But our progress today is comparable to hiking sixteen miles on the John Muir Trail,[3] a fantastic achievement for one twelve-hour stretch.

Bahía Snug is open like Hanga Roa Bay and doesn't seem to afford much protection, but the Pilot says it's protected from any seas and "no squalls are experienced." Don says, "I'm not sure how appropriate this name is! But Slocum stayed here, so perhaps we'll have his luck." We'll see.

Only 60 miles to Punta Arenas. We could probably do it in one day, but since Don wants to arrive midday to clear customs and immigration, we'll spend tomorrow night in Puerto del Hambre. I write "tomorrow night" so glibly. Haven't I learned that nothing in this Strait is certain?

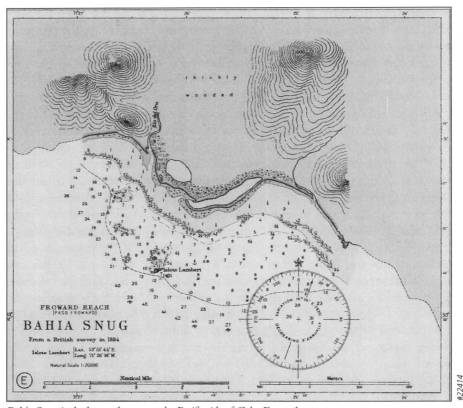

Bahía Snug is the last anchorage on the Pacific side of Cabo Froward

I took our rubber-banded Slocum out of the book slot above our berth and thumbed to the page where he'd mentioned Bahía Snug. His attempt to anchor here in 1896 was brief; however, his problems were not with the weather but with human beings. He wrote:

> The savages on comparatively fine days ventured forth on their marauding excursions, and in boisterous weather disappeared from sight, their wretched canoes being frail and undeserving the name of craft at all . . . I anchored to find, when broad day appeared, that two canoes which I had eluded by sailing all night were now entering the same bay stealthily under the shadow of the high headland. They were well manned, and the savages were well armed with spears and bows. At a shot from my rifle across the bows [*Sic*], both turned aside into a small creek out of range. In danger now of being flanked by the savages in the bush close aboard, I was obliged to hoist the sails, which I had barely lowered, and make across to the opposite side of the strait, a distance of six miles.[4]

Lack of sleep was telling on Don's face. His eyes were red, his face was drained of color. I appreciated the comfort and care he'd taken to ease my mind, but I was concerned that he'd pushed himself too long. He was teetering at the edge again, and if he made a miscalculation we could end up by going down within sight of our first port.

"God, I'd give anything for one night of uninterrupted sleep," he said. "That and a hot bath. That's what I'm *really* looking forward to. More than a steak, more than fresh fruit, more than ice cream. Twelve hours' sleep and I think I'd be raring to go again."

"Go to bed now," I ordered. "I'll stay up and keep an eye on things." I promised to wake him if the barometer started to drop or if I noticed any change in conditions. He looked at me dubiously, as if about to argue. "Go on," I said, firmly. He turned around and headed for bed.

I stretched my legs on the galley settee, prepared to finish the long letter-journal I'd been writing to my parents. But snatches of conversations the two of us had been having recently, and thoughts of the past and future, wafted in and out of my mind like the mists in the Strait. I wrote in my diary instead.

"You've changed a lot on this trip," Don has told me many times lately. Do you feel the changes in yourself?" Yes, I do feel the changes, but I was curious to see what changes he'd observed in me, and asked.

He says I've become much more observant and questioning. That I study the land and water and sky and can interpret nature's signals now. That I don't take for granted what I read in the Pilot. That I'm more sure of myself when I take the helm—that I don't let it take over.

Yes, I had become more sure of myself, more competent, more observant. I'd learned a lot from Don. I had *let* myself learn. I hadn't fought it, the way I used to. I'd also become less afraid of taking charge or making my point clear.

I thought about how I used to be, about the life I came from, about Mother and Daddy: so genteel in comparison!

Dress nicely, keep your house and your yard beautiful, care for the antique furniture handed down from generations (even if it's uncomfortable!). Daddy's a true Victorian gentleman—takes his hat off in the presence of a woman, seats her at the dinner table, walks on the curb side of the sidewalk, takes her arm crossing the street—never any vulgarity. (Thank God, he's never heard Don's sarcastic attacks on me, or my replies!) Mom and Dad speculate about politics, religion, anthropology—anything but economics and our power-driven society. I've talked their line for years—"business" is a dirty word; power is evil.

I thought about how these and other aspects of my upbringing had often interfaced with my relationship with Don—how, for example, I'd sometimes valued form to the exclusion of substance.

I've made fun of Don's grammatical errors, as if how he says something is more important than the idea behind it. I need to show him that I respect him, even if he does on occasion murder the language. I need to let him know how much I appreciate his love of ideas and concepts. And how much I love him for making life exciting. He's not the only one who needs to make changes. I need to also. I have begun to let go of my childhood. God, I'm forty-two. It's time!

Letting go of childhood habits and ideas was easier in fantasy than in practice. I thought of some other changes I wanted to make—and they weren't going to be easy at all. I would have to learn new ways of demanding Don's emotional support when I needed it, and how to softly discourage him from giving me "rational" solutions unless I asked for them. (Blowing my own whistle, even emotionally, did not come easily.) I would have to accept my own part in provoking Don's anger, and ignore it when it was misplaced. And sooner or later, I would have to test myself by "going to the wall" with Don, to fight for my own desires, instead of stifling them and giving way to his.

But some of these tests will have to wait, until we return home and resume our normal rhythm of life on land. Timing is everything.

I had been writing so long that my leg had fallen asleep. I got up and stretched, then sat back down and continued.

Our life has revolved around sailing for the past five years. I want to do other things now. Go to France, lead trips of my own, continue my graduate studies. And I definitely want to go home this fall, to teach—to spend time with Mother and Daddy while I can, to be with Sean before he goes off to college. My own life has been on hold too long.

After I finished writing, I closed my journal and sighed. It wasn't as if everything were now clear and simple, but I had the feeling that something, besides our voyage, was ending, and something new was beginning. I felt good. I checked the barometer, the anchor line, the weather. It was clear. Everything seemed to warrant the name "Snug."

When I climbed into bed after midnight, Don moaned, "Everything okay?" and turned over.

"Everything's okay," I whispered, just the way he always did.

APRIL 1

Thick fog had moved in by the next morning, and we had to wait until it had partially lifted before we could move. As we hugged the northern coast of the Strait, Chilean Navy Cruiser 45 passed abeam and signaled in Morse code with their signal light.

"Good grief! They're sending the message too fast," Don said. "I caught only the first letter—A." Nevertheless, it was reassuring to know the navy was keeping track of us.

A while after the navy ship had passed, Cabo Froward loomed out of the fog, an immense receding forehead like that of an Easter Island *moai*. It was the real turning point—the southernmost tip of the South American continent, the point in the V-shaped strait where we turned north. Named by the pirate Thomas Cavendish in 1587, Froward in six-teenth-century English meant "adverse" or "unfavorable." It deserved its name. The fog hanging over it made it look forbidding and gloomy; even the highest peaks behind it were obscured.

Don dashed below and reappeared with the Scotch and a cup. "Here, take a swig. We've got to toast to the bloody south end of the Andes! A toast to you, to us."

To celebrate our arrival, the fog lifted after noon, and the sun scrubbed the landscape clean. Above the shore, we spotted a few rustic cabins, and cows, sheep, and horses grazing on treeless slopes. Rivers here and there pushed out small alluviums of yellow sand and pebbles. The majestic, glacier-covered twin peaks of Monte Sarmiento—the highest on Tierra del Fuego across the Strait to the south—dazzled our eyes. Not a cloud spoiled the blue at that moment.

During his 1834 voyage here on the *Beagle*, Charles Darwin wrote:

> The country on both sides of this part of the Strait consists of nearly level plains, like those of [Argentine] Patagonia . . . On the east coast, south of the Strait, broken park-like scenery in a like manner connects these two countries, which are opposed to each other in almost every feature. It is truly surprising to find in a space of twenty miles such a change in the land-scape. If we take a rather greater distance, as between Port Famine and Gregory Bay [north], that is about sixty miles, the difference is still more wonderful. At the former place, we have rounded mountains concealed by impervious forests, which are drenched with the rain, brought by an end-less succession of gales; while at Cape Gregory, there is a clear and bright blue sky over the dry and.[5]

By midafternoon we were securely anchored behind Punta Santa Ana in Puerto del Hambre. On the chart, Punta Santa Ana looked like a long, thin pig's snout that could snuff out any north wind. Silt from a small stream and from the Rio San Juan at the southwest corner of the bay cre-ated a shallow bank along shore.

The site of a tragic and disastrous attempt by Pedro Sarmiento to establish a Spanish colony in 1584, Puerto del Hambre (Port Famine) acquired its name when Cavendish sailed through the area in 1587.[6] He found several survivors out of the original three hundred colonists starving to death on shore. Much later, in 1843, when Chile first took possession of the region, a fort and settlement were built on Punta Santa Ana. But the area was found unsuitable for a town, and after a few years the settlement was moved to its present site at Punta Arenas. A replica of the original Fuerte Bulnes (Fort Bulnes) and its village had been built at the original site in the middle of this century. Later we would visit it, but at the moment we had to be content with studying what we could see

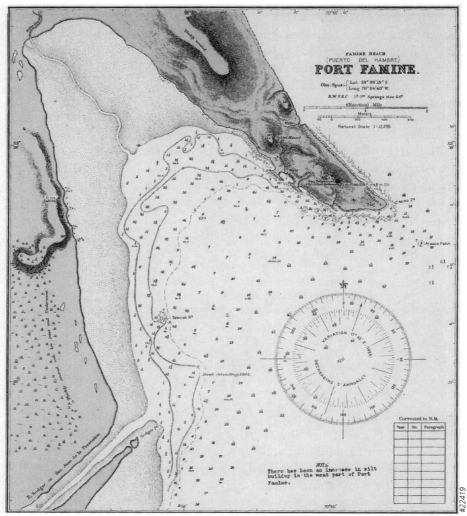

Puerto del Hambre (Port Famine), now called San Juan de la Posesión, was our last anchorage before Punta Arenas

Fuerte Bulnes as it looks now

After Francis Drake sailed through the Strait in the late 1570s and sacked Spanish colonies on the west coast of South America, Spain ordered Pedro Sarmiento (then assistant to the viceroy in Peru) to fortify the Strait. He returned to Spain to gather an armada of twenty-three ships and over three thousand men and women. After a voyage plagued by shipwrecks, disease, and desertions, the expedition—consisting of five remaining vessels—arrived at the eastern entrance of the Strait where three hundred survivors set foot on shore in February 1584.

In short order, three frigates mutinied and headed home, Sarmiento's flag ship broke up on the rocks, and natives attacked. The settlers endured, however, and within four weeks they set up a village called Nombre de Jesus.

Sarmiento saw this settlement as a military outpost only. Several summers earlier he had passed Punta Santa Ana where he noticed a brook and river that flowed into the Strait. He set out with a hundred soldiers to look for this hospitable land, ordering the men of the María, his one remaining ship, to head to Punta Santa Ana and begin felling trees for the new settlement.

For two weeks he and his men struggled down the windy, coastal plain, chopping their way through brush and forest, till they came to the bay where the Rio Santa Ana flows into the Strait. Christening their second settlement Rey Don Felipe, after King Philip II, they set about building a new town.

Realizing that his people would need food and supplies to survive the winter of 1584, Sarmiento left the Strait and set sail for Brazil to secure fresh provisions. Several years' efforts to return to the Strait ended in disaster, and his people were left to starve.

through binoculars—a cha-
pel, a large log building,
several small cabins, and two
cannons pointed toward the
bay.

The bronze statue of
Sarmiento looking across
the Strait toward the peaks
named in his honor seemed
totally out of place.

Later, too, we would
come across a humble white
wooden cross, a memorial
to Pringle Stokes, first captain of the *Beagle,* who
committed suicide in 1828.

Before supper, I record-
ed more mundane details:

> We saw our first signs of
> civilization on shore this
> afternoon. A small
> group of tourists gath-
> ered by the log houses
> stared at us through

A memorial to Pringle Stokes

> binoculars. After we anchored, a yellow fishing boat, towing a skiff, headed
> toward us. We thought they were coming to talk to us, and Don started to
> put the fenders over so they could come alongside. But they circled complete-
> ly around us, and after they had stared, they went on their way, without
> even a sign of acknowledgment. It was strange and disappointing. Maybe
> they're cut out of the same dough as the captains of the Anaconda Valley
> and Cheun On.
>
> Tonight the water's calm as a pond. We shall have a good night's sleep.
> Badly needed. We're preparing for re-entry: this afternoon I trimmed Don's
> beard and mustache and washed my hair. It doesn't seem possible that we're
> almost there.

APRIL 2

We did not leave as planned the next day. Although no surprises disturbed
us during the night, and we slept well between anchor checks, at dawn
the barometer began a Cossack's dance that lasted all day.

Balls of mist moved in and out across the bay, then intense, short-

lived rain showers flew diagonally across the bay. After they passed
through, the barometer would shoot up, and we did our own dance—up
and down the companionway ladder—as hurricane force winds swooped
across Punta Santa Ana. To check the anchor, Don had to crawl the
length of the deck; it was impossible to stand. I wrote:

> Start the engine, jam it into full forward rpms. Test the anchor line, adjust it;
> let out more line when the wind increases; pull it in when the wind decreas-
> es; re-tie lines. Resecure the mizzen sail; verify that main boom and self-
> steering vane remain in place on deck. Keep an eye peeled on the shrouds
> and stays, and pray they don't beat themselves to death. Feel the mast shake
> the boat from stem to stern, and pray it will hold. Watch the sea spouts rage
> across the bay. See the trees bow horizontal on shore. (No tourists today.)

Between hurricane acts, squalls attacked counterclockwise. Sometimes,
the sun pierced the stunning dark clouds, and a blue hole would appear in
the sky. Then the play would resume, the same act, the same lines. By
midnight, Don had filled every line of the logbook, just as he had in
Puerto Tamar.

At the western end of the Strait—somewhere off Cabo Pilar—masses
of purple clouds were permanently stationed, while at Puerto del
Hambre, through thick and thin, we were treated to a rainbow that hung
over Tierra del Fuego to the south all afternoon. A Magellanic cloud cap,
curving and windswept, indicated extreme winds over Monte Sarmiento.

In late afternoon, the sky finally cleared, but the wind continued to
howl. Don logged: "Here—the opposite of the western channels—a
falling barometer does *not* bring heavy winds. But an upswing in the
barometer brings storm winds from the east side of Cabo Froward, and
it's incredible to see what these winds do to the surface of the water! We
took photos of the bay at its worst, but I doubt that a man-made lens can
record this amount of energy."

APRIL 3

> We tried again. Up at 0530 for an early start. I made hot cereal and, in
> the dim light, added what I thought was cinnamon. Wrong! It was curry.
> I'd just been congratulating myself on my early-rising efficiency when I had
> to feed the whole batch to the fish.
>
> We raised anchor and motored out past Punta Santa Ana. But, like
> trying to get out of Caleta Notch, we made no headway against the north
> wind—the knotmeter registered zero at 2300 rpms. Big swells rolled toward
> us and broke over the bow. "No good," Don yelled, as he wheeled the helm
> around and headed back to reanchor. "Red sky in morning, sailors take
> warning." We should have known better.

We checked the Strait frequently through the binoculars, hoping the spray would subside and the seas would calm. No such luck. The horizon was a bumpy line of breakers that raced before the wind.

A small coastal steamer, hugging the coast as it headed south with the wind at its back, signaled us with a light as it passed. This friendliness made up for the disappointment I'd felt after the fishing boat slighted us. In the afternoon Don said. "Okay, we *have* to get to port tomorrow — we're out of toilet paper."

APRIL 4

This was our day! We weighed anchor at early dawn and began motoring. Less than 30 miles to go. "We'll be there by noon, babe!" Don said, excited, but intense and nervous.

The idea of people—immigration officials, port officials, naval officials, and who knew who else—after so many weeks presented its own worries. Would we be welcomed or seen as a problem? Would we be able to get *le Dauphin* repaired? Would communication with the States be difficult? Would anyone in Punta Arenas be able to help us track down the chronometer? What if we encountered the same type of incompetent official as the governor of Rapa Nui?

We had done nothing but worry about anchoring for the past four months. Now, docking would present a different set of problems. Punta Arenas was an unsheltered roadstead, open to the winds and swells of the Strait. Freighters and large vessels with hundreds of feet of chain can anchor off the pier, but even heavy ships have gone aground in those waters. A photo I'd seen in a travel brochure showed a steel sailing ship lying permanently on its side near shore—a fatality of the weather.

Before we arrived, anchor lines had to be restowed in their own lockers. Dock lines, fenders, and boat hook had to be dug out of the lazaret, and the Chilean and American flags out of the abandon-ship locker.

"Get out the United Nations flag, too," I told Don. "We're going to fly it, by God."

Houses and small shacks began to appear along shore. Wooden fishing skiffs, painted yellow, blue, or brown lay on pebbly beaches. Cows grazed on green hills neatly divided by split-log fences. Here and there, a handsome, sturdy farmhouse stood out against a hill above shore. Once in a while an automobile was visible, heading north toward town on a dirt road. I was overcome with emotion—the scenery resembled a Wisconsin landscape and brought tears to my eyes.

Then, before noon, we saw a mass of houses in the distance. Square buildings, lines of streets perpendicular to the Strait, and a long pier jutting out at the foot of the city came into view. I'd been at the helm for four hours, and the wind had made my cheeks raw, my body chilled. But it was excitement that now made me shiver.

1230 HOURS

"Get the binoculars and see if anything's tied up on the north side of the pier. I want to dock there, if we can, since the wind's coming from the west."

Tied up at the dock in Punta Arenas (oil on bow from Don's try at calming the water after our pitchpole)

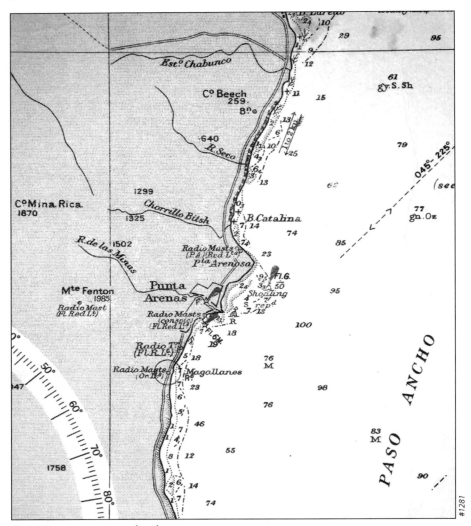

Punta Arenas—an open roadstead

Two freighters appeared to be loading on the south side, and I could make out a naval cruiser on the north, but the space in front of the navy ship looked free. We headed for that side.

I kept studying the pier with the binoculars. "There's a huge crowd on the pier," I said. "I wonder what's going on."

We approached the pier, and naval dockworkers motioned us to the north side of the pier. Men and women in civilian dress lined the pier; children in school uniforms, military in olive drab and navy blue, camera-

Our first radio contacts with our families

men with a television camera, and reporters with note pads. They shouted and waved.

"They're here to greet us!" I began to cry.

We pulled in front of Navy Cruiser 60, where sailors hung over the
bow and cheered, and we tied up along the pier against huge black truck
tires.

"I'll take care of the dock lines," Don said, throwing off a bowline.
"You talk to them."

I was so overcome, I didn't know how I could manage to squeak out
anything—in Spanish, English, or any language.

I went to the port rail. A man in navy blue serge leaned over the edge
of the pier, introduced himself as the port captain's assistant, and handed
me an armful of mail. Mail for us. (Mail, we learned later, that had been
accumulating since late February.) God, how badly I wanted to tear open
those envelopes.

From all sides we were bombarded with the same question, "What
can we do for you?" The port captain's assistant offered to drive us to the
admiral's office; someone else offered the use of his washing machine; a
member of the amateur Radio Club asked if we'd like to contact our
family in the States; a teacher from the English school wanted to show us
around town immediately.

A television cameraman leaned over the edge of the pier and stuck a
microphone in my face. The newspaper reporters clicked away on their

35-millimeter cameras while the *jefe de prensa* (chief of the press) of Canal Seís plied me for details of our accident.

"Pitchpole" wasn't in my Spanish vocabulary. I described what I could—"terrible storm," "waves of huge dimensions," "turned over," "much damage," "lost our little boat, our motor, our radio"—using a lot of gestures.

Then there were more questions:

"When did you leave the States?"

"What was your itinerary?"

"How long did it take you from Acapulco to Isla de Pascua?"

"How much time did you spend there?"

"Were you there for the visit of our president?"

I struggled to answer. Accustomed to two months of English, my mouth didn't seem able to form Spanish sentences.

"What do you plan to do now?"

We didn't know, I replied. "Everything depends on getting the boat repaired."

Then the question that completely overwhelmed me: "How do you feel now?"

About to break down, I took a deep breath and managed, "We are . . . very . . . very . . . happy . . . to be here!" Then my tears let loose. I turned to look at Don. He had just finished adjusting the lines. I pulled him toward me, hugged him, and with the microphone still in my face, said, *"Mi esposo es muy buen marinero! My husband is a great sailor!"*

NOTES

1. Telltales are strips of fabric hung from shrouds or stays to indicate the direction of the wind.

2. *Sailing Alone Around the World,* pp. 126–27

3. California's 221-mile long John Muir Trail runs along the spine of the Sierra Nevada mountain range with elevations running between 7000 and 14, 900.

4. *Ibid.,* pp. 137–38.

5. *The Voyage of the Beagle,* p. 232

6. The Chilean government has recently officially renamed the harbor San Juan de la Posesión to honor the place where Chile first took possession in 1843.

CHAPTER 17

Epilogue to the First Edition

W hat mattered before counts less now, even doesn't
count at all. And there are things which were unimportant which
now count a lot. Time and material things do not have the same
dimension they had when I left.

—Bernard Moitessier (After having circumnavigated
the world via the Great Southern Ocean)[1]

1984

I tightened my seat belt, settled back in the seat of the Boeing 727, and
glanced at my watch. Two hours till we landed in Punta Arenas, from
where my friend Katherine Wells and I would cross the Strait of Magellan
and begin a mountain bicycling trip that would push our middle-aged
bodies and bikes to the ultimate—nearly 500 kilometers round trip across
Tierra del Fuego, "the Uttermost End of the World." It would be a first
for women.

This was not only a sentimental homecoming to Magallanes—to the
friends who had treated us so warmly after Don and I limped into Punta
Arenas with our broken boat in 1975—it was also a test.

A test for myself, to see what I could accomplish with another
woman whose mental and physical skills were similar to mine. I had spent
all seventeen years of my marriage to Don going along with him, at his
driven pace, on his terms—and always lagging behind. (No wonder at
times I felt inadequate.)

In addition, I had a compulsion to revisit this raw land we had called
home for three months nine years before. I had to return—I had no
choice. I had to know if this land was as harsh as I remembered it. Had I

From Punta Arenas to Ushuaia and back

romanticized its severity in the years since *le Dauphin Amical* pitchpoled, 800 miles northwest of Cape Horn? Or was everything I'd recorded in my journal about the weather and the williwaws and the storm-force winds true? I had to know, before I could write this book.

There was yet another reason. When I had first come up with a plan for "the test" in 1983, Don had dismissed the idea, "You'll never do it. You can't train for something like that in six months—it's too hard. You don't have the drive." That was enough to spur me on. I'd show him! As I had on our second date when I rappelled down the overhanging cliff. But this time it would be on *my* terms, not his.

He wanted to come along, but I "uninvited" him. He pushed, he pressured, he prodded. I held my ground. And finally, when he saw how serious I was, he became my support team. It was a major turning point in our partnership.

I looked out the window as the pilot announced that we were over Puerto Montt and would soon be passing over the Canales de Patagonia. I was nervous and excited. Nervous—wondering if the weather would hold, wondering if the 727 could handle those terrific Magellanic winds.

Memories crammed my mind as I looked down on Golfo de Peñas—the northernmost entry to the channels, 150 miles north of Canal Trinidad. My throat filled as I studied the channels and fjords below. *Don should be with me,* I thought. *He'd be thrilled to see this region from an airplane.*

His nose would be glued against the window; he'd be giving me a running account of what he recognized. Maybe I'd been too hard, insisting on making this my trip alone. *No. I won't let myself think that way. I have a goal to complete, and I have to do it in my own way.*

I thought ahead to Punta Arenas, wondering what changes I might find. In 1975, we'd had such trouble communicating from there with the outside world—the telephone system was antiquated, and we had relied on a ham radio friend to patch us to our families. I wondered if a new port had been built. Our stay there had been a nightmare of a different

The weather was every bit as bad as I remembered, at times we had to walk our bikes

sort. The naval dock, fully exposed to the furious winds of the Strait, had not provided safety. Whenever we left *le Dauphin,* we had to be on call.

I wondered, too, if the repair facilities had been expanded. Although we had been able to make minor repairs, facilities for repairing a sailboat of our size were inadequate, and we were forced to head to Buenos Aires—a thousand miles to the north—in order to haul the boat out and make major repairs. (We'd been lucky to find good crew in Punta Arenas: Alfonso, a Chilean fisherman, and Margaret and Trevor—tourists from Capetown who were ready for a sailing adventure.)

"If you look out the right side of the plane"—the pilot's voice jogged me back to the present—"you can see Canal Trinidad and Isla Madre de Dios." I scrambled over and looked down upon a jigsaw puzzle—green and dazzling white, surrounded by blue waters. *It's so beautiful!* I thought. And somewhere down there was Dársena Aid, whose williwaws we had dreaded every night at anchor.

We were beginning our descent across Canal Sarmiento, then over Seno Union, and would be landing in Punta Arenas in forty-five minutes. Chills ran through me. We were nearly there! I was almost as excited as I had been when we pulled up to the naval pier in April 1975. *I was coming home, and the big test was about to begin!*

"Would you do it again?" "What did you learn about yourself?" "How did the trip change you?" People asked me these questions in 1975, then again in 1984, after Kathy and I had successfully completed our cycling expedition.

Would I do it again? Cape Horn in a sailboat? *No, never! Not in those open waters.* That I could answer unequivocally. I had been out of my element, and without Don I could never have made it. Another cycling trip? *Yes!* In spite of the rain, the hail, the snow, the storm-force winds that had knocked us and our bicycles flat—the weather was every bit as bad as I had remembered—I would do it again.

What had I learned about myself? I had learned from our sailing nightmare that the will to survive is the strongest instinct I have—that when my life depended on it I could push myself far beyond what I'd ever believed possible. But that I had no desire to keep testing life "for adventure," as Don had—life was too fragile. On the other hand, the cycling trip taught me that I could choose my own challenges and derive deep satisfaction out of pushing myself within my own self-defined limits. And I had proved that, in my own element, on land, I could take care of myself. Other answers would take shape over the months and the years to come.

A year on my own in 1976 gave me time to reflect. I realized I did not want to live without him. We had been through too much in our near-death experience to "hang it up." We had a greater appreciation of each other, of the ways in which we complemented one another. He needed my softness, my social antennae, my attention to detail, my ability to bring him down to earth when his dreams got too lofty. I needed his enthusiasm and optimism; his ability to plan, to face confrontations, and make hard bargains. Although we would never lead the conventional life my family had, that no longer bothered me.

How else had I changed? I had become less tolerant of administrators, teachers, and students who wasted time. Of people who refused to take responsibility for their own actions. (Eventually, the lack of discipline in education frustrated me, and I went into business with Don.) City life had lost its luster—I had lived too long in the open air. I wanted to live where the air was perfumed with sage and Jeffrey pine, where visibility was fifty miles every day. Where I could watch the sun's diurnal changes over the ridge of a mountain, or along the horizon of the sea. Where seasonal changes were crisp and definite.

And I wanted a land base. A place that didn't rock. A place with room for the familiar things I love—a piano, my books, a painting, my favorite chair. I wanted a permanent nest, a home I could return to when I tired of wandering. That would provide sanctuary when the rest of the world seemed cold. Where I could meet with old friends, among a few treasured belongings passed down from another generation that anchor me to my past.

And now, many years later, I have the best of two worlds—I share with Don both a home in the Great Basin and a 32-foot diesel trawler in which we make annual trips through the Inside Passage of British Columbia and Alaska. The high-latitude environment has become part of my blood. The forested islands, the winds, the rain, and the sea are similar to those I grew to love in the Canales de Patagonia. And yes, I sometimes get seasick when we cross the open waters of Queen Charlotte Sound and the boat pitches and rolls, and the seas crash over the pilothouse. But these days, when the captain teases me about my "mental illness" I can hold my own.

NOTE

1. Quote from a flier Moitessier distributed at a slide show he gave in Ventura, California, 1981.

CHAPTER 18

Epilogue to the Second Edition

Whathat happened after you arrived in Punta Arenas?"
. . . "Where did you go after you left Chile?" . . . "What happened
to the kids?" These are questions readers of Cape Horn have asked
over the years since the First Edition of Cape Horn was published.
The following is a summary of our experience after we arrived in
Punta Arenas in April 1975. The "kids," who are now adults with
children of their own, were kind enough to write their own stories
which follow this Epilogue.

Arrival in Punta Arenas, while an overwhelming joy and relief, did not
guarantee the end of our nightmare. The city is an open roadstead and
the pier that was to be our home for nearly three months is totally
exposed to wind and seas. We were the guests of the Chilean Navy, and
we are still grateful for their unconditional help.

Chile was under military rule when we arrived and we had to
observe a midnight curfew any time we left *Le Dauphin Amical* for more
than an hour. The tempestuous weather prevented any overnight travel
and, wherever we went, we had to remain in constant telephone contact
with the Naval authorities in case the wind changed direction, forcing us
to move from one side of the pier to the other or—in extreme cases—to
anchor out.

Soon after our arrival, we learned that Punta Arenas lacked facilities
to haul out a boat of our size.[1] Until we decided what the next step was,
major work would have to wait. Our immediate concerns were to assure
our families that we were safe and healthy, to deal with the insurance
claim, to replace critical electronic equipment that had been damaged in

Réanne and Don on the Strait of Magellan

our pitchpole and make enough repairs that would allow us to continue. Admiral Allen, chief of Chile's Patagonia region, assigned us his right-hand man who was able to cut through the formalities that met us at every turn; he was even able to locate our "missing" chronometer.[2]

The residents of the city welcomed us with open arms. We were bombarded with invitations and offers of help. Humberto Gaete, a ham radio operator, provided our first radio contact with the States; the Irwin Korn family came weekly to pick up our dirty laundry; others ensured we had gourmet dinners or hot baths. I was invited to give talks at both primary and secondary schools where the pupils knew more about the States than most American teenagers. The Chilean Navy cited us as examples for their midshipmen, and we made lifelong friends with whom we still correspond and visit when we can.

Living in a country under military rule was a new experience for us. Although Punta Arenas was far removed from the centers of political activity, the army prowled every street corner, and we were aware that just across the Strait lay the infamous Dawson Island which, according to stateside editorials, housed *desaparecidos* and tortured prisoners. One holiday, during a military parade on the pier, we flew our United Nations flag along with our U.S. and Chilean flags generating tight-lipped looks from army officers. At a party on another occasion, Don asked an army colonel how Pinochet could rationalize "giving freedom" to Chile under the present regime. Our host—who feared instant repercussions—was livid, but the colonel responded politely to each of Don's questions and, the next day, his staff delivered a sack of coal for our fireplace, along with a three-page list contrasting Allende's socialist government policies with Pinochet's.

We decided that continuing our original itinerary was out of the question and that the best plan would be to head to Buenos Aires, 1000 miles to the north, where we would find not only the necessary facilities for repairing *Le Dauphin,* but also a warmer climate. The Navy was reluctant to let us leave without major repairs and suggested the possibility of towing us to Valparaíso. However, with the approach of winter, they deemed this idea unsafe, and we prepared to sail up the coast of Argentina. In the meantime, we hired carpenters and steel workers who crafted a beautiful replacement spreader, and repaired the masts, booms and stanchions.

Both Don and I were concerned about continuing with just the two of us aboard. Rafting frequently side by side along a Chilean fishing vessel, we befriended Alfonso Bahamonde, one of the crew, whose sense of responsibility and skill impressed us. Because the fishing industry was in a severe recession at the time, Alfonso's captain encouraged our asking him to join us. We also invited Trevor Dwyer and Margaret Manzoni, a young couple from South Africa who had been trekking around Chile. Although neither Alfonso, Trev or Margaret had any offshore sailing experience, they caught on fast. We worked amazingly well together, and our relationships grew into enduring friendships.

As winter approached in the "Ultimate South," it snowed frequently, ice formed on the deck creating hazardous conditions, and we had to feed coal non-stop to our stove to keep cabin temperatures above freezing. We anticipated leaving Punta Arenas the first of June. However, a raging, week-long storm prevented our departure.

On June 7, our Naval liaison told us that the *Bendoran* was expected to arrive later that day. Since our encounter in Sarmiento Canal, nine weeks earlier, the ship had made a round-trip through the Panama Canal to Germany and back. For once, we were happy that the gale-force winds had prevented our leaving.

The *Bendoran* docked just 20 feet away from us and Captain Addison and Don finally met. When the winds forced us to move to the lee of the pier, the captain came to our rescue a second time. He took the helm and led us around. Then he, his engineer and Don talked "dreams" for a few hours over a new bottle of Scotch he brought us.

This second encounter was a fitting send-off from the Strait of Magellan. As we cast off our lines the next day, the crew of the *Bendoran* joined ranks with the friends, Naval officers, dockworkers and townspeople who came to see us off. It was a tearful farewell to a city that had welcomed us in our time of need.

We were also saying good-bye to a military regime that was ostensibly trying to restore order, encourage private enterprise, increase production and establish economic stability; and, as we began our three-week passage up the coast of Argentina, we quickly realized we were entering a country of the opposite bent.

Argentina was out of control. Under Peron's widow, Isabella, inflation was rampant, strikes were constant, food and paper goods were in short supply or non-existent, except on the *mercado paralelo* (black market), and authorities could be bought.

We were invited into middle and upper class homes where a small bunker inside their entrance concealed a machine gun or rifle. Our hosts turned their radios up full blast when we discussed politics over coffee and flan. They warned Don, "When you hear the radio play Beethoven's *Missa Solemnis,* don't leave your boat!" It would mean a coup was starting.

Our insurance settlement check, sent in care of the port captain, mysteriously disappeared. Then, with the help of an influential friend, just as mysteriously reappeared, cancelled, but with a note from the authorities that if we showed up at a certain bank and asked for a certain manager, our check would be made good—in U.S. dollars, cash. And it was, much to our surprise.

Despite all the uncertainty and unrest, Don proceeded to repair the boat under the direction of Manuel Campos, one of the world's great naval architects. However, the process took another six months and my sabbatical leave had run out. As the austral winter neared its end, summer in the Northern Hemisphere was also coming to an end and classes would soon resume in the States. It was time for me to fly home to be with Sean (our last teenager) and take up my teaching job again.

Alfonso, Trevor and Margaret would carry on, helping Don sail the boat to Capetown, South Africa, then back across the South Atlantic with stops at Tristan da Cunha and Saint Helena Island, and through the Panama Canal. Don had to fly home on three occasions to solve problems with our business, Wilderness Group, delaying *Le Dauphin's* return by another six months. When Don and the crew finally returned to California in June 1976, we sold our house to pour the money into our business and moved aboard *Le Dauphin Amical.*

Having lived apart for a year, adjusting once again to togetherness brought its own challenges. Don was not ready to live on land yet and I resented taking my "home" to Southern California's offshore islands every weekend with charter guests aboard, or cruising to Mexico in the

Don joined Mahina Tiare *for a trip to Cape Horn*

winter. It took nearly a decade before we became "real partners." Despite our differences, we never considered splitting up—we'd been through tougher times at sea. As Don mellowed over the years, and I became more sure of myself, our marriage strengthened.

We sold *Le Dauphin* in 1987[3] and, a year later, Wilderness Group. We continued to enjoy backpacking and cross-country skiing in our Sierra Nevada home where we originated our publishing venture.

In the latter part of the 1990s, Don and I returned to Chile where he joined friends, John and Amanda Neal, on their sailboat *Mahina Tiare,* for a trip to Cape Horn. After more than two decades, his dream became reality when he signed the register at the top of Horn Island![4] And, in Valparaíso, he was made an honorary member of the International Society of Cape Horners.

The two of us have continued our bicycling and boating adventures, turning our explorations into a lively and successful publishing business. Although we loved the mountains of the Sierra Nevada, we prefer the higher latitudes and decided to move to Fidalgo Island in Washington State where we have become aficionados of wilderness cruising in the Northwest and Alaskan waters on our Nordhavn trawler, *Baidarka.* As I gained more expertise over the years, Don's Mongolian scowl became less and less essential and, these days, we rarely argue about decisions. And yes, he still *is* the captain. Despite the current vogue of co-captaining, I believe there can be only one captain—especially in high-stress situations.

A friend of mine who had read this book before she met Don, looked him straight in the eye when I introduced them and said, "I didn't like you at all when I read Cape Horn, but I decided that if I ever had to go to the Southern Ocean I wouldn't go with anyone but you."

I have that same faith in Don. He is a magnificent explorer and navigator. And, together, we have now logged over 160,000 nautical miles and we plan to continue as long as we can!

NOTES

1 Punta Arenas now has complete marine facilities for large vessels.

2 The second chronometer was damaged beyond repair, and we had to send for a third, which arrived safely in care of the Navy just days before our departure.

3 In 2001 we received news from the most recent owner of *Le Dauphin Amical* that she had sunk in a hurricane in American Samoa and now rests at the bottom of the South Pacific Ocean.

4 We also had an emotional reunion with Alfonso Bahamonde who is now a successful businessman on the island of Chiloe.

And Now the "Kids"

THE DREAM—*JEFF*

There are those of us that become, at one time or another, "infected" by our dreams. It is this very infection that has allowed otherwise normal men to go beyond what prudent men think reasonable or safe. And for the lucky few that have the disease, it's a driving force that has beckoned us to go beyond ourselves. To walk outside while others are content just to look through the window. That is the story of *Le Dauphin Amical*, one man's dream and his never-ending drive to reach the other side.

Having had the opportunity to crew on the boat that was so much a central part of my father's dream, I'd like to leave a few words of my own. Going to sea for any length of time will try even the best relations. When four of those relations are teenage boys, I think most captains would agree that trying to round the Horn would be the lesser of the two challenges. Although my shipmates may have other feelings, I would suggest that each is a better person for the voyage we made, and we each came away with a picture that is uniquely our own.

The picture I remember best is that of an 18-year old sailing between La Paz and Puerto Vallarta. Caught in a two-day storm, alone at the helm strapped into his safety harness, just him, the storm and the trusted *Le Dauphin Amical*. He was facing something larger than himself, yet confident in his abilities to handle whatever was thrown to him. When the clouds cleared and the sun returned he knew that he had passed a test.

That young man was me. Without knowing it, somewhere in the middle of that long dark night I crossed the line in life and became stronger.

One of the hardest decisions I've ever made was the decision to leave *le Dauphin Amical* and return to the States. Letting my father down was no small thing. Although this was my father's dream, and he takes center stage, I think the real unsung hero here is my mother. It took great courage for her to adopt my father's dream and follow him down through the Roaring Forties and into the Screaming Fifties. My father could not have asked for a better first mate either for this voyage or for life.

SEAN

I started the voyage on *Le Dauphin* at age 14, and left her at age 15 just six weeks later. I think I lasted two weeks longer than my best friend, Carl, and my brother Mike, and a few weeks less than the final rat to jump ship—my brother Jeff. After leaving the boat in Puerto Vallarta, I returned home to Southern California, where I lived for a number of months with Carl so that I could finish high school. My journal at that time reflected my thoughts:

When Carl said he wasn't ready to live away from his dad, I guess I didn't understand. Now I do and I'm discovering that it's really hard to live without your parents when you're not through with high school and you're trying to support yourself. Unlike Carl, I have no place to run: where I

Réanne & Sean—sea trials on Liddie Mae, *future* le Dauphin Amical

have friends, parents, and a house to come home to. . . . It's a big job growing up, something fierce when it's thrust upon you, and I think I've done more growing up in the last year than all of my life before. I suppose I was as well prepared as just about anybody, but I hope I [can] teach my own kids well.

After my high school graduation, I went on to college, and then graduate school. I'm now an economist living in the Washington D.C. area with my wife, Margaret, and our three kids, Kevin, Kathleen, and Shelley. I never took to sailing, perhaps because of my congenitally weak stomach, and neither my wife nor kids are sailors.

With hindsight, and the benefit of adult- and parenthood, I would offer the following advice for anyone thinking of embarking on a long cruise with a family. First, wait until your kids are out of high school. Next, start simple. Invite them along on the trip for a week or two, with boy- or girlfriend or fiancée or spouse in tow, and a bail-out plan with plane tickets to home. That, in effect, is what Margaret and I did when— as part of our "modern-type" honeymoon—we spent a week cruising the Queen Charlotte Sound with my parents, Don and Réanne, on a rented power boat in 1990. The boat was a real tub, but the sun was out, the weather hot, the wind dead-calm, the deep-blue water like glass, the drinks cold, the company good, and the scenery breathtaking. All things considered, it was one of the most memorable trips I've taken (and just right for a landlubber!).

CARL KOWALSKI

Share the dream? Maybe Jeff or Mike or even Sean saw the odyssey of the *Le Dauphin Amical* as the fulfillment of a shared dream, but I was focused on something inside me—my weakness. Admitting this has been one of the hardest realizations of my life and one of the best lessons in many respects.

I understood that Don had a dream, but it was never something to share as far as I could tell. But we could be part of it. Looking back, had we accepted it as the gift it was, things could have been different. Simultaneously I feel bitter about it and very sorry that I let everyone down. I didn't see the experience for what it was. I now realize how hard it must have been for Don and Réanne. The logistics of the trip must have been overwhelming and my actions didn't make it any easier.

For all of the hard work, discomfort, and sacrifice, I wouldn't have missed the opportunity for anything. I am grateful for having been part of the crew, and grateful to the Douglass family for accepting me, especially Sean. Sailing is now something I share with my wife, Linda, and my three daughters. I think more important than sailing is that we share our dreams. It is a lesson I am still trying to learn.

Stateside Headlines: Missing at Sea
by Katherine Wells

"Cucamongans Missing at Sea," screamed the March 20 headline in the *Daily Report,* the Ontario, California newspaper. The size of the type used should have been reserved for the Second Coming, but it reflected the bold face of my feelings. Réanne and I had been close friends for more than ten years. We met when we were both first-year teachers at Montclair High School and had helped each other through that difficult time. I had done considerable hand holding when Réanne was a single mother with little confidence, less money, and two small, hard-to-control boys. I had listened to her misgivings about relinquishing her own dreams to accommodate Don's when they got married. I'd tracked her excitement, complaints, and anxieties as they bought and prepared *le Dauphin Amical* to pursue Don's life-long obsession to sail the world and challenge Cape Horn.

Now, years later, I look out onto a sea of golden grass in northern New Mexico. Mesas and plains roll outside my window as far as the eye can see. Across the valley the Sangre de Cristo Mountains rise under a burden of snow. My notes clutter the room. The typewriter covers the dining table. The wind buffets the house as I haul up memories submerged for decades, feelings that gnawed at the rigging of my soul those days and nights when I thought I might never see Réanne again.

Early in the Douglasses' married life, my husband Geza and I had co-owned a 29-foot sloop with them. We bought it together so that each couple could work on sailing skills. Being an experienced sailor already, Don was itching to move on to a bigger craft as soon as Réanne and their kids had learned the basics of seamanship.

There was a further connection between us, and two reasons to be angry at Don for pursuing his hazardous dream. Not only had he put Réanne in harm's way, he had left Wilderness Group Incorporated, his fledgling manufacturing and retail sporting goods business, in which Geza and I had invested considerable money and time. It was growing like crazy but in dire straits. Don's chutzpah and tenacity, which we admired on one level, transmogrified into villainy in the eyes of Réanne's friends.

We had feared that something was wrong for weeks because Don and Réanne had missed their prearranged radio contact schedules. But the newspaper and television reports, however sensationalized, made it harder to pretend that everything was okay. I was the last to talk to Réanne and Don on a phone patch on February 21. She had sounded upbeat through the static, but I detected concern in her voice about the size of the waves they were experiencing in the Southern Ocean.

Then the pile of silent days began. Radio contact dates came and went. Silence. Grim silence. Worry spread like an oil slick surging darkly under the surface of my consciousness, choking off reason. "Maybe it's just that the radio is on the fritz," said my rational self. "But you know they don't have a chronometer to fix their position with," the angry, fearful counterpart answered. "You know they're in the Screaming Fifties and that the captain is an irresponsible asshole."

I mentally screamed at Don for letting his drivenness, rather than prudence, run the show. He gave lip service to the risks, but it was clear that he would go on with his monomaniacal quest no matter what the cost. I cursed him for wanting to go around the Horn in the first place and especially for going on with only Réanne as crew after the kids jumped ship in Mexico. I yelled at Réanne for not following her intuition and not having the guts to say no to him, excoriated myself for having encouraged her to marry him.

But my anger was no match for the hot lump of rubber growing in the pit of my stomach. Marble-sized at first, it had expanded to baseball dimensions, a constant companion, like Réanne's seasickness on the first leg of their voyage. Images of steep, black waves crashed in my mind. The shock of cold water, hard and opaque. Thoughts I could not keep at bay. Twin strands of anger and fear twisted themselves into a sturdy rope. I visualized Don hanging from the yard arm.

Even after several radio contacts had been missed I continued to go out to General Dynamics in Pomona when I could. Radio schedules had been kept there regularly on a bi-weekly basis since their departure. In that way they had been able to maintain a tether to home, and their friends and family could follow their progress. In the ham shack, Tex Porter faithfully continued to observe the schedule calling K6KWS over and over on the powerful 20-meter ham band. For me it had the quality of a vigil. Though I lit no candles, it was as though my being there might communicate some light, some caring spark across the Pacific's great expanse.

Two or three other friends and Wilderness Group people gathered in GD's ham shack too, anxiously listening to the radio's crackle and static, the repeated chant of the call letters, hoping for some word, some sound of reassurance answering the silence from the Southern Ocean. Nothing. Not a sound.

At home I wasn't alone in my worries or my anger. Geza's long-standing friend/foe relationship with Don reached a new intensity. They were competitors in business prowess, in feats of accomplishment in nature, and in their ability to milk those feats in stories related to our mutual friends.

On the one hand Geza recited a litany of what might have gone wrong technically to keep *le Dauphin* incommunicado: radio malfunction, antenna malfunction that could be repaired only on deck or aloft. Perhaps the weather and sea conditions were too bad for Don to go on deck or up the mast. Or there might be electrical problems of various kinds. Or battery failures.

Then he'd rail at Don for being a macho idiot, for putting Réanne and himself at such risk on purpose, for leaving Easter Island without a chronometer. He knew and respected Don's sailing abilities, but perhaps among the Douglasses' friends he understood best the hazards they faced because of his own knowledge of sailing and the frailties of boats and their electronic equipment. We had our own dream of long distance cruising, but it paled by the day as we waited for word of our friends' fate.

Geza, one of the directors of Wilderness Group, and I—and all those who had an investment in the enterprise—were doubly angry at Don. He had placed the struggling business in jeopardy by leaving it in the first place and now by the prospect of what would become of it if *le Dauphin Amical* had gone down.

"That son-of-a bitch," Geza yelled. "He left the company in a period of rapid growth, flux, and expansion, just when the presence of a president is most needed. He rationalized everything." Geza jammed his hands in his pockets and shook his head. "That son-ov-a-beech," he repeated in his Hungarian accent (which became more pronounced when he was angry.)

I agreed with him but I didn't want to hear it. He reminded me too much of Don when he launched into a tirade. But he and the other WGI directors had to consider the "gory details" to be dealt with if the Douglasses were indeed "lost at sea," i.e., dead.

The company was already on financially shaky ground, and because of a continuing 50 percent annual growth rate its cash flow was always marginal. The prospect of struggling with banks and bank loans to which Don personally was committed—as well as the company—was chilling in the extreme. There were lots of unknowns and many of them were discussed at a board meeting on March 20. Who would receive or control the Douglasses' shares of stock? How would creditors and shareholders react when word got out that the Douglasses were "missing at sea?" The tone of the meeting's minutes was businesslike, but gloom was palpable. Don's vision and drive were missing and needed. Even though he might be dead, there were few charitable words for him. If *le Dauphin* had gone down, the business would surely follow. Fear and anger, the lengthening rope.

The fabric of hope began to fray, the waves in my mind grew higher and colder. At school each day teachers, friends, and Réanne's former students asked for any news. There was none to give. One day I stood outside my classroom commiserating with Ray Rayburn—a guidance counselor and Wilderness Group investor. Phil Gosswiller, our vice-principal and Réanne's good friend, happened by and joined us. "I'm going to kill that SOB if anything has happened to Réanne," he said. His usually relaxed, handsome face was tight, his eyes narrow. He could have recruited several accomplices for the deed within the high school.

I was concerned about Réanne's parents too, especially her father, who had been diagnosed with cancer since their departure. Réanne was so close to her family, her disappearance would kill her father with grief. The Hemingways were political liberals, but conservative in a very fundamental sense. Not risk takers. They didn't understand Don's drive in business and recreation, his need to dance on the edge of the knife. Thrill seeking was not in their lexicon. They would have been much happier had Réanne married a staid history professor or an architect who played bridge or golf, rather than a kamikaze like Don. But that may have been what attracted her to him in the first place, a rebellion against always playing it safe.

We all worried about the boys and lamented their decisions to abandon ship. We wondered how they'd handle the grief and guilt if the worst were true. What would happen to them now? Sean seemed to be avoiding the subject as much as possible, going on as though he were unconcerned. Inside he must have been churning. Jeff's reaction made us all feel hopeful though. A little sunshine to puncture our gloom. "I refuse to believe they're not okay," he stated one day in the ham shack at General Dynamics. He counted off on his fingers all the extra safety and reinforcing features Don had built into the boat, all the back-up emergency equipment and supplies on board and the safety drills his dad had put the crew through.

Listening to him speak, hearing Don's intonation in his voice, seeing Don's mannerisms, the same facial planes, the same crooked teeth, was eerie; reassuring in some respects, disconcerting in others. Jeff had a much cooler head than his father, and he knew better than anyone how well prepared *le Dauphin* was for Cape Horn. While the rest of us were condemning Don as an irresponsible adventurer, Jeff stood resolutely behind his dad and was confident that his careful preparation of the boat and his abilities as a navigator and sailor would see them through anything.

I tried to keep Jeff's optimism in my mind, but it was hard in the face of the priority telegram from the State Department in Washington, D.C., to Réanne's parents listing the Douglasses as "lost at sea." Hope sank like a stone.

It's all over, I thought. The telegram was based on reports from the Chilean navy. Those three terse little words, "lost at sea," and waves pounding in my brain, churning in my stomach, held sway, until one night I lay in bed thinking about that last conversation. I tried to remember the sound of their voices. Suddenly I had a bright, clear image of Réanne's face as though it flashed on a TV screen. She was squinting into the sunlight.

She's okay, I thought jubilantly, though the information materialized out of nowhere. The skeptic in me immediately assigned the experience to the wishful-thinking pile, but the feeling stuck, and the force of the waves in my mind diminished. I wondered if Réanne were trying to send telepathic messages to her friends.

When we got the news three days later that they had been sighted in the Patagonian channels I was euphoric. It seemed almost anticlimactic, however, because I was already convinced at the intuitive level that they would be found okay. I wanted to say, "I know. I heard from Réanne already." Still, the call from the Hemingways saying they'd received a radio message from the HMS *Bendoran* sent voltage through my system like no other I have ever received. It was a joy to stop worrying about whether or not they were alive and to start making a mental list of the hundreds of questions I wanted to ask them.

Now, gazing up at the Sangre de Cristos, I think back on my friendship with Réanne and Don, a friendship that might have ended tragically in 1975 but instead has lasted into the twenty-first century. Part of me is still mad at Don for his pigheadedness and insistence on having his own way, no matter the cost. I'm happy to report that he has mellowed. He still has a maddening zeal to be right and dominate any discussion. But if you say "Excuse me, I've had enough of your tirade," he will back off with grace and good humor.

He has learned to value Réanne for the amazing partner she is. He could never have built the publishing business they've created post-Cape Horn without her considerable writing and editing skills and her ability to keep on top of the innumerable details of the enterprise. He's learned to count his blessings.

Réanne continues to amaze and mystify me because she's stayed with him in spite of turmoil and chaos that would have done in other women. I know there are rewards for her. Continued boating adventures she still loves despite the nightmare of Cape Horn. An interesting business in which she can exercise many of her talents and a lot of excitement, like Don's contagious enthusiasm and endless flow of ideas. And a circle of friends who are adventurers like they are. With Don she also has a life of interesting travel, much variety and hard work. Their partnership stretches her in ways that are meaningful as well as challenging. Despite the difficulties I know she finally decided that the balance in their marriage lay on the positive side and that life would be more interesting with him than without him.

And looking back now on that day in 1975 when I received the news she was alive, I understand Réanne better. I remember that I wanted to hug Don. Though I still blamed him for getting them into the mess, I was sure his skills must have played a big part in getting them out of it.

Appendices

A. Original two-year itinerary of le Dauphin Amical

STOP	ARRIVE	LEAVE	DISTANCE (in miles)
Los Angeles		Oct. 12, 10 a.m.	60
Pyramid Cove		Oct. 13	400
Turtle Bay	Oct. 17	Oct. 21	240
Magdalena Bay	Oct. 22	Oct. 24	180
Cabo San Lucas	Oct. 26	Oct. 30	440
Manzanillo	Nov. 3	Nov. 6	360
Acapulco	Nov. 9	Nov. 12	240
Puerto Angel (Mexico)	Nov. 14	Nov. 16	400
San José (Guatamala)	Nov. 20	Nov. 24	900
Galapagos	Dec. 4	Dec. 20	2,000
Easter Island	Jan. 8, 1975	Jan. 15	2,500
Punta Arenas (Chile) (post–Cape Horn)	Feb. 12	Feb. 17	700
Falkland Islands	Feb. 28	Mar. 3	3,000
Tristan da Cunha	Apr. 1	Apr. 5	1,600
Cape Town (So. Africa)	Apr. 20	May 10	2,300
Mauritius	June 3	June 15	300
La Réunion	June 18	June 30	900
Madagascar	July 10	July 30	

Stops on return trip planned for:
Durban, Perth, Melbourne, Hobart, Wellington, Christ Church, Easter Island, Marquesas, Tahiti, Honolulu, San Francisco, Los Angeles

Radio call K6KWS, maintaining radio watch 14,300 mcs, 7 a.m. and 7 p.m. Pacific Time

B. *Le Dauphin Amical—Specifications*

Le Dauphin Amical
Documented number: 524917
William Garden Porpoise Class Ketch
42 ft. on deck (not including bowsprit and dinghy davits)
13 ft. beam
5½ ft. draft
20 tons gross, 19 tons net

Hull
Strip-planked Port Orford cedar over oak ribs
Oak frames
Full-length composite cement and iron keel
Hull built in Victoria, B.C., Canada
Finished in Port Angeles, Washington (1969)

Rigging
Spruce masts
Stainless steel standing rigging
Dacron running rigging (six sail halyards, three signal halyards)

Accommodations
Sleeps six
Double bunk amidships to starboard
Single pilot berth to port
Two each, single quarter berths (port and starboard)
Galley settee converts to single berth
Single pipe berth in forepeak
Berths have either bunkboards or weather clothes

Engine
Perkins 4-107 diesel (with factory spares)
Five batteries charged from two alternators
Three separate fuel filters
100+ gallon iron fuel tank

Sails
Dacron main, yankee working jib, forestaysail (self-tending) and mizzen
Genoa, two each twin spinnaker jibs with forespar running poles mounted
    to mast
Mizzen staysail (cotton, antique)

Galley
Shipmate two-burner with oven (kerosene)
Sink, deep double-compartment, stainless steel

Fresh and saltwater manual pumps
Water capacity: three stainless tanks, 120 gallons, plus plastic jerry
      jugs backup
Gimballed table, solid teak, with L-shaped settee to starboard
Cabin sole: Armstrong vinyl with stainless steel trim

Head
Wilcox Crittenden mounted fore and aft
Sink and cupboards

Forepeak
Workbench to port with vise and tool rack
Single pipe berth mounted to starboard
Three chain lockers

Ground Tackle
Anchors: 65 lb. Danforth, 60 lb. CQR, 50 lb. fisherman,
                 50 lb. yachtsman, 20 lb. Danforth
Anchor winch: Simpson Lawrence, two-speed
Rodes: 300 ft. BBB ⅜ in. chain
                 300 ft. ⅞ in. nylon
                 300 ft. ⅝ in. nylon
Various spare lines, chain, and shackles

Heater
Shipmate fireplace (coal- or wood-burning)
Stainless steel full reflector and chimney

Winches
Four halyard winches mounted on masts
Two each two-speed Barlow sheet winches

Lifelines
Double stainless steel, plastic-covered lifelines
Full bow and stern pulpits, stainless
Port and starboard lifeline harnesses on deck, stainless

Navigation
Seafarer echo sounder
Salem quartz crystal chronometer
6 in. Danforth Constellation compass
2 in. Tell Tale compass
V.D.O. knotmeter and sumlog
Walker taffrail log
Single sideband transceiver for ham bands
300 charts of world ports, Plath sextant, stopwatch,
      hand-bearing compass, misc.

Survival Gear
Eight-man Avon life raft
Special abandon-ship locker with equipment
Three fire extinguishers
Eight life jackets
Two life rings with xenon lights
Two man-overboard poles

Vane
Self-steering custom-built auxiliary trim tab (wind-operated)
Miscellaneous
Permanent boom gallows (main and mizzen)
Booms with downhaul, outhauls, topping lifts and preventers with block
    and tackle
Two large full-length sun shades
Fourteen opening portlights (most with mesh screens)
Lazaret aft of wheel steering
Three hatches for ventilation (includes main companionway)
Bosun's box of spare parts
Variety of jerry jugs for water, diesel, and kerosene
Two spotlights
Two boat hooks
Two Whale gusher bilge pumps (one mounted on desk)
Sailing dinghy

C. State Department Telegram

```
                        UNCLASSIFIED        SCS408

   PAGE 01  SANTIA 01646  182243Z

   70
   ACTION SCSE-00

   INFO  OCT-01  ARA-10  ISO-00  SCA-01  EB-07  CG-00  DOTE-00

         CIAE-00  DODE-00  INR-07  NSAE-00  PA-02  USIA-15  PRS-01

         SP-02  /046 W
                         ---------------------        10966Y
   P 182227Z MAR 75
   FM AMEMBASSY SANTIAGO
   TO SECSTATE WASHDC PRIORITY 2545

   UNCLAS SANTIAGO 1646

   EO 11652: N/A
   TAGS: CASC, CI (DOUGLAS, DONALD AND REANNE NEE HEMINGWAY)
   SUBJECT: W/W: US YACHT "LE DAULPHIN AMICAL" LOST AT SEA

   1.  SANTIAGO DAILY "LA TERCERA" ARTICLE OF 18 MARCH REFERRED
   TO OFFICIAL REPORTS FROM THE CHILEAN NAVY INDICATING THAT A
   U.S. REGISTRY YACHT "LA DAUPHIN AMICAL" IS LOST AT SEA. THE
   ARTICLE STATED THAT THE YACHT LAST ADVISED ITS POSITION, SOME
   600 MILES OFF THE WESTERN ENTRY TO THE MAGELLAN STRAITS, ON
   25 FEBRUARY. "LA TERCERA" ALSO COMMENTED THAT THE YACHT·S CREW
   OF TWO INFORMED THE AUTHORITIES ON WT FEBRUARY THAT IT WAS
   NAVAGATING WITHOUT A CHRONOMETER, THAT ITS MAGNETIC COMPASS
   WAS DESTROYED AND THAT THE VESSEL HAD PROBLEMS WITH ITS
   STEERING SYSTEM.

   2.  AFTER AN INITIAL ALERT ON 12 MARCH THAT THE YACHT WAS
   OVERDUE, DEFENSE ATTACHE OFFICE RECEIVED A MESSAGE 17 MARCH
   FROM U.S. PACIFIC COMMAND HEADQUARTERS, HONOLULU, REQUESTING
   THAT CHILEAN AUTHORITIES ATTEMPT LOCATE VESSEL. SINCE THAT
   TIME, DAO HAS CONTACTED AIR FORCE AND NAVY AUTHORITIES AND
   CURRENTLY A JOINT SEARCH AND RESCUE EFFORT IS UNDERWAY WITH
   THE AIR FORCE SANTIAGO SEARCH AND RESCUE CENTER COORDINATING
   ALL ACTIVITIES. PRELIMINARY REPORTS BY CHILEAN COAST GUARD
   INDICATE THAT A SHIP SIMILAR TO THE DAUPHIN HAS BEEN REPORTED
   SIGHTED AT CANAL SARMIENTO, NEAR ISLA INOCENTES. WE ARE
   AWAITING FURTHER CONFIRMATION AND WILL ADVISE SOONEST.
                        UNCLASSIFIED
```

```
                        UNCLASSIFIED

   PAGE 02  SANTIA 01646  182243Z

   3.  ON 13 FEBRUARY CONSULATE RECEIVED A LETTER FROM MRS.
   J. RENE HEMINGWAY, 37 EAST SANTA INEZ AVE., SAN MATEO,
   CALIFORNIA 94401, REQUESTING HELP IN LOCATING A CHRONOMETER
   FOR THE "LE DAUPHIN AMICAL" SHIPPED TO EASTER ISLAND, THEN
   FORWARDED TO CUSTOMS AUTHORITIES IN VALPARAISO.
   MRS. HEMINGWAY ADVISED THAT HER DAUGHTER, REANNE HEMINGWAY
   DOUGLASS AND SON-IN-LAW DONAL D DOUGLASS, CREWED THE 42-FOOT
   KETCH, AND WERE PLANNING TO DEPART EASTER ISLAND FOR PUNTA
   ARENAS. SEVERAL DIFFERENT CHECKS BY EMBASSY WITH CUSTOMS
   AUTHORITIES IN VALPARAISO TO LOCATE THE MISSING CHRONOMETER
   HAVE BEEN UNSUCCESSFUL.

   4.  REQUEST DEPARTMENT TELEPHONE MRS. HEMINGWAY TO ADVISE
   HER OF THE SITUATION AND EFFORTS BEING MADE BY EMBASSY AND
   CHILEAN AUTHORITIES. IF MRS. HEMINGWAY WISHES CONTACT EMBASSY
   BY TELEPHONE, DEPARTMENT MAY WISH REFER HER TO CONSULAR
   SECTION.
   POPPER
```

D. *Newspaper articles from Ontario* Daily Report &
La Prensa Austral

THE DAILY REPORT

HOME FINAL

VOL. LXV NO. 79   ONTARIO-UPLAND, CALIFORNIA, THURSDAY, MARCH 20, 1975   TEN CENTS

Cucamongans missing at sea

Search launched after distress signals received

By SUE MANNING

A Cucamonga couple is reportedly missing at sea and has not been heard from since Feb. 22 in the Pacific Ocean between Easter Island and Punta Arenas, on the southeast tip of South America.

Tom Douglass, president of the Backpacker Shop in Claremont, and his wife, Reanne, a foreign language teacher at Montclair High School, have become the objects of both air and sea searches.

Mrs. Douglass' parents, in Palo Alto, received a message from the State Department Wednesday, night, indicating that a distress call had been received from the couple's sailboat on Feb. 27. The distress signal was picked up 2 Hawaii and Santiago, the message said.

They went in quest of their dream

By STEVE PAPINCHAK

The quest for adventure is what drew Don and Reanne Douglass on a 18-month around-the-world sailing voyage — a trip marred by reports the Cucamonga couple are missing in the high seas between Chile and Easter Island.

Shortly before departing, San Pedro on Oct. 12, Douglass was asked what distinguished a journey on the high seas that was sure to produce potential dangers.

"Human beings are different because they do things for love and for fun," replied the owner of the Backpacker Shop in Claremont.

As for the risks, he said the trip would involve less danger than a Fourth of July auto drive.

The message also indicated the Chilean government had conducted an extensive air search, but had called the search off at March 18 after being unable to find anything at sea.

John Porter, Douglass boat operator in Claremont, said "it appears they may be lost at sea or at least their radio is out.

Porter talked to Douglass on Feb. 16 when Douglass told him he would talk to him on Feb. 26 because he was on the tail end of a gale, Porter said.

He did not indicate he couldn't get to port, Porter said. He did change his port because of steering vane problems. Porter said, but notified the captain aboard the Hero, a United States research

recovered from the couple's sailboat on Feb. 27. This picture was taken on their boat shortly before they left, in of the couple and two of their children. They are, from left, Michael, Tom, Reanne and Sean Douglass.

Israel ponders policy in marathon meeting

JERUSALEM (UPI) — ...

Mansfield bill would increase 1974 rebates

WASHINGTON (UPI) — The

Face deportation
33 illegal aliens held in Chino

Thirty-three illegal aliens were arrested in Chino Wednesday during a roundup, of 40 aliens throughout the West End, Border Patrol authorities said.

El Centro Border Patrol investigator Bill Glenn said the roundup was not a "raid" but a periodic routine operation.

A four-man detail remained in the West End today as the operation continued.

The four-man team doubled the size of the Riverside-based station, charged with deporting illegal aliens from the West End area, Glenn said.

Boxes pick up the aliens and haul about any place they go in productive for us," Glenn said.

Usually the Riverside office is a busy busy gathering up aliens arrested by local police during each night Glenn explained.

"Most days that's all they can accomplish, harvesting the aliens department, coop." he said.

But with the extra team, the Border Patrol officers are able to get out and check the agricultural areas, train yards and light industrial areas, Glenn said.

a landscaping firm, a packing plant, a chemical company and a sheet working firm, Glenn said.

Others were picked up hitchhiking or waiting for rides along the road, he added.

Many declined to tell the Border Patrol where they had been working and very few showed United States addresses, Glenn said.

Most of the aliens picked up Wednesday had been in the United States from four to 30 days, several had been here from one to six months and some had been here longer than six months, Glenn said.

A couple of the aliens were picked up at the new Chino county civic center site where demolition is currently in progress.

Border Patrol authorities could not say whether the men were employed by the contractor working for the city or whether they just happened to be near the site when picked up.

Committee ok's repeal

LA PRENSA AUSTRAL

DIARIO INDEPENDIENTE IMPULSOR DEL PROGRESO NACIONAL

...ESIMO CUARTO AÑO — Nº 9.654.—   Punta Arenas, Sábado 5 de Abril de 1975.—

62 DIAS DE VIAJE— Después de una serie de dificultades recién ayer pudo arribar a nuestro puerto el yate norteamericano "Le Dauphin Amical", tripulado por el matrimonio formado por Donald Douglass y esposa Reanne Douglass. A su llegada a Punta Arenas la pareja señaló que habían tenido muchos inconvenientes en alta mar, derivados de fallas en los instrumentos de comunicación, de navegación y del motor. El crucero lo iniciaron en Los Angeles, EE. UU., prosiguiendo a Acapulco México, Isla de Pascua y Punta Arenas. Aún no han decidido el curso del itinerario porque el yate se encuentra en malas condiciones.

E. Damage Report by Lloyd's of London Insurance Agent Punta Arenas, May 1975

NO 5/75
YACHT "LE DAUPHIN-AMICAL"
MORRO BAY, CALIFORNIA

Emilio Cabrera A.
Engineer & Surveyor
Punta Arenas, Chile

Damage suffered by the boat

1.- This is to Certify that I:

The undersigned surveyor did. At the request of Messrs Wilson King & Co Ltd. Lloyd's Agent at this Port, proceed to the above named boat to survey and report on damage suffered by the tilt and inmundation of the hull on February 27th at 02.00 hours in navegation at 50° S and 89° W, on the 28st April 1975 at 10 and 17 hours.

2.- In found that

2.1 SPARS AND RIGGING

1) Mast head top block split and twisted to starboard
2) Wind direction vane bent and missing counter weight
3) Mast tang for starboard staysail backstay torn downward 3/4 inch
4) Starboard spreader with light and 2 signal halyards carried away
5) Port spreader bent backward 10°
6) Starboard lower stay tang torn Downward 1/3 inch.
7) Port lower stay turnbuckle bent
8) Mainsail boom carriage bent
9) Mainsail boom carried away
10) Starboard light board carried away
11) Port starboard spinnaker pole chocks carried away
12) Starboard mizzen pinrail askew
13) H.F. radio antenna lead-in carried away
14) Mizzen mast forward stay tang moved up 1/2 inch pinching mast
15) Lateral crack mizzen mast
16) Mizzen boom cracked and delaminating
17) Mizzen boom gallows bent foward 15°

- 2 -

18) Main boom gallows bent foward 5°
19) 2 Aft stay chainplates starboard cracked
20) Staysail boom carried away
21) Starboard upper stay kinked (Replace Both Port and Starboard)

2.2 HULL

1) Seam opening below water line to allow 200 gallons per Day leak when under way
2) Chaff at waterline starboard bow from storm jib luff cable
3) Paint covered by oil used to cam breaking seas
4) Missing letters from home port
5) Self steering vane aux. rudder shaft bent 20° - control rod inside bent also.
6) Stern pulpit bent
7) 3 stanstions of lifeline carried away
8) Cabin portlight blown out
9) Cabin deck joint opened up
10) Deck comming joint cracked
11) Port cat head broken
12) Bocesprit lifted up 1/2 inch from deck and loose
13) Prot catwalk cracked
14) Bobstay chain plate bent and bobstay loose
15) Dolphin striker bent

2.3 SAILS AND RUNNING RIGGING

1) Working jib torn and hanks missing
2) Staysail jib torn
3) Mainmail torn and stretched
4) Mizzen sail torn and stretched
5) 60 feet 1/2" nylon jib sheet carried away
6) 60 feet 1/2" nylon stay sail sheet carried away
7) 200 feet of 5/8 nylon dock line carried away or badey chuffed
8) Mizzen staysail torn
9) Spm jib carried away

Damage Report (continued)

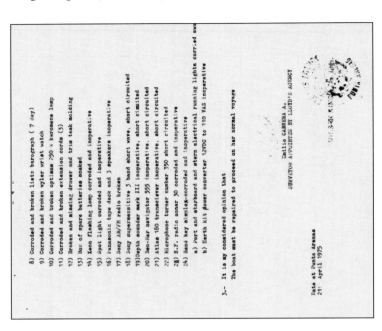

- 3 -

2.4 MISC. OUTSIDE
1) 1 Hawse pipe cover carried away
2) 2 fiberglass dingy (with sail center board, rudder and oars) carried away
3) 7 feet fiberglass surf board carried away
4) Various Brooms and mops carried away
5) 8 feet boat hook carried away
6) 3 spreader lights on main mast and 1 on mizzen mast are inoperative
7) Dingy tie down straps carried away

2.5 FOREPEAK
1) Various hand tools (3 boxes full) corroded many beyond use
2) Spare handswum broken, corroded or lost to bilge
3) Paint cans corroded
4) Canned engine oil corroded

2.6 MAIN CABIN
1) Corroded canned meats, vegetables and fruits for 18 month voyage
2) Cabin light broken
3) Kerosene lamp broken
4) Charts, H.O. Publications and Books soaked beyond use
5) Various nicks in woodwork
6) Battery charger corroded

2.7 GALLEY
1) Corroded canned meats as in main cabin
2) Wet cushions (Bilge water and Kerosene) corroded zippers
3) Broken battery selector switch
4) 2 inoperative florescent light fixtures
5) Broken chart light fixture
6) Various corroded and inoperative hinges on cupboard doors and settee
7) Corroded and inoperative salem quartz Chronometer

8) Corroded and broken lietz barograph (7 day)
9) Corroded and broken wyler wrist watch
10) Corroded and broken optimus 250 x kerosene lamp
11) Corroded and broken extension cords (3)
12) Broken and missing drawer and trim teak molding
13) Box of spare batteries soaked
14) Xeon flashing lamp corroded and inoperative
15) Spot light corroded and inoperative
16) Panasonic tape deck and 3 speakers inoperative
17) Sony AM/FM radio broken
18) Sony supersensitive 3 band short wave, short circuited
19) Depth sounder mark III inoperative, short cicmited
20) Ben-Mar navigator 555 inoperative, short circuited
21) Atlas 180 transceiver inoperative, short circuited
22) Microphone turner number 350 short circuited
23) H.F. radio sonar 30 corroded and inoperative
24) Hand key simplex-corroded and inoperative
   a) Port and starboard and stern electrical running lights carried away
   b) Herth kit power converter 12VDC to 110 VA2 inoperative

3.-- It is my considered opinion that
The boat must be repaired to proceed on her normal voyage

Date at Punta Arenas
21 April 1975

Emilio CABRERA A.
SURVEYOR APPOINTED BY LLOYD'S AGENCY

F. Beaufort Scale

Sir Francis Beaufort (1774–1857) developed the wind scale, which also describes sea and land conditions accompanying the wind force.

Beaufort Number	Descriptive Term	Mean wind speed equivalent in knots	Deep Sea Criterion	Probable mean wave height in metres
0	Calm	>1	Sea like a mirror	—
1	Light air	1 – 3	Ripples with the appearance of scales are formed, but without foam crests	0·1 (0·1)
2	Light breeze	4 – 6	Small wavelets, still short but more pronounced; crests have a glassy appearance and do not break	0·2 (0·3)
3	Gentle breeze	7 – 10	Large wavelets; crests begin to break; foam of glassy appearance; perhaps scattered white horses	0·6 (1)
4	Moderate breeze	11 – 16	Small waves, becoming longer; fairly frequent white horses	1 (1·5)
5	Fresh breeze	17 – 21	Moderate waves, taking a more pronounced long form; many white horses are formed (chance of some spray)	2 (2·5)
6	Strong breeze	22 – 27	Large waves begin to form; the white foam crests are more extensive everywhere (probably some spray)	3 (4)
7	Near gale	28 – 33	Sea heaps up and white foam from breaking waves begins to be blown in streaks along the direction of the wind	4 (5·5)
8	Gale	34 – 40	Moderately high waves of greater length; edges of crests begin to break into spindrift; foam is blown in well-marked streaks along the direction of the wind	5·5 (7·5)
9	Strong gale	41 – 47	High waves; dense streaks of foam along the direction of the wind; crests of waves begin to topple, tumble, and roll over; spray may affect visibility	7 (10)
10	Storm	48 – 55	Very high waves with long overhanging crests; the resulting foam, in great patches, is blown in dense white streaks along the direction of the wind; on the whole, the surface of the sea takes a white appearance; the tumbling of the sea becomes heavy and shock-like; visibility affected	9 (12·5)
11	Violent Storm	56 – 63	Exceptionally high waves (small and medium-sized ships might be for a time lost to view behind the waves); the sea is completely covered with long white patches of foam lying along the direction of the wind; everywhere the edges of the wave crests are blown into froth; visibility affected	11·5 (16)
12	Hurricane	64 and over	The air is filled with foam and spray; sea completely white with driving spray; visibility very seriously affected	14 (—)

G. Captain's Notes about the Ultimate Wave

Wind speed estimates by small boat skippers are notorious for being overstated and generally reflect the peak values rather than more conventional averages used in weather forecasting. For this reason I went out of my way to keep from overstating wind speeds in our logbook.

The wind speeds we have reported are based upon actual readings taken at cabin level by a hand-held anemometer which means that the reported speeds need to be increased for the ocean current (about 2 knots in the Roaring Forties), the breaking forward motion of surface water, a height correction of approximately 10% increase because the Weather Service measures wind speed at a standard altitude of 35 feet above the surface. The readings we took are also understated because most readings at sea are taken in a wave trough that acts as a shield against the wind.

For this reason, most of our recorded readings should be increased to bring them in line with other references. This understatement explains why small vessels often report carrying canvas well into gale force and, in some cases, storm force, which seems unlikely based on our experience.

I believe that even a heavy, well-constructed, full displacement sailboat of moderate size cannot carry even a handkerchief-sized sail during force 10 storm winds (48 to 55 knots).

My attempt to measure the actual wind speed of the approaching storm, about 8 hours before our pitchpoling, taken at 5-second intervals with the anemometer held just outside the hatch, showed rapid fluctuations with reading of 40, 45, 28, 35, 44, 55, 52, 40, 42, 48, 32, 51, 38, 46 knots.

Given the foregoing correction-factors, I judged the wind at the time to be a steady 50 knots, gusting from 60 to 70 knots; when I stood on deck, holding the anemometer it frequently pegged at 65 knots on top of a wave, indicating that we were indeed experiencing 64-knot hurricane-force winds of 12 on the Beaufort Scale.

So, at that point, it was impossible for either of us to remain on deck. There was nothing to do but heave-to, tie the helm (tiller) to leeward and go below.

The British Hydrographic Office states that Beaufort scale winds of 12, over unlimited fetch generate the highest sea state of value 9, with an average wave height of 45 feet. They use the term *phenomenal* for describe such a wave. My research before leaving on our voyage indicated that it was scientifically impossible for a wave to reach a reported height of 100 feet. However, the day after our pitchpole, I saw five truly phenomenal waves that dramatically dwarfed our 55-foot main mast.

I estimated them to be at least 100 feet high as they heaped up and broke. Recent measurements off North Sea oil rigs have confirmed that 100-foot waves do exist during full storms. I believe that it must have been one of these phenomenal waves that dropped us vertically, carrying away the horizontal spars and damaging the vertical ones.

Glossary

ahu: a ceremonial stone platform; one of the oldest of the Easter Island art forms

anchor rode: anchor system that includes anchor and chain or line

angostura: narrows

backwind a sail: to push the sail out to one side to catch the wind on its back side until the boat turns the opposite way

backstay: a stay that runs from the masthead to the stern

bahía: bay

bare poles (to barepole): to sail downwind without any sails in very strong winds where the spars and hull provide adequate surface to propel the boat

bend a sail: install a sail

bobstay: a lower steel support that offsets pressure on the jib stay (mounted below bowsprit)

boom: horizontal spar

boom gallows: a frame that holds the boom stationary after the sail is lowered

bowsprit: fixed spar projecting from the bow

broach: a sudden, uncontrolled turning of a boat broadside to the wind or seas, which usually results in a capsize

bulkhead: a transverse wall of a boat

cable: 600 feet

caleta: cove

catheads: timber "arms" to which the bowsprit stays are secured

close (the coast): to draw near or approach the coast

come about: to turn from one tack to the other, with the bow passing through the eye of the wind

companionway: entranceway (also see: hatch)

dársena: basin

deckhead: the ceiling of the interior cabin

doghouse: that part of the cabin which sits above deck (also known as deckhouse)

dolphin striker: a nearly vertical rod which helps tension the bobstay

douse the sails: to take down the sails

draw: when a sail fills with wind

drogue: a sea anchor or object towed off the stern of a vessel to keep the vessel end-on to a heavy sea

fall off: to turn downwind (by letting out the sheets)

fetch: the distance waves travel in open water before they reach a certain
  point; the longer the fetch, the higher the waves

fiordo: fjord

forepeak: the forward most part of the sailboat

forestay: a stay that runs from high on the mast to the foredeck

frames: the ribs of a boat

galley: the kitchen

gimbals: pivoting rings that hold a stove, compass, or table to allow it to
  tip or rotate so that it remains level

halyard: a line used to hoist a sail, or other things, aloft

hand the sail: to take down, furl, and stow a sail

hatch: an opening in the deck

hawse pipe: a deck fitting through which anchor lines can be run

head: toilet

headstay: steel stay which runs from the bow (or bowsprit) to the top of
  the foremast; usually supports the jib sails

heave to: to remove sail or engine power so as to remain nearly stationary
  in the water

helm: the wheel or tiller of a boat

irons, in: loss of headway

isla: island

jibe: to change direction so that the wind comes from the opposite quarter and the stern moves across the eye of the wind; this maneuver can
  be dangerous to the boat and crew, unless it is carefully controlled

kedge: to move a vessel by dropping an anchor with a line attached and
  winching the boat in to the anchor

keel haul: old-world punishment whereby a sailor was dragged under the
  keel by means of ropes

lazaret: storage compartment in the stern of a boat

let out: to pay out a line in the direction of the tension

lie ahull: a "last-ditch" maneuver used when weather conditions are so
  severe that the boat or crew can't cope with continuing to sail and
  stand watch; the boat looks after itself under bare poles and assumes
  its own position with regard to the wind and the waves; usually handled by lashing the helm, closing all hatches, and going below

lifelines: lines run through the stanchions along the sides of a deck to prevent crew from falling overboard; also, a safety line run along the
  length of deck which a crew member can hook into

lightboards: boards which hold the running lights of a ship (ours looked
  like a teak bookshelf)

luff: the leading edge of a sail; to luff: to come into the wind, causing the
  sails to wave back and forth

mast: a vertical spar

mizzen mast: the aft mast on a ketch-rigged sailboat

moai (Easter Island): the large stone statues that resemble the upper torso of a human

moai kava kava (Easter Island): small wooden carving of a cadaverous human male

paso: passage or pass

pitch: the fore and aft plunging and rising of a boat

point into the wind: to sail toward the direction of the wind

port: the left side of a boat looking toward the bow

portlight: porthole

puerto: port, harbor

rail: the edge of the deck, usually raised

rano: (literally, a hill); the original word used by Easter Islanders for crater

Rapa Nui: the language and native people of Easter Island

roll: the sideways motion of a boat

salon: the main living area

Samson post: a heavy post and bitt on the foredeck used to fasten the anchor line

seno: sound

sheets: lines that control the lateral movement of a sail

shrouds: stays that run from either side of the mast to the deck

sole: cabin floor

spars: the general term for masts, booms, or gaffs, etc.

spreaders: horizontal struts used to tension the shrouds

stanchions: metal posts used to hold the lifelines along the deck

starboard: the right side of a boat looking toward the bow

staysail: a small sail attached to the forward side of the mast, aft of the jib

step: where the base (heel) of a mast is set

strakes: lines of planking

taffrail: railing around the stern

trailing log/recording log/patent log: a trailing spinner connected to a revolving counter mounted on the transom of a boat which indicates how far in nautical miles a boat has travelled (we frequently referred to ours as the taffrail log, since it was mounted on the taffrail

unhand the sail: to fully remove a sail from its track

warp: a heavy line used in towing a drogue

wear around: to bring a sailing vessel onto the opposite tack by bringing the wind around the stern (a form of controlled jibe used by square riggers)

williwaw: wind of high velocity that sweeps down the sides of a mountain

yaw: to swing horizontally off course, as when a boat is running with a quartering sea

Bibliography & Suggested Reading

Aebi, Tania. *Maiden Voyage.* New York: Simon and Schuster, 1989.

Bailey, Maurice and Maralyn. 117 Days Adrift. London: Sheridan House, 1992

Bascom, Willard. *Waves and Beaches.* New York: Doubleday & Company, Inc., 2000.

Campbell, Ramón. *El Misterioso Mundo de Rapanui.* Buenos Aires, Argentina: Editorial Francisco de Aguirre, S.A., 1973.

————. *La herencia musical de Rapanui.* Santiago, Chile: Editorial Andrés Bello, 1971.

Chichester, Sir Francis. *Gipsy Moth Circles the World.* New York: Pocket Books, 1969.

————. *The Lonely Sea and the Sky.* New York: Ballantine Books, 1969.

Clark, Miles. *High Endeavours.* Vancouver, B.C.: Douglas & McIntyre, 1991.

Coffey, D. J. *Dolphins, Whales and Porpoises.* New York: Macmillan Publishing Co., Inc., 1977.

Coles, K. Adlard. *Heavy Weather Sailing.* Tuckahoe, New York: John de Graff, Inc., 1971.

Darwin, Charles. *The Voyage of the Beagle.* Edited by Leonard Engel. New York: Natural History Library and Doubleday/Anchor, 1962.

Dumas, Vito. *Alone Through the Roaring Forties.* From *Great Voyages in Small Boats: Solo Circumnavigations.* Camden: International Marine, 2001 [reissue]

Farrington, Tony. *Rescue in the Pacific: A True Story of disaster and Survival in a Force 12 Storm.* Camden: International Marine, 1996.

Fuentes, Jordi. *Dictionary & Grammar of the Easter Island Language/ Diccionario y Gramática de la lengua de la Isla de Pascua.* Santiago, Chile: Editorial Andres Bello, 1960.

Goodall, Rae Natalie Prosser. *Tierra del Fuego.* Buenos Aires, Argentina: Instituto Salesiano de Artes Gráficas, 1978.

Guzzwell, John. *Trekka Round the World.* Bishop: Fine Edge Productions, 1999.

Heyerdahl, Thor. *Aku-Aku.* New York: Rand McNally & Company, 1958.

————. *Easter Island, the Mystery Solved.* New York, Random House, 1989.

Hough, Richard. *The Blind Horn's Hate.* New York: W. W. Norton & Company, 1971.

Janichon, Gérard. *Damien, l'Antarctique à la voile, 2e Edition.* Paris: Transboréal. 1998. [included in *Damien Autour du Monde*]

Jung, Carl G. *Man and His Symbols.* New York: Doubleday & Company, Inc., 1964.

Junger, Sebastian. *The Perfect Storm.* New York: W.W. Norton, 1997.

Lansing, Alfred. *Endurance.* New York: Carroll & Graf Publishers, Inc., 1986.

Maloney, Elbert S. *Chapman Piloting.* 59th Edition. New York: Hearst Marine Books, 1989.

The Mariner's Handbook. Fourth Edition. Somerset, England: Hydrographer of the Navy, 1973.

Métraux, Alfred. *Ethnology of Easter Island.* Honolulu, Hawaii: Bishop Museum Press, 1971.

Moitessier, Bernard. *Cap Horn à la voile.* Paris: B. Arthaud, 1971.

Moorehead, Alan. *Darwin and the Beagle.* New York: Harper & Row, 1969.

Morison, Samuel Eliot. *The European Discovery of America: the Southern Voyages.* New York: Oxford University Press, 1974.

————. *The European Discovery of America: the Northern Voyages.* New York: Oxford University Press, 1971.

Mundle, Rob. *Fatal Storm.* Camden: International Marine, 1999.

Nouveau Cours de Navigation des Glénans. Seuil, 1982.

Ocean Passages for the World. Somerset, England: Hydrographer of the Navy, Third Edition, 1973.

The Oxford Companion to Ships & the Sea. Edited by Peter Kemp. London: Oxford University Press, 1988.

Raban, Jonathan, Ed. *The Oxford Book of the Sea.* Oxford: Oxford University Press, 1992.

Robb, Frank. *Handling Small Boats in Heavy Weather.* Chicago: Quadrangle Books, 1965. [out of print]

Robertson, Dougal. *Survive the Savage Sea.* New York: Praeger Publishers, Inc., 1973.

Roth, Hal. *Always a Distant Anchorage.* New York: W. W. Norton & Company, 1988.

————. *Chasing the Long Rainbow.* New York: W. W. Norton & Company, 1990.

————. *Two Against Cape Horn.* New York: W. W. Norton & Company, 1978.

Sill, Edward Rowland. *Around the Horn.* New Haven: Yale University Press, 1944.

Slocum, Joshua. *Sailing Alone Around the World and Voyage of the Liberdade.* Edited by Walter Magnes Teller. New York: Collier Books, 1962.

Smeeton, Miles. *Once Is Enough.* London: Grafton, 1986.

South America Pilot. Somerset, England: Hydrographer of the Navy, Vol. II, Fifteenth Edition, 1971, and Supplement No. 12, 1990.

Stevenson, Janet. *Woman Aboard.* Novato, California: Chandler & Sharp Publishers, Inc., 1981.

Street, Donald. *The Ocean Sailing Yacht.* New York: W. W. Norton & Company, Inc., 1978.

Tilman, H. W. *Mischief in Patagonia.* London: Grafton Books, 1988.

Tomalin, Nicholas, and Hall, Ron. *The Strange Last Voyage of Donald Crowhurst.* Camden: International Marine, 1995.

Villiers, Alan. *Captain James Cook.* New York: Charles Scribner's Sons, 1967.

Acknowledgments

Over the course of the years, I have many people to thank for their encouragement and support. Some, unfortunately, did not live to see the final product. Among the latter are my father, J. Rene Hemingway, who died two years after I returned home; my mother, Marian SeCheverell Hemingway—journalist and English instructor—whose cogent comments and help I sorely missed as I completed the final draft; the late Roberto (Bobby) Uriburu, Argentine sailor, who urged me to write this book because "raising a child and writing a book are two of the most beautiful tasks in the world"; the late Manuel (Manolo) Campos, world renowned naval architect, whose invaluable help in repairing *le Dauphin Amical* in Buenos Aires allowed Don to bring the boat safely back to California.

Special thanks to our friend, Al Ryan, whose skill and integrity in preparing *le Dauphin Amical* for high latitude sailing before we set out, saved our lives. To our Douglass-Collins brood who helped prepare *le Dauphin*, and who encouraged our parents to have faith when reports of "missing at sea" circulated at home.

Thanks, also, to Captain Adam Addison and his crew of the *Bendoran*; to the many people of Punta Arenas and Porvenir, Chile, who welcomed us into their homes—in particular, Erwin and Flora Korn, Rina and Sergio Araneda, Berta and the late Humberto Gaete, Gabriela and Alfonso Jara, and the Ruíz families; to Admiral Eduardo Allen and Captain Carlos Toledo (now retired Admiral), of the Chilean navy, both of whom cut through miles of red tape for our benefit; to Dr. Ramón Campbell for providing good-humored balance on Easter Island when we most needed it. To our cheerful, dependable, and vigilant crew who made life-after-Punta Arenas fun and safe: Alfonso Bahamonde of Castro, Chiloë, Chile; Margaret and Trevor Dwyer of Capetown, South Africa. To the dedicated amateur radio operators—named and unnamed worldwide—who provided essential communications along our entire voyage.

To the following people for their helpful criticism in reading earlier versions of my manuscript, as well as this Second Edition: the late Lloyd Dennis, Leanna Jean Douglass, Will Durant, Dorothy Gilbertson, Jean Gillingwators, Alexandra Hollowell, Genny House, Sue Irwin, Honeydew Murray, Rod Nash, and Margaret Sweeney, Linda Schreiber, Laurie and Warren Miller. To Lois SeCheverell Buell, Geza Dienes, Alan Remes, and Ray Rayburn for providing their "stateside recollections." To the late Ann Belknap Benner and Juanita Pacifico Clarke for their moral support when my mother could no longer give hers.

And, my sincerest thanks to those who helped me pull this project together—my long-time friend, Katherine Wells; Alice Klein, editor of the First Edition—who gave helpful suggestions at the very times mine seemed to have played out; to my friend, Kathryn Wilkens, for her editorial assistance with this Second Edition, as well as her critique of the original manuscript; to Sue Irwin and Pat Eckart for their help in preparing the original manuscript; to Melanie Haage for her project management and book design; to my granddaughters, Christa and Amanda Collins for their patience and helpfulness during the last stages of the First Edition; and to Jeff, Sean and Carl—our teen-age crew members, now adults—for their willingness to add their own comments to this Second Edition. And—most important—to my husband, Don, for his technical and editorial suggestions, his daily galley duty, and his loving support throughout this entire adventure—First as well as Second Editions. Without the help of each of these individuals, this project might have become another nightmare!